Extraordinary Praise for *A History of Reading*

"A highly entertaining overview that leaves us with both a new appreciation of our own bibliomania and a deeper understanding of the role that the written word has played throughout history."
—*The New York Times*

"Manguel's digressions are delightful, his anecdotes appealing, and his stories scintillating. What might have been no more than one damned thing after another turns out to be, at the hands of this splendid raconteur, one divine thing after another. . . . It is all utterly beguiling." —*The Boston Sunday Globe*

"Impressionistic, engrossing." —*Time*

"An entertaining, provocative, and informative book."
—*The Washington Post*

"Sweeping and personal, erudite and intimate, *A History of Reading* is an altogether charming book. . . . [Manguel] may be the last romantic in a world where the goat counters are winning out." —*New York Newsday*

"Tickles, surprises, and amuses." —*The Philadelphia Inquirer*

"Impressive, engaging." —*The Washington Times*

"Erudite and original." —*The Miami Herald*

"Enormously entertaining." —*San Francisco Chronicle*

"A wonderful merger of scholarship and personal essay. . . . Manguel writes so beautifully and felicitously that he infects us with his enthusiasm again and again." —Philip Lopate

"Manguel's urbane, unpretentious tone recalls that of a friend eager to share his knowledge and enthusiasm. His book, digressive, witty, surprising, is a pleasure." —*Kirkus Reviews*

"Highly enjoyable. . . . I finished the book with a sense of gratitude to have shared this journey through time in the company of a mind so lively, knowledgeable, and sympathetic."
—P.D. James

"An eclectic and deeply felt history of reading. It is a history illuminated by an acute sensibility. . . . An unfailingly engaging work."
—*School Library Journal*

"Unique, enlightening, and as captivating as a celebration of reading should be."
—*Booklist*

"Interesting, intriguing, and entertaining."
—*Library Journal*

"A distinctly personal work, the culmination of a lifetime of reading and reposing. Manguel's witty, intellectual, accessible prose infects the reader with his passion."
—*The Bergen Record*

"One of the most important and fascinating books published this year. Maybe any year."
—*Red Rock News*

"Erudition and memoir are beautifully wed in this stimulating and provocative book."
—*Virginia Quarterly Review*

"An enjoyable blend of classical studies, psychology, narrative history, anecdotal essay, memoir, and fantasy, all in celebration of the history of reading and books. . . . Will enlighten and entertain any lover of books and reading. Manguel has produced a classic of his own."
—*Mobile Register*

PENGUIN BOOKS

A HISTORY OF READING

Alberto Manguel is a writer, translator, and editor of international reputation; his many books include *The Dictionary of Imaginary Places* (with Gianni Guadalupi), the award-winning novel *News From a Foreign Country Came*, and the short story anthologies *Black Water*, *The Gates of Paradise*, and (with Craig Stephenson) *In Another Part of the Forest*. Born in Buenos Aires, Manguel has traveled extensively and is now a Canadian citizen.

A

HISTORY

of

READING

by

ALBERTO

MANGUEL

PENGUIN BOOKS

TO CRAIG STEPHENSON,

That day she put our heads together,
Fate had her imagination about her,
My head so much concerned with outer
Yours with inner weather.

— After Robert Frost —

PENGUIN BOOKS
Published by the Penguin Group
Penguin Putnam Inc., 375 Hudson Street,
New York, New York 10014, U.S.A.
Penguin Books Ltd, 27 Wrights Lane, London W8 5TZ, England
Penguin Books Australia Ltd, Ringwood, Victoria, Australia
Penguin Books Canada Ltd, 10 Alcorn Avenue,
Toronto, Ontario, Canada M4V 3B2
Penguin Books (N.Z.) Ltd, 182–190 Wairau Road,
Auckland 10, New Zealand

Penguin Books Ltd, Registered Offices:
Harmondsworth, Middlesex, England

First published in Great Britain by HarperCollins Publishers 1996
First published in the United States of America by
Viking Penguin, a division of Penguin Books USA Inc. 1996
Published in Penguin Books 1997

1   3   5   7   9   10   8   6   4   2

Illustration credits appear on pages 357–59.

THE LIBRARY OF CONGRESS HAS CATALOGUED THE VIKING HARDCOVER AS FOLLOWS:
Manguel, Alberto.
A history of reading/Alberto Manguel.
p.   cm.
ISBN 0-670-84302-4 (hc.)
ISBN 0 14 01.6654 8 (pbk.)
1. Books and reading—History.   I. Title.
Z1003.M292   1996
028′.9—dc20   96–2703

Printed in the United States of America
Set in Perpetua
Designed by Paul Hodgson

ACKNOWLEDGEMENTS

Over the seven years that this book was in the making,
I've accumulated a fair number of debts of gratitude. The notion of
writing a history of reading began with an attempt
to write an essay; Catherine Yolles suggested that the subject deserved
a whole book — my gratitude to her for her confidence.
Thanks to my editors — Louise Dennys, most gracious of readers,
whose friendship has supported me since the faraway days of
The Dictionary of Imaginary Places; Nan Graham, who stood by the book
at the very beginning, and Courtney Hodell, whose enthusiasm
accompanied it to the end; Philip Gwyn Jones, whose encouragement
helped me read on through difficult passages.
Painstakingly and with Sherlockian skill, Gena Gorrell and
Beverley Beetham Endersby copyedited my manuscript: to them
my thanks, as usual. Paul Hodgson designed the book with
intelligent care. My agents Jennifer Barclay and Bruce Westwood kept
wolves, bank managers and tax collectors from my door.
A number of friends made kind suggestions — Marina Warner,
Giovanna Franci, Dee Fagin, Ana Becciú, Greg Gatenby,
Carmen Criado, Stan Persky, Simone Vauthier. Professor Amos Luzzatto,
Professor Roch Lecours, M. Hubert Meyer and Fr. F.A. Black
generously agreed to read and correct a few individual chapters;
the errors remaining are all my own. Sybel Ayse Tuzlac
did some of the early research. My heartfelt thanks to the library staff
who dug out odd books for me and patiently answered my
unacademic questions at the Metro Toronto Reference Library, Robarts
Library, Thomas Fisher Rare Book Library — all in Toronto —
Bob Foley and the staff of the library at the Banff Centre for the Arts,
the Bibliothèque Humaniste in Sélestat, the Bibliothèque
Nationale in Paris, the Bibliothèque Historique de la Ville de Paris,
the American Library in Paris, the Bibliothèque de
l'Université de Strasbourg, the Bibliothèque Municipale in Colmar,

the Huntington Library in Pasadena, California, the
Biblioteca Ambrosiana in Milan, the London Library and the
Biblioteca Nazionale Marciana in Venice. I also wish to
thank the Maclean Hunter Arts Journalism Programme and
the Banff Centre for the Arts, and Pages Bookstore in
Calgary, where parts of this book were first read.

It would have been impossible for me to complete this book
without financial assistance from the pre-Harris Ontario
Arts Council, and the Canada Council, as well
as from the George Woodcock fund.

In memoriam Jonathan Warner,
whose support and advice I very much miss.

TO THE READER

Reading has a history.

ROBERT DARNTON
The Kiss of Lamourette, 1990

*For the desire to read, like all the other desires which
distract our unhappy souls, is capable of analysis.*

VIRGINIA WOOLF
"Sir Thomas Browne", 1923

But who shall be the master? The writer or the reader?

DENIS DIDEROT
Jaques le Fataliste et son maître, 1796

CONTENTS

A universal fellowship of readers. *From left to right, top to bottom:* the young Aristotle by Charles Degeorge, Virgil by Ludger tom Ring the Elder, Saint Dominic by Fra Angelico, Paolo and Francesca by Anselm Feuerbach, two Islamic students by an anonymous illustrator, the Child Jesus lecturing in the Temple by disciples of Martin Schongauer, the tomb of Valentine Balbiani by Germain Pilon, Saint Jerome by a follower of Giovanni Bellini, Erasmus in his study by an unknown engraver.

THE LAST
PAGE

Read in order to live.

GUSTAVE FLAUBERT
Letter to Mlle de Chantepie, June 1857

One hand limp by his side, the other to his brow, the young Aristotle languidly reads a scroll unfurled on his lap, sitting on a cushioned chair with his feet comfortably crossed. Holding a pair of clip glasses over his bony nose, a turbaned and bearded Virgil turns the pages of a rubricated volume in a portrait painted fifteen centuries after the poet's death. Resting on a wide step, his right hand gently holding his chin, Saint Dominic is absorbed in the book he holds unclasped on his knees, deaf to the world. Two lovers, Paolo and Francesca, are huddled under a tree, reading a line of verse that will lead them to their doom: Paolo, like Saint Dominic, is touching his chin with his hand; Francesca is holding the book open, marking with two fingers a page that will never be reached. On their way to medical school, two Islamic students from the twelfth century stop to consult a passage in one of the books they are carrying. Pointing to the right-hand page of a book open on his lap, the Child Jesus explains his reading to the elders in the Temple while they, astonished and unconvinced, vainly turn the pages of their respective tomes in search of a refutation.

Beautiful as when she was alive, watched by an attentive lap-dog, the Milanese noblewoman Valentina Balbiani flips through the pages of her marble book on the lid of a tomb that carries, in bas-relief, the image of her emaciated body. Far from the busy city, amid sand and parched rocks, Saint Jerome, like an elderly commuter awaiting a train, reads a tabloid-sized manuscript while, in a corner, a lion lies listening. The great humanist scholar Desiderius Erasmus shares with his friend Gilbert Cousin a joke in the book he is reading, held open on the lectern in front of him. Kneeling among oleander blossoms, a seventeenth-century Indian poet strokes his beard as he reflects on the verses he's just read out loud to himself to catch their full flavour,

From left to right, top to bottom: a Mogul poet by Muhammad Ali, the library at the Haeinsa Temple in Korea, Izaak Walton by an anonymous nineteenth-century English artist, Mary Magdalene by Emmanuel Benner, Dickens giving a reading, a young man on the Paris *quais*.

clasping the preciously bound book in his left hand. Standing next to a long row of roughly hewn shelves, a Korean monk pulls out one of the eighty thousand wooden tablets of the seven-centuries-old *Tripitaka Koreana* and holds it in front of him, reading with silent attention. "Study To Be Quiet" is the advice given by the unknown stained-glass artist who portrayed the fisherman and essayist Izaak Walton reading a little book by the shores of the River Itchen near Winchester Cathedral.

Stark naked, a well-coiffed Mary Magdalen, apparently unrepentant, lies on a cloth strewn over a rock in the wilderness, reading a large illustrated volume. Drawing on his acting talents, Charles Dickens holds up a copy of one of his own novels, from which he is going to read to an adoring public. Leaning on a stone parapet overlooking the Seine, a young man loses himself in a book (what is it?) held open in front of him. Impatient or merely bored, a mother holds up a book for her red-haired son as he tries to follow the words with his right hand on the page. The blind Jorge Luis Borges screws up his eyes the better to hear the words of an unseen reader. In a dappled forest, sitting on a mossy

From left to right: a mother teaching her son to read by Gerard ter Borch, Jorge Luis Borges by Eduardo Comesaña, a forest scene by Hans Toma.

trunk, a boy holds in both hands a small book from which he's reading in soft quiet, master of time and of space.

All these are readers, and their gestures, their craft, the pleasure, responsibility and power they derive from reading, are common with mine.

I am not alone.

I first discovered that I could read at the age of four. I had seen, over and over again, the letters that I knew (because I had been told) were the names of the pictures under which they sat. The boy drawn in thick black lines, dressed in red shorts and a green shirt (that same red and green cloth from which all the other images in the book were cut, dogs and cats and trees and thin tall mothers), was also somehow, I realized, the stern black shapes beneath him, as if the boy's body had been dis-membered into three clean-cut figures: one arm and the torso, **b**; the severed head so perfectly round, **o**; and the limp, low-hanging legs, **y**. I drew eyes in the round face, and a smile, and filled in the hollow cir-cle of the torso. But there was more: I knew that not only did these shapes mirror the boy above them, but they also could tell me pre-cisely what the boy was doing, arms stretched out and legs apart. **The boy runs**, said the shapes. He wasn't jumping, as I might have thought, or pretending to be frozen into place, or playing a game whose rules and purpose were unknown to me. **The boy runs**.

And yet these realizations were common acts of conjuring, less interesting because someone else had performed them for me. Another reader — my nurse, probably — had explained the shapes and now, every time the pages opened to the image of this exuberant boy, I knew what the shapes beneath him meant. There was pleasure in this, but it wore thin. There was no surprise.

Then one day, from the window of a car (the destination of that journey is now forgotten), I saw a billboard by the side of the road. The sight could not have lasted very long; perhaps the car stopped for a moment, perhaps it just slowed down long enough for me to see, large and looming, shapes similar to those in my book, but shapes that I had never seen before. And yet, all of a sudden, I knew what they were; I heard them in my head, they metamorphosed from black lines and white spaces into a solid, sonorous, meaningful reality. I had done this all by myself. No one had performed the magic for me. I and the shapes were alone together, revealing ourselves in a silently respectful dialogue. Since I could turn bare lines into living reality, I was all-powerful. I could read.

What that word was on the long-past billboard I no longer know (vaguely I seem to remember a word with several *A*s in it), but the impression of suddenly being able to comprehend what before I could only gaze at is as vivid today as it must have been then. It was like acquiring an entirely new sense, so that now certain things no longer consisted merely of what my eyes could see, my ears could hear, my tongue could taste, my nose could smell, my fingers could feel, but of what my whole body could decipher, translate, give voice to, read.

The readers of books, into whose family I was unknowingly entering (we always think that we are alone in each discovery, and that every experience, from death to birth, is terrifyingly unique), extend or concentrate a function common to us all. Reading letters on a page is only one of its many guises. The astronomer reading a map of stars that no longer exist; the Japanese architect reading the land on which a house is to be built so as to guard it from evil forces; the zoologist reading the spoor of animals in the forest; the card-player reading her partner's gestures before playing the winning card; the dancer reading the choreographer's notations, and the public reading the dancer's movements on the stage; the weaver reading the intricate design of a carpet being woven; the organ-player reading various simultaneous strands of music orchestrated on the page; the parent reading the baby's face for signs of joy or fright, or wonder; the Chinese fortune-teller reading the ancient marks on the shell of a tortoise; the lover blindly reading the loved one's body at night, under the sheets; the psychiatrist helping patients read their own bewildering dreams; the Hawaiian fisherman reading the ocean currents by plunging a hand into the water; the farmer reading the weather in the sky — all these share with book-readers the craft of deci-phering and translating signs. Some of these readings are coloured by the knowledge that the thing read was created for this specific purpose by other human beings — music nota-tion or road signs, for instance — or by the gods — the tortoise shell, the sky at night. Others belong to chance.

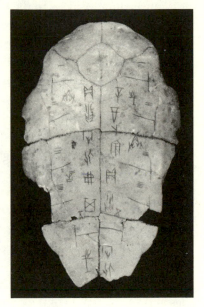

An example of *Chia-ku-wen*, or "bone-and-shell script", on a tortoise carapace, *c.* 1300–1100 BC.

And yet, in every case, it is the reader who reads the sense; it is the reader who grants or recognizes in an object, place or event a certain possi-ble readability; it is the reader who must attribute meaning to a system of signs, and then decipher it. We all read ourselves and the world around us in order to glimpse what and where we are. We read to understand, or to begin to understand. We cannot do but read. Reading, almost as much as breathing, is our essential function.

I didn't learn to write until much later, until I was seven. I could perhaps live without writing. I don't think I could live without reading. Reading — I discovered — comes before writing. A society can exist — many do exist — without writing,[1] but no society can exist with-out reading. According to the ethnologist Philippe Descola,[2] societies without writing have a linear sense of time, while in societies called lit-erate the sense of time is cumulative; both societies move within those different but equally complex times by reading the multitude of signs the world has to offer. Even in societies that set down a record of their passing, reading precedes writing; the would-be writer must be able to recognize and decipher the social system of signs before setting them down on the page. For most literate societies — for Islam, for Jewish and Christian societies such as my own, for the ancient Mayas, for the vast Buddhist cultures — reading is at the beginning of the social con-tract; learning how to read was my rite of passage.

Once I had learned to read my letters, I read everything: books, but also notices, advertisements, the small type on the back of tramway tickets, letters tossed into the garbage, weathered newspapers caught under my bench in the park, graffiti, the back covers of magazines held by other readers in the bus. When I found that Cervantes, in his fondness for reading, read "even the bits of torn paper in the street",[3] I knew exactly what urge drove him to this scavenging. This worship of the book (on scroll, paper or screen) is one of the tenets of a literate society. Islam takes the notion even further: the Koran is not only one of the creations of God but one of His attributes, like His omnipresence or His compassion.

Experience came to me first through books. When later in life I came across an event or circumstance or character similar to one I had read about, it usually had the slightly startling but disappointing feeling of *déjà vu*, because I imagined that what was now taking place had already happened to me in words, had already been named. The earliest extant Hebrew text of systematic, speculative thought — the *Sefer Yezirah*, written sometime in the sixth century — states that God created the world by means of thirty-two secret paths of wisdom, ten *Sefirot* or numbers and twenty-two letters.[4] From the *Sefirot* were created all abstract things; from the twenty-two letters were created all the real beings in the three strata of the cosmos — the world, time and the human body. The universe, in Judaeo-Christian tradition, is conceived of as a written Book made from numbers and letters; the key to understanding the universe lies in our ability to read these properly and master their combination, and thereby learn to give life to some part of that colossal text, in imitation of our Maker. (According to a fourth-century legend, the Talmudic scholars Hanani and Hoshaiah would once a week study the *Sefer Yezirah* and, by the right combination of letters, create a three-year-old calf which they would then have for dinner.)

My books were to me transcriptions or glosses of that other, colossal Book. Miguel de Unamuno,[5] in a sonnet, speaks of Time, whose source is in the future; my reading life gave me that same impression of flowing against the current, living out what I had read. The street outside the house was full of malignant men going about their murky business. The desert, which lay not far from our house in Tel Aviv, where I lived until the age of six, was prodigious because I knew there was a City of Brass buried under its sands, just beyond the asphalt road. Jelly was a mysterious substance which I had never seen but which I knew about

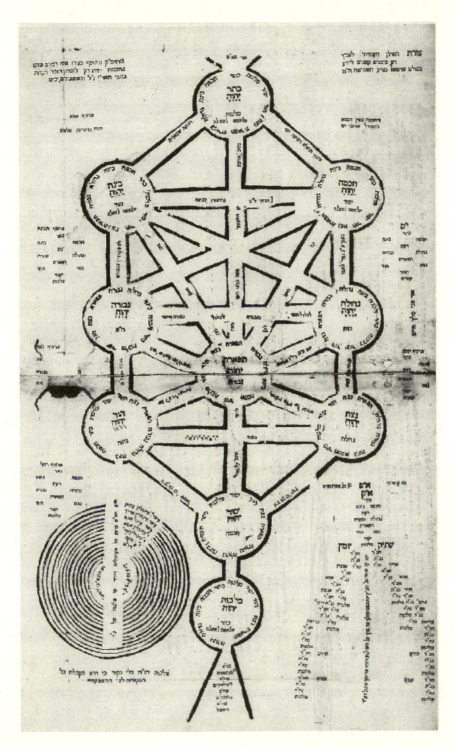

A page from the kabbalistic text *Pa'amon ve-Rimmon*, printed in Amsterdam in 1708, showing the ten *Sefirot*.

from Enid Blyton's books, and which never matched, when I finally tasted it, the quality of that literary ambrosia. I wrote to my far-away grandmother, complaining about some minor misery and thinking she'd be the source of the same magnificent freedom my literary orphans found when they discovered long-lost relatives; instead of rescuing me from my sorrows, she sent the letter to my parents, who found my complaints mildly amusing. I believed in sorcery, and was certain that one day I'd be granted three wishes which countless stories had taught me how not to waste. I prepared myself for encounters with ghosts, with death, with talking animals, with battle; I made complicated plans for travel to adventurous islands on which Sinbad would become my bosom friend. Only when, years later, I touched for the first time my lover's body did I realize that literature could sometimes fall short of the actual event.

The Canadian essayist Stan Persky once said to me that "for readers, there must be a million autobiographies", since we seem to find, in book after book, the traces of our lives. "To write down one's impressions of *Hamlet* as one reads it year after year," wrote Virginia Woolf, "would be virtually to record one's own autobiography, for as we know more of life, so Shakespeare comments upon what we know."[6] For me it was somewhat different. If books were autobiographies, they were so before the event, and I recognized later happenings from what I had read earlier in H.G. Wells, in *Alice in Wonderland*, in Edmondo De Amicis's lacrimose *Cuore*, in the adventures of Bomba, the Jungle Boy. Sartre, in his memoirs, confessed to much the same experience. Comparing the flora and fauna discovered in the pages of the *Encyclopédie Larousse* with their counterparts in the Luxembourg Gardens, he found that "the apes in the zoo were less ape, the people in the Luxembourg Gardens were less people. Like Plato, I passed from knowledge to its subject. I found more reality in the idea than in the thing because it was given to me first and because it was given as a thing. It was in books that I encountered the universe: digested, classified, labelled, meditated, still formidable."[7]

Reading gave me an excuse for privacy, or perhaps gave a sense to the privacy imposed on me, since throughout my childhood, after we returned to Argentina in 1955, I lived apart from the rest of my family, looked after by my nurse in a separate section of the house. Then my favourite reading-place was on the floor of my room, lying on my stomach, feet hooked under a chair. Afterwards, my bed late at night became the safest, most secluded place for reading in that nebulous region between being awake and being asleep. I don't remember ever feeling lonely; in fact, on the rare occasions when I met other children I found their games and their talk far less interesting than the adventures and dialogues I read in my books. The psychologist James Hillman argues that those who have read stories or had stories read to them in childhood "are in better shape and have a better prognosis than those to whom story must be introduced. . . . Coming early with life it is already a perspective on life." For Hillman, these first readings become "something lived in and lived through, a way in which the soul finds itself in life."[8] To these readings, and for that reason, I've returned again and again, and return still.

Since my father was in the diplomatic service, we travelled a great deal; books gave me a permanent home, and one I could inhabit exactly as I felt like, at any time, no matter how strange the room in which I had to sleep or how unintelligible the voices outside my door. Many nights I would turn on my bedside lamp, while my nurse either worked away at her electric knitting-machine or slept snoring in the bed across from mine, and try both to reach the end of the book I was reading, and to delay the end as much as possible, going back a few pages, looking for a section I had enjoyed, checking details that I thought had escaped me.

I never talked to anyone about my reading; the need to share came afterwards. At the time, I was superbly selfish, and I identified completely with Stevenson's lines:

This was the world and I was king;
For me the bees came by to sing,
For me the swallows flew.[9]

Each book was a world unto itself, and in it I took refuge. Though I knew myself incapable of making up stories such as my favourite authors wrote, I felt that my opinions frequently coincided with theirs, and (to use Montaigne's phrase) "I took to trailing far behind them, murmuring, 'Hear, hear.'"[10] Later I was able to dissociate myself from their fiction; but in my childhood and much of my adolescence, what the book told me, however fantastical, was true at the time of my reading, and as tangible as the stuff of which the book itself was made. Walter Benjamin described the same experience. "What my first books were to me — to remember this I should first have to forget all other knowledge of books. It is certain that all I know of them today rests on the readiness with which I then opened myself to books; but whereas now content, theme and subject-matter are extraneous to the book, earlier they were solely and entirely in it, being no more external or independent of it than are today the number of its pages or its paper. The world that revealed itself in the book and the book itself were never, at any price, to be divided. So with each book its content, too, its world, was palpably there, at hand. But equally, this content and this world transfigured every part of the book. They burned within it, blazed from it; located not merely in its binding or its pictures, they were enshrined in chapter headings and opening letters, paragraphs and columns. You did not read books through; you dwelt, abided between their lines and, reopening them after an interval, surprised yourself at the spot where you had halted."[11]

Later, as an adolescent in my father's largely unused library in Buenos Aires (he had instructed his secretary to furnish the library, and she had bought books by the yard and sent them to be bound to the height of the shelves, so that the titles at the page-tops were in many cases trimmed, and sometimes even the first lines were missing), I made another discovery. I had begun to look up, in the elephantine Espasa-Calpe Spanish encyclopedia, the entries that somehow or other I imagined related to sex: "Masturbation", "Penis", "Vagina", "Syphilis", "Prostitution". I was always alone in the library, since my father used it only on the rare occasions when he had to meet someone at home rather than at his office. I was twelve or thirteen; I was curled up in one of the big armchairs, engrossed in an article on the devastating effects of gonorrhoea, when my father came in and settled himself at his desk. For a moment I was terrified that he would notice what it was I was reading, but then I realized that no one — not even my father, sitting barely a few steps away — could enter my reading-space, could make out what I was being lewdly told by the book I held in my hands, and that nothing except my own will could enable anyone else to know. The small miracle was a silent one, known only to myself. I finished the article on gonorrhoea more elated than shocked. Still later, in that same library, to complete my sexual education, I read Alberto Moravia's *The Conformist*, Guy Des Cars's *The Impure*, Grace Metalious's *Peyton Place*, Sinclair Lewis's *Main Street* and Vladimir Nabokov's *Lolita*.

There was privacy not only in my reading, but also in determining what I would read, in choosing my books in those long-vanished bookstores of Tel Aviv, of Cyprus, of Garmisch-Partenkirchen, of Paris, of Buenos Aires. Many times I chose books by their covers. There were moments that I remember even now: for instance, seeing the matte jackets of the Rainbow Classics (offered by the World Publishing Company of Cleveland, Ohio), and being delighted by the stamped bindings underneath, and coming away with *Hans Brinker or The Silver Skates* (which I never liked and never finished), *Little Women* and *Huckleberry Finn*. All these had May Lamberton Becker's introductions, called "How This Book Came to Be Written", and their gossip still seems to me one of the most exciting ways of talking about books. "So one cold morning in September, 1880, with a Scotch rain hammering at the windows, Stevenson drew close to the fire and began to write," read Ms Becker's introduction to *Treasure Island*. That rain and that fire accompanied me throughout the book.

I remember, in a bookstore in Cyprus, where our ship had stopped for a few days, a windowful of Noddy stories with their shrill-coloured covers, and the pleasure of imagining building Noddy's house with him from a box of building-blocks depicted on the page. (Later on, with no shame at all, I enjoyed Enid Blyton's *The Wishing Chair* series, which I didn't then know English librarians had branded "sexist and snobbish".) In Buenos Aires I discovered the pasteboard Robin Hood series, with the portrait of each hero outlined in black against the flat yellow background, and read there the pirate adventures of Emilio Salgari — *The Tigers of Malaysia* — the novels of Jules Verne and Dickens's *The Mystery of Edwin Drood*. I don't remember ever reading blurbs to find out what the books were about; I don't know if the books of my childhood had any.

I think I read in at least two ways. First, by following, breathlessly, the events and the characters without stopping to notice the details, the quickening pace of reading sometimes hurtling the story beyond the last page — as when I read Rider Haggard, the *Odyssey*, Conan Doyle and the German author of Wild West stories, Karl May. Secondly, by careful exploration, scrutinizing the text to understand its ravelled meaning, finding pleasure merely in the sound of the words or in the clues which the words did not wish to reveal, or in what I suspected was hidden deep in the story itself, something too terrible or too marvellous to be looked at. This second kind of reading — which had something of the quality of reading detective stories — I discovered in Lewis Carroll, in Dante, in Kipling, in Borges. I also read according to what I thought a book was *supposed* to be (labelled by the author, by the publisher, by another reader). At twelve I read Chekhov's *The Hunt* in a series of detective novels and, believing Chekhov to be a Russian thriller writer, then read "Lady with a Lapdog" as if it had been composed by a rival of Conan Doyle's — and enjoyed it, even though I thought the mystery rather thin. In much the same way, Samuel Butler tells of a certain William Sefton Moorhouse who "imagined he was being converted to Christianity by reading Burton's *Anatomy of Melancholy*, which he had got by mistake for Butler's *Analogy*, on the recommendation of a friend. But it puzzled him a good deal."[12] In a story published in the 1940s, Borges suggested that to read Thomas à Kempis's *Imitation of Christ* as if it had been written by James Joyce "would be sufficient renewal for those tenuous spiritual exercises."[13]

Spinoza, in his 1650 *Tractatus Theologico-Politicus* (denounced by the Roman Catholic Church as a book "forged in hell by a renegade Jew and the devil"), had already observed: "It often happens that in different books we read histories in themselves similar, but which we judge very differently, according to the opinions we have formed of the authors. I remember once to have read in some book that a man named Orlando Furioso used to ride a kind of winged monster through the air, fly over any country he liked, kill unaided vast numbers of men and giants, and other such fancies which from the point of view of reason are obviously absurd. I read a very similar story, in Ovid, of Perseus, and also, in the books of Judges and Kings, of Samson, who alone and unarmed killed thousands of men, and of Elijah, who flew through the air and at last went up to heaven in a chariot of fire, with fiery horses. All these stories are obviously alike, but we judge them very differently. The first one sought to amuse, the second had a political object, the third a religious one."[14] I too, for the longest time, attributed purposes to the books I read, expecting, for instance, that Bunyan's *Pilgrim's Progress* would preach to me because it was, I was told, a religious allegory — as if I were able to listen to what was taking place in the author's mind at the moment of creation, and to gain proof that the author was indeed speaking the truth. Experience and a degree of common sense have not yet completely cured me of this superstitious vice.

Sometimes the books themselves were talismans: a certain two-volume set of *Tristram Shandy*, a Penguin edition of Nicholas Blake's

The Beast Must Die, a tattered copy of Martin Gardner's *Annotated Alice* which I had bound (at the cost of a whole month's allowance) at a shady bookseller's. These I read with special care, and kept for special moments. Thomas à Kempis instructed his students to take "a book into thine hands as Simeon the Just took the Child Jesus into his arms to carry him and kiss him. And thou hast finished reading, close the book and give thanks for every word out of the mouth of God; because in the Lord's field thou hast found a hidden treasure."[15] And Saint Benedict, writing at a time when books were comparatively rare and expensive, ordered his monks to hold "if possible" the books they read "in their left hands, wrapped in the sleeve of their tunics, and resting on their knees; their right hands shall be uncovered with which to grip and turn the pages."[16] My adolescent reading did not entail such deep veneration or such careful rituals, but it possessed a certain secret solemnity and importance that I will not now deny.

I wanted to live among books. When I was sixteen, in 1964, I found a job, after school, at Pygmalion, one of the three Anglo-German bookstores of Buenos Aires. The owner was Lily Lebach, a German Jew who had fled the Nazis and settled in Buenos Aires in the late 1930s, and who set me the daily task of dusting each and every one of the books in the store — a method by which she thought (quite rightly) I would quickly get to know the stock and its location on the shelves. Unfortunately, many of the books tempted me beyond cleanliness; they wanted to be held and opened and inspected, and sometimes even that was not enough. A few times I stole a tempting book; I took it home with me, stashed away in my coat pocket, because I not only had to read it; I had to have it, to call it mine. The novelist Jamaica Kincaid, confessing to the similar crime of stealing books from her childhood library in Antigua, explained that her intention was not to steal; it was "just that once I had read a book I couldn't bear to part with it."[17] I too soon discovered that one doesn't simply read *Crime and Punishment* or *A Tree Grows in Brooklyn*. One reads a certain edition, a specific copy, recognizable by the roughness or smoothness of its paper, by its scent, by a slight tear on page 72 and a coffee ring on the right-hand corner of the back cover. The epistemological rule for reading, established in the second century, that the most recent text replaces the previous one, since it is supposed to contain it, has rarely been true in my case. In the early Middle Ages, scribes would supposedly "correct" errors they might perceive in the text they were copying, thereby producing a "better" text;

for me, however, the edition in which I read a book for the first time became the *editio princeps*, with which all others must be compared. Printing has given us the illusion that all readers of *Don Quixote* are reading the same book. For me, even today, it is as if the invention of printing had never taken place, and each copy of a book remains as singular as the phoenix.

And yet, the truth is that particular books lend certain characteristics to particular readers. Implicit in the possession of a book is the history of the book's previous readings — that is to say, every new reader is affected by what he or she imagines the book to have been in previous hands. My second-hand copy of Kipling's autobiography, *Something of Myself*, which I bought in Buenos Aires, carries a handwritten poem on the flyleaf, dated the day of Kipling's death. The impromptu poet who owned this copy, was he an ardent imperialist? A lover of Kipling's prose who saw the artist through the jingoist patina? My imagined predecessor affects my reading because I find myself in dialogue with him, arguing this or that point. A book brings its own history to the reader.

Miss Lebach must have known that her employees pilfered books, but I suspect that, as long as she felt we did not exceed certain unspoken limits, she would allow the crime. Once or twice she saw me engrossed in a new arrival, and merely told me to get on with my work and to keep the book and read it at home, on my own time. Marvellous books came my way at her store: Thomas Mann's *Joseph and His Brothers*, Saul Bellow's *Herzog*, Pär Lagerkvist's *The Dwarf*, Salinger's *Nine Stories*, Broch's *The Death of Virgil*, Herbert Read's *The Green Child*, Italo Svevo's *Confessions of Zeno*, the poems of Rilke, of Dylan Thomas, of Emily Dickinson, of Gerard Manley Hopkins, the Egyptian love lyrics translated by Ezra Pound, the epic of Gilgamesh.

One afternoon, Jorge Luis Borges came to the bookstore accompanied by his eighty-eight-year-old mother. He was famous, but I had read only a few of his poems and stories and I did not feel overwhelmed by his literature. He was almost completely blind and yet he refused to carry a cane, and he would pass a hand over the shelves as if his fingers could see the titles. He was looking for books to help him study Anglo-Saxon, which had become his latest passion, and we had ordered for him Skeat's dictionary and an annotated version of *Battle of Maldon*. Borges's mother grew impatient; "Oh Georgie," she said. "I don't know why you waste your time with Anglo-Saxon, instead of studying something useful like Latin or Greek!" In the end, he turned and asked me for several books. I found a few and made note of the others and then, as he was about to leave, he asked me if I was busy in the evenings because he needed (he said this very apologetically) someone to read to him, since his mother now tired very easily. I said I would.

Over the next two years I read to Borges, as did many other fortunate and casual acquaintances, either in the evenings or, if school allowed it, in the mornings. The ritual was always very much the same. Ignoring the elevator, I would climb the stairs to his apartment (stairs similar to the ones Borges had once climbed carrying a newly acquired copy of *The Arabian Nights*; he failed to notice an open window and received a bad cut which turned septic, leading him to delirium and to the belief that he was going mad); I would ring the bell; I would be led by the maid through a curtained entrance into the small sitting-room where Borges would come and meet me, soft hand outstretched. There were no preliminaries; he would sit expectantly on the couch while I took my place in an armchair, and in a slightly asthmatic voice he would suggest that night's reading. "Shall we choose Kipling tonight? Eh?" And of course he didn't really expect an answer.

In that sitting-room, under a Piranesi engraving of circular Roman ruins, I read Kipling, Stevenson, Henry James, several entries of the Brockhaus German encyclopedia, verses of Marino, of Enrique Banchs, of Heine (but these last ones he knew by heart, so I would barely have begun my reading when his hesitant voice picked up and recited from memory; the hesitation was only in the cadence, not in the words themselves, which he remembered unerringly). I had not read many of these authors before, so the ritual was a curious one. I would discover a text by reading it out loud, while Borges used his ears as other readers use their eyes, to scan the page for a word, for a sentence, for a paragraph that would confirm a memory. When I read he'd interrupt, commenting on the text in order (I think) to take note of it in his mind.

Stopping me after a line he found side-splitting in Stevenson's *New Arabian Nights* ("dressed and painted to represent a person connected with the Press in reduced circumstances" — "How can someone be dressed like that, eh? What do you think Stevenson had in mind? Being impossibly precise? Eh?"), he proceeded to analyse the stylistic device of defining someone or something by means of an image or category that, while appearing to be exact, forces the reader to make up a personal definition. He and his friend Adolfo Bioy Casares had played on that idea in an eleven-word short story: "The stranger climbed the stairs in the dark: tick-tock, tick-tock, tick-tock."

Listening to my reading of Kipling's story "Beyond the Pale", Borges interrupted me after a scene in which a Hindu widow sends a message to her lover, made up of different objects collected in a bundle. He remarked on the poetic appropriateness of this, and wondered out loud whether Kipling had invented this concrete and yet symbolic language.[18] Then, as if scouring a mental library, he compared it to John Wilkins's "philosophical language" in which each word is a definition of itself. For instance, Borges noted that the word *salmon* does not tell us anything about the object it represents; *zana*, the corresponding word in Wilkins's language, based on pre-established categories, means "a scaly river fish with reddish flesh":[19] *z* for fish, *za* for river fish, *zan* for scaly river fish and *zana* for the scaly river fish with reddish flesh. Reading to Borges always resulted in a mental reshuffling of my own books; that evening, Kipling and Wilkins stood side by side on the same imaginary shelf.

Another time (I can't remember what it was I had been asked to read), he began to compile an impromptu anthology of bad lines by famous authors, which included Keats's "The owl, for all his feathers, was a-cold", Shakespeare's "O my prophetic soul! My uncle!" (Borges found "uncle" an unpoetic, inappropriate word for Hamlet to utter — he would have preferred "My father's brother!" or "My mother's kin!"), Webster's "We are merely the stars' tennis-balls" from *The Duchess of Malfi* and Milton's last lines in *Paradise Regained* — "he unobserv'd / Home to his Mother's house private return'd" — which made Christ out to be (Borges thought) an English gentleman in a bowler hat coming home to his mum for tea.

Sometimes he'd make use of the readings for his own writing. His discovery of a ghost tiger in Kipling's "The Guns of 'Fore and 'Aft", which we read shortly before Christmas, led him to compose one of his last stories, "Blue Tigers"; Giovanni Papini's "Two Images in a Pond" inspired his "August 24, 1982", a date which was then still in the future; his irritation with Lovecraft (whose stories he had me start and abandon half a dozen times) made him create a "corrected" version of a Lovecraft story and publish it in *Dr. Brodie's Report*. Often he'd ask me to write something down on the endpaper pages of the book we were reading — a chapter reference or a thought. I don't know how he made use of these, but the habit of speaking of a book behind its back became mine too.

There is a story by Evelyn Waugh in which a man, rescued by another in the midst of the Amazonian jungle, is forced by his rescuer to read Dickens out loud for the rest of his life.[20] I never had the sense of merely fulfilling a duty in my reading to Borges; instead, the experience felt like a sort of happy captivity. I was enthralled not so much by the texts he was making me discover (many of which eventually became my own favourites) as by his comments, which were vastly but unobtrusively erudite, very funny, sometimes cruel, almost always indispensable. I felt I was the unique owner of a carefully annotated edition, compiled for my exclusive sake. Of course, I wasn't; I (like many others) was simply his notebook, an *aide-mémoire* which the blind man required in order to assemble his ideas. I was more than willing to be used.

Before meeting Borges, either I had read silently on my own, or someone had read aloud to me a book of my choice. Reading out loud to the blind old man was a curious experience because, even though I felt, with some effort, in control of the tone and pace of the reading, it was nevertheless Borges, the listener, who became the master of the text. I was the driver, but the landscape, the unfurling space, belonged to the one being driven, for whom there was no other responsibility than that of apprehending the country outside the windows. Borges chose the book, Borges stopped me or asked me to continue, Borges interrupted to comment, Borges allowed the words to come to him. I was invisible.

I quickly learned that reading is cumulative and proceeds by geometrical progression: each new reading builds upon whatever the reader has read before. I began by making assumptions about the stories Borges chose for me — that Kipling's prose would be stilted, Stevenson's childish, Joyce's unintelligible — but very soon prejudice gave way to experience, and the discovery of one story made me look forward to another, which in turn became enriched by the memory of both Borges's reactions and my own. The progression of my reading never followed the conventional sequence of time. For instance, reading out loud to him texts that I had read before on my own modified those earlier solitary readings, widened and suffused my memory of them, made me perceive what I had not perceived at the time but seemed to recall now, triggered by his response. "There are those who, while reading a book, recall, compare, conjure up emotions from other, previous readings," remarked the Argentinian writer Ezequiel

Martínez Estrada. "This is one of the most delicate forms of adultery."[21] Borges disbelieved in systematic bibliographies and encouraged such adulterous reading.

Aside from Borges, a few friends, several teachers and a review here and there have suggested titles now and again, but largely my encounters with books have been a matter of chance, like meeting those passing strangers who in the fifteenth canto of Dante's Hell "eye one another when the daylight fades to dusk and a new moon is in the sky", and who suddenly find in an appearance, a glance, a word, an irresistible attraction.

I first kept my books in straight alphabetical order, by author. Then I began dividing them by genre: novels, essays, plays, poems. Later on I tried grouping them by language, and when, during the course of my travels, I was obliged to keep only a few, I separated them into those I hardly ever read, those I read all the time and those I was hoping to read. Sometimes my library obeyed secret rules, born from idiosyncratic associations. The Spanish novelist Jorge Semprún kept Thomas Mann's *Lotte in Weimar* among his books on Buchenwald, the concentration camp in which he had been interned, because the novel opens with a scene at Weimar's Elephant Hotel, where Semprún was taken after his liberation.[22] Once I thought it would be amusing to construct from such groupings a history of literature, exploring, for instance, the relationships between Aristotle, Auden, Jane Austen and Marcel Aymé (in my alphabetical order), or between Chesterton, Sylvia Townsend Warner, Borges, Saint John of the Cross and Lewis Carroll (among those I most enjoy). It seemed to me that the literature taught at school — in which links were explained between Cervantes and Lope de Vega based on the fact that they shared a century, and in which Juan Ramón Jiménez's *Platero y yo* (a purple tale of a poet's infatuation with a donkey) was considered a masterpiece — was as arbitrary or as permissible a selection as the literature I could construct myself, based on my findings along the crooked road of my own readings and the size of my own bookshelves. The history of literature, as consecrated in school manuals and official libraries, appeared to me to be nothing more than the history of certain readings — albeit older and better informed than mine, but no less dependent on chance and on circumstance.

One year before graduating from high school, in 1966, when the military government of General Onganía came to power, I discovered yet another system by which a reader's books can be arranged. Under suspicion of being Communist or obscene, certain titles and certain authors were placed on the censor's list, and in the ever-increasing police checks in cafés, bars and train stations, or simply on the street, it became as important not to be seen with a suspicious book in hand as it was to carry proper identification. The banned authors — Pablo Neruda, J.D. Salinger, Maxim Gorky, Harold Pinter — formed another, different history of literature, whose links were neither evident nor everlasting, and whose communality was revealed exclusively by the punctilious eye of the censor.

But not only totalitarian governments fear reading. Readers are bullied in schoolyards and in locker-rooms as much as in government offices and prisons. Almost everywhere, the community of readers has an ambiguous reputation that comes from its acquired authority and perceived power. Something in the relationship between a reader and a book is recognized as wise and fruitful, but it is also seen as disdainfully exclusive and excluding, perhaps because the image of an individual curled up in a corner, seemingly oblivious of the grumblings of the world, suggests impenetrable privacy and a selfish eye and singular secretive action. ("Go out and live!" my mother would say when she saw me reading, as if my silent activity contradicted her sense of what it meant to be alive.) The popular fear of what a reader might do among the pages of a book is like the ageless fear men have of what women might do in the secret places of their body, and of what witches and alchemists might do in the dark behind locked doors. Ivory, according to Virgil, is the material out of which the Gate of False Dreams is made; according to Sainte-Beuve, it is also the material out of which is made the reader's tower.

Borges once told me that, during one of the populist demonstrations organized by Perón's government in 1950 against the opposing intellectuals, the demonstrators chanted, "Shoes yes, books no." The retort, "Shoes yes, books yes," convinced no one. Reality — harsh, necessary reality — was seen to conflict irredeemably with the evasive dreamworld of books. With this excuse, and with increasing effect, the artificial dichotomy between life and reading is actively encouraged by those in power. Demotic regimes demand that we forget, and therefore they brand books as superfluous luxuries; totalitarian regimes demand that we not think, and therefore they ban and threaten and censor; both, by and large, require that we become stupid and that we accept

our degradation meekly, and therefore they encourage the consumption of pap. In such circumstances, readers cannot but be subversive.

And so I ambitiously proceed from my history as a reader to the history of the act of reading. Or rather, to *a* history of reading, since any
such history — made up of particular intuitions and private circumstances — must be only one of many, however impersonal it may try
to be. Ultimately, perhaps, the history of reading is the history of each
of its readers. Even its starting-point has to be fortuitous. Reviewing a
history of mathematics published sometime in the mid-thirties, Borges
wrote that it suffered "from a crippling defect: the chronological order
of its events doesn't correspond to its logical and natural order. The
definition of its elements very frequently comes last, practice precedes
theory, the intuitive labours of its precursors are less comprehensible
for the profane reader than those of the modern mathematicians."[23]
Much the same can be said of a history of reading. Its chronology cannot be that of political history. The Sumerian scribe for whom reading
was a much-valued prerogative had a keener sense of responsibility
than the reader in today's New York or Santiago, since an article of law
or a settling of accounts depended on his exclusive interpretation. The
reading methods of the late Middle Ages, defining when and how to
read, distinguishing, for instance, between the text to be read aloud
and the text to be read silently, were much more clearly established
than those taught in *fin-de-siècle* Vienna or in Edwardian England. Nor
can a history of reading follow the coherent succession of the history of
literary criticism; the qualms expressed by the nineteenth-century
mystic Anna Katharina Emmerich (that the printed text never equalled
her experience)[24] were even more strongly expressed two thousand
years earlier by Socrates (who found books an impediment to learning)[25] and in our time by the German critic Hans Magnus Enzensberger
(who praised illiteracy and proposed a return to the original creativity
of oral literature).[26] This position was refuted by the American essayist
Allan Bloom,[27] among many others; with splendid anachronism, Bloom
was amended and improved by his precursor, Charles Lamb, who in
1833 confessed that he loved to lose himself "in other men's minds.
When I am not walking," he said, "I am reading; I cannot sit and think.
Books think for me."[28] Neither does the history of reading correspond
to the chronologies of the histories of literature, since the history of

reading one particular author often finds a beginning not with that author's first book but with one of the author's future readers: the Marquis de Sade was rescued from the condemned shelves of pornographic literature, where his books had sat for over 150 years, by the bibliophile Maurice Heine and the French surrealists; William Blake, ignored for over two centuries, begins in our time with the enthusiasm of Sir Geoffrey Keynes and Northrop Frye, which made him obligatory reading on every college curriculum.

Told that we are threatened with extinction, we, today's readers, have yet to learn what reading is. Our future — the future of the history of our reading — was explored by Saint Augustine, who tried to distinguish between the text seen in the mind and the text spoken out loud; by Dante, who questioned the limits of the reader's power of interpretation; by Lady Murasaki, who argued for the specificity of certain readings; by Pliny, who analysed the performance of reading, and the relationship between the writer who reads and the reader who writes; by the Sumerian scribes, who imbued the act of reading with political power; by the first makers of books, who found the methods of scroll-reading (like the methods we now use to read on our computers) too limiting and cumbersome, and offered us instead the possibility of flipping through pages and scribbling in margins. The past of that history lies ahead of us, on the last page in that cautionary future described by Ray Bradbury in *Fahrenheit 451*, in which books are carried not on paper but in the mind.

Like the act of reading itself, a history of reading jumps forward to our time — to me, to my experience as a reader — and then goes back to an early page in a distant foreign century. It skips chapters, browses, selects, rereads, refuses to follow conventional order. Paradoxically, the fear that opposes reading to active life, that urged my mother to move me from my seat and my book out into the open air, recognizes a solemn truth: "You cannot embark on life, that one-off coach ride, once again when it is over," writes the Turkish novelist Orhan Pamuk in *The White Castle*, "but if you have a book in your hand, no matter how complex or difficult to understand that book may be, when you have finished it, you can, if you wish, go back to the beginning, read it again, and thus understand that which is difficult and, with it, understand life as well."[29]

ACTS

of

READING

Reading means approaching something
that is just coming into being.

ITALO CALVINO
If on a winter's night a traveller, 1979

READING SHADOWS

OPPOSITE

Teaching optics
and the laws of
perception in
a sixteenth-
century Islamic
school.

LEFT

Two
pictographic
tablets from
Tell Brak,
Syria, similar to
the ones in the
Archeological
Museum in
Baghdad.

I n 1984, two small clay tablets of vaguely rectangular shape were found in Tell Brak, Syria, dating from the fourth millennium BC. I saw them, the year before the Gulf War, in an unostentatious display case in the Archeological Museum of Baghdad. They are simple, unimpressive objects, each bearing a few discreet markings: a small indentation near the top and some sort of stick-drawn animal in the centre. One of the animals may be a goat, in which case the other is probably a sheep. The indentation, archeologists say, repre-

sents the number ten. All our history begins with these two modest tablets.[1] They are — if the war spared them — among the oldest examples of writing we know.[2]

There is something intensely moving in these tablets. Perhaps, when we stare at these pieces of clay carried by a river which no longer exists, observing the delicate incisions portraying animals turned to dust thousands and thousands of years ago, a voice is conjured up, a thought, a message that tells us, "Here were ten goats," "Here were ten sheep," something spoken by a careful farmer in the days when the deserts were green. By the mere fact of looking at these tablets we have prolonged a memory from the beginnings of our time, preserved a thought long after the thinker has stopped thinking, and made ourselves

participants in an act of creation that remains open for as long as the incised images are seen, deciphered, read.[3]

Like my nebulous Sumerian ancestor reading the two small tablets
on that inconceivably remote afternoon, I too am reading, here in my
room, across centuries and seas. Sitting at my desk, elbows on the
page, chin on my hands, abstracted for a moment from the changing
light outside and the sounds that rise from the street, I am seeing,
listening to, following (but these words don't do justice to what is
taking place within me) a story, a description, an argument. Nothing
moves except my eyes and my hand occasionally turning a page, and
yet something not exactly defined by the word "text" unfurls,
progresses, grows and takes root as I read. But how does this process
take place?

Reading begins with the eyes. "The keenest of our senses is the
sense of sight," wrote Cicero, noting that when we see a text we remember it better than when we merely hear it.[4] Saint Augustine
praised (and then condemned) the eyes as the world's point of entry,[5]
and Saint Thomas Aquinas called sight "the greatest of the senses
through which we acquire knowledge".[6] This much is obvious to any
reader: that letters are grasped through sight. But by what alchemy do
these letters become intelligible words? What takes place inside us
when we are faced with a text? How do the things seen, the "sub-
stances" that arrive through the eyes to our internal laboratory, the
colours and shapes of objects and of letters, become readable? What, in
fact, is the act we call reading?

Empedocles, in the fifth century BC, described the eye as born
from the goddess Aphrodite, who "confined a fire in membranes and
delicate cloths; these held back the deep water flowing around, but let
through the inner flames to the outside."[7] More than a century later,
Epicurus imagined these flames to be thin films of atoms that flowed
from the surface of every object and entered our eyes and minds like a
constant and ascending rain, drenching us in all the qualities of the object.[8] Euclid, Epicurus's contemporary, proposed the contrary theory:
that rays are sent out of the observer's eyes to apprehend the object
observed.[9] Seemingly insurmountable problems riddled both theories.
For instance, in the case of the first, the so-called "intromission" theory, how could the film of atoms emitted by a large object — an elephant or Mount Olympus — enter so small a space as the human
eye? As to the second, the "extromission" theory, what ray could issue

from the eyes and in a fraction of a second reach the distant stars we see every night?

A few decades earlier Aristotle had suggested another theory. Anticipating and correcting Epicurus, he had argued that the qualities of the thing observed — rather than a film of atoms — travelled through air (or some other medium) to the eye of the observer, so that what was apprehended was not the actual dimensions but the relative size and shape of a mountain. The human eye, according to Aristotle, was like a chameleon, taking in the form and colour of the observed object and passing this information, via the eye's humours, on to the all-powerful innards (*splanchna*),[10] a conglomerate of organs that included the heart, liver, lungs, gall-bladder and blood vessels, and held dominion over motion and senses.[11]

Six centuries later, the Greek physician Galen offered a fourth solution, contradicting Epicurus and following Euclid. Galen proposed that a "visual spirit", born in the brain, crossed the eye through the optic nerve and flowed out into the air. The air itself then became capable of perception, apprehending the qualities of the objects perceived however far away they might happen to be. These qualities were re-transmitted back through the eye to the brain, and down the spinal cord to the nerves of sense and motion. For Aristotle, the observer was a passive entity receiving through the air the thing observed, which was then communicated to the heart, seat of all sensations — including vision. For Galen, the observer, rendering the air sentient, held an active role, and the root from which vision stemmed lay deep in the brain.

Medieval scholars, for whom Galen and Aristotle were the fountainheads of scientific learning, generally believed that a hierarchical relation could be found between these two theories. It was not a question of one theory overriding the other; what mattered was to extract from each an understanding of how the different parts of the body related to perceptions of the outside world — and also how these parts related to one another. The fourteenth-century Italian doctor Gentile da Foligno decreed that such an understanding was "as essential a step in medicine as learning the alphabet is in reading,"[12] and recalled that Saint Augustine, among other early Fathers of the Church, had already considered the question carefully. For Saint Augustine, both the brain and the heart functioned as shepherds of that which the senses stored in our memory, and he used the verb *colligere* (meaning

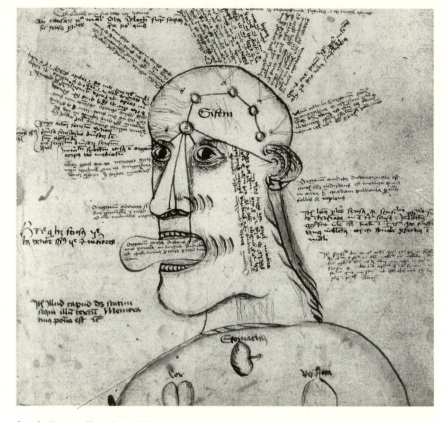

both "to collect" and "to summarize") to describe how these impressions were gathered from memory's separate compartments, and "shepherded out of their old lairs, because there is no other place where they could have gone".[13]

Memory was only one of the functions that benefited from this husbandry of the senses. It was commonly accepted by medieval scholars that (as Galen had suggested) sight, sound, smell, taste and touch fed into a general sensorial repository located in the brain, an area sometimes known as "common sense", from which derived not only memory but also knowledge, fantasy and dreams. This area, in turn, was connected to Aristotle's *splanchna*, now reduced by the medieval commentators to just the heart, the centre of all feeling. Thus the senses were ascribed a direct kinship with the brain while the heart was declared the body's ultimate ruler.[14] A late-fifteenth-century manuscript in German, of Aristotle's treatise on logic and natural philosophy, depicts the head of a man, eyes and mouth open, nostrils flaring,

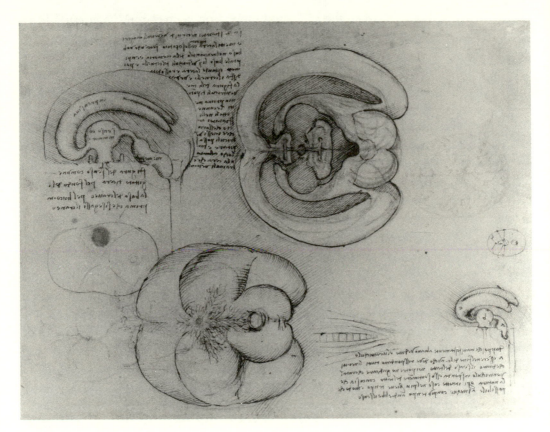

one ear carefully underlined. Inside the brain are five small connected circles representing, from left to right, the principal site of common sense, and then the sites of imagination, fantasy, cogitative power and memory. According to the accompanying gloss, the circle of common sense is related as well to the heart, also depicted in the drawing. This diagram is a fair example of how the process of perception was imagined in the late Middle Ages, with one small addendum: though it was not represented in this illustration, it was commonly supposed (going back to Galen) that at the base of the brain was a "marvellous net" — *rete mirabile* — of small vessels that acted as communication channels when whatever reached the brain was refined. This *rete mirabile* appears in a drawing of a brain that Leonardo da Vinci made around the year 1508, clearly marking the separate ventricles and attributing to different sections the various mental faculties. According to Leonardo, "the *senso comune* [common sense] is that which judges the impressions transmitted by the other senses . . . and its place is in the middle of the

Leonardo Da Vinci's drawing of a brain, showing the *rete mirabile.*

31

head, between the *impresiva* [impression centre] and the *memoria* [centre of memory]. The surrounding objects transmit their images to the senses and the senses pass these on to the *impresiva*. The *impresiva* communicates them to the *senso comune* and, from there, they are imprinted in the memory where they become more or less fixed, according to the importance and force of the object in question."[15] The human mind, in Leonardo's time, was seen as a small laboratory where the material gathered in by the eyes, ears and other organs of perception became "impressions" in the brain that were channelled through the centre of common sense and then transformed into one or several faculties — such as memory — under the influence of the supervising heart. The sight of black letters (to use an alchemical image) became through this process the gold of knowledge.

But one fundamental question remained unsolved: did we, the readers, reach out and capture letters on a page, according to the theories of Euclid and Galen? Or did the letters reach out to our senses, as Epicurus and Aristotle had maintained? For Leonardo and his contemporaries, the answer (or hints towards an answer) could be found in a thirteenth-century translation of a book written two hundred years earlier (so long are sometimes the hesitancies of scholarship) in Egypt, by the Basra scholar al-Hasan ibn al-Haytham, known to the West as Alhazen.

Egypt flourished in the eleventh century under Fatimid rule, drawing its wealth from the Nile valley and from trade with its Mediterranean neighbours, while its sandy frontiers were protected by an army recruited from abroad — Berbers, Sudanese and Turks. This heterogenous arrangement of international trade and mercenary warfare gave Fatimid Egypt all the advantages and aims of a truly cosmopolitan state.[16] In 1004 the caliph al-Hakim (who had become ruler at the age of eleven and disappeared mysteriously during a solitary walk twenty-five years later) founded a large academy in Cairo — the Dar al-Ilm or House of Science — modelled on pre-Islamic institutions, making a gift to the people of his own important collection of manuscripts and decreeing that "all and sundry might come here to read, transcribe and be instructed".[17] Al-Hakim's eccentric decisions — he prohibited the game of chess and the sale of scaleless fish — and his notorious bloodthirstiness were tempered in the popular imagination by his administrative success.[18] His purpose was to make Fatimid Cairo not only the symbolic centre of political power but also the capital of artistic

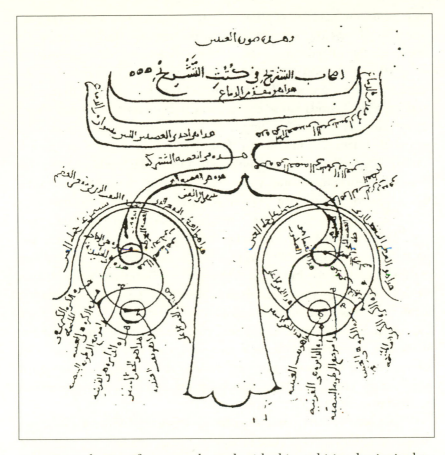

Al-Haytham's
visual system
as depicted in
the eleventh-
century *Kitab
al-manazir*,
drawn by the
author's son-
in-law, Ahmad
ibn Jafar.

pursuits and scientific research, and with this ambition he invited to
court many celebrated astronomers and mathematicians, among them
al-Haytham. Al-Haytham's official mission was to study a method of
regulating the flow of the Nile. This he did, unsuccessfully, but he also
spent his days preparing a refutation of Ptolemy's astronomical theories (which his enemies argued was "less a refutation than a new set of
doubts") and his nights writing the bulky study of optics on which his
fame was to rest.

According to al-Haytham, all perception from the outside world
involves a certain deliberate inference that stems from our faculty of
judgement. To develop this theory, al-Haytham followed the basic
argument of Aristotle's intromission theory — that the qualities of
what we see enter the eye by means of the air — and he supported his
choice with accurate physical, mathematical and physiological explanations.[19] But more radically, al-Haytham made a distinction between

"pure sensation" and "perception", the former being unconscious or in-voluntary — seeing the light outside my window and the changing shapes of the afternoon — the latter requiring a voluntary act of recognition — following a text on the page.[20] The importance of al-Haytham's argument was that it identified for the first time, in the act of perceiving, a gradation of conscious action that proceeds from "see-ing" to "deciphering" or "reading".

Al-Haytham died in Cairo in 1038. Two centuries later, the English scholar Roger Bacon — attempting to justify the study of optics to Pope Clement IV at a time when certain factions within the Catholic Church were violently arguing that scientific research was contrary to Christian dogma — offered a revised summary of al-Haytham's the-ory.[21] Following al-Haytham (while at the same time underplaying the importance of Islamic scholarship), Bacon explained to His Holiness the mechanics of the intromission theory. According to Bacon, when we look at an object (a tree or the letters *SUN*) a visual pyramid is formed that has its base on the object itself and its apex at the centre of the curvature of the cornea. We "see" when the pyramid enters our eye and its rays are arranged on the surface of our eyeball, refracted in such a way that they do not intersect. Seeing, for Bacon, was the active process by which an image of the object entered the eye and was then grasped through the eye's "visual powers".

But how does this perception become reading? How does the act of apprehending letters relate to a process that involves not only sight and perception but inference, judgement, memory, recognition, knowledge, experience, practice? Al-Haytham knew (and Bacon no doubt agreed) that all these elements necessary to perform the act of reading lent it an astounding complexity, which required for its suc-cessful performance the co-ordination of a hundred different skills. And not only these skills but the time, place, and tablet, scroll, page or screen on which the act is performed affect the reading: for the anony-mous Sumerian farmer, the village near where he tended his goats and sheep, and the rounded clay; for al-Haytham, the new white room of the Cairo academy, and the scornfully read Ptolemy manuscript; for Bacon, the prison cell to which he was condemned for his unorthodox teaching, and his precious scientific volumes; for Leonardo, the court of King François I, where he spent his last years, and the notebooks he kept in a secret code which can be read only if held up to a mirror. All these bewilderingly diverse elements come together in that one act;

this much, al-Haytham had surmised. But how it all took place, what intricate and formidable connections these elements established among themselves, was a question that, for al-Haytham and for his readers, remained unanswered.

The modern study of neurolinguistics, the relationship between brain and language, begins almost eight and a half centuries after al-Haytham, in 1865. That year, two French scientists, Michel Dax and Paul Broca,[22] suggested in simultaneous but separate studies that the vast majority of humankind, as a result of a genetic process which begins at conception, is born with a left cerebral hemisphere that will eventually become the dominant part of the brain for encoding and decoding language; a much smaller proportion, mostly left-handers or ambidextrous people, develop this function in the right cerebral hemisphere. In a few cases (in people genetically predisposed to a dominant left hemisphere), early damage to the left hemisphere results in a cerebral "reprogramming" and leads to development of the language function in the right hemisphere. But neither hemisphere will act as encoder and decoder until the person is actually exposed to language.

By the time the first scribe scratched and uttered the first letters, the human body was already capable of the acts of writing and reading that still lay in the future; that is to say, the body was able to store, recall and decipher all manner of sensations, including the arbitrary signs of written language yet to be invented.[23] This notion, that we are capable of reading before we can actually read — in fact, before we have even seen a page open in front of us — harks back to Platonic ideas of knowledge existing within us before the thing is perceived. Speech itself apparently evolves along the same pattern. We "discover" a word because the object or idea it represents is already in our mind, "ready to be linked up with the word".[24] It is as if we are offered a gift from the outside world (by our elders, by those who first speak to us) but the ability to grasp the gift is our own. In that sense, the words spoken (and, later on, the words read) belong neither to us nor to our parents, to our authors; they occupy a space of shared meaning, a communal threshold which lies at the beginning of our relationship to the arts of conversation and reading.

According to Professor André Roch Lecours of Côte-des-Neiges Hospital in Montreal, exposure to oral language alone may not be enough for either hemisphere to develop the language functions fully; it may be that, for our brains to allow this development, we must be taught to recognize a shared system of visual signs. In other words, we must learn to read.[25]

In the 1980s, while working in Brazil, Professor Lecours came to the conclusion that the genetic program leading to the more common left cerebral dominance was less implemented in the brains of those who had not learned to read than in those who had. This suggested to him that the process of reading could be explored through cases of patients in whom the reading faculty had become impaired. (Galen long ago argued that a disease not only indicates the failure of the body to perform but also sheds light on the absent performance itself.) A few years later, studying patients suffering from speech or reading impediments in Montreal, Professor Lecours was able to make a series of observations regarding the mechanisms of reading. In examples of aphasia, for instance — where the patient has partially or completely lost the power or understanding of the spoken word — he found that specific lesions to the brain caused particular speech handicaps that were curiously restricted: some patients became incapable of reading or writing only irregularly spelled words (such as "rough" or "though" in English); others could not read invented words ("tooflow" or "boojum"); yet others could see but not pronounce certain oddly assorted words, or words unevenly disposed on the page. Sometimes these patients could read whole words but not syllables; sometimes they read by replacing certain words with others. Lemuel Gulliver, describing the Struldbruggs of Laputa, noted that at age ninety these elderly worthies can no longer amuse themselves with reading, "because their Memory will not serve to carry them from the Beginning of a Sentence to the End; and by this Defect they are deprived of the only Entertainment whereof they might otherwise be capable."[26] Several of Professor Lecours' patients suffered from just such a disorder. To complicate matters, in similar studies in China and Japan researchers observed that patients accustomed to reading ideograms as opposed to phonetic alphabets reacted differently to the investigations, as if these specific language functions were predominant in different areas of the brain.

Agreeing with al-Haytham, Professor Lecours concluded that the process of reading entailed at least two stages: "seeing" the word, and "considering" it according to learned information. Like the Sumerian scribe thousands of years ago, I face the words. I look at the words, I see the words, and what I see organizes itself according to a code or system which I have learned and which I share with other readers of my time and place — a code that has settled in specific sections of my brain. "It is," Professor Lecours argues, "as if the information received from the page by the eyes travels through the brain through a series of conglomerates of specialized neurons, each conglomerate occupying a certain section of the brain and effecting a specific function. We don't yet know what exactly each of these functions is, but in certain cases of brain lesions one or several of these conglomerates become, so to speak, disconnected from the chain and the patient becomes incapable of reading certain words, or a certain type of language, or of reading out loud, or replaces one set of words with another. The possible disconnections seem endless."[27]

Neither is the primary act of scanning the page with our eyes a continuous, systematic process. It is usually assumed that, when we are reading, our eyes travel smoothly, without interruptions, along the lines of a page, and that, when we are reading Western writing, for instance, our eyes go from left to right. This isn't so. A century ago, the French ophthalmologist Émile Javal discovered that our eyes actually jump about the page; these jumps or saccades take place three or four times per second, at a speed of about 200 degrees per second. The speed of the eye's motion across the page — but not the motion itself — interferes with perception, and it is only during the brief pause between movements that we actually "read". Why our sense of reading is related to the continuity of the text on the page or to the scrolling of the text on the screen, assimilating entire sentences or thoughts, and not to the actual saccadic movement of the eyes, is a question which scientists have not yet been able to answer.[28]

Analysing the cases of two clinical patients — one an aphasic who could make eloquent speeches in a language that was gibberish, and the other an agnosic who could use ordinary language but was incapable of imbuing it with tone or emotion — Dr. Oliver Sacks argued that "speech — natural speech — does not consist of words alone. . . . It consists of utterance — an uttering-forth of one's whole meaning with one's whole being — the understanding of which involves infinitely more than mere word-recognition."[29] Much the same can be said of reading: following the text, the reader utters its meaning through a vastly entangled method of learned significances, social conventions, previous readings, personal experience and private taste. Reading in

The language-
sense divided
according to its
functions, as
recorded in
photographs of
the human brain
taken at the
Washington
University
School of
Medicine.

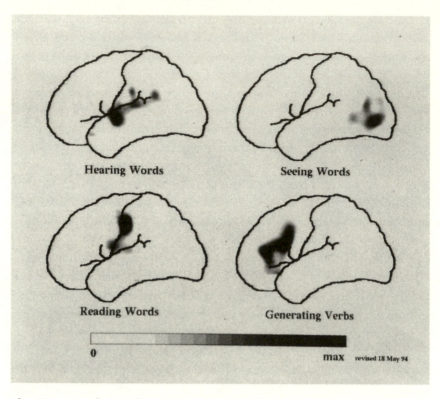

Hearing Words

Seeing Words

Reading Words

Generating Verbs

0

max   revised 18 May 94

the Cairo academy, al-Haytham was not alone; reading over his shoul-
der, as it were, hovered the shadows of the Basra scholars who had
taught him the Koran's sacred calligraphy in the Friday Mosque, of
Aristotle and his lucid commentators, of the casual acquaintances with
whom al-Haytham would have discussed Aristotle, of the various al-
Haythams who throughout the years became at last the scientist that al-
Hakim invited to his court.

What all this seems to imply is that, sitting in front of my book, I,
like al-Haytham before me, do not merely perceive the letters and
blank spaces of the words that make up the text. In order to extract a
message from that system of black and white signs, I first apprehend
the system in an apparently erratic manner, through fickle eyes, and
then reconstruct the code of signs through a connecting chain of processing neurons in my brain — a chain that varies according to the nature of the text I'm reading — and imbue that text with something —
emotion, physical sentience, intuition, knowledge, soul — that depends on who I am and how I became who I am. "To comprehend a
text," wrote Dr. Merlin C. Wittrock in the 1980s, "we not only read it,

in the nominal sense of the word, we construct a meaning for it." In this complex process, "readers attend to the text. They create images and verbal transformations to represent its meaning. Most impressively, they generate meaning as they read by constructing relations between their knowledge, their memories of experience, and the written sentences, paragraphs and passages."[30] Reading, then, is not an automatic process of capturing a text in the way photosensitive paper captures light, but a bewildering, labyrinthine, common and yet personal process of reconstruction. Whether reading is independent from, for instance, listening, whether it is a single distinctive set of psychological processes or consists of a great variety of such processes, researchers don't yet know, but many believe that its complexity may be as great as that of thinking itself.[31] Reading, according to Dr. Wittrock, "is not an idiosyncratic, anarchic phenomenon. But neither is it a monolithic, unitary process where only one meaning is correct. Instead, it is a generative process that reflects the reader's disciplined attempt to construct one or more meanings within the rules of language."[32]

"To completely analyse what we do when we read," the American researcher E.B. Huey admitted at the turn of our century, "would almost be the acme of the psychologist's achievements, for it would be to describe very many of the most intricate workings of the human mind."[33] We are still far from an answer. Mysteriously, we continue to read without a satisfactory definition of what it is we are doing. We know that reading is not a process that can be explained through a mechanical model; we know that it takes place in certain defined areas of the brain but we also know that these areas are not the only ones to participate; we know that the process of reading, like that of thinking, depends on our ability to decipher and make use of language, the stuff of words which makes up text and thought. The fear that researchers seem to express is that their conclusion will question the very language in which they express it: that language may be in itself an arbitrary absurdity, that it may communicate nothing except in its stuttering essence, that it may depend almost entirely not on its enunciators but on its interpreters for its existence, and that the role of readers is to render visible — in al-Haytham's fine phrase — "that which writing suggests in hints and shadows".[34]

THE SILENT

READERS

I n AD 383, almost half a century after Constantine the Great, first emperor of the Christian world, was baptized on his death-bed, a twenty-nine-year-old professor of Latin rhetoric whom future centuries would know as Saint Augustine arrived in Rome from one of the empire's outposts in North Africa. He rented a house, set up a school and attracted a number of students who had heard about the qualities of this provincial intellectual, but it wasn't long before it became clear to him that he wasn't going to be able to earn his living as a teacher in the imperial capital. Back home in Carthage his students had been rioting hooligans, but at least they had paid for their lessons; in Rome his pupils listened quietly to his dis-quisitions on Aristotle and Cicero until it came time to settle the fee, and then transferred *en masse* to another teacher, leaving Augustine empty-handed. So when, a year later, the Prefect of Rome offered him the opportunity of teaching literature and elocution in the city of Milan, and included travelling expenses in the offer, Augustine accepted gratefully.[1]

Perhaps because he was a stranger to the city and wanted intellec-tual company, or perhaps because his mother had asked him to do so, in Milan Augustine paid a visit to the city's bishop, the celebrated Am-brose, friend and adviser to Augustine's mother, Monica. Ambrose (who, like Augustine, was later to be canonized) was a man in his late forties, strict in his orthodox beliefs and unafraid of even the highest earthly powers; a few years after Augustine's arrival in Milan, Ambrose

OPPOSITE

An eleventh-
century
depiction of
Saint Augustine
at his lectern.

forced the emperor Theodosius I to show public repentance for ordering a massacre of the rioters who had killed the Roman governor of
Salonica.[2] And when the empress Justina requested that the bishop hand
over a church in his city so that she could worship according to the rites
of Arianism, Ambrose organized a sit-in, occupying the site night and day until she desisted.

A portrait of Saint Ambrose in the church that bears his name, in Milan.

According to a fifth-century mosaic, Ambrose was a small, clever-
looking man with big ears and a neat
black beard that diminished rather
than filled out his angular face. He
was an extremely popular speaker;
his symbol in later Christian iconography was the beehive, emblematic
of eloquence.[3] Augustine, who considered Ambrose fortunate to be
held in such high regard by so many
people, found himself unable to ask
the old man the questions about matters of the faith that were troubling
him because, when Ambrose was not
eating a frugal meal or entertaining
one of his many admirers, he was
alone in his cell, reading.

Ambrose was an extraordinary
reader. "When he read," said Augustine, "his eyes scanned the page and
his heart sought out the meaning, but
his voice was silent and his tongue
was still. Anyone could approach him
freely and guests were not commonly announced, so that often, when
we came to visit him, we found him reading like this in silence, for he
never read aloud."[4]

Eyes scanning the page, tongue held still: that is exactly how I
would describe a reader today, sitting with a book in a café across from
the Church of St. Ambrose in Milan, reading, perhaps, Saint Augustine's
Confessions. Like Ambrose, the reader has become deaf and blind to the
world, to the passing crowds, to the chalky flesh-coloured façades of

the buildings. Nobody seems to notice a concentrating reader: with-drawn, intent, the reader becomes commonplace.

To Augustine, however, such reading manners seemed sufficiently strange for him to note them in his *Confessions*. The implication is that this method of reading, this silent perusing of the page, was in his time something out of the ordinary, and that normal reading was performed out loud. Even though instances of silent reading can be traced to ear-lier dates, not until the tenth century does this manner of reading be-come usual in the West.[5]

Augustine's description of Ambrose's silent reading (including the remark that he *never* read aloud) is the first definite instance recorded in Western literature. Earlier examples are far more uncertain. In the fifth century BC, two plays show characters reading on stage: in Euripi-des' *Hippolytus*, Theseus reads in silence a letter held by his dead wife; in Aristophanes' *The Knights*, Demosthenes looks at a writing-tablet sent by an oracle and, without saying out loud what it contains, seems taken aback by what he has read.[6] According to Plutarch, Alexander the Great read a letter from his mother in silence in the fourth century BC, to the bewilderment of his soldiers.[7] Claudius Ptolemy, in the sec-ond century AD, remarked in *On the Criterion* (a book that Augustine may have known) that sometimes people read silently when they are concentrating hard, because voicing the words is a distraction to thought.[8] And Julius Caesar, standing next to his opponent Cato in the Senate in 63 BC, silently read a little billet-doux sent to him by Cato's own sister.[9] Almost four centuries later, Saint Cyril of Jerusalem, in a catechetical lecture probably delivered at Lent of the year 349, en-treated the women in church to read, while waiting during the cere-monies, "quietly, however, so that, while their lips speak, no other ears may hear what they say"[10] — a whispered reading, perhaps, in which the lips fluttered with muffled sounds.

If reading out loud was the norm from the beginnings of the writ-ten word, what was it like to read in the great ancient libraries? The As-syrian scholar consulting one of the thirty thousand tablets in the library of King Ashurbanipal in the seventh century BC, the unfurlers of scrolls at the libraries of Alexandria and Pergamum, Augustine himself looking for a certain text in the libraries of Carthage and Rome, must have worked in the midst of a rumbling din. However, even today not all libraries preserve the proverbial silence. In the seventies, in Milan's beautiful Biblioteca Ambrosiana, there was nothing like the stately

silence I had noticed in the British Library in London or the Bibliothèque Nationale in Paris. The readers at the Ambrosiana spoke to one
another from desk to desk; from time to time someone would call out
a question or a name, a heavy tome would slam shut, a cartful of books
would rattle by. These days, neither the British Library nor the Bibliothèque Nationale is utterly quiet; the silent reading is punctuated by
the clicking and tapping of portable word-processors, as if flocks of
woodpeckers lived inside the book-lined halls. Was it different then, in
the days of Athens or Pergamum, trying to concentrate with dozens of
readers laying out tablets or unfurling scrolls, mumbling away to themselves an infinity of different stories? Perhaps they didn't hear the din;
perhaps they didn't know that it was possible to read in any other way.
In any case, we have no recorded instances of readers complaining of
the noise in Greek or Roman libraries — as Seneca, writing in the first
century, complained of having to study in his noisy private lodgings.[11]

Augustine himself, in a key passage of the *Confessions*, describes a
moment in which the two readings — voiced and silent — take place
almost simultaneously. Anguished by indecision, angry at his past sins,
frightened that at last the time of his reckoning has come, Augustine
walks away from his friend Alypius, with whom he has been reading
(out loud) in Augustine's summer garden, and flings himself down
under a fig-tree to weep. Suddenly, from a nearby house, he hears the
voice of a child — boy or girl, he can't say — singing a song whose
refrain is *tolle, lege*, "take up and read".[12] Believing that the voice is
speaking to him, Augustine runs back to where Alypius is still sitting
and picks up the book he has left unfinished, a volume of Paul's *Epistles*.
Augustine says, "I took hold of it and opened it, and in silence I read
the first section on which my eyes fell."The passage he reads *in silence* is
from Romans 13 — an exhortation to "make not provision for the
flesh" but to "put ye on [i.e., 'like an armour'] the Lord Jesus Christ".
Thunderstruck, he comes to the end of the sentence. The "light of
trust" floods his heart and "the darkness of doubt" is dispelled.

Alypius, startled, asks Augustine what has affected him so. Augustine (who, in a gesture so familiar to us across those alien centuries, has
marked the place he was reading with a finger and closed the book)
shows his friend the text. "I pointed it out to him and he read [aloud,
presumably] beyond the passage which I had read. I had no idea what
followed, which was this: *Him that is weak in the faith receive ye.*" This admonition, Augustine tells us, is enough to give Alypius the longed-for

spiritual strength. There in that garden in Milan, one day in August of the year 386, Augustine and his friend read Paul's *Epistles* much as we would read the book today: the one silently, for private learning; the other out loud, to share with his companion the revelation of a text. Curiously, while Ambrose's prolonged wordless perusal of a book had seemed to Augustine unexplainable, he did not consider his own silent reading surprising, perhaps because he had merely looked at a few essential words.

Augustine, a professor of rhetoric who was well versed in poetics and the rhythms of prose, a scholar who hated Greek but loved Latin, was in the habit — common to most readers — of reading anything he found written for sheer delight in the sounds.[13] Following the teachings of Aristotle, he knew that letters, "invented so that we might be able to converse even with the absent", were "signs of sounds" and these in turn were "signs of things we think".[14] The written text was a conversation, put on paper so that the absent partner would be able to pronounce the words intended for him. For Augustine the spoken word was an intricate part of the text itself — bearing in mind Martial's warning, uttered three centuries earlier:

The verse is mine; but friend, when you declaim it,
It seems like yours, so grievously you maim it.[15]

Written words, from the days of the first Sumerian tablets, were meant to be pronounced out loud, since the signs carried implicit, as if it were their soul, a particular sound. The classic phrase *scripta manent, verba volant* — which has come to mean, in our time, "what is written remains, what is spoken vanishes into air" — used to express the exact opposite; it was coined in praise of the word said out loud, which has wings and can fly, as compared to the silent word on the page, which is motionless, dead. Faced with a written text, the reader had a duty to lend voice to the silent letters, the *scripta*, and to allow them to become, in the delicate biblical distinction, *verba*, spoken words — spirit. The primordial languages of the Bible — Aramaic and Hebrew — do not differentiate between the act of reading and the act of speaking; they name both with the same word.[16]

In sacred texts, where every letter and the number of letters and their order were dictated by the godhead, full comprehension required not only the eyes but also the rest of the body: swaying to the cadence of the sentences and lifting to one's lips the holy words, so that nothing of the divine could be lost in the reading. My grandmother read the Old Testament in this manner, mouthing the words and moving her body back and forth to the rhythm of her prayer. I can see her in her dim apartment in the Barrio del Once, the Jewish neighbourhood of Buenos Aires, intoning the ancient words from her bible, the only book in her house, whose black covers had come to resemble the texture of her own pale skin grown soft with age. Among Muslims too the entire body partakes of the holy reading. In Islam, the question of whether a sacred text is to be heard or read is of essential importance. The ninth-century scholar Ahmad ibn Muhammad ibn Hanbal phrased it in this manner: since the original Koran — the Mother of the Book, the Word of God as revealed by Allah to Muhammad — is uncreated and eternal, did it become present only in its utterance in prayer, or did it multiply its being on the perused page for the eye to read, copied out in differ-ent hands throughout the human ages? We do not know whether he re-ceived an answer, because in 833 his question earned him the condemnation of the *mihnah*, or Islamic inquisition, instituted by the Abassid caliphs.[17] Three centuries later, the legal scholar and theologian Abu Hamid Muhammad al-Ghazali established a series of rules for studying the Koran in which reading and hearing the text read became part of the same holy act. Rule number five established that the reader must follow the text slowly and distinctly in order to reflect on what he was reading. Rule number six was "for weeping. . . . If you do not weep naturally, then force yourself to weep", since grief should be im-plicit in the apprehension of the sacred words. Rule number nine de-manded that the Koran be read "loud enough for the reader to hear it himself, because reading means distinguishing between sounds", thereby driving away distractions from the outside world.[18]

The American psychologist Julian Jaynes, in a controversial study on the origin of consciousness, argued that the bicameral mind — in which one of the hemispheres becomes specialized in silent reading — is a late development in humankind's evolution, and that the process by which this function develops is still changing. He suggested that the earliest instances of reading might have been an aural rather than a visual perception. "Reading in the third millennium BC may therefore have been a matter of *hearing* the cuneiform, that is, hallucinating the speech from looking at its picture-symbols, rather than visual reading of syllables in our sense."[19]

This "aural hallucination" may have been true also in the days of Augustine, when the words on the page did not just "become" sounds as soon as the eye perceived them; they *were* sounds. The child who sang the revelatory song in the garden next door to Augustine's, just like Augustine before him, had no doubt learned that ideas, descriptions, true and fabricated stories, anything the mind could process, possessed a physical reality in sounds, and it was only logical that these sounds, represented on the tablet or scroll or manuscript page, be uttered by the tongue when recognized by the eye. Reading was a form of thinking and of speaking. Cicero, offering consolation to the deaf in one of his moral essays, wrote, "If they happen to enjoy recitations, they should first remember that before poems were invented, many wise men lived happily; and second, that much greater pleasure can be had in reading these poems than in hearing them."[20] But this is only a booby-prize tendered by a philosopher who can himself delight in the sound of the written word. For Augustine, as for Cicero, reading was an oral skill: oratory in the case of Cicero, preaching in the case of Augustine.

Until well into the Middle Ages, writers assumed that their readers would hear rather than simply see the text, much as they themselves spoke their words out loud as they composed them. Since comparatively few people could read, public readings were common, and medieval texts repeatedly call upon the audience to "lend ears" to a tale. It may be that an ancestral echo of those reading practices persists in some of our idioms, as when we say, "I've heard from So-and-so" (meaning "I've received a letter"), or "So-and-so says" (meaning "So-and-so wrote"), or "This text doesn't sound right" (meaning "It isn't well written").

Because books were mainly read out loud, the letters that composed them did not need to be separated into phonetic unities, but were strung together in continuous sentences. The direction in which the eyes were supposed to follow these reels of letters varied from place to place and from age to age; the way we read a text today in the Western world — from left to right and from top to bottom — is by no means universal. Some scripts were read from right to left (Hebrew and Arabic), others in columns, from top to bottom (Chinese and Japanese); a few were read in pairs of vertical columns (Mayan); some had alternate lines read in opposite directions, back and forth — a method called *boustrophedon*, "as an ox turns to plough", in ancient

Greek. Yet others meandered across the page like a game of Snakes and Ladders, the direction being signalled by lines or dots (Aztec).[21]

The ancient writing on scrolls — which neither separated words nor made a distinction between lower-case and upper-case letters, nor used punctuation — served the purposes of someone accustomed to

reading aloud, someone who would allow the ear to disentangle what to the eye seemed a continuous string of signs. So important was this continuity that the Athenians supposedly raised a statue to a certain Phillatius, who had invented a glue for fastening together leaves of parchment or papyrus.[22] Yet even the continuous scroll, while making the reader's task easier, would not have helped a great deal in disentangling the clusters of sense. Punctuation, traditionally ascribed to Aristophanes of Byzantium (*circa* 200 BC) and developed by other scholars of the Library of Alexandria, was at best erratic. Augustine, like Cicero before him, would have had to practise a text before reading it out loud, since sight-reading was in his day an unusual skill and often led to errors of interpretation. The fourth-century grammarian Servius criticized his colleague Donat for reading, in Virgil's *Aeneid*, the words *collectam ex Ilio pubem* ("a people gathered from Troy") instead of *collectam exilio pubem* ("a people gathered for exile").[23] Such mistakes were common when reading a continuous text.

Paul's *Epistles* as read by Augustine were not a scroll but a codex, a bound papyrus manuscript in continuous writing, in the new uncial or semi-uncial hand which had appeared in Roman documents in the last years of the third century. The codex was a pagan invention; according to Suetonius,[24] Julius Caesar was the first to fold a roll into pages, for dispatches to his troops. The early Christians adopted the codex because they found it highly practical for carrying around, hidden away in their clothes, texts that were forbidden by the Roman authorities. The pages could be numbered, which allowed the reader easier access to the sections, and separate texts, such as Paul's *Epistles*, could easily be bound in one convenient package.[25]

The separation of letters into words and sentences developed very gradually. Most early scripts — Egyptian hieroglyphs, Sumerian cuneiform, Sanskrit — had no use for such divisions. The ancient scribes were so familiar with the conventions of their craft that they apparently needed hardly any visual aids, and the early Christian monks often knew by heart the texts they were transcribing.[26] In order to help those whose reading skills were poor, the monks in the scriptorium made use of a writing method known as *per cola et commata*, in which the text was divided into lines of sense — a primitive form of punctuation that helped the unsteady reader lower or raise the voice at the end of a block of thought. (This format also helped a scholar seeking a certain passage to find it with greater ease.)[27] It was Saint Jerome who, at the end of the fourth century, having discovered this method in copies of Demosthenes and Cicero, first described it in his introduction to his translation of the Book of Ezekiel, explaining that "what is written *per cola et commata* conveys more obvious sense to the readers".[28]

Punctuation remained unreliable, but these early devices no doubt assisted the progress of silent reading. By the end of the sixth century, Saint Isaac of Syria was able to describe the benefits of the method: "I practise silence, that the verses of my readings and prayers should fill me with delight. And when the pleasure of understanding them silences my tongue, then, as in a dream, I enter a state when my senses and thoughts are concentrated. Then, when with prolonging of this silence the turmoil of memories is stilled in my heart, ceaseless waves of joy are sent me by inner thoughts, beyond expectation suddenly arising to delight my heart."[29] And in the mid-seventh century, the theologian Isidore of Seville was sufficiently familiar with silent reading to be able to praise it as a method for "reading without effort, reflecting on that which has been read, rendering their escape from memory less easy".[30] Like Augustine before him, Isidore believed that reading made possible a conversation across time and space, but with one important distinction. "Letters have the power to convey to us *silently* the sayings of those who are absent,"[31] he wrote in his *Etymologies*. Isidore's letters did not require sounds.

The avatars of punctuation continued. After the seventh century, a combination of points and dashes indicated a full stop, a raised or high point was equivalent to our comma, and a semicolon was used as we use it today.[32] By the ninth century, silent reading was probably common enough in the scriptorium for scribes to start separating each word from its encroaching neighbours to simplify the perusal of a text — but perhaps also for aesthetic reasons. At about the same time, the Irish scribes, celebrated throughout the Christian world for their skill, began isolating not only parts of speech but also the grammatical constituents within a sentence, and introduced many of the punctuation marks we use today.[33] By the tenth century, to further ease the silent reader's task, the first lines of the principal sections of a text (the books of the Bible, for example) were ordinarily written in red ink, as well as the *rubrics* (from the Latin for "red"), explanations independent of the text proper. The ancient practice of beginning a new paragraph with a dividing stroke (*paragraphos* in Greek) or wedge (*diple*) continued; later the first letter of the new paragraph was written in a slightly larger or upper-case character.

The first regulations requiring scribes to be silent in the monastic scriptoriums date from the ninth century.[34] Until then, they had worked either by dictation or by reading to themselves out loud the text they were copying. Sometimes the author himself or a "publisher" dictated the book. An anonymous scribe, concluding his copying sometime in the eighth century, writes this: "No one can know what efforts are demanded. Three fingers write, two eyes see. One tongue speaks, the entire body labours."[35] *One tongue speaks* as the copyist works, enunciating the words he is transcribing.

Once silent reading became the norm in the scriptorium, communication among the scribes was done by signs: if a scribe required a new book to copy, he would pretend to turn over imaginary pages; if he specifically needed a psalter, he'd place his hands on his head in the shape of a crown (in reference to King David); a lectionary was indicated by wiping away imaginary wax from candles; a missal, by the sign of the cross; a pagan work, by scratching his body like a dog.[36]

Reading out loud with someone else in the room implied shared reading, deliberate or not. Ambrose's reading had been a solitary act. "Perhaps he was afraid," Augustine mused, "that if he read out loud, a difficult passage by the author he was reading would raise a question in the mind of an attentive listener, and he would then have to explain what it meant or even argue about some of the more abstruse points."[37] But with silent reading the reader was at last able to establish an unrestricted relationship with the book and the words. The words no longer needed to occupy the time required to pronounce them. They could exist in interior space, rushing on or barely begun, fully deciphered or only half-said, while the reader's thoughts inspected them at leisure, drawing new notions from them, allowing comparisons from memory or from other books left open for simultaneous perusal. The reader had time to consider and reconsider the precious words whose sounds — he now knew — could echo just as well within as without. And the text itself, protected from outsiders by its covers, became the reader's own possession, the reader's intimate knowledge, whether in the busy scriptorium, the market-place or the home.

Some dogmatists became wary of the new trend; in their minds, silent reading allowed for day-dreaming, for the danger of accidie — the sin of idleness, "the destruction that wasteth at noonday".[38] But silent reading brought with it another danger the Christian fathers had not foreseen. A book that can be read privately, reflected upon as the eye unravels the sense of the words, is no longer subject to immediate clarification or guidance, condemnation or censorship by a listener. Silent reading allows unwitnessed communication between the book and the reader, and the singular "refreshing of the mind", in Augustine's happy phrase.[39]

Until silent reading became the norm in the Christian world, heresies had been restricted to individuals or small numbers of dissenting congregations. The early Christians were preoccupied both with condemning the unbelievers (the pagans, the Jews, the Manicheans and, after the seventh century, the Muslims) and with establishing a common dogma. Arguments digressing from orthodox belief were either vehemently rejected or cautiously incorporated by Church authorities, but because these heresies had no large followings, they were treated with considerable leniency. The catalogue of these heretical voices includes several remarkable imaginations: in the second century the Montanists claimed (already) to be returning to the practices and beliefs of the primitive Church, and to have witnessed the second coming of Christ in the form of a woman; in the second half of that century the Monarchianists concluded from the definition of the Trinity that it was God the Father who had suffered on the Cross; the Pelagians, contemporaries of Saint Augustine and Saint Ambrose, rejected the notion of original sin; the Apollinarians declared, in the last years of the fourth century, that the Word, and not a human soul, was united with Christ's flesh in the Incarnation; in the fourth century the Arians objected to the word *homoousios* (of same substance) to describe the stuff of which the Son was made and (to quote a contemporary *jeu de mots*) "convulsed the Church by a diphthong"; in the fifth century the Nestorians opposed the ancient Apollinarians and insisted that Christ was two beings, a god and also a man; the Eutychians, contemporaries of the Nestorians, denied that Christ had suffered as all humans suffer.[40]

Even though the Church instituted the death penalty for heresy as early as 382, the first case of burning a heretic at the stake did not occur until 1022, in Orléans. On that occasion the Church condemned a group of canons and lay nobles who, believing that true instruction could only come directly from the light of the Holy Spirit, rejected the Scriptures as "the fabrications which men have written on the skins of animals".[41] Such independent readers were obviously dangerous. The interpretation of heresy as a civil offence punishable by death was not given legal basis until 1231, when the emperor Frederick II decreed it as such in the Constitutions of Melfi, but by the twelfth century the Church was already enthusiastically condemning large and aggressive heretical movements that argued not for ascetic withdrawal from the world (which the earlier dissenters had proposed) but for a challenge to corrupt authority and the abusive clergy, and for an individual reckoning with the Divinity. The movements spread through tortuous byways, and crystallized in the sixteenth century.

A contemporary portrait of Martin Luther by Lucas Cranach the Elder.

On October 31, 1517, a monk who, through his private study of the Scriptures, had come to believe that the divine grace of God superseded the merits of acquired faith, nailed to the door of All Saints Church in Wittenberg ninety-five theses against the practice of indulgences — the selling of remission from temporal punishment for condemned sins — and other ecclesiastical abuses. With this act Martin Luther became an outlaw in the eyes of the empire and an apostate in those of the Pope. In 1529 the Holy Roman emperor Charles V rescinded the rights granted to Luther's followers, and fourteen free cities of Germany, together with six Lutheran princes, caused a protest to be read against the imperial decision. "In matters which concern God's honour and salvation and the eternal life of our souls, everyone must stand and give account before God for himself," argued the protesters or, as they were later to be known, Protestants. Ten years earlier, the Roman theologian Silvester Prierias had stated that the book upon which the Church was founded needed to remain a mystery, interpreted only through the authority and power of the Pope.[42] The heretics, on the other hand, maintained that people had the right to read the word of God for themselves, without witness or intermediary.[43]

Centuries later, beyond a sea that for Augustine would have been at the limits of the earth, Ralph Waldo Emerson, who owed his faith to those ancient protesters, took advantage of the art that had so surprised the saint. In church, during the lengthy and often tedious sermons which he attended out of a sense of social responsibility, he silently read Pascal's *Pensées*. And at night, in his cold room in Concord, "covered with blankets to the chin", he read to himself the *Dialogues* of Plato. ("He associated Plato," noted a historian, "ever after, with the smell of wool.")[44] Even though he thought there were too many books to be read, and thought readers should share their findings by reporting to one another the gist of their studies, Emerson believed that reading a book was a private and solitary business. "All these books," he wrote, drawing up a list of "sacred" texts that included the Upanishads and the *Pensées*, "are the majestic expressions of the universal conscience, and are more to our daily purpose than this year's almanac or this day's newspaper. But they are for the closet, and are to be read on the bended knee. Their communications are not to be given or taken with the lips and the end of the tongue, but out of the glow of the cheek, and with the throbbing heart."[45] In silence.

Observing the reading of Saint Ambrose that afternoon in 384, Augustine could hardly have known what was before him. He thought he was seeing a reader trying to avoid intrusive visitors, sparing his voice for teaching. In fact he was seeing a multitude, a host of silent readers who over the next many centuries would include Luther, would include Calvin, would include Emerson, would include us, reading him today.

THE BOOK

OF MEMORY

I am standing on the ruins of Carthage, in Tunisia. The stones are Roman, bits of walls built after the city was destroyed by Scipio Aemilianus in 146 BC, when the Carthaginian empire became a Roman province and was renamed Africa. Here Saint Augustine, as a young man, taught rhetoric before travelling to Milan. In his late thirties he crossed the Mediterranean once again, to settle in Hippo, in what is today Algeria; he died there in AD 430 as the invading Vandals were laying siege to the town.

I've brought with me my school edition of the *Confessions*, a thin, orange-covered volume of the Classiques Roma, which my Latin teacher preferred to all other series. Standing here with the book in my hand, I feel a certain camaraderie with the great Renaissance poet Francesco Petrarca, whom his Anglo-Saxon readers called Petrarch, and who always used to carry with him a pocket-sized edition of Augustine. Reading the *Confessions*, he felt that Augustine's voice spoke to him so intimately that, towards the end of his life, he composed three imaginary dialogues with the saint, which were published posthumously as the *Secretum meum*. A pencilled note in the margin of my Roma edition comments on Petrarch's comments, as if continuing those imaginary dialogues.

It is true that something in Augustine's tone suggests a comfortable intimacy, propitious for the sharing of secrets. When I open the book, my marginal scribbles bring to mind the roomy classroom of the Colegio Nacional de Buenos Aires, where the walls were painted the colour

OPPOSITE

Socrates in conversation depicted on the lateral face of a second-century sarcophagus.

of Carthaginian sand, and I find myself recalling the voice of my teacher reciting Augustine's words, and our pompous debates (were we fourteen, fifteen, sixteen?) about political responsibility and metaphysical reality. The book preserves the memory of that far-away adolescence, of my teacher (now dead), of Petrarch's readings of Augustine, which our teacher read to us approvingly, but also of Augustine and his classrooms, of the Carthage that was built on the Carthage that was destroyed, only to be destroyed once again. The dust of these ruins is far, far older than the book, but the book contains it too. Augustine observed and then wrote what he recalled. Held in my hand, the book twice remembers.

Perhaps it was his very sensuality (which he tried so hard to repress) that made Saint Augustine such a keen observer. He seems to have spent the latter part of his life in a paradoxical state of discovery and distraction, marvelling at what his senses taught him and yet asking God to remove from him the temptations of physical pleasure. Ambrose's silent reading habits were observed because Augustine bowed to the curiosity of his eyes, and the words in the garden were heard because he indulged in the scent of the grass and the song of invisible birds.

Not only the possibility of silent reading surprised Augustine. Writing about an early schoolmate, he remarked on the man's extraordinary memory, which enabled him to compose and recompose texts which he

had once read and learned by heart. He was capable, Augustine said, of quoting the next to last verse of each book of Virgil, "quickly, in order and from memory. . . . If we then asked him to recite the verse before each of those, he did. And we believed that he could recite Virgil backwards. . . . If we wanted even prose passages from whatever Cicero oration he had committed to memory, that also he could do."[1] Reading either in silence or aloud, this man was able to impress the text (in Cicero's phrase, which Augustine liked to quote) "on the wax tablets of memory",[2] to be recalled and recited at will in whatever order he chose, as if he were flipping through the pages of a book. By recalling a text, by bringing to mind a book once held in the hands, such a reader can *become* the book, from which he and others can read.

In 1658, the eighteen-year-old Jean Racine, studying at the Abbey of Port-Royal under the watchful eye of the Cistercian monks, discovered by chance an early Greek novel, *The Loves of Theogonis and Charicles*, whose notions of tragic love he may have recalled years later, when writing *Andromaque* and *Bérénice*. He took the book into the forest surrounding the abbey, and had begun to read it voraciously when he was surprised by the sexton, who pulled the book from the boy's hands and threw it into a bonfire. Shortly afterwards, Racine managed to find a second copy, which was also discovered and condemned to the flames. This encouraged him to buy a third copy and learn the whole novel by heart. Then he handed it over to the

A Florentine school of the twelfth century. The students can be seen sharing their texts in groups of three.

57

fiery sexton, saying, "Now you can burn this one too, just as you did the others."[3]

This quality of reading, which enables a reader to acquire a text not simply by perusing the words but by actually making them part of the reader's self, was not always considered a blessing. Twenty-three centuries ago, just beyond the walls of Athens, in the shade of a tall plane tree by the edge of the river, a young man of whom we know little more than his name, Phaedrus, read out to Socrates a speech by a certain Lycias, whom Phaedrus passionately admired. The young man had heard the speech (on the duties of a lover) several times, and in the end had obtained a written version of it which he studied over and over again, until he had learned it by heart. Then, longing to share his discovery (as readers so often do), he had sought an audience with Socrates. Socrates, guessing that Phaedrus was holding the text of the speech hidden under his cloak, asked him to read the original rather than recite it for him. "I won't let you practise your oratory on me," he said to the young enthusiast, "when Lycias himself is here present."[4]

The ancient dialogue dealt, above all, with the nature of love, but the conversation happily drifted and, towards the end, the subject happened to be the craft of letters. Once upon a time, Socrates told Phaedrus, the god Thoth of Egypt, inventor of dice, checkers, numbers, geometry, astronomy and writing, visited the King of Egypt and offered him these inventions to pass on to his people. The king discussed the merits and disadvantages of each of the god's gifts, until Thoth came to the art of writing. "Here," said Thoth, "is a branch of learning that will improve their memories; my discovery provides a recipe for both memory and wisdom." But the king was not impressed. "If men learn this," he told the god, "it will implant forgetfulness in their souls; they will cease to exercise memory because they will rely on that which is written, calling things to remembrance no longer from within themselves, but by means of external marks. What you have discovered is a recipe not for memory, but for reminder. And it is no true wisdom that you offer your disciples, but only its semblance, for by telling them of many things without teaching them anything, you will make them seem to know much, while for the most part they will know nothing. And as men filled not with wisdom but with the conceit of wisdom, they will be a burden to their fellow-men." A reader, Socrates admonished Phaedrus, "must be singularly simple-minded to believe that written words can do anything more than remind one of what one already knows."

Phaedrus, convinced by the old man's reasoning, agreed. And Socrates continued: "You know, Phaedrus, that's the strange thing about writing, which makes it truly analogous to painting. The painter's work stands before us as though the paintings were alive, but if you question them, they maintain a most majestic silence. It is the same with written words; they seem to talk to you as though they were intelligent, but if you ask them anything about what they say, from a wish to know more, they go on telling you the same thing over and over again forever." For Socrates, the text read was nothing but its words, in which sign and meaning overlapped with bewildering precision. Interpretation, exegesis, gloss, commentary, association, refutation, symbolic and allegorical senses, all rose not from the text itself but from the reader. The text, like a painted picture, said only "the moon of Athens"; it was the reader who furnished it with a full ivory face, a deep dark sky, a landscape of ancient ruins along which Socrates once walked.

Towards the year 1250, in the preface to *Bestiaire d'amour*, the chancellor of the Cathedral of Amiens, Richard de Fournival, disagreed with Socrates' contention and suggested that, since all of humankind desires knowledge and has but a short time to live, it must rely on the knowledge gathered by others to increase the wealth of its own. To this effect, God gave the human soul the gift of memory, to which we gain access through the senses of sight and hearing. De Fournival then elaborated on Socrates' notion. The road to sight, he said, consisted of *peintures* or pictures; the road to hearing of *paroles* or words.[5] The merit of these was found not in merely stating an image or text with no progress or variation, but in re-creating in the reader's own time and space that which had been conceived and rendered into pictures or words in another age and under different skies. "When one sees painted a story, whether of Troy or something else," argued de Fournival, "one sees those noble deeds which were done in the past exactly as though they were still present. And it is the same thing with hearing a text, for when one hears a story read aloud, listening to the events one sees them in the present. . . . And when you read, this writing with its *peinture* and *parole* will make me present to your memory, even when I am not physically before you."[6] Reading, according to de Fournival, enriched the present and actualized the past; memory prolonged these qualities into the future. For de Fournival, the book, not the reader, preserved and passed on memory.

The written text, in Socrates' time, was not a common tool. While books existed in Athens in considerable numbers in the fifth century

BC, and a trade in books had begun to develop, the practice of private reading did not become fully established until at least a century later, in the time of Aristotle — one of the first readers to assemble an important collection of manuscripts for his own use.[7] Talk was the means by which people learned and passed on learning, and Socrates belongs to a line of oral masters that includes Moses, Buddha and Jesus Christ, who only once, we are told, wrote a few words in the sand and then effaced them.[8] For Socrates, books were aids to memory and knowledge but true scholars were to do without them. A few years later, his disciples Plato and Xenophon recorded his disparaging opinion of books in a book, and their memory of his memory was thereby preserved for us, his future readers.

In de Fournival's day, students commonly used books as memory aids, setting the open pages in front of them in class, usually one copy for several students.[9] In school I studied in the same manner, holding the book open in front of me while the teacher lectured, marking the main passages that I would later try to memorize (though a few teachers — followers of Socrates, I suppose — didn't like us opening the books in class). There was, however, one curious difference between my fellow students in the Buenos Aires high school and the students depicted in the illustrations of de Fournival's time. We marked passages in our books in pen (if we were brave) or pencil (if we were squeamish), making notes in the margins to remind us of the teacher's comments. The thirteenth-century students in the old illustrations are mostly shown without any writing material whatsoever;[10] they stand or sit in front of the open codexes, memorizing the position of a paragraph, the disposition of the letters, committing a sequence of essential points to memory instead of entrusting them to the page. Unlike myself and my contemporaries, who would study for a particular exam from the underlined and annotated passages (which would then, after the exam, be largely forgotten, in the safe knowledge that the book would be there for consultation if it was ever needed), de Fournival's students relied on the library stored in their heads, from which, thanks to the laborious mnemotechnics taught from their earliest years, they would be able to pick chapter and verse as easily as I can find a given subject in a reference library of microchips and paper. They even believed that memorizing a text was physically beneficial, and cited as an authority the second-century Roman doctor Antyllus, who had written that those who have never learned verses by heart and must instead

resort to reading them in books sometimes have great pains in elimi-
nating, through abundant perspiration, the noxious fluids that those
with a keen memory of texts eliminate merely through breathing.[11]

I instead confidently rely on the ability of computerized services to
hunt through libraries vaster than Alexandria's for a remote piece of information, and my word-processor
can "access" all manner of books. En-
terprises such as Project Gutenberg
in the United States file on diskettes
everything from Shakespeare's Complete Works to the *CIA World Factbook*
and *Roget's Thesaurus*, and the Oxford
Text Archive in England offers electronic versions of the major Greek
and Latin authors, plus several classics in various other languages. The
medieval scholars relied on their
own memory of the books they had
read, whose pages they could conjure up like living ghosts.

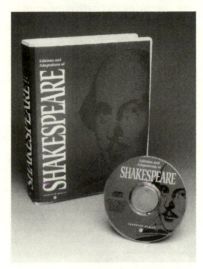

A single
diskette of
the complete
works of
Shakespeare in
its various
editions and
adaptations,
and its
codex-shaped
packaging.

Saint Thomas Aquinas was a contemporary of de Fournival's. Following recommendations made by Cicero to improve the rhetorician's
ability to recall, he elaborated a series of memory rules for readers:
placing the things one wished to remember in a certain order, developing an "affection" for them, transforming them into "unusual similitudes"
that would render them easy to visualize, repeating them frequently.
Eventually the scholars of the Renaissance, improving on Aquinas's
method, suggested the mental construction of architectural models —
palaces, theatres, cities, the realms of heaven and hell — in which to
lodge whatever they wished to remember.[12] These models were highly
elaborate constructions, erected in the mind over time and made sturdy
through use, and proved for centuries to be immensely efficient.

For me, reading today, the notes I take while reading are held in
the vicarious memory of my word-processor. Like the Renaissance
scholar who could wander at will through the chambers of his memory
palace to retrieve a quotation or a name, I blindly enter the electronic
maze buzzing behind my screen. With the help of its memory I can
remember more accurately (if accuracy is important) and more copi-
ously (if quantity seems valuable) than my illustrious ancestors, but I

must still be the one to find an order in the notes and to draw conclusions. Also, I work in fear of losing a "memorized" text — a fear which for my ancestors came only with the dilapidations of age, but which for me is always present: fear of a power surge, a misdirected key, a glitch in the system, a virus, a defective disk, any of which might erase from my memory everything for ever.

About a century after de Fournival completed his *Bestiaire*, Petrarch, who had apparently followed Aquinas's mnemotechnic devices the better to pursue his voluminous readings, imagined in the *Secretum meum* entering a conversation with his beloved Augustine on the subject of reading and memory. Petrarch had led, like Augustine, a turbulent life in his younger days. His father, a friend of Dante's, had been banished like the poet from his native Florence, and shortly after Petrarch's birth had moved his family to the court of Pope Clement V in Avignon. Petrarch attended the universities of Montpellier and Bologna, and at the age of twenty-two, after his father's death, he settled again in Avignon, a rich young man. But neither the wealth nor the

A portrait of Petrarch in a fourteenth-century manuscript of *De viris illustribus*.

youth lasted long. In a few years of riotous living he squandered all of his father's inheritance, and was obliged to enter a religious order. The discovery of books by Cicero and Saint Augustine awoke a taste for literature in the newly ordained priest, and for the rest of his life he read voraciously. He started writing seriously in his mid-thirties, composing two works, *De viris illustribus* (*Of Famous Men*) and the poem *Africa*, in which he acknowledged his debt to the ancient Greek and Latin authors, and for which he was crowned with a laurel wreath by the Senate and the people of Rome — a wreath which he later placed on the high altar at St. Peter's. Pictures of him at this time show a gaunt, irritable-looking man with a large nose and nervous eyes, and one imagines that age must have done little to appease his restlessness.

In the *Secretum meum*, Petrarch (under his Christian name, Francesco) and Augustine sit and talk in a garden, watched by the unwavering eye of Lady Truth. Francesco confesses that he is weary of the vain bustle of the city; Augustine replies that Francesco's life is a book like those in the poet's library, but one that Francesco does not yet know how to read, and reminds him of several texts on the subject of madding crowds — including Augustine's own. "Don't these help you?" he asks. Yes, Francesco answers, at the time of reading they are very helpful, but "as soon as the book leaves my hands, all my feeling for it vanishes."

Augustine: This manner of reading is now quite common; there's such a mob of lettered men. . . . But if you'd jot down a few notes in their proper place, you'd easily be able to enjoy the fruit of your reading.

Francesco: What kind of notes do you mean?

Augustine: Whenever you read a book and come across any wonderful phrases which you feel stir or delight your soul, don't merely trust the power of your own intelligence, but force yourself to learn them by heart and make them familiar by meditating on them, so that whenever an urgent case of affliction arises, you'll have the remedy ready as if it were written in your mind. When you come to any passages that seem to you useful, make a firm mark against them, which may serve as lime in your memory, less otherwise they might fly away.[13]

What Augustine (in Petrarch's imagining) suggests is a new manner of reading: neither using the book as a prop for thought, nor trusting it as one would trust the authority of a sage, but taking from it an idea, a phrase, an image, linking it to another culled from a distant text preserved in memory, tying the whole together with reflections of one's own — producing, in fact, a new text authored by the reader. In the introduction to *De viris illustribus*, Petrarch remarked that this book was to serve the reader as "a sort of artificial memory"[14] of "dispersed" and "rare" texts, and that he not only had collected them but, more important, had lent them an order and a method. To his readers in the fourteenth century, Petrarch's claim was astonishing, since the authority of a text was self-established and the reader's task was that of an outside observer; a couple of centuries later, Petrarch's personal, re-creative, interpretative, collating form of reading would become the common method of scholarship throughout Europe. Petrarch comes upon this method in the light of what he calls "divine truth": a sense which the reader must possess, must be blessed with, to pick and choose and interpret his way through the temptations of the page. Even the author's intentions, when surmised, are not of any particular value in judging a text. This, Petrarch suggests, must be done through one's own recollection of other readings, into which flows the memory which the author set down on the page. In this dynamic process of give and take, of pulling apart and piecing together, the reader must not exceed the ethical boundaries of truth — whatever the reader's conscience (we would say common sense) dictates these to be. "Reading," wrote Petrarch in one of his many letters, "rarely avoids danger, unless the light of divine truth shines upon the reader, teaching what to seek and what to avoid."[15] This light (to follow Petrarch's image) shines differently on all of us, and differently also at the various stages of our lives. We never return to the same book or even to the same page, because in the varying light we change and the book changes, and our memories grow bright and dim and bright again, and we never know exactly what it is we learn and forget, and what it is we remember. What is certain is that the act of reading, which rescues so many voices from the past, preserves them sometimes well into the future, where we may be able to make use of them in brave and unexpected ways.

When I was ten or eleven, one of my teachers in Buenos Aires tutored me in the evenings in German and European history. To improve my German pronunciation, he encouraged me to memorize poems by Heine, Goethe and Schiller, and Gustav Schwab's ballad "Der Ritter und der Bodensee", in which a rider gallops across the frozen Lake of Constance and, on realizing what he has accomplished, dies of fright on the far shore. I enjoyed learning the poems but I didn't understand of what use they might possibly be. "They'll keep you company on the day you have no books to read," my teacher said. Then he told me that his father, murdered in Sachsenhausen, had been a famous scholar who knew many of the classics by heart and who, during his time in the concentration camp, had offered himself as a library to be read to his fellow inmates. I imagined the old man in that murky, relentless, hopeless place, approached with a request for Virgil or Euripides, opening himself up to a given page and reciting the ancient words for his bookless readers. Years later, I realized that he had been immortalized as one of the crowd of roaming book-savers in Bradbury's *Fahrenheit 451*.

A text read and remembered becomes, in that redemptive rereading, like the frozen lake in the poem I memorized so long ago — as solid as land and capable of supporting the reader's crossing, and yet, at the same time, its only existence is in the mind, as precarious and fleeting as if its letters were written on water.

L E A R N I N G   T O   R E A D

R eading out loud, reading silently, being able to carry in the
mind intimate libraries of remembered words, are astounding
abilities that we acquire by uncertain methods. And yet, before these abilities can be acquired, a reader needs to learn the
basic craft of recognizing the common signs by which a society has
chosen to communicate: in other words, a reader must learn to read.
Claude Lévi-Strauss tells how, when he was travelling among the Nambikwara Indians of Brazil, his hosts, seeing him write, took his pencil
and paper and drew squiggly lines in imitation of his letters and demanded that he "read" what they had written. The Nambikwara expected their scribbles to be as immediately significant to Lévi-Strauss
as those he drew himself.[1] For Lévi-Strauss, taught to read in a European school, the notion that a system of communication should be
immediately comprehensible to any other person seemed absurd. The
methods by which we learn to read not only embody the conventions
of our particular society regarding literacy — the channelling of information, the hierarchies of knowledge and power — they also determine and limit the ways in which our ability to read is put to use.

I lived for a year in Sélestat, a small French town twenty miles
south of Strasbourg, in the middle of the Alsatian plain between the
Rhine River and the Vosges Mountains. There, in the small municipal
library, are two large handwritten notebooks. One is 300 pages long,
the other 480; in both the paper has yellowed over the centuries, but
the writing, in different colours of ink, is still surprisingly clear. Later

OPPOSITE

The illustrious
reader Beatus
Rhenanus,
book-collector
and editor.

6 7

in life, their owners had the notebooks bound in order to preserve them better, but when they were in use they were little more than bundles of folded pages, probably bought at a bookseller's stall in one of the local markets. Open to the gaze of the library's visitors, they are — a typed card explains — the notebooks of two of the students who attended the Latin school of Sélestat in the last years of the fifteenth century, from 1477 to 1501: Guillaume Gisenheim, of whose life nothing is known except what his schoolboy's notebook tells us, and Beatus Rhenanus, who was to become a leading figure in the humanist movement and the editor of many of the works of Erasmus.

In Buenos Aires, in the first few grades, we too had "reading" notebooks, laboriously handwritten and painstakingly illustrated with coloured crayons. Our desks and benches were fixed to each other by cast-iron brackets and set in long rows of two, leading (the symbol of power did not escape us) up to the teacher's desk, high on a wooden platform, behind which loomed the blackboard. Each desk was pierced to hold a white porcelain inkpot into which we plunged the metal nibs of our pens; we were not allowed to use fountain-pens until grade three. Centuries from now, if some scrupulous librarian were to exhibit those notebooks as precious objects in glass cases, what would a visitor discover? From the patriotic texts copied out in tidy paragraphs, the visitor might deduce that in our education the rhetoric of politics superseded the niceties of literature; from our illustrations, that we learned to transform these texts into slogans ("The Malvinas Belong To Argentina" became two hands linked around a pair of ragged islands; "Our Flag Is The Emblem Of Our Homeland", three strips of colour blowing in the wind). From the identical glosses the visitor might learn that we were taught to read not for pleasure or for knowledge but merely for instruction. In a country where inflation was to attain a monthly 200 per cent, this was the only way to read the fable of the grasshopper and the ant.

In Sélestat there were several different schools. A Latin school had existed since the fourteenth century, lodged on church property and maintained by both the municipal magistrate and the parish. The original school, the one attended by Gisenheim and Rhenanus, had occupied a house on the Marché-Vert, in front of the eleventh-century church of St. Foy. In 1530 the school had become more prestigious and had moved to a larger building across from the thirteenth-century church of St. George, a two-storey house that carried on its façade an inspiring fresco depicting the nine muses sporting in the sacred fountain of Hippocrene, on Mount Helicon.[2] With the transfer of the school, the name of the street changed from Lottengasse to Babilgasse, in reference to the babbling (in Alsatian dialect, *bablen*, "to babble") of the students. I lived only a couple of blocks away.

From the beginnings of the fourteenth century, there exist full records of two German schools in Sélestat; then, in 1686, the first French school was opened, thirteen years after Louis XIV took possession of the town. These schools taught reading, writing, singing and a little arithmetic in the vernacular, and were open to all. An admission contract for one of the German schools, around the year 1500, notes that the teacher would instruct "members of the guilds and others from the age of twelve on, as well as those children unable to attend the Latin school, boys as well as girls."[3] Unlike those attending the German schools, students were admitted to the Latin school at the age of six, and remained there until they were ready for university at thirteen or fourteen. A few became assistants to the teacher and stayed on until the age of twenty.

Though Latin continued to be the language of bureaucracy, ecclesiastical affairs and scholarship in most of Europe until well into the seventeenth century, by the early sixteenth century the vernacular languages were gaining ground. In 1521, Martin Luther began publication of his German Bible; in 1526, William Tyndale brought out his English translation of the Bible in Cologne and Worms, having been forced to leave England under threat of death; in 1530, in both Sweden and Denmark, a government decree prescribed that the Bible was to be read in church in the vernacular. In Rhenanus's days, however, the prestige and official use of Latin continued not only in the Catholic Church, where priests were required to conduct services in Latin, but also in universities such as the Sorbonne, which Rhenanus wished to attend. Latin schools were therefore still in great demand.

Schools, Latin and otherwise, provided a certain degree of order in the chaotic existence of students in the late Middle Ages. Because scholarship was seen as the seat of a "third power" positioned between the Church and the State, students were granted a number of official privileges from the twelfth century on. In 1158, the German Holy Roman emperor Frederick Barbarossa exempted them from the jurisdiction of secular authorities except in serious criminal cases, and guaranteed them safe conduct when travelling. A privilege accorded by King

Philippe Auguste of France in 1200 forbade the Provost of Paris to imprison them under any excuse. And from Henry III onwards, each English monarch guaranteed secular immunity to the students at Oxford.[4]

To attend school, students had to pay tax-fees, and they were taxed according to their *bursa*, a unit based on their weekly bed and board. If they were unable to pay, they had to swear that they were "without means of support" and sometimes they were granted fellowships assured by subventions. In the fifteenth century, poor students accounted for 18 per cent of the student body in Paris, 25 per cent in Vienna and 19 per cent in Leipzig.[5] Privileged but penniless, anxious to preserve their rights but uncertain about how to make a living, thousands of students roamed the land, living off alms and larceny. A few survived by pretending to be fortune-tellers or magicians, selling miraculous trinkets, announcing eclipses or catastrophes, conjuring up spirits, predicting the future, teaching prayers to rescue souls from purgatory, giving out recipes to guard crops against hail and cattle against disease. Some claimed to be descendants of the Druids and boasted that they had entered the Mountain of Venus, where they had been initiated into the secret arts; as a sign of this, they wore capes of yellow netting over their shoulders. Many went from town to town following an older cleric whom they served and from whom they sought instruction; the teacher was known as a *bacchante* (not from "Bacchus" but from the verb *bacchari*, "to roam"), and his disciples were called *Schützen* (protectors) in German or *bejaunes* (dunces) in French. Only those who were determined to become clerics or to enter some form of civil service would seek the means to leave the road and enter a learning establishment[6] like the Latin school in Sélestat.

The students who attended the Latin school in Sélestat came from different parts of Alsace and Lorraine, and even farther, from Switzerland. Those who belonged to rich bourgeois or noble families (as was the case with Beatus Rhenanus) could choose to be lodged in the boarding-house run by the rector and his wife, or to stay as paying guests at the house of their private tutor, or even at one of the local inns.[7] But those who had sworn that they were too poor to pay their fees had great difficulties in finding room and board. The Swiss Thomas Platter, who arrived at the school in 1495 at the age of eighteen "knowing nothing, unable even to read [the best-known of medieval grammar primers, the *Ars de octo partibus orationis* by Aelius] Donat", and who felt, among the younger students, "like a hen among the chicks", described in his autobiography how he and a friend had set off in search of instruction. "When we reached Strasbourg, we found many poor students there, who told us that the school was not good, but that there was an excellent school in Sélestat. We set off for Sélestat. On the way we met a nobleman who asked us, 'Where are you going?' When he heard that we were headed for Sélestat, he advised us against it, telling us that there were many poor students in that town and that the inhabitants were far from rich. Hearing this, my companion burst into bitter tears, crying, 'Where can we go?' I comforted him by saying, 'Rest assured, if some can find the means of obtaining food in Sélestat, I'll certainly manage to do so for both of us.'" They managed to stay in Sélestat for a few months, but after Pentecost "new students arrived from all parts, and I no longer was able to find food for both of us, and we left for the town of Soleure."[8]

In every literate society, learning to read is something of an initiation, a ritualized passage out of a state of dependency and rudimentary communication. The child learning to read is admitted into the communal memory by way of books, and thereby becomes acquainted with a common past which he or she renews, to a greater or lesser degree, in every reading. In medieval Jewish society, for instance, the ritual of learning to read was explicitly celebrated. On the Feast of Shavuot, when Moses received the Torah from the hands of God, the boy about to be initiated was wrapped in a prayer shawl and taken by his father to the teacher. The teacher sat the boy on his lap and showed him a slate on which were written the Hebrew alphabet, a passage from the Scriptures and the words "May the Torah be your occupation." The teacher read out every word and the child repeated it. Then the slate was covered with honey and the child licked it, thereby bodily assimilating the holy words. Also, biblical verses were written on peeled hard-boiled eggs and on honey cakes, which the child would eat after reading the verses out loud to the teacher.[9]

Though it is difficult to generalize over several centuries and across so many countries, in the Christian society of the late Middle Ages and the early Renaissance learning to read and write — outside the Church — was the almost exclusive privilege of the aristocracy and (after the thirteenth century) the upper bourgeoisie. Even though there were aristocrats and *grands bourgeois* who considered reading and writing menial tasks suitable only for poor clerics,[10] most boys and quite a few girls born to these classes were taught their letters very early. The child's nurse, if she could read, initiated the teaching, and for that reason had to be chosen with utmost care, since she was not only to provide milk but also to ensure correct speech and pronunciation.[11] The great Italian humanist scholar Leon Battista Alberti, writing between 1435 and 1444, noted that "the care of very young children is women's work, for nurses or the mother,"[12] and that at the earliest possible age they should be taught the alphabet. Children learned to read phonetically by repeating letters pointed out by their nurse or mother in a hornbook or alphabet sheet. (I myself was taught this way, by my nurse reading out to me the bold-type letters from an old English picture-book; I was made to repeat the sounds again and again.) The image of the teaching mother-figure was as common in Christian iconography as the female student was rare in depictions of the classroom. There are numerous representations of Mary holding a book in

Two fifteenth-century mothers teaching their children to read: *left*, the Virgin and Child; *right*, Saint Anne with the young Mary.

front of the Child Jesus, and of Anne teaching Mary, but neither Christ nor His Mother was depicted as learning to write or actually writing; it was the notion of Christ *reading* the Old Testament that was considered essential to make the continuity of the Scriptures explicit.

Quintilian, a first-century Roman lawyer from northern Spain who became the tutor of the Emperor Domitian's grand-nephews, wrote a twelve-volume pedagogical manual, the *Institutio oratoria*, which was highly influential throughout the Renaissance. In it, he advised: "Some hold that boys should not be taught to read till they are seven years old, that being the earliest age at which they can derive profit from instruction and endure the strain of learning. Those however who hold that a child's mind should not be allowed to lie fallow for a moment are wiser. Chrysippus, for instance, though he gives the nurses a three years' reign, still holds the formation of the child's mind on the best principles to be a part of their duties. Why, again, since children are capable of moral training, should they not be capable of literary education?"[13]

After the letters had been learned, male teachers would be brought in as private tutors (if the family could afford them) for the boys, while the mother busied herself with the education of the girls. Even though, by the fifteenth century, most wealthy houses had the space, quiet and equipment to provide teaching at home, most scholars recommended that boys be educated away from the family, in the company of other boys; on the other hand, medieval moralists hotly debated the benefits of education — public or private — for girls. "It is not appropriate for girls to learn to read and write unless they wish to become nuns, since they might otherwise, coming of age, write or receive amorous missives,"[14] warned the nobleman Philippe de Novare, but several of his contemporaries disagreed. "Girls should learn to read in order to learn the true faith and protect themselves from the perils that menace their soul," argued the Chevalier de la Tour Landry.[15] Girls born in richer households were often sent to school to learn reading and writing, usually to prepare them for the convent. In the aristocratic households of Europe, it was possible to find women who were fully literate.

Before the mid-fifteenth century, the teaching at the Latin school of Sélestat had been rudimentary and undistinguished, following the conventional precepts of the scholastic tradition. Developed mainly in the twelfth and thirteenth centuries, by philosophers for whom "thinking is a craft with meticulously fixed laws",[16] scholasticism proved a useful method for reconciling the precepts of religious faith with the arguments of human reason, resulting in a *concordia discordantium* or "harmony among differing opinions" which could then be used as a further point of argument. Soon, however, scholasticism became a method of preserving rather than eliciting ideas. In Islam it served to establish the official dogma; since there were no Islamic councils or synods set up for this purpose, the *concordia discordantium*, the opinion that survived all objections, became orthodoxy.[17] In the Christian world, though varying considerably from university to university, scholasticism adamantly followed the precepts of Aristotle by way of early Christian philosophers such as the fifth-century Boethius, whose *De consolatione philosophiae* (which Alfred the Great translated into English) was a great favourite throughout the Middle Ages. Essentially, the scholastic method consisted in little more than training the students to consider a text according to certain pre-established, officially approved criteria which were painstakingly and painfully drilled into them. As far as the teaching of reading was concerned, the success of the method depended more on the students' perseverance than on their intelligence. Writing in the mid-thirteenth century, the learned Spanish king Alfonso el Sabio belaboured the point: "Well and truly must the teachers show their learning to the students by reading to them books and making them understand to the best of their abilities; and once they begin to read, they must continue the teaching until they have come to the end of the books they have started; and while in health they must

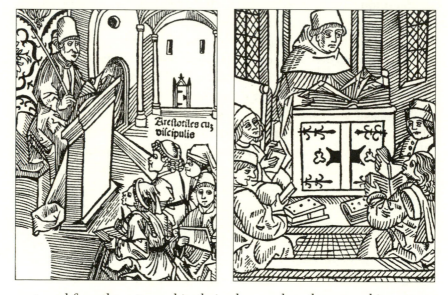

Two school scenes from the turn of the fifteenth century showing the hierarchical relationship between teachers and students: *left*, Aristotle and his disciples; *right*, an anonymous class.

not send for others to read in their place, unless they are asking someone else to read in order to show him honour, and not to avoid the task of reading."[18]

Well into the sixteenth century, the scholastic method was prevalent in universities and in parish, monastic and cathedral schools throughout Europe. These schools, the ancestors of the Latin school of Sélestat, had begun to develop in the fourth and fifth centuries after the decline of the Roman educational system, and had flourished in the

ninth, when Charlemagne ordered all cathedrals and churches to provide schools for training clerics in the arts of reading, writing, chant and calculus. In the tenth century, when the resurgence of the towns made it essential to have centres of basic learning, schools established themselves around the figure of a particularly gifted teacher on whom the school's fame then depended.

The physical aspect of the schools did not change much from the times of Charlemagne. Classes were conducted in a large room. The teacher usually sat at an elevated lectern, or sometimes at a table, on an ordinary bench (chairs did not become common in Christian Europe until the fifteenth century). A marble sculpture from a Bolognese tomb, from the mid-fourteenth century, shows a teacher seated on a bench, a book open on the desk in front of him, looking out at his students. He is holding a page open with his left hand, while his right hand seems to be stressing a point, perhaps explaining the passage he has just read out loud. Most illustrations show the students sitting on benches, holding lined pages or wax tablets for taking notes, or standing around the teacher with open books. One signboard advertising a school in 1516 depicts two adolescent students working on a bench, hunched over their texts, while on the right a woman seated at a lectern is guiding a much younger child by pointing a finger at a page; on the left a student,

A signboard advertising a school, painted in 1516 by Ambrosius Holbein.

probably in his early teens, stands at a lectern, reading from an open book, while the teacher behind him holds a bundle of birches to his buttocks. The birch, as much as the book, would be the teacher's emblem for many centuries.

In the Latin school of Sélestat, students were first taught to read and write, and later learned the subjects of the *trivium*: grammar above all, rhetoric and dialectics. Since not all students arrived with a knowledge of their letters, reading would begin with an ABC or primer and collections of simple prayers such as the Lord's Prayer, Hail Mary and Apostles' Creed. After this rudimentary learning, the students were taken through several reading manuals common in most medieval schools: Donat's *Ars de octo partibus orationis*, the *Doctrinale puerorum* by the Franciscan monk Alexandre de Villedieu and the *Handbook of Logic* by Peter the Spaniard. Few students were rich enough to buy books,[19] and often only the teacher possessed these expensive volumes. He would copy the complicated rules of grammar onto the blackboard — usually without explaining them, since, according to scholastic pedagogy, understanding was not a requisite of knowledge. The students were then forced to learn the rules by heart. As might be expected, the results were often disappointing.[20] One of the students who attended the Sélestat Latin school in the early 1450s, Jakob Wimpfeling (who was to become, like Rhenanus, one of the most noted humanists of his age), commented years later that those who had studied under the old system "could neither speak Latin nor compose a letter or a poem, nor even explain one of the prayers used at Mass."[21] Several factors made reading difficult for a novice. As we have seen, punctuation was still erratic in the fifteenth century, and upper-case letters were used inconsistently. Many words were abbreviated, sometimes by the student hastening to take notes, but often as the common manner of writing out a word — perhaps to save paper — so the reader not only had to be able to read phonetically but also had to recognize what the abbreviation stood for. Finally, spelling was not uniform; the same word could appear under several different guises.[22]

An illuminated miniature showing a teacher ready to punish his student, in a late fifteenth-century French translation of Aristotle's *Politics*.

Following the scholastic method, students were taught to read through orthodox commentaries that were the equivalent of our potted lecture notes. The original texts — whether those of the Church Fathers or, to a far lesser extent, those of the ancient pagan writers — were not to be apprehended directly by the student but to be reached through a series of preordained steps. First came the *lectio*, a grammatical analysis in which the syntactic elements of each sentence would be identified; this would lead to the *littera* or literal sense of the text. Through the *littera* the student acquired the *sensus*, the meaning of the text according to different established interpretations. The process ended with an exegesis — the *sententia* — in which the opinions of approved commentators were discussed.[23] The merit of such a reading lay not in discovering a private significance in the text but in being able to recite and compare the interpretations of acknowledged authorities, and thus becoming "a better man". With these notions in mind, the fifteenth-century professor of rhetoric Lorenzo Guidetti summed up the purpose of teaching proper reading: "For when a good teacher undertakes to explicate any passage, the object is to train his pupils to speak eloquently and to live virtuously. If an obscure phrase crops up which serves neither of these ends but is readily explicable, then I am in favour of his explaining it. If its sense is not immediately obvious, I will not consider him negligent if he fails to explicate it. But if he insists on digging out trivia which require much time and effort to be expended in their explication, I shall call him merely pedantic."[24]

In 1441, Jean de Westhus, priest of the Sélestat parish and the local magistrate, decided to appoint a graduate of Heidelberg University — Louis Dringenberg — to the post of director of the school. Inspired by the contemporary humanist scholars who were questioning the traditional instruction in Italy and The Netherlands, and whose extraordinary influence was gradually reaching France and Germany, Dringenberg introduced fundamental changes. He kept the old reading manuals of Donat and Alexandre, but made use of only certain sections of their books, which he opened for discussion in class; he explained the rules of grammar, rather than merely forcing his students to memorize them; he discarded the traditional commentaries and glosses, which he found did "not help students to acquire an elegant language",[25] and worked instead with the classic texts of the Church Fathers themselves. By largely disregarding the conventional stepping-stones of the scholastic annotators, and by allowing the class to discuss the texts being taught (while still maintaining a strict guiding hand over the discussions), Dringenberg granted his students a greater degree of reading freedom than they had ever known before. He was not afraid of what Guidetti dismissed as "trivia". When he died in 1477, the basis for a new manner of teaching children to read had been firmly established in Sélestat.[26]

Dringenberg's successor was Crato Hofman, also a graduate of Heidelberg, a twenty-seven-year-old scholar whose students remembered him as "joyfully strict and strictly joyful",[27] who was quite ready to use the cane on anyone not sufficiently dedicated to the study of letters. If Dringenberg had concentrated his efforts on acquainting his students with the Church Fathers' texts, Hofman preferred the Roman and Greek classics.[28] One of his students noted that, like Dringenberg, "Hofman abhorred the old commentaries and glosses";[29] rather than take the class through a morass of grammatical rules, he proceeded very quickly to the reading of the texts themselves, adding to them a wealth of archeological, geographical and historical anecdotes. Another student recalled that, after Hofman had guided them through the works of Ovid, Cicero, Suetonius, Valerius Maximus, Antonius Sabellicus and others, they reached the university "perfectly fluent in Latin and with a profound knowledge of grammar".[30] Although calligraphy, "the art of writing beautifully", was never neglected, the ability to read fluently, accurately and intelligently, deftly "milking the text for every drop of sense", was for Hofman the utmost priority.

But even in Hofman's class, the texts were never left entirely open to the students' chance interpretation. On the contrary, they were systematically and rigorously dissected; from the copied words a moral was extracted, as well as politeness, civility, faith and warnings against vices — every sort of social precept, in fact, from table manners to the pitfalls of the seven deadly sins. "A teacher," wrote a contemporary of Hofman's, "must not only teach reading and writing, but also Christian virtues and morals; he must strive to seed the child's soul with virtue; this is important, because, as Aristotle says, a man behaves in later life according to the education he has received; all habits, especially good habits, having taken root in a man during his youth, cannot afterwards be uprooted."[31]

The Sélestat notebooks of Rhenanus and Gisenheim begin with Sunday prayers and selections from the Psalms which the students would copy from the blackboard on the first day of class. These they probably already knew by heart; in copying them out mechanically — not yet knowing how to read — they would have associated the series of words with the sound of the memorized lines, as in the "global" method for teaching reading laid out two centuries later by Nicolas Adam in his *A Trustworthy Method of Learning Any Language Whatsoever*: "When you show a child an object, a dress for instance, has it ever occurred to you to show him separately first the frills, then the sleeves, after that the front, the pockets, the buttons, etc.? No, of course not; you show him the whole and say to him: this is a dress. That is how children learn to speak from their nurses; why not do the same when teaching them to read? Hide from them all the ABCs and all the manuals of French and Latin; entertain them with whole words which they can understand and which they will retain with far more ease and pleasure than all the printed letters and syllables."[32]

In our time, the blind learn to read in a similar manner, by "feeling" the entire word — which they know already — rather than deciphering it letter by letter. Recalling her education, Helen Keller said that as soon as she had learned to spell, her teacher gave her slips of cardboard on which whole words were printed in raised letters. "I quickly learned that each printed word stood for an object, an act or a quality. I had a frame in which I could arrange the words in little sentences; but before

I ever put sentences in the frame I used to make them into objects. I found the slips of paper which represented, for example, *doll*, *is*, *on*, *bed* and placed each name on its object; then I put my doll on the bed with the words *is*, *on*, *bed* arranged beside the doll, thus making a sentence of the words, and at the same time carrying out the idea of the sentence with the things themselves."[33] For the blind child, since words were con-

crete objects that could actually be touched, they could be supplanted, as language signs, by the objects they were made to represent. This, of course, was not the case for the Séle-stat students, for whom the words on the page remained abstract signs.

The same notebook was used over several years, possibly for economic reasons, because of the cost of paper, but more probably because Hofman wanted his students to keep a progressive record of their lessons. Rhenanus's handwriting shows hardly any change as he copies out texts over the years. Set in the centre of the page, leaving large margins and broad spaces between lines for later glosses and comments, his handwriting imitates the Gothic script of German fifteenth-century manuscripts, the elegant hand that Gutenberg was to copy when cutting the letters for his Bible. Strong and clear, in bright purple ink, the handwriting allowed Rhenanus to follow the text with growing ease. Decorated initials appear on several pages (they remind me of the elaborate lettering with which I used to illumine my homework in the hope of better marks). After the devotions and brief quotations from the Church Fathers — all annotated with grammatical or etymological notes in black ink in the margins and between the lines, and sometimes with critical comments probably added later in the students' career — the notebooks progress to the study of certain classical writers.

Hofman stressed the grammatical perfection of these texts, but from time to time he was moved to remind his students that their reading was to be not only studiously analytical but also from the heart. Because he himself had found beauty and wisdom in those ancient texts, he encouraged his students to seek, in the words set down by souls long vanished, something that spoke to them personally, in their own place and time. In 1498, for instance, when they were studying books IV, V and VI of Ovid's *Fasti*, and the year after, when they copied out the opening sections of Virgil's *Bucolics* and then the complete *Georgics*, a

The school notebook of the adolescent Beatus Rhenanus, preserved at the Humanist Library in Sélestat.

jotted word of praise here and there, an enthusiastic gloss added to the margin, allows us to imagine that at that precise verse Hofman stopped his students to share his admiration and delight.

Looking at Gisenheim's notes, appended to the text in both Latin and German, we can follow the analytical reading that took place in Hofman's class. Many of the words Gisenheim wrote in the margins of his Latin copy are synonyms or translations; at times the note is a specific explanation. For instance, over the word *prognatos* the student has written the synonym *progenitos*, and then explained, in German, "those who are born from yourself". Other notes offer the etymology of a word, and its relation to its German equivalent. A favourite author at Sélestat was Isidore of Seville, the seventh-century theologian whose *Etymologies*, a vast work in twenty volumes, explained and discussed the meaning and use of words. Hofman seems to have been particularly concerned with instructing his students in using words correctly, being respectful of their meaning and connotations, so that they could interpret or translate with authority. At the end of the notebooks he had the students compile an *Index rerum et verborum* (Index of Things and Words) listing and defining the subjects they had studied, a step which no doubt gave them a sense of the progress they were making, and tools to use in other readings done on their own. Certain passages bear Hofman's comments on the texts. In no case are the words translated phonetically, which might lead one to suppose that, before copying down a text, Gisenheim, Rhenanus and the other students had repeated it out loud a sufficient number of times to memorize its pronunciation. Nor do the sentences in the notebooks carry stresses, so we don't know whether Hofman demanded a certain cadence in the reading or whether this was left to chance. In poetic passages, no doubt, a standard cadence would be taught, and we can imagine Hofman reading out in a booming voice the ancient and resonant lines.

The evidence that emerges from these notebooks is that, in the mid-fifteenth century, reading, at least in a humanist school, was gradually becoming the responsibility of each individual reader. Previous authorities — translators, commentators, annotators, glossers, cataloguers, anthologists, censors, canon-makers — had established official hierarchies and ascribed intentions to the different works. Now the readers were asked to read for themselves, and sometimes to determine value and meaning on their own in light of those authorities. The change, of course, was not sudden, nor can it be fixed to a single place and date. As early as the thirteenth century, an anonymous scribe had written in the margins of a monastic chronicle, "You should make it a habit, when reading books, to attend more to the sense than to the words, to concentrate on the fruit rather than the foliage."[34] This sentiment was echoed in Hofman's teaching. In Oxford, in Bologna, in Baghdad, even in Paris, the scholastic teaching methods were questioned and then gradually changed. This was brought on in part by the sudden availability of books soon after the invention of the printing press, but also by the fact that the somewhat simpler social structure of previous European centuries, of the Europe of Charlemagne and the later medieval world, had been economically, politically and intellectually fractured. To the new scholar — to Beatus Rhenanus, for instance — the world seemed to have lost its stability and grown in bewildering complexity. As if things weren't bad enough, in 1543 Copernicus's controversial treatise *De revolutionibus orbium coelestium* (*Of the Movement of Heavenly Bodies*) was published, which placed the sun at the centre of the universe — displacing Ptolemy's *Almagest*, which had assured the world that the earth and humankind were at the centre of all creation.[35]

The passage from the scholastic method to more liberated systems of thought brought another development. Until then, the task of a scholar had been — like that of the teacher — the search for knowledge, inscribed within certain rules and canons and proven systems of learning; the responsibility of the teacher had been felt to be a public one, making texts and their different levels of meaning available to the vastest possible audience, affirming a common social history of politics, philosophy and faith. After Dringenberg, Hofman and the others, the products of those schools, the new humanists, abandoned the classroom and the public forum and, like Rhenanus, retired to the closed space of the study or library, to read and think in private. The teachers of the Latin school at Sélestat passed on orthodox precepts that implied an established "correct" and common reading but also offered students the vaster and more personal humanist perspective; the students eventually reacted by circumscribing the act of reading to their own intimate world and experience and by asserting their authority as individual readers over every text.

THE MISSING
FIRST PAGE

In my last year of high school, at the Colegio Nacional de Buenos Aires, a teacher whose name I don't care to remember stood in front of the class and read to us the following:

All that allegories intend to say is merely that the incomprehensible is incomprehensible, and that we already know. But the problems we struggle with every day are a different matter. On this subject, a man once asked: "Why such stubbornness? If you only followed the allegories, you yourselves would become allegories and in that way solve all your everyday problems."

Another said: "I bet that is also an allegory."
The first said: "You have won."
The second said: "But alas, only allegorically."
The first said: "No, in real life. Allegorically you have lost."[1]

The short text, which our teacher never tried to explain, troubled us and provoked many discussions in the smoky café La Puerto Rico, just around the corner from the school. Franz Kafka wrote it in Prague in 1922, two years before his death. Forty-five years later, it left us, inquisitive adolescents, with the unsettling feeling that any single interpretation, any conclusion, any sense of having "understood" him and his allegories, was wrong. What those few lines suggested was not only that every text can be read as an allegory (and here the distinction between "allegory" and the less dogmatic concept of "symbol" becomes blurred),[2] revealing elements outside the text itself, but that every reading is in itself allegorical, the object of other readings. Without having heard of the critic Paul de Man, for whom "allegorical narratives tell the story of the *failure* to read",[3] we were in agreement with him that no reading can ever be final. With one important difference: what de Man saw as anarchic failure, we saw as proof of our freedom as readers. If, in reading, there was no such thing as "the last word", then no authority could impose a "correct" reading on us. With time we realized that some readings were better than others — more informed, more lucid, more challenging, more pleasurable, more disturbing. But the newly discovered sense of freedom never left us, and even now, enjoying a book which a certain reviewer has condemned or casting aside another which has been hotly praised, I think I can recall that rebellious feeling quite vividly.

Socrates affirmed that only that which the reader already knows can be sparked by a reading, and that knowledge cannot be acquired through dead letters. The early medieval scholars sought in reading a multiplicity of voices that ultimately echoed one single voice, God's *logos*. For the humanist teachers of the late Middle Ages, the text (including Plato's reading of Socrates' argument) and the successive comments of changing generations of readers, tacitly implied that not one but a near infinity of readings was possible, feeding upon one another. Our classroom reading of Lycias's speech was informed by centuries that Lycias never suspected — as he might not have suspected Phaedrus's enthusiasm or Socrates' sly comments. The books on my shelves do not know me until I open them, yet I am certain that they address me — me and every other reader — by name; they await our comments and opinions. I am presumed in Plato as I am presumed in every book, even in those I'll never read.

Around the year 1316, in a famous letter to the imperial vicar Can Grande della Scala, Dante argued that a text has at least two readings, "for we obtain one meaning from the letter of it, and another from that which the letter signifies; and the first is called *literal*, but the other *allegorical* or *mystical*". Dante goes on to suggest that the allegorical sense comprises three other readings. Setting as an example the biblical verse "When Israel came out of Egypt and the House of Jacob from among a strange people, Judah was his sanctuary and Israel his dominion," Dante explains: "For if we regard *the letter alone*, what is set before us is the exodus of the Children of Israel from Egypt in the days of Moses; if the *allegory*, our redemption wrought by Christ; if the *analogical* sense, we are shown the conversion of the soul from the grief and wretchedness of sin to the state of grace; if the *anagogical*, we are shown the departure of the holy soul from the thraldom of this corruption to the liberty of eternal glory. And although these mystical meanings are called by various names, they may all be called in general *allegorical*, since they differ from the literal and the historical."[4] All these are possible readings. Some readers may find one or several of them false: they may distrust a "historical" reading if they lack the context of the passage; they may object to the "allegorical" reading by regarding the reference to Christ as anachronistic; they may find the "analogical" (through analogy) and "anagogical" (through biblical interpretations) readings too fanciful or farfetched. Even a "literal" reading may be suspect. What does "came out" mean, exactly? Or "House"? Or "dominion"? It would seem that, in order to read at even a skin-deep level, the reader re-

Dante holding open his *Divine Comedy*, a mid-fifteenth-century mural by Domenico di Michelino in Florence Cathedral.

quires information about the text's creation, historical background, specialized vocabulary and even that most mysterious of things, what Saint Thomas Aquinas called *quem auctor intendit*, the author's intention. And yet, provided reader and text share a common language, any reader can make *some* sense out of any text: dada, horoscopes, hermetic poetry, computer manuals, even political bombast.

In 1782, just over four and a half centuries after Dante's death, Emperor Joseph II promulgated an edict, the *Toleranzpatent*, that theoretically abolished most barriers between Jews and non-Jews in the Holy

Roman Empire, with the intention of assimilating them into the Christian population. The new law made it compulsory for Jews to adopt German names and surnames, to use German in all official documents, to enrol for military service (from which they had up to then been excluded) and to attend secular German schools. A century later, on September 15, 1889, in the city of Prague, six-year-old Franz Kafka was taken by the family cook to the Deutsche Volks- und Bürgerschule on the Meatmarket,[5] a German-language establishment run largely by Jews in the midst of a Czech nationalist environment, to begin his schooling according to the wishes of the long-dead Habsburg emperor.

Kafka hated both the elementary school and, later, the Altstädter Gymnasium, or high school. He felt that, in spite of his successes (he passed all his grades easily), he had merely managed to deceive his elders and "to sneak from the first into the second Gymnasium grade, then into the third, and so on up the line. But," he added, "now that I had at last aroused their attention, I would of course be immediately thrown out, to the immense satisfaction of all righteous men delivered from a nightmare."[6]

Out of the ten months of the high-school year, one-third was devoted to classical languages and the rest to German, geography and history. Arithmetic was considered a subject of little importance, and Czech, French and physical education were optional. Students were expected to memorize their lessons and regurgitate them on demand. The philologist Fritz Mautner, Kafka's contemporary, noted that "of the forty students in my class, some three or four finally reached the point where, with infinite pains, they could just about handle a syllable-by-syllable translation of some ancient classic. . . . This certainly did not convey to them even the remotest notion of the spirit of the antique, its incomparable and inimitable strangeness. . . . As for the rest, the remaining 90 per cent of the class, they managed to pass the finals without ever deriving the slightest pleasure from their tag ends of Greek and Latin, promptly forgotten in any case right after graduation."[7] The teachers, in turn, seem to have blamed the students for their lack of appreciation, and by and large treated them with contempt. In a letter to his fiancée years later, Kafka wrote, "I am reminded of a teacher who, on reading the *Iliad* to us, often used to say: 'Too bad one has to read this with the likes of you. You cannot possibly understand it, and even when you think you do, you don't understand a thing. One has to have lived a great deal in order to understand even a tiny snippet.'" Throughout his life, Kafka read with the feeling that he lacked the experience and knowledge necessary to achieve even the beginning of an understanding.

According to Kafka's friend and biographer, Max Brod, religious teaching at the gymnasium was very poor. Since the Jewish students outnumbered the Protestants and Catholics, they were the ones who remained in the classroom to be taken through a digest of Jewish history in German and the recitation of prayers in Hebrew, a language of which most of them knew nothing. Only later did Kafka discover in his own notions of reading a common ground with the ancient Talmudists, for whom the Bible encoded a multiplicity of meanings whose continuous pursuit was the purpose of our voyage on earth. "One reads in order to ask questions," Kafka once told a friend.[8]

According to the Midrash — a collection of scholarly investigations into the possible meanings of the sacred texts — the Torah that God gave Moses on Mount Sinai was both a written text and an oral gloss. During the forty days Moses spent in the wilderness before returning to his people, he read the written word during the day and studied the oral commentary during the night. The notion of this double text — the written word and the reader's gloss — implied that the Bible allowed an ongoing revelation, based on but not limited to the Scriptures themselves. The Talmud — composed of the Mishna, a written collection of so-called oral laws supplementing the central five books of the Old Testament or Pentateuch, and the Gemara, its elaboration in the form of a debate — was developed to preserve the diverse layers of reading over many hundreds of years, from the fifth and sixth centuries (in Palestine and Babylonia, respectively) to modern times, when the standard scholarly edition of the Talmud was produced in Vilna in the late nineteenth century.

Two different ways of reading the Bible developed among Jewish scholars in the sixteenth century. One, centred around the Sephardic schools of Spain and North Africa, preferred to summarize the contents of a passage with little discussion of the details that composed it, concentrating on the literal and grammatical sense. The other, in the Ashkenazi schools based largely in France, Poland and the Germanic countries, analysed every line and every word, searching for every possible sense. Kafka belonged to this latter tradition.

Since the purpose of the Ashkenazi Talmudic scholar was to explore and elucidate the text on every conceivable level of meaning, and to comment on the commentaries all the way back to the original text,

Talmudic literature developed into self-regenerating texts that un-folded under progressive readings, not superseding but rather includ-ing all previous ones. When reading, the Ashkenazi Talmudic scholar commonly made use of four simultaneous levels of meaning, different from those proposed by Dante. The four levels were encoded in the acronym *PaRDeS*: *Pshat* or literal sense, *Remez* or limited meaning, *Drash* or rational elaboration and *Sod* or occult, secret, mystical mean-ing. Therefore reading was an activity that could never be completed. Rabbi Levi Yitzhak of Berdichev, one of the great eighteenth-century Hasidic masters, was asked why the first page of each of the treatises in the Babylonian Talmud was missing, so that the reader was forced to begin on page two. "Because however many pages the studious man reads," the rabbi answered, "he must never forget that he has not yet reached the very first page."[9]

For the Talmudic scholar, the reading of the text proceeds through a number of possible methods. Let us look at one small example. Follow-ing a system known as *gematria*, in which the letters of the sacred text are translated into numerical equivalents, one of the most famous Talmudic commentators, the eleventh-century rabbi Shlomo Yitzhak, known as Rashi, explained the reading of Genesis 17, when God tells Abraham that his aged wife, Sarah, will bear a son called Isaac. In Hebrew, "Isaac" is written *Y.tz.h.q*. Rashi aligned each letter with a number:

Y: 10, the ten times Abraham and Sarah tried unsuccessfully to
    have a child.
TZ: 90, Sarah's age at Isaac's birth.
H: 8, the eighth day, when the child is to be circumcised.
Q: 100, Abraham's age at Isaac's birth.

Decoded, one of the levels on which the text is read reveals Abra-ham's answer to God:

"Are we to have a child after ten years of waiting?
What! She is ninety years old!
A child who must be circumcised after eight days?
I, who am already one hundred years old?"[10]

Centuries after Rashi, in the confluence of German, Czech and Jewish cultures where Hasidism had once thrived, on the eve of the

Holocaust which would attempt to wipe all Jewish wisdom from the face of the earth, Kafka developed a manner of reading that allowed him to decipher words while at the same time questioning his ability to decipher them, persisting to understand the book and yet not confusing the circumstances of the book with his own circumstances — as if he was responding both to the classics teacher who sneered at his lack of experience which prevented him from understanding the text, and to his rabbinical ancestors for whom a text must continuously tempt a reader with revelation.

What were Kafka's books? As a child, we are told,[11] he read fairy-tales, Sherlock Holmes stories, travel narratives of foreign lands; as a young man, the works of Goethe, Thomas Mann, Hermann Hesse, Dickens, Flaubert, Kierkegaard, Dostoevsky. In his room, where the family bustle constantly intruded, or in his office on the second floor of the Workmen's Accident Insurance Institution, he would often try, on stolen time, to pore over whatever book he had with him: searching for meanings, each meaning neither more nor less valid than the next; constructing a whole library of texts unfurled like a scroll on the open page in front of him; proceeding like a Talmudic scholar from commentary to commentary; allowing himself to drift away from and at the same time bore into the original text.

Walking through Prague one day with the son of a colleague, he stopped outside a bookstore and looked in the window. Seeing his young companion bend his head right and left, trying to read the titles of the lined-up books, he laughed. "So you too are a lunatic about books, with a head that wags from too much reading?" The friend assented: "I don't think I could exist without books. To me, they're the whole world." Kafka grew serious. "That's a mistake," he said. "A book cannot take the place of the world. That is impossible. In life, everything has its own meaning and its own purpose, for which there cannot be any permanent substitute. A man can't, for instance, master his own experience through the medium of another personality. That is how the world is in relation to books. One tries to imprison life in a book, like a songbird in a cage, but it's no good."[12]

Kafka's intuition that if the world has coherence, it is one that we can never fully comprehend — that if it offers hope, it is (as he once replied to Max Brod) "not for us" — led him to see, in this very irre-solvability, the essence of the world's richness.[13] Walter Benjamin noted in a celebrated essay that in order to understand Kafka's view of

the world "one must keep in mind Kafka's way of reading",[14] which
Benjamin compared to that of Dostoevsky's Grand Inquisitor in the
allegorical tale in *The Brothers Karamazov*: "We have before us," says the
Inquisitor, speaking to Christ returned to earth, "a mystery which we
cannot grasp. And precisely because it is a mystery we have had the
right to preach it, to teach the people that what matters is neither freedom nor love, but the riddle, the secret, the mystery to which they
have to bow — without reflection and even without conscience."[15] A
friend who saw Kafka reading at his desk said that he reminded him of
the anguished figure depicted in the painting *A Reader of Dostoevsky* by
the Czech expressionist Emil Filla, who seems to have fallen into a
trance while reading the book he still holds in his grey hand.[16]

Kafka famously asked his friend Max Brod to burn his writings
after his death; Brod famously disobeyed. Kafka's request has been seen
as a self-deprecating gesture, the obligatory "I'm not worthy" of the
writer who expects Fame to answer, "But yes, yes, you are." Perhaps

Emil Filla's
*A Reader of
Dostoevsky*.

there is another explanation. It
may be that since Kafka realized
that, for a reader, every text must
be unfinished (or abandoned, as
Paul Valéry suggested), that in fact
a text can be read only *because* it is
unfinished, thus allowing room
for the reader's work, he wished
for his own writing the immortal-
ity that generations of readers
have granted to the volumes
burned in the Library of Alexandria, the eighty-three lost plays of
Aeschylus, the lost books of Livy,
the first draft of Carlyle's *The
French Revolution*, which a friend's maid accidentally tipped into the fire,
the second volume of Gogol's *Dead Souls*, which a fanatical priest condemned to the flames. Perhaps for the same reason, Kafka never completed many of his writings: there is no last page to *The Castle* because
K., the hero, must never reach it, so that the reader can continue into
the multilayered text for ever. A novel by Judith Krantz or Elinor Glyn
locks itself into one exclusive, airtight reading, and the reader cannot
escape without knowingly exceeding the limits of common sense

(there are few who read *Princess Daisy* as an allegory of the voyage of the soul, or *Three Weeks* as a nineteenth-century *Pilgrim's Progress*). This we realized back in Buenos Aires, together with that early sense of freedom: that the authority of the reader is never limitless. "The limits of interpretation," Umberto Eco has noted in a useful epigram, "coincide with the rights of the text."[17]

Ernst Pawel, at the end of his lucid biography of Kafka, written in 1984, observed that "the literature dealing with Kafka and his work currently comprises an estimated 15,000 titles in most of the world's major languages."[18] Kafka has been read literally, allegorically, politically, psychologically. That readings always outnumber the texts that breed them is a trite observation, and yet something revealing about the creative nature of the act of reading lies in the fact that one reader can despair and another can laugh at exactly the same page. My daughter Rachel read *Metamorphosis* at thirteen and thought it humorous; Gustav Janouch, Kafka's friend, read it as a religious and ethical parable;[19] Bertolt Brecht read it as the work of "the only true Bolshevist writer";[20] the Hungarian critic György Lukács read it as the typical product of a decadent bourgeois;[21] Borges read it as a retelling of the paradoxes of Zeno;[22] the French critic Marthe Robert read it as an example of the German language at its clearest;[23] Vladimir Nabokov read it (partly) as an allegory on adolescent *Angst*.[24] The fact is that Kafka's stories, nourished by Kafka's reading experience, offer and take away, at the same time, the illusion of understanding; they undermine, as it were, the craft of Kafka the writer in order to satisfy Kafka the reader.

"Altogether," Kafka wrote in 1904 to his friend Oskar Pollak, "I think we ought to read only books that bite and sting us. If the book we are reading doesn't shake us awake like a blow on the skull, why bother reading it in the first place? So that it can make us happy, as you put it? Good God, we'd be just as happy if we had no books at all; books that make us happy we could, in a pinch, also write ourselves. What we need are books that hit us like a most painful misfortune, like the death of someone we loved more than we love ourselves, that make us feel as though we had been banished to the woods, far from any human presence, like a suicide. A book must be the axe for the frozen sea within us. That is what I believe."[25]

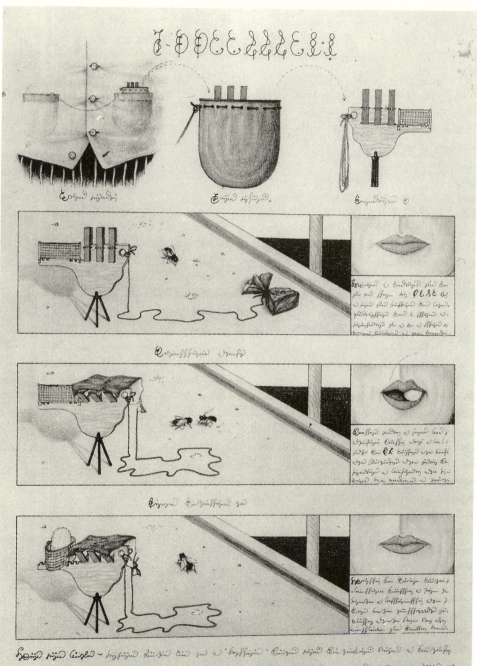

One summer afternoon in 1978, a voluminous parcel arrived in the offices of the publisher Franco Maria Ricci in Milan, where I was working as foreign-language editor. When we opened it we saw that it contained, instead of a manuscript, a large collection of illustrated pages depicting a number of strange objects and detailed but bizarre operations, each captioned in a script none of the editors recognized. The accompanying letter explained that the author, Luigi Serafini, had created an encyclopedia of an imaginary world along the lines of a medieval scientific compendium: each page precisely depicted a specific entry, and the annotations, in a nonsensical alphabet which Serafini had also invented during two long years in a small apartment in Rome, were meant to explain the illustrations' intricacies. Ricci, to his credit, published the work in two luxurious volumes with a delighted introduction by Italo Calvino; they are one of the most curious examples of an illustrated book I know. Made entirely of invented words and pictures, the *Codex Seraphinianus*[1] must be read without the help of a common language, through signs for which there are no meanings except those furnished by a willing and inventive reader.

This is, of course, a brave exception. Most of the time, a sequence of signs follows an established code, and only my ignorance of the code makes it impossible for me to read it. Even so, I wander through an exhibition at the Rietberg Museum in Zurich, of Indian miniatures depicting mythological scenes of stories with which I'm not familiar, and

OPPOSITE

An explanatory page from the *Codex Seraphinianus*.

attempt to reconstruct their sagas; I sit in front of the prehistoric paintings on the rocks of the Tessali Plateau in the Algerian Sahara and try to imagine what menace pursues the fleeing giraffe-like creatures; I flip through a Japanese comic book at Narita Airport and make up a narrative for characters who speak in a script I have never learned. Attempting to read a book in a language I don't know — Greek, Russian, Cree, Sanskrit — reveals of course nothing to me; but if the book is illustrated, even if I can't read the captions I can usually assign a meaning — though not necessarily the one explained in the text. Serafini counted on his readers' creative skill.

Serafini had a reluctant precursor. In the last few years of the fourth century, Saint Nilus of Ancyra (now Ankara, the capital of Turkey) founded a monastery near his native town. Of Nilus we know almost nothing: that his feast day is November 12, that the year of his death was *circa* 430, that he was the author of several sententious and ascetical treatises intended for his monks and of more than a thousand letters to his superiors, his friends and his congregation, and that, in the days of his youth, he studied under the famous Saint John Chrysostom in Constantinople.[2] For centuries, until scholarly detectives stripped the saint's life down to these bare bones, Saint Nilus had been the hero of a prodigiously unusual story.[3] According to the *Septem narrationes de caede monarchorum et de Theodulo filio*, a sixth-century compilation once read as a hagiographical chronicle and now shelved among romances and fictional tales of adventure, Nilus was born in Constantinople of a noble family and was appointed officer and prefect to the court of Emperor Theodosius the Great. He married and had two children but, filled with spiritual longings, abandoned his wife and daughter and in 390 or 404 (retellings of his story vary in their imaginative precision)[4] entered the ascetic congregation of Mount Sinai, where he and his son, Theodulus, led pious and reclusive lives. According to the *Narrationes*, the virtue of Saint Nilus and his son was such that "it provoked demons to hatred and angels to envy". As a result of this angelic and demonic displeasure, in 410 a horde of Saracen bandits attacked the hermitage, massacred a number of monks and took others away as slaves, among them the young Theodulus. By divine grace Nilus escaped both the sword and the chains, and set off in search of his son. He found him in a town somewhere between Palestine and Arabia Petrea, where the local bishop, moved by the saint's devotion, ordained both father and son as priests. Saint Nilus returned to Mount Sinai, where he died at a pleasant old age, lulled by bashful angels and repentant demons.[5]

We do not know what Saint Nilus's monastery was like, or where exactly it was located, but in one of his many letters[6] he describes certain ideal features of ecclesiastical decoration which we may assume he used in his own chapel. Bishop Olympidorus had consulted him about the erection of a church which he wished to decorate with images of saints, hunting scenes, birds and animals. Saint Nilus, while approving the depiction of saints, condemned the hunting scenes and the fauna as "trifling and unworthy of a manly Christian soul" and suggested instead scenes from the Old and New Testament "painted by the hand of a gifted artist". These, he argued, set up on either side of the Holy Cross, would "serve as books for the unlearned, teach them scriptural history and impress on them the record of God's mercies."[7]

Saint Nilus imagined the illiterate faithful coming to these scenes in his functional church and reading them as if they were the words of a book. He imagined them looking up at decorations that were no longer "trifling adornments"; he imagined them identifying the precious images, linking one with another in their minds, inventing stories for them or recognizing in the familiar pictures associations with sermons they had heard or, if they happened to be not totally "unlearned", with exegeses from the Scriptures. Two centuries later, Pope Gregory the Great would echo Saint Nilus's views: "It is one thing to worship a picture, it is another to learn in depth, by means of pictures, a venerable story. For that which writing makes present to the reader, pictures make present to the illiterate, to those who only perceive visually, because in pictures the ignorant see the story they ought to follow, and those who don't know their letters find that they can, after a fashion, read. Therefore, especially for the common folk, pictures are the equivalent of reading."[8] In 1025 the Synod of Arras stated that "what simple people could not grasp through reading the scriptures could be learned by means of contemplating pictures."[9]

Although the Second Commandment given by God to Moses specifically forbids the making of graven images of "any likeness of any thing that is in the heaven above, or that is in the earth beneath, or that is in the water under the earth",[10] Jewish artists decorated religious sites and objects as far back as Solomon's Temple in Jerusalem.[11] At times though, the interdiction prevailed, and Jewish artists resorted to inventive compromises, such as giving the forbidden human figures bird heads so as not to depict the human face. The controversy was resurrected in Christian Byzantium during the eighth and ninth centuries, when Emperor Leo III and later the iconoclastic emperors Constantine V and Theophilus banned the depiction of images throughout the empire.

From a fourteenth-century German *Haggadah*, a cantor at the reading desk in the synagogue, his face replaced by that of a bird to satisfy the Old Testament's injunction against representing the human figure.

For the ancient Romans, the symbol of a god (the eagle for Jupiter, for instance) was a substitute for the god himself. In the rare cases when Jupiter is represented together with his eagle, the eagle is not a repetition of the god's presence but becomes his attribute, like his thunderbolt. For the early Christians symbols had this double quality, standing not merely for the subjects (the lamb for Christ, the dove for the Holy Spirit) but also for specific aspects of the subjects (the lamb as the sacrificial Christ, the dove as the Holy Spirit's promise of deliverance).[12] They were not meant to be read as synonyms of the concepts or mere duplicates of the deities. Instead they graphically expanded certain qualities of the central image, commented on them, underlined them, turned them into subjects in their own right.

Eventually, the basic symbols of early Christianity appear to have lost some of their symbolic function and become in fact little more than ideograms: the crown of thorns standing for the Passion of Christ, the dove for the Holy Spirit. These elementary images were gradually complemented by vaster and more complex ones, so that entire episodes of the Bible became symbols of various aspects of Christ, of the Holy Spirit, of the life of the Virgin, as well as becoming illustrations of certain readings of other sacred episodes. Perhaps this richness of meaning is what Saint Nilus had in mind when he suggested counterpointing the New and Old Testament by depicting them on either side of the Holy Cross.

The fact that images from the Old and New Testament could complement one another and continue each other's narrative, teaching "the unlearned" the Word of God, had already been suggested by the evangelists themselves. In his gospel, Matthew explicitly linked the Old and New Testament at least eight times: "Now all this was done, that it might be fulfilled which was spoken of the Lord by the prophet."[13] And

Christ Himself said that "all things must be fulfilled, which were written in the law of Moses, and in the prophets, and in the psalms, concerning me."[14] There are 275 literal quotations of the Old Testament in the New, plus 235 specific references.[15] This concept of a spiritual continuity was not new even then; a contemporary of Christ, the Jewish philosopher Philo of Alexandria, had developed the idea of an all-pervading mind manifesting itself throughout the ages. That single and omniscient spirit is present in Christ's words, which described it as a wind that "bloweth where it listeth", and links past to present and future. Origen, Tertullian, Saint Gregory of Nyssa and Saint Ambrose all wrote imaginatively of common images in both testaments, and elaborated complex and poetic explanations in which no single element of the Bible passed by unremarked or unexplained. "The New Testament," wrote Saint Augustine in a much-quoted couplet, "lies hidden in the Old, while the Old is disclosed in the New."[16] And Eusebius of Caesarea, who died in 340, proclaimed that "every prophet, every ancient writer, every revolution of the state, every law, every ceremony of the Old Covenant points only to Christ, announces only Him, represents only Him.... He was in Father Adam, progenitor of the saints; He was innocent and virginal like a martyr in Abel, a renewer of the world in Noah, blessed in Abraham, the high priest in Melchisedec, a willing sacrifice in Isaac, chief of the elect in Jacob, sold by His brothers in Joseph, powerful in work in Egypt, a giver of laws in Moses, suffering and forsaken in Job, hated and persecuted in most of the prophets."[17]

By the time of Saint Nilus's recommendation, the iconography of the Christian Church was already developing conventional pictures of the Spirit's ubiquity. One of the earliest examples can be seen on a

Christ as the Lamb that washes away the sins of the world, in the famous Ghent Altarpiece by H. and J. Van Eyck.

two-panelled door carved in Rome in the fourth century and installed in the Church of St. Sabina. The panels depict corresponding scenes from the Old and New Testament which can be read simultaneously. The workmanship is somewhat rough and the details have been blurred

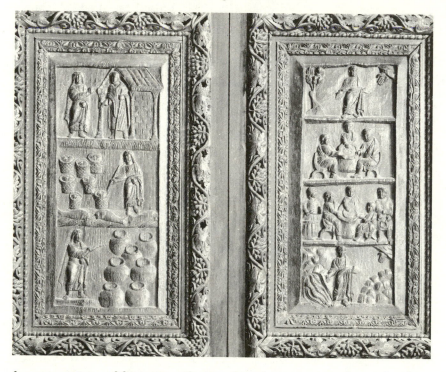

Two panels from the doors of the Church of Saint Sabina in Rome contrasting, to the left, three miracles of Christ, and, to the right, those of Moses.

by generations of fingering pilgrims, but the scenes can be easily identified. On one side are three of the miracles attributed to Moses: the sweetening of the waters of Marah, the provision of manna during the flight from Egypt (depicted in two sections) and the striking of water from a rock. On the other are three of the miracles of Christ: the restoring of sight to the blind man, the multiplication of the loaves and fishes and the turning of water into wine for the wedding at Cana.

What would a Christian, looking upon the doors of St. Sabina in the mid-fifth century, have read? The tree with which Moses sweetened the bitter waters of Marah would have been recognized as the Cross, symbol of Christ Himself. The spring, like Christ, was a fount of living water giving life to the Christian flock. The desert rock that Moses struck would also have been read as an image of Christ, the Saviour from whose side flows both the blood and the water.[18] The manna foreshadowed the food of Cana and of the Last Supper.[19] An unbeliever, however, not instructed in the Christian faith, would read the images on the doors of St. Sabina much as Serafini intended his readers to understand his fantastical encyclopedia: by making up, from the depicted elements, a story and a vocabulary for themselves.

This, of course, was not what Saint Nilus had in mind. In 787, the Seventh Church Council in Nicaea made it clear that not only was the congregation not free to interpret the pictures shown in church, but neither was the painter free to lend his work any private significance or resolution. "The execution of pictures is not an invention of the painter," the council declared, "but a recognized proclamation of the laws and tradition of the overall Church. The ancient fathers caused them to be executed on the walls of the churches: it is their thought and tradition that we see, not that of the painter. To the painter belongs the art, but the arrangement belongs to the Church fathers."[20]

When Gothic art began to flourish in the thirteenth century, and painting on church walls was abandoned in favour of pictorial windows and carved columns, the biblical iconography was transferred from plaster to stained glass, wood and stone. The lessons of the Scriptures now shone with light and stood out in rounded forms, narrating to the faithful stories in which the New and the Old Testament subtly mirrored each other.

Then, sometime in the early fourteenth century, the images Saint Nilus had intended for the faithful to read on the walls were reduced and collected in the shape of a book. In the regions of the Lower Rhine, several illuminators and woodblock engravers began to depict the echoing images on parchment and paper. The books they created were made almost entirely out of juxtaposed scenes, with just a few words, sometimes as captions on the sides of the page and sometimes issuing from the mouths of characters in banner-like cartouches, like the balloons in today's comic strips.

By the end of the fourteenth century these books of images had become hugely popular, and they were to remain so throughout the Middle Ages, in all their various guises: volumes of full-page drawings, meticulous miniatures, hand-tinted woodblock prints and finally, in the fifteenth century, printed tomes. The first such volume we possess dates from 1462.[21] In time, these extraordinary books came to be known as Bibliae Pauperum, or Bibles of the Poor.

Essentially, these "Bibles" were large picture-books in which each page was divided to allow for two or more scenes. For instance, in the

A sequential
page from the
Heidelberg
Biblia pauperum.

so-called Biblia Pauperum of Heidelberg,[22] from the fifteenth century,
the pages are divided into two halves, upper and lower. The lower half
of one of the first pages depicts the Annunciation, and would have been
shown to the faithful on that liturgical date. Surrounding the scene are
the four Old Testament prophets who foresaw the coming of Christ:

David, Jeremiah, Isaiah and Ezekiel. Above them, in the upper half, are two Old Testament scenes: God cursing the snake in the Garden of Eden, with Adam and Eve standing coyly to one side (Genesis, 3); and the angel calling Gideon to action, while Gideon lays the fleece on the ground to find out if God will save Israel (Judges, 6).

Chained to a lectern, opened to an appropriate page, the Biblia Pauperum would display its double images to the faithful sequentially, day after day, month after month. Many would not be able to read the words in Gothic script surrounding the depicted personages; few would grasp the several meanings of each image in their historical, moral and allegorical significance. But the majority of the people would recognize most of the characters and scenes, and be able to "read" in those images a relationship between the stories of the Old Testament and the stories of the New, simply because of their juxtaposition on the page. Preachers and priests would no doubt gloss upon these images, and retell the events portrayed, linking them in an edifying manner, embroidering on the sacred narration. And the sacred texts themselves would be read, day in, day out, all through the year, so that in the course of their lives people would likely hear much of the Bible many times. It has been suggested that the main purpose of the Biblia Pauperum was not to provide reading for the unlettered flock but to lend the priest a sort of prompter or thematic guide, a starting-place for sermons or addresses, helping him to demonstrate the unity of the Bible.[23] If this was so (no document exists to confirm its purpose), then, like most books, it had a variety of users and uses.

Almost certainly, "Biblia Pauperum" was not the name by which these books were known by their first readers. The misnomer was discovered late in the eighteenth century by the German writer Gotthold Ephraim Lessing, himself a devoted reader who believed that "books explain life". In 1770, poor and sick, Lessing accepted the badly paid post of librarian to the stolid Duke of Braunschweig, at Wolfenbüttel. There he spent eight miserable years, wrote his most famous play, *Emilia Galotti*, and in a series of critical essays discussed the relationship between different forms of artistic representation.[24] One of the books in the Duke's library was a Biblia Pauperum. Lessing found, scribbled on one of the margins by a later hand, the inscription *Hic incipitur bibelia* [sic] *pauperum*. He deduced from this that the book, in order to be catalogued, had required some sort of name, and that an ancient librarian, inferring from the many illustrations and the sparseness of text that it was intended for the illiterate, that is, the poor, had given it a title that future generations took to be authentic.[25] As Lessing remarked, however, several examples of such bibles were far too ornate and costly to be meant for the poor. Perhaps what mattered was not ownership — what belonged to the Church might be considered to belong to all —

Gotthold
Ephraim
Lessing.

but access; with its pages open on the appropriate days for all to inspect, the fortuitously named Biblia Pauperum escaped confinement among the learned and became popular among the faithful, who were hungry for stories.

Lessing also drew attention to the similarities between the book's parallel iconography and that of the stained glass in the windows of the Hirschau cloister. He suggested that the illustrations in the book were copies of those in the windows; he also dated the windows from the time of Abbot Johan von Calw (1503 to 1524), almost half a century before the Wolfenbüttel copy of the Biblia Pauperum was executed. Modern research indicates that it was not a copy,[26] but whether the iconography of both the book and the windows merely followed a fashion that had gradually established itself over several centuries is impossible to say. Lessing, however, was right in noting that the "reading" of the pictures in the Biblia Pauperum and on the stained-glass windows was essentially the same act, and that both were different from reading a description in words on a page.

For the literate Christian of the fourteenth century, a page of an ordinary bible had a multiplicity of meanings through which the reader could progress according to the guiding gloss of the author or the reader's own knowledge. A reader would pace this reading at will, over an hour or a year, with interruptions or delays, skipping sections or devouring the whole page at one sitting. But the reading of an illustrated page in the Biblia Pauperum was almost instantaneous, since the "text" was offered iconographically as a whole, without semantic gradations, and the time of the narration in pictures necessarily coincided with that of the reader's own reading. "It is relevant to consider," wrote Marshall McLuhan, "that the old prints and woodcuts, like the modern comic strip and comic book, provide very little data about any particular moment in time, or aspect in space, of an object. The viewer, or reader, is compelled to participate in completing and interpreting the few hints provided by the bounding lines. Not unlike the character of the woodcut and the cartoon is the TV image, with its very low degree of data on objects, and the resulting high degree of participation by the viewer in order to complete what is only hinted at in the mosaic mesh of dots."[27]

A 1994 ad for Absolut vodka.

For me, centuries away, the two kinds of reading converge when I go over the morning newspaper: on the one hand, there is the slow progress through the news, continued sometimes on a distant page, related to other items hidden away in different sections, written in varying styles from the apparently unemotional to the blatantly ironic; on the other, the almost involuntary grasping of the ads read at a single glance, each story told within precise and limited frames, through familiar characters and symbols — not the tormented Saint Catherine or the dinner at Emmaus, but the vicissitudes of the latest Peugeot or the epiphany of Absolut Vodka.

Who then were my ancestors, these distant picture-readers? The great majority, like the authors of the pictures they read, were silent, anonymous, unsung, but from those shifting crowds a few individuals can be rescued.

In October 1461, after being released from prison by the chance passing of King Louis XI through the town of Meung-sur-Loire, the poet François Villon composed a long poetic medley which he called his *Testament*.[28] One of the pieces, a prayer to the Virgin Mary written (so he tells us) at his mother's request, put in his mother's mouth these words:

I am a woman poor and aged,
I know nothing at all; letters I never read;
At my parish monastery I saw
A painted Paradise with harps and lutes,
And also Hell wherein the damned are boiled:
One gave me fright; the other, joyfulness.[29]

Every article of the religious service displayed a story. The faithful would be able to follow the terrors of the Last Judgement when the priest turned his back to pray (as on this fifteenth-century Italian chasuble, *opposite page*) or as they passed behind the altarpiece (*right*, painted panels by Jorg Kandel of Biberach *c.* 1525).

Villon's mother would have seen images of a serene and musical heaven, and a fiery, bubbling hell, and she would have known that, after her death, her soul was destined to enter one or the other. Obviously she would not, in seeing these images — however dextrously painted, however long her eyes busied themselves on the many excruciating details — have recognized in them the arduous theological arguments developed by the Church Fathers over the past fifteen centuries. She probably knew the French version of the popular Latin maxim *Salvandorum paucitas, damnandorum multitudo* ("Few are saved, many are damned"); she probably did not know that Saint Thomas Aquinas had determined that the proportion of those to be saved was equivalent to that of Noah and his family in relation to the rest of humankind. Church sermons would have glossed some of those images, and her imagination would have done the rest.

Like Villon's mother, thousands of people lifted their eyes to the images that adorned the church walls and later the windows, columns, pulpits, even the back of the priest's cha-suble as he was saying mass or the panels at the rear of the altar where they sat during confession, and saw in those images myriad stories or a single, never-ending story. There is no reason to think that it was otherwise with the Biblia Pauperum. But several modern scholars disagree. According to the German critic Maurus Berve, for instance, the Biblia Pauperum was "absolutely unintelligible to illiterate people". Instead, Berve suggests that "they were probably intended for scholars or clerics who could not afford to

purchase a complete Bible or who being 'poor in spirit' [arme in Geiste] lacked a more demanding level of education and contented themselves with these extracts."[30] Consequently the name "Biblia Pauperum" would not have meant "Bible of the Poor" but would have stood instead for Biblia Pauperum Praedicatorum, or Poor Preachers' Bible.[31]

Whether these images were intended for the poor or for their preachers, it is certain that they stood open on the lectern, in front of the flock, day after day throughout the liturgical year. For the illiterate, excluded from the realm of the written word, seeing the sacred texts represented in a book in images they could recognize or "read" must have induced a feeling of belonging, of sharing with the wise and powerful the material presence of God's word. Seeing these scenes in a book — in that almost magical object that belonged exclusively to the learned clerics and scholars of the day — was very different from seeing them in the popular decorations of the church, as they always had in the past. It was as if suddenly the holy words which had until then appeared to be the property of a few, to share or not with the flock at will, had been translated into a language that anyone, even an uninstructed woman "poor and aged" like Villon's mother, could understand.

T he pictures of medieval Europe offered a syntax without words, to which the reader silently added a narration. In our time, deciphering the pictures of advertising, of video art, of cartoons, we too lend a story not only a voice but a vocabulary. I must have read like that at the very beginning of my reading, before my encounter with letters and their sounds. I must have constructed, out of the water-colour Peter Rabbits, the brazen Struwwelpeters, the large, bright creatures in *La Hormiguita Viajera*, stories that explained and justified the different scenes, linking them in a possible narrative that took every one of the depicted details into account. I didn't know it then, but I was exercising my freedom to read almost to the limit of its possibilities: not only was the story mine to tell, but nothing forced me to repeat the same tale time after time for the same illustrations. In one version the anonymous hero was a hero, in another he was a villain, in the third he bore my name.

On other occasions I relinquished all these rights. I delegated both words and voice, gave up possession — and sometimes even the choice — of the book and, except for the odd clarifying question, became nothing but hearing. I would settle down (at night, but also often during the day, since frequent bouts of asthma kept me trapped in my bed for weeks) and, propped up high against the pillows, listen to my nurse read the Grimms' terrifying fairy-tales. Sometimes her voice put me to sleep; sometimes, on the contrary, it made me feverish with excitement, and I urged her on in order to find out, more quickly than the

OPPOSITE

Reading in public fulfilled a social function in eighteenth-century France, as depicted in this contemporary engraving by Marillier.

109

author had intended, what happened in the story. But most of the time I simply enjoyed the luxurious sensation of being carried away by the words, and felt, in a very physical sense, that I was actually travelling somewhere wonderfully remote, to a place that I hardly dared glimpse on the secret last page of the book. Later on, when I was nine or ten, I was told by my school principal that being read to was suitable only for small children. I believed him, and gave up the practice — partly because being read to gave me enormous pleasure, and by then I was quite ready to believe that anything that gave pleasure was somehow unwholesome. It was not until much later, when my lover and I decided to read to each other, over a summer, *The Golden Legend*, that the long-lost delight of being read to came back to me. I didn't know then that the art of reading out loud had a long and itinerant history, and that over a century ago, in Spanish Cuba, it had established itself as an institution within the earthbound strictures of the Cuban economy.

Cigar-making had been one of Cuba's main industries since the seventeenth century, but in the 1850s the economic climate changed. The saturation of the American market, rising unemployment and the cholera epidemic of 1855 convinced many workers that the creation of a union was necessary to improve their conditions. In 1857 a Mutual Aid Society of Honest Workers and Day Labourers was founded for the benefit of white cigar-makers only; a similar Mutual Aid Society was founded for free black workers in 1858. These were the first Cuban workers' unions, and the precursors of the Cuban labour movement of the turn of the century.[1]

In 1865, Saturnino Martínez, cigar-maker and poet, conceived the idea of publishing a newspaper for the workers in the cigar industry, which would contain not only political features but also articles on science and literature, poems and short stories. With the support of several Cuban intellectuals, Martínez brought out the first issue of *La Aurora* on October 22 of that year. "Its purpose," he announced in the first editorial, "will be to illuminate in every possible way that class of society to which it is dedicated. We will do everything to make ourselves generally accepted. If we are not successful, the blame will lie in our insufficiency, not in our lack of will." Over the years, *La Aurora* published work by the major Cuban writers of the day, as well as translations of European authors such as Schiller and Chateaubriand, reviews of books and plays, and exposés of the tyranny of factory owners and of the workers' sufferings. "Do you know," it asked its readers on

June 27, 1866, "that at the edge of La Zanja, according to what people say, there is a factory owner who puts shackles on the children he uses as apprentices?"[2]

But, as Martínez soon realized, illiteracy was the obvious stumbling-block to making *La Aurora* truly popular; in the mid-nineteenth century barely 15 per cent of the working population of Cuba could read. In order to make the paper accessible to all workers, he hit on the idea of a public reader. He approached the director of the Guanabacoa high school and suggested that the school assist readings in the working-place. Full of enthusiasm, the director met with the workers of the fac-tory El Fígaro and, after obtaining the owner's permission, convinced them of the usefulness of the enterprise. One of the workers was chosen as the reader, the official *lector*, and the others paid for his efforts out of their own pockets. On January 7, 1866, *La Aurora* reported, "Reading in the shops has begun for the first time among us, and the initiative be-longs to the honoured workers of El Fígaro. This constitutes a giant step in the march of progress and the general advance of the workers, since in this way they will gradually become familiar with books, the source of everlasting friendship and great entertainment."[3] Among the books read were the historical compendium *Battles of the Century*, didactic novels such as *The King of the World* by the now long forgotten Fernández y González and a manual of political economy by Flórez y Estrada.[4]

Eventually other factories followed the example of El Fígaro. So successful were these public readings that in very little time they acquired a reputation for "being subversive". On May 14, 1866, the Political Governor of Cuba issued the following edict:

> 1. It is forbidden to distract the workers of the tobacco shops, workshops and shops of all kinds with the reading of books and newspapers, or with discussions foreign to the work in which they were engaged. 2. The police shall exercise constant vigilance to enforce this decree, and put at the disposal of my authority those shop owners, representatives or managers who disobey this mandate so that they may be judged by the law according to the gravity of the case.[5]

In spite of the prohibition, clandestine readings still took place for a time in some form or other; however, by 1870 they had virtually dis-appeared. In October 1868, with the outbreak of the Ten Years War, *La*

The earliest known sketch of a *lector*, in the *Practical Magazine*, New York, 1873.

Aurora too came to an end. And yet the readings were not forgotten. As early as 1869 they were resurrected, on American soil, by the workers themselves.

The Ten Years War of Independence began on October 10, 1868, when a Cuban landowner, Carlos Manuel de Céspedes, and two hundred poorly armed men took over the city of Santiago and proclaimed the country's independence from Spain. By the end of the month, after Céspedes had offered to free all slaves joining the revolution, his army had recruited twelve thousand volunteers; in April of the following year, Céspedes was elected president of the new revolutionary government. But Spain held strong. Four years later Céspedes was deposed *in absentia* by a Cuban tribunal, and in March 1874 he was trapped and shot by Spanish soldiers.[6] In the meantime, anxious to disrupt Spain's restrictive trade measures, the U.S. government had loudly supported the revolutionaries, and New York, New Orleans and Key West had opened their ports to thousands of fleeing Cubans. As a result, Key West was transformed in a few years from a small fishing village into a major cigar-producing community, the new Havana-cigar capital of the world.[7]

The workers who immigrated to the United States took with them, among other things, the institution of the *lector*: an illustration in the American *Practical Magazine* of 1873 shows one such *lector*, wearing glasses and a large-brimmed hat, sitting with legs crossed and a book in his hands while a row of workers (all male) in waistcoats and shirtsleeves go about their cigar-rolling with what appears to be rapt attention.

"El lector" by Mario Sánchez.

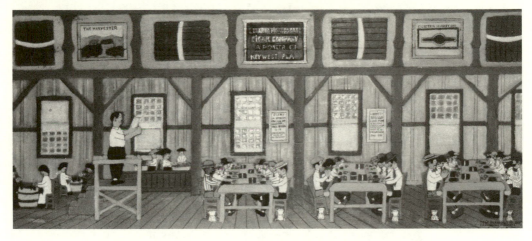

The material for these readings, agreed upon in advance by the workers (who, as in the days of El Fígaro, paid the *lector* out of their own earnings), ranged from political tracts and histories to novels and collections of poetry both modern and classical.[8] They had their favourites: Alexandre Dumas's *The Count of Monte Cristo*, for instance, became such a popular choice that a group of workers wrote to the author shortly before his death in 1870, asking him to lend the name of his hero to one of their cigars. Dumas consented.

According to Mario Sánchez, a Key West painter who in 1991 could still recall *lectores* reading to the cigar-rollers in the late twenties, the readings took place in concentrated silence, and comments or questions were not allowed until the session was over. "My father," Sánchez reminisced, "was the reader in the Eduardo Hidalgo Gato cigar factory in the early 1900s until the 1920s. In the mornings, he read the news which he translated from the local newspapers. He read international news directly from Cuban newspapers brought daily by boat from Havana. From noon until three in the afternoons, he read from a novel. He was expected to interpret the characters by imitating their voices, like an actor." Workers who had spent several years at the shops were able to quote from memory long passages of poetry and even prose. Sánchez mentioned one man who was able to remember the entire *Meditations* of Marcus Aurelius.[9]

Being read to, as the cigar workers found out, allowed them to overlay the mechanical, mind-numbing activity of rolling the dark scented tobacco leaves with adventures to follow, ideas to consider, reflections to make theirs. We don't know whether, in the long workshop hours, they regretted that the rest of their body was excluded from the reading ritual; we don't know if the fingers of those who could read longed for a page to turn, a line to follow; we don't know if those who had never learned to read were prompted to do so.

One night a few months before his death *circa* 547 — some thirteen centuries before the Cuban *lectors* — Saint Benedict of Nursia had a vi-

An eleventh-century manuscript illumination showing Saint Benedict offering his *Rules* to an abbot.

sion. As he was praying by his open window, looking out into the darkness, "the whole world appeared to be gathered into one sunbeam and thus brought before his eyes".[10] In that vision, the old man must have seen, with tears in his eyes, "that secret and conjectural object whose name men have seized upon but that no man has ever beheld: the inconceivable universe".[11]

Benedict had renounced the world at the age of fourteen and relinquished the fortunes and titles of his wealthy Roman family. Around 529 he had founded a monastery on Monte Cassino — a craggy hill towering fifteen hundred feet over an ancient pagan shrine halfway between Rome and Naples — and composed a series of rules for his friars[12] in which the authority of a code of laws replaced the absolute will of the monastery's superior. Perhaps because he sought in the Scriptures the all-encompassing vision that would be granted to him years later, or perhaps because he believed, like Sir Thomas Browne, that God offered us the world under two guises, as nature and as a book,[13] Benedict decreed that reading would be an essential part of the monastery's daily life. Article 38 of his Rule laid out the procedure:

> At the meal time of the brothers, there should always be reading; no one may dare to take up the book at random and begin to read there; but he who is about to read for the whole week shall begin his duties on Sunday. And, entering upon his office after Mass and Communion, he shall ask all to pray for him, that God may avert from him the spirit of elation. And this verse shall be said in the oratory three times by all, he however beginning it: "O Lord, open Thou my lips, and my mouth shall show forth Thy praise." And thus, having received the benediction, he shall enter upon his duties as reader. And there shall be the greatest silence at table, so that no whispering or any voice save the reader's may be heard. And whatever is needed, in the way of food, the brethren should pass to each other in turn, so that no one need ask for anything.[14]

As in the Cuban factories, the book to be read was not chosen at random; but unlike the factories, where the titles were chosen by consensus, in the cloister the choice was made by the community's authorities. For the Cuban workers, the books could become (many times did become) the intimate possession of each listener; but for the disciples of Saint Benedict, elation, personal pleasure and pride were to be avoided, since the joy of the text was to be communal, not individual. The prayer to God, asking Him to open the reader's lips, placed the act of reading in the hands of the Almighty. For Saint Benedict the text — the Word of God — was beyond personal taste, if not beyond understanding. The text was immutable and the author (or Author) the definitive authority. Finally, the silence at table, the audience's lack of response, was necessary not only to ensure concentration but also to preclude any semblance of private commentary on the sacred books.[15]

Later, in the Cistercian monasteries founded throughout Europe from the early twelfth century onwards, the Rule of Saint Benedict was used to ensure an orderly flow of monastic life in which personal agonies and desires were submitted to communal needs. Violations of the rules were punished with flagellation, and the offenders were separated from the fold, isolated from their brothers. Solitude and privacy were considered punishments; secrets were common knowledge; individual pursuits of any kind, intellectual or otherwise, were strongly discouraged; discipline was the reward of those who lived well within the community. In ordinary life, the Cistercian monks were never alone. At meals, their spirits were distracted from the pleasures of the flesh and joined in the holy word by Saint Benedict's prescribed reading.[16]

Coming together to be read to also became a necessary and common practice in the lay world of the Middle Ages. Up to the invention of printing, literacy was not widespread and books remained the property of the wealthy, the privilege of a small handful of readers. While some of these fortunate lords occasionally lent their books, they did so to a limited number of people within their own class or family.[17] People who wished to acquaint themselves with a certain book or author often had a better chance of hearing the text recited or read out loud than of holding the precious volume in their own hands.

There were different ways to hear a text. Beginning in the eleventh century, throughout the kingdoms of Europe, travelling *joglars* would recite or sing their own verses or those composed by their master troubadours, which the *joglars* would have stored in their prodigious memories. These *joglars* were public entertainers who performed at fairs and market-places, as well as before the courts. They were mostly of lowly birth and were usually denied both the protection of the law and the sacraments of the Church.[18] Troubadours, such as Guillaume of Aquitaine, grandfather of Eleanor, and Bertran de Born, Lord of Hautefort, were of noble birth and wrote formal songs in praise of their unreachable love. Of the hundred or so troubadours known by name from the early twelfth to the early thirteenth century, when the fashion flourished, some twenty were women. It seems that, in general, the *joglars* were more popular than the troubadours, so that highbrow artists such as Peter Pictor complained that "some of the high ecclesiasts would rather listen to the fatuous verses of a joglar than to the well-composed stanzas of a serious Latin poet"[19] — meaning himself.

Being read to from a book was a somewhat different experience. A *joglar*'s recital had all the obvious characteristics of a performance, and its success or failure largely depended upon the performer's skill at varying expressions, since the subject-matter was rather predictable. While a public reading also depended on the reader's ability to "perform", it laid the stress on the text rather than on the reader. The audience at a recital would watch a *joglar* perform the songs of a specific troubadour such as the celebrated Sordello; the audience at a public reading could listen to the anonymous *History of Reynard the Fox* read by any literate member of the household.

In the courts, and sometimes also in humbler houses, books were read aloud to family and friends for instruction as well as for entertainment. Being read to at dinner was not intended to distract from the joys of the palate; on the contrary, it was meant to enhance them with imaginative entertainment, a practice carried over from the days of the Roman empire. Pliny the Younger mentioned in one of his letters that, when eating with his wife or a few friends, he liked to have an amusing book read out loud to him.[20] In the early fourteenth century the Countess Mahaut of Artois travelled with her library packed into large leather bags, and in the evenings she had a lady-in-waiting read from them, whether philosophical works or entertaining accounts of foreign lands such as the *Travels* of Marco Polo.[21] Literate parents read to their children. In 1399 the Tuscan notary Ser Lapo Mazzei wrote to a friend, the merchant Francesco di Marco Datini, asking him for the loan of *The Little Flowers of Saint Francis* to read aloud to his sons. "The boys would take delight in it on winter evenings," he explained, "for it is, as you know, very easy reading."[22] In Montaillou, in the early fourteenth century, Pierre Clergue, the village priest, read out loud on different occasions from a so-called *Book of the Faith of the Heretics*, to those sitting around the fire in people's homes; in the village of Aix-les-Thermes, at about the same time, the peasant Guillaume Andorran was discovered reading a heretic Gospel to his mother and tried by the Inquisition.[23]

The fifteenth-century *Évangiles des quenouilles* (*Gospels of the Distaffs*) shows how fluid these informal readings could be. The narrator, an old learned man, "one night after supper, during the long winter nights between Christmas and Candlemas", visits the house of an elderly lady, where several of the neighbourhood women often gather "to spin and talk about many happy and minor things". The women, remarking that the men of their time "incessantly write defamatory lampoons and infectious books against the honour of the female sex," ask the narrator to attend their meetings — a sort of reading group *avant la lettre* — and act as scrivener, while the women read out certain passages on the sexes, love affairs, marital relationships, superstitions and local customs, and comment on them from a female point of view. "One of us will begin her reading and read a few chapters to all the others present," one of the spinners explains with enthusiasm, "so as to hold them and fix them permanently in our memories."[24] Over six days the

An early
reading-group
depicted in
the sixteenth-
century *Les
Evangiles des
quenouilles*.

women read, interrupt, comment, object and explain, and seem to enjoy themselves immensely, so much so that the narrator finds their laxity tiresome and, though faithfully recording their words, judges their comments "lacking rhyme or reason". The narrator is, no doubt, accustomed to more formal scholastic disquisitions by men.

Informal public readings at casual gatherings were quite ordinary occurrences in the seventeenth century. Stopping at an inn in search of the errant Don Quixote, the priest who has so diligently burnt the books in the knight's library explains to the company how reading novels of chivalry has upset Don Quixote's mind. The innkeeper objects to this statement, confessing that he very much enjoys listening to these stories in which the hero valiantly battles giants, strangles monstrous serpents and single-handedly defeats huge armies. "During harvest time," he says, "during the festivities, many of the labourers gather here, and there are always a few among them who can read, and one of them will pick up one of these books in his hands, and more than thirty strong we will collect around him, and listen to him with such delight that our white hairs turn young again." His daughter too is part of the audience, but she dislikes the scenes of violence; she prefers "to hear the lamentations the knights make when their ladies are absent, which in truth sometimes make me weep with pity for them". A fellow traveller, who happens to have with him a number of novels of chivalry (which the priest wants to burn at once), also carries in his bags the manuscript of a novel. Somewhat against his will, the priest agrees to read it out loud for all those present. The title of the novel is, appropriately, *The Curious Impertinent*,[25] and its reading occupies the three following chapters, while everyone feels free to interrupt and comment at will.[26]

So relaxed were these gatherings, so free of the strictures of institutionalized readings, that the listeners (or the reader) could mentally transfer the text to their own time and place. Two centuries after Cervantes, the Scottish publisher William Chambers wrote the biography of his brother Robert, with whom he had founded in 1832 the famous Edinburgh company that bears their name, and recollected certain such readings in their boyhood town of Peebles. "My brother and I," he wrote, "derived much enjoyment, not to say instruction, from the singing of old ballads, and the telling of legendary stories, by a kind old female relative, the wife of a decayed tradesman, who dwelt in one of the ancient closes. At her humble fireside, under the canopy of a huge chimney, where her half-blind and superannuated husband sat dozing in a chair, the battle of Corunna and other prevailing news was strangely mingled with disquisitions on the Jewish wars. The source of this interesting conversation was a well-worn copy of L'Estrange's translation of Josephus, a small folio of date 1720. The envied possessor of the work was Tam Fleck, 'a flichty chield', as he was considered, who, not particularly steady at his legitimate employment, stuck out a sort of profession by going about in the evening with his Josephus, which he read as the current news; the only light he had for doing so being usually that imparted by the flickering blaze of a piece of parrot coal. It was his practice not to read more than from two or three pages at a time, interlarded with sagacious remarks of his own by way of foot-notes, and in this way he sustained an extraordinary interest in the narrative. Retailing the matter with great equability in different households, Tam kept all at the same point of information, and wound them up with a corresponding anxiety as to the issue of some moving event in Hebrew annals. Although in this way he went through a course of Josephus yearly, the novelty somehow never seemed to wear off."[27]

> "Weel, Tam, what's the news the nicht?" would old Geordie Murray say, as Tam entered with his Josephus under his arm, and seated himself at the family fireside.
> "Bad news, bad news," replied Tam. "Titus has begun to besiege Jerusalem — it's gaun to be a terrible business."[28]

During the act of reading (of interpreting, of reciting), possession of a book sometimes acquires talismanic value. In the north of France, even today, village story-tellers use books as props; they memorize the text, but then show authority by pretending to read from the book, even if they are holding it upside down.[29] Something about the possession of a book — an object that can contain infinite fables, words of wisdom, chronicles of times gone by, humorous anecdotes and divine revelation — endows the reader with the power of creating a story, and the listener with a sense of being present at the moment of creation. What matters in these recitations is that the moment of reading be fully re-enacted — that is, with a reader, an audience and a book — without which the performance would not be complete.

In Saint Benedict's day being read to was considered a spiritual exercise; in later centuries this lofty purpose could be used to conceal other, less seemly functions. For instance, in the early nineteenth century, when the notion of a scholarly woman was still frowned upon in Britain, being read to became one of the socially accepted ways of studying. The novelist Harriet Martineau lamented in her *Autobiographical Memoir*, published after her death in 1876, that "when she was young it was not thought proper for a young lady to study very conspicuously; she was expected to sit down in the parlour with her sewing, listen to a book read aloud, and hold herself ready for callers. When the callers came, conversation often turned naturally on the book just laid down, which must therefore be very carefully chosen lest the shocked visitor should carry to the house where she paid her next call an account of the deplorable laxity shown by the family she had left."[30]

On the other hand, one might read out loud so as to *produce* this much-regretted laxity. In 1781, Diderot wrote amusingly about "curing" his bigoted wife, Nanette, who said she would not touch a book unless it contained something spiritually uplifting, by submitting her over several weeks to a diet of raunchy literature. "I have become her Reader. I administer three pinches of *Gil Blas* every day: one in the morning, one after dinner and one in the evening. When we have seen the end of *Gil Blas* we shall go on to *The Devil on Two Sticks* and *The Bachelor of Salamanca* and other cheering works of the same class. A few years and a few hundred such readings will complete the cure. If I were sure of success, I should not complain at the labour. What amuses me is that she treats everyone who visits her to a repeat of what I have just read her, so conversation doubles the effect of the remedy. I have always spoken of novels as frivolous productions, but I have finally discovered that they are good for the vapours. I will give Dr Tronchin the formula next time I see him. *Prescription*: eight to ten pages of Scarron's *Roman comique*; four chapters of *Don Quixote*; a well-chosen paragraph from Rabelais; infuse in a reasonable quantity of *Jacques the Fatalist* or *Manon Lescaut*, and vary these drugs as one varies herbs, substituting others of roughly the same qualities, as necessary."[31]

Being read to allows the listener a confidential audience for the reactions which must usually take place unheard, a cathartic experience which the Spanish novelist Benito Pérez Galdós described in one of his *Episodios Nacionales*. Doña Manuela, a nineteenth-century middle-class reader, retires to bed with the excuse of not wishing to become feverish by reading fully dressed under the light of the drawing-room lamp during a warm Madrid summer night. Her gallant admirer, General Leopoldo O'Donnell, offers to read to her out loud until she falls asleep, and chooses one of the pot-boilers that delight the lady, "one of those convoluted and muddled plots, badly translated from the French". Guiding his eyes with his index finger, O'Donnell reads her the description of a duel in which a young blond man wounds a certain Monsieur Massenot:

> "How wonderful!" Doña Manuela exclaimed, enraptured. "That blond fellow, don't you remember, is the artilleryman who came from Brittany disguised as a pedlar. By his looks, he must be the natural son of the duchess. . . . Carry on. . . . But according to what you just read," Doña Manuela observed, "you mean to say he cut off Massenot's nose?"
>
> "So it seems. . . . It says clearly: 'Massenot's face was covered with blood which ran like two rivulets across his greying moustache.'"
>
> "I'm delighted. . . . Serves him right, and let him come back for more. Now let's see what else the author will tell us."[32]

Because reading out loud is not a private act, the choice of reading material must be socially acceptable to both the reader and the audience. At Steventon rectory, in Hampshire, the Austen family read to one another at all times of the day and commented on the appropriateness of each selection. "My father reads Cowper to us in the mornings, to which I listen when I can," Jane Austen wrote in 1808. "We have got the second volume of [Southey's] *Espriella's Letters* and I read it aloud by candlelight." "Ought I to be very pleased with [Sir Walter Scott's] *Marmion*? As yet I am not. James [the eldest brother] reads it aloud every evening — the short evening, beginning about ten, and broken by supper." Listening to Madame de Genlis's *Alphonsine*, Austen is outraged: "We were disgusted in twenty pages, as, independent of a bad translation, it has indelicacies which disgrace a pen hitherto so pure; and we changed it for [Lennox's] the *Female Quixote*, which now makes our evening amusement, to me a very high one, as I find the work quite equal to what I remember it."[33] (Later, in Austen's writings, there will be echoes of these books she has heard read out loud, in direct references made by characters defined through their bookish likes or dislikes: Sir Edward Denham dismisses Scott as "tame" in *Sanditon*, and in

Northanger Abbey John Thorpe remarks, "I never read novels" — though he immediately confesses to finding Fielding's *Tom Jones* and Lewis's *The Monk* "tolerably decent".)

Being read to for the purpose of purifying the body, being read to for pleasure, being read to for instruction or to grant the sounds supremacy over the sense, both enrich and diminish the act of reading. Allowing someone else to speak the words on a page for us is an experience far less personal than holding the book and following the text with our own eyes. Surrendering to the reader's voice — except when the listener's personality is overwhelming — removes our ability to establish a certain pace for the book, a tone, an intonation that is unique to each person. It condemns the ear to someone else's tongue, and in that act a hierarchy is established (sometimes made apparent in the reader's privileged position, in a separate chair or on a podium) which places the listener in the reader's grip. Even physically, the listener will often follow the reader's cue. Describing a reading among friends, Diderot wrote in 1759, "Without conscious thought on either's part, the reader disposes himself in the manner he finds most appropriate, and the listener does the same. . . . Add a third character to the scene, and he will submit to the law of the two former: it is a combined system of three interests."[34]

At the same time, the act of reading out loud to an attentive listener often forces the reader to become more punctilious, to read without skipping or going back to a previous passage, fixing the text by means of a certain ritual formality. Whether in the Benedictine monasteries or the winter rooms of the late Middle Ages, in the inns and kitchens of the Renaissance or the drawing-rooms and cigar factories of the nineteenth century — even today, listening to an actor read a book on tape as we drive down the highway — the ceremony of being read to no doubt deprives the listener of some of the freedom inherent in the act of reading — choosing a tone, stressing a point, returning to a best-loved passage — but it also gives the versatile text a respectable identity, a sense of unity in time and an existence in space that it seldom has in the capricious hands of a solitary reader.

THE SHAPE
OF THE BOOK

OPPOSITE

Master-printer
Aldus Manutius.

M y hands, choosing a book to take to bed or to the reading-desk, for the train or for a gift, consider the form as much as the content. Depending on the occasion, depending on the place where I've chosen to read, I prefer something small and cosy or ample and substantial. Books declare themselves through their titles, their authors, their places in a catalogue or on a bookshelf, the illustrations on their jackets; books also declare themselves through their size. At different times and in different places I have come to expect certain books to look a certain way, and, as in all fashions, these changing features fix a precise quality onto a book's definition. I judge a book by its cover; I judge a book by its shape.

From the very beginning, readers demanded books in formats adapted to their intended use. The early Mesopotamian tablets were usually square but sometimes oblong pads of clay, approximately 3 inches across, and could be held comfortably in the hand. A book consisted of several such tablets, kept perhaps in a leather pouch or box, so that a reader could pick up tablet after tablet in a predetermined order. It is possible that the Mesopotamians also had books bound in much the same way as our volumes; neo-Hittite funerary stone monuments depict some objects resembling codexes — perhaps a series of tablets bound together inside a cover — but no such book has come down to us.

Not all Mesopotamian books were meant to be held in the hand. There exist texts written on much larger surfaces, such as the Middle

Assyrian Code of Laws, found in Ashur and dating from the twelfth century BC, which measures 67 square feet and carries its text in columns on both sides.[1] Obviously this "book" was not meant to be handled, but to be erected and consulted as a work of reference. In this case, size must also have carried a hierarchic significance; a small tablet might suggest a private transaction; a book of laws in such a large for- mat surely added, in the eyes of the Mesopotamian reader, to the au- thority of the laws themselves.

Of course, whatever a reader might have desired, the format of a book was limited. Clay was convenient for manufacturing tablets, and papyrus (the dried and split stems of a reed-like plant) could be made into manageable scrolls; both were relatively portable. But neither was suitable for the form of book that superseded tablet and scroll: the codex, or sheaf of bound pages. A codex of clay tablets would have been heavy and cumbersome, and although there were codexes made of papyrus pages, papyrus was too brittle to be folded into booklets. Parchment, on the other hand, or vellum (both made from the skins of animals, through different procedures), could be cut up or folded into all sorts of different sizes. According to Pliny the Elder, King Ptolemy of Egypt, wishing to keep the production of papyrus a national secret in order to favour his own Library of Alexandria, forbade its export, thereby forcing his rival, Eumenes, ruler of Pergamum, to find a new material for the books in his library.[2] If Pliny is to be believed, King Ptolemy's edict led to the invention of parchment in Pergamum in the second century BC, although the earliest parchment booklets known to us today date from a century earlier.[3] These materials were not used exclusively for one kind of book: there were scrolls made out of parch- ment and, as we have said, codexes made out of papyrus; but these were rare and impractical. By the fourth century, and until the appear- ance of paper in Italy eight centuries later, parchment was the pre- ferred material throughout Europe for the making of books. Not only was it sturdier and smoother than papyrus, it was also cheaper, since a reader who demanded books written on papyrus (notwithstanding King Ptolemy's edict) would have had to import the material from Egypt at considerable cost.

The parchment codex quickly became the common form of books for officials and priests, travellers and students — in fact for all those who needed to transport their reading material conveniently from one place to another, and to consult any section of the text with ease.

Furthermore, both sides of the leaf could hold text, and the four margins of a codex page made it easier to include glosses and commentaries, allowing the reader a hand in the story — a participation that was far more difficult when reading from a scroll. The organization of the texts themselves, which had previously been divided according to the capacity of a scroll (in the case of Homer's *Iliad*, for instance, the division of the poem into twenty-four books probably resulted from the fact that it normally occupied twenty-four scrolls), was changed. The text could now be organized according to its contents, in books or chapters, or could become itself a component when several shorter works were conveniently collected under a single handy cover. The unwieldy scroll possessed a limited surface — a disadvantage we are keenly aware of today, having returned to this ancient book-form on our computer screens, which reveal only a portion of text at a time as we "scroll" upwards or downwards. The codex, on the other hand, allowed the reader to flip almost instantly to other pages, and thereby retain a sense of the whole — a sense compounded by the fact that the entire text was usually held in the reader's hands throughout the reading. The codex had other extraordinary merits: originally intended to be transported with ease, and therefore necessarily small, it grew in both size and number of pages, becoming, if not limitless, at least much vaster than any previous book. The first-century poet Martial wondered at the magical powers of an object small enough to fit in the hand and yet containing an infinity of marvels:

> Homer on parchment pages!
> The *Iliad* and all the adventures
> Of Ulysses, foe of Priam's kingdom!
> All locked within a piece of skin
> Folded into several little sheets![4]

The codex's advantages prevailed: by AD 400, the classical scroll had been all but abandoned and most books were being produced as gathered leaves in a rectangular format. Folded once, the parchment became a folio; folded twice, a quarto; folded once again, an octavo. By the sixteenth century, the formats of the folded sheets had become official: in France, in 1527, François I decreed standard paper sizes throughout his kingdom; anyone breaking this rule was thrown into prison.[5]

Of all the shapes that books have acquired through the ages, the most popular have been those that allowed the book to be held comfortably in the reader's hand. Even in Greece and Rome, where scrolls were normally used for all kinds of texts, private missives were usually written on small, hand-held reusable wax tablets, protected by raised edges and decorated covers. In time, the tablets gave way to a few gathered leaves of fine parchment, sometimes of different colours, for the purpose of jotting down quick notes or doing sums. In Rome, towards the third century AD, these booklets lost their practical value and became prized instead for the look of their covers. Bound in finely decorated flats of ivory, they were offered as gifts to high officials on their nomination to office; eventually they became private gifts as well, and wealthy citizens began giving each other booklets in which they would inscribe a poem or dedication. Soon, enterprising booksellers started manufacturing small collections of poems in this manner — little gift books whose merit lay less in the contents than in the elaborate embellishments.[6]

Engraving copied from a bas-relief showing a method for storing scrolls in ancient Rome. Note the name-tags hanging from the ends of the scrolls.

The size of a book, whether it was a scroll or a codex, determined the shape of the place in which it was kept. Scrolls were put away either in wooden scroll boxes (which resembled hat-boxes of a sort) with labels which were made of clay in Egypt and of parchment in Rome, or in bookcases with their tags (the *index* or *titulus*) showing, so that the book could be easily identified. Codexes were stored lying flat, on shelves made for that purpose. Describing a visit to a country house in Gaul around AD 470, Gaius Sollius Apollinaris Sidonius, Bishop of Auvergne, mentioned a number of bookcases which varied according to the sizes of the codexes they were meant to hold: "Here too were books in plenty; you might fancy you were looking at the breast-high bookshelves (*plantei*) of the grammarians, or the wedge-shaped cases (*cunei*) of the Atheneum, or the well-filled cupboards (*armaria*) of the booksellers."[7] According to Sidonius, the books he found there were of two kinds: Latin classics for the men and books of devotion for the women.

Since much of the life of Europeans in the Middle Ages was spent in religious offices, it is hardly surprising that one of the most popular books of the time was the personal prayer-book, or Book of Hours, which was commonly represented in depictions of the Annunciation. Usually handwritten or printed in a small format, in many cases illuminated with exquisite richness by master artists, it contained a collection of short services known as "the Little Office of the Blessed Virgin Mary", recited at various times of the night and day.[8] Modelled on the Divine Office — the fuller services said daily by the clergy — the Little Office comprised Psalms and other passages from the Scriptures, as well as hymns, the Office of the Dead, special prayers to the saints and a calendar. These small volumes were eminently portable tools of devotion which the faithful could use either in public church services or in private prayers. Their size made them suitable for children; around 1493, the Duke Gian Galeazzo Sforza of Milan had a Book of Hours designed for his three-year-old son, Francesco Maria Sforza, "Il Duchetto", depicted on one of the pages as being led by a guardian angel through a night-time wilderness. The Books of Hours were richly but variably decorated, depending on who the customers were and how much they could afford to pay. Many depicted the commissioning of the family's coat-of-arms, or a portrait of the reader. Books of Hours became conventional wedding gifts for the nobility and, later, for the rich bourgeoisie. By the end of the fifteenth century, the book illuminators of Flanders dominated the European market, sending trade delegations throughout Europe to establish the equivalent of our wedding-gift lists.[9] The beautiful Book of

A personalized illumination showing the child Francesco Maria Sforza with his guardian angel in a Book of Hours made especially for him.

Hours commissioned for the wedding of Anne of Brittany in 1490 was made to the size of her hand.[10] It is designed for a single reader absorbed in both the words of the prayers repeated month after month and year after year, and the ever-surprising illustrations, whose details would never be utterly deciphered and whose urbanity — the Old and New Testament scenes took place in modern landscapes — brought the sacred words into a setting contemporary with the reader herself.

In the same way that small volumes served specific purposes, large volumes met other readers' demands. Around the fifth century, the Catholic Church began producing huge service-books — missals, chorales, antiphonaries — which, displayed on a lectern in the middle of the choir, allowed readers to follow

the words or musical notes with as much ease as if they were reading a monumental inscription. There is a beautiful antiphonary in the Abbey Library of St. Gall, containing a selection of liturgical texts in lettering so large that it can be read at a fair distance, to the cadence of melodic chants, by choirs of up to twenty singers;[11] standing several feet back from it, I can make out the notes with absolute clarity, and I wish my own reference books could be consulted with such ease from afar. Some of these service-books were so immense that they had to be laid on rollers so they could be moved. But they were moved very rarely. Decorated with brass or ivory, protected with corners of metal, closed by gigantic clasps, they were books to be read communally and at a distance, disallowing any intimate perusal or sense of personal possession.

In order to be able to read a book comfortably, readers invented ingenious improvements on the lectern and the desk. There is a statue of Saint Gregory the Great, made of pigmental stone in Verona sometime in the fourteenth century and preserved in the Victoria and Albert Museum in London, showing the saint at a sort of articulated reading-desk which would have enabled him to prop the lectern at different angles or raise it in order to leave his seat. A fourteenth-century engraving shows a scholar in a book-lined library writing at an elevated, octagonal desk-cum-lectern that allows him to work on one side, then swivel the desk and read the books laid ready for him on the seven other sides. In 1588 an Italian engineer, Agostino Ramelli, serving under the King of France, published a book describing a series of useful machines. One of these is a "rotary reading desk" which Ramelli describes as "a beautiful and ingenious machine, which is very useful and convenient to every person who takes pleasure in study, especially those who are suffering from indisposition or are subject to gout: for with this sort of machine a man can see and read a great quantity of books, without moving his place: besides, it has this fine convenience, which is, of occupying little space in the place where it is set, as any person of understanding can appreciate from the drawing".[12] (A full-scale model of this marvellous reading-wheel appeared in Richard Lester's 1974 film *The Three Musketeers*.) Seat and reading-desk could be combined in a single piece of furniture. The ingenious cockfighting chair (so called because it was depicted in illustrations of cockfighting) was made in England in the early eighteenth century, specifically for libraries. The reader sat astride it, facing the desk at the back of the chair while leaning on the broad armrests for support and comfort.

Mahogany cockfighting chair with leather upholstery, *c.* 1720.

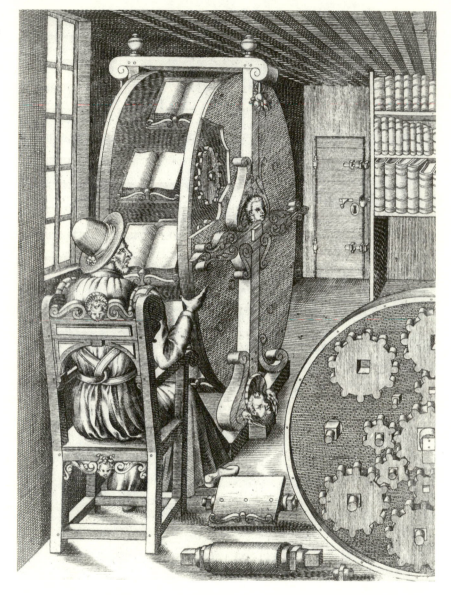

Sometimes a reading-device would be invented out of a different
kind of necessity. Benjamin Franklin relates that, during Queen Mary's
reign, his Protestant ancestors would hide their English bible, "fastened
open with tapes under and within the cover of a joint-stool". Whenever
Franklin's great-great-grandfather read to the family, "he turned up the
joint-stool upon his knees, turning over the leaves then under the
tapes. One of the children stood at the door to give notice if he saw the

apparitor coming, who was an officer of the spiritual court. In that case the stool was turned down again upon its feet, when the Bible remained concealed under it as before."[13]

Crafting a book, whether the elephantine volumes chained to the lecterns or the dainty booklets made for a child's hand, was a long, laborious process. A change that took place in mid-fifteenth-century Europe not only reduced the number of working-hours needed to produce a book, but dramatically increased the output of books, altering for ever the reader's relationship to what was no longer an exclusive and unique object crafted by the hands of a scribe. The change, of course, was the invention of printing.

Sometime in the 1440s, a young engraver and gem-cutter from the Archbishopric of Mainz, whose full name was Johannes Gensfleisch zur Laden zum Gutenberg (which the practicalities of the business world trimmed down to Johann Gutenberg), realized that much could be gained in speed and efficiency if the letters of the alphabet were cut in the form of reusable type rather than as the woodcut blocks which were then being used occasionally for printing illustrations. Gutenberg experimented over several years, borrowing large sums of money to finance his enterprise. He succeeded in devising all the essentials of printing as they were employed until the twentieth century: metal prisms for moulding the faces of the letters, a press that combined features of those used in wine-making and bookbinding, and an oil-based ink — none of which had previously existed.[14] Finally, between 1450 and 1455, Gutenberg produced a bible with forty-two lines to each page — the first book ever printed from type[15] — and took the printed pages with him to the Frankfurt Trade Fair. By an extraordinary stroke of luck, we have a letter from a certain Enea Silvio Piccolomini to the Cardinal of Carvajal, dated March 12, 1455, in Wiener Neustadt, telling His Eminence that he has seen Gutenberg's bible at the fair:

> I did not see any complete Bibles, but I did see a certain number of five-page booklets [signatures] of several of the books of the Bible, with very clear and very proper lettering, and without any faults, which Your Eminence would have been able to read effortlessly with no glasses. Various witnesses told me that 158 copies had been completed, while others say there were

180. I am not certain of the quantity, but about the books'
completion, if people can be trusted, I have no doubts whatsoever. Had I known your wishes, I would certainly have bought
a copy. Several of these five-page booklets were sent to the
Emperor himself. I shall try, as
far as possible, to have one of
these Bibles delivered for sale
and I will purchase one copy for
you. But I am afraid that this may
not be possible, both because of
the distance and because, so they
say, even before the books were
finished, there were customers
ready to buy them.[16]

The effects of Gutenberg's invention were immediate and extraordi-
narily far-reaching, for almost at
once many readers realized its great
advantages: speed, uniformity of
texts and relative cheapness.[17] Barely
a few years after the first bible had
been printed, printing presses were
set up all over Europe: in 1465 in
Italy, 1470 in France, 1472 in Spain,
1475 in Holland and England, 1489
in Denmark. (Printing took longer
to reach the New World: the first
presses were established in 1533 in Mexico City and in 1638 in Cambridge, Massachusetts.) It has been calculated that more than 30,000
incunabula (a seventeenth-century Latin word meaning "related to the
cradle" and used to describe books printed before 1500) were produced on these presses.[18] Considering that fifteenth-century print-runs
were usually of fewer than 250 copies and hardly ever reached 1,000,
Gutenberg's feat must be seen as prodigious.[19] Suddenly, for the first
time since the invention of writing, it was possible to produce reading
material quickly and in vast quantities.

It may be useful to bear in mind that printing did not, in spite of the
obvious "end-of-the-world" predictions, eradicate the taste for hand-

written text. On the contrary, Gutenberg and his followers attempted to emulate the scribe's craft, and most *incunabula* have a manuscript appearance. At the end of the fifteenth century, even though printing was by then well established, care for the elegant hand had not died out, and some of the most memorable examples of calligraphy still lay in the future. While books were becoming more easily available and more people were learning to read, more were also learning to write, often stylishly and with great distinction, and the sixteenth century became not only the age of the printed word but also the century of the great manuals of handwriting.[20] It is interesting to note how often a technological development — such as Gutenberg's — promotes rather than eliminates that which it is supposed to supersede, making us aware of old-fashioned virtues we might otherwise have either overlooked or dismissed as of negligible importance. In our day, computer technology and the proliferation of books on CD-ROM have not affected — as far as statistics show — the production and sale of books in their old-fashioned codex form. Those who see computer development as the devil incarnate (as Sven Birkerts portrays it in his dramatically titled *Gutenberg Elegies*)[21] allow nostalgia to hold sway over experience. For example, 359,437 new books (not counting pamphlets, magazines and periodicals), were added in 1995 to the already vast collections of the Library of Congress.

The sudden increase in book production after Gutenberg emphasized the relation between the contents of a book and its physical form. For instance, since Gutenberg's bible was intended to imitate the expensive handmade volumes of the time, it was bought in gathered sheets and bound by its purchasers into large, imposing tomes — usually quartos measuring about 12 by 16 inches,[22] meant to be displayed on a lectern. A bible of this size in vellum would have required the skins of more than two hundred sheep ("a sure cure for insomnia," commented the antiquarian bookseller Alan G. Thomas).[23] But cheap and quick production led to a larger market of people who could afford copies to read privately, and who therefore did not require books in large type and format, and Gutenberg's successors eventually began producing smaller, pocketable volumes.

In 1453 Constantinople fell to the Ottoman Turks, and many of the Greek scholars who had established schools on the shores of the Bosphorus left for Italy. Venice became the new centre of classical

An elegant
example of
Aldus's work:
the sober beauty
of Cicero's
*Epistolae
Familiares*.

learning. Some forty years later the Italian humanist Aldus Manutius, who had instructed such brilliant students as Pico della Mirandola in Latin and Greek, finding it difficult to teach without scholarly editions of the classics in practical formats, decided to take up Gutenberg's craft and established a printing-house of his own where he would be able to produce exactly the kind of books he needed for his courses. Aldus chose to establish his press in Venice in order to take advantage of the presence of the displaced Eastern scholars, and probably employed as correctors and compositors other exiles, Cretan refugees who had formerly been scribes.[24] In 1494 Aldus began his ambitious publishing program, which was to produce some of the most beautiful volumes in the history of printing: first in Greek — Sophocles, Aristotle, Plato, Thucydides — and then in Latin — Virgil, Horace, Ovid. In Aldus's view, these illustrious authors were to be read "without intermediaries" — in the original tongue, and mostly without annotations or glosses — and to make it possible for readers to "converse freely with the glorious dead" he published grammar books and dictionaries alongside the classical texts.[25] Not only did he seek the services of local experts, he also invited eminent humanists from all over Europe — including such luminaries as Erasmus of Rotterdam — to stay with him in Venice. Once a day these scholars would meet in Aldus's house to discuss what titles would be printed and what manuscripts would be used as reliable sources, sifting through the collections of classics established in the previous centuries. "Where medieval humanists accumulated," noted the historian Anthony Grafton, "Renaissance ones discriminated."[26] Aldus discriminated with an unerring eye. To the list of classical writers he added the works of the great Italian poets, Dante and Petrarch among others.

As private libraries grew, readers began to find large volumes not only difficult to handle and uncomfortable to carry, but inconvenient to store. In 1501, confident in the success of his first editions, Aldus responded to readers' demands and brought out a series of pocket-sized books in octavo — half the size of quarto — elegantly printed and meticulously edited. To keep down the production costs he decided to print a thousand copies at a time, and to use the page more economically he employed a newly designed type, "italic", created by the Bolognese punch-cutter Francesco Griffo, who also cut the first roman type in which the capitals were shorter than the ascending (full-height) letters of the lower case to ensure a better-balanced line. The result was a book that appeared much plainer than the ornate manuscript editions popular throughout the Middle Ages, a volume of elegant sobriety. What counted above all, for the owner of an Aldine pocket-book, was the text, clearly and eruditely printed — not a preciously decorated object. Griffo's italic type (first used in a woodcut illustrating a collection of letters of Saint Catherine of Siena, printed in 1500) gracefully drew the reader's attention to the delicate relationship between letters; according to the modern English critic Sir Francis Meynell, italics slowed down the reader's eye, "increasing his capacity to absorb the beauty of the text".[27]

Since these books were cheaper than manuscripts, especially illuminated ones, and since an identical replacement could be purchased if a copy was lost or damaged, they became, in the eyes of the new readers, less symbols of wealth than of intellectual aristocracy, and essential tools for study. Booksellers and stationers had produced, both in the days of ancient Rome and in the early Middle Ages, books as merchandise to be

On the open book and on the heart held by Saint Catherine, the earliest use of Griffo's italics, in an Aldine edition of the Saint's letters.

traded, but the cost and pace of their production weighed upon the readers with a sense of privilege in owning something unique. After Gutenberg, for the first time in history, hundreds of readers possessed identical copies of the same book, and (until a reader gave a volume private markings and a personal history) the book read by someone in Madrid was the same book read by someone in Montpellier. So successful was Aldus's enterprise that his editions were soon being imitated throughout Europe: in France by Gryphius in Lyons, as well as Colines and Robert Estienne in Paris, and in The Netherlands by Plantin in Antwerp and Elzevir in Leiden, The Hague, Utrecht and Amsterdam. When Aldus died in 1515, the humanists who attended his funeral erected all around his coffin, like erudite sentinels, the books he had so lovingly chosen to print.

The example of Aldus and others like him set the standard for at least a hundred years of printing in Europe. But in the next couple of centuries the readers' demands once again changed. The numerous editions of books of every kind offered too large a choice; competition between publishers, which up to then had merely encouraged better editions and greater public interest, began producing books of vastly impoverished quality. By the mid-sixteenth century, a reader would have been able to choose from well over eight million printed books, "more perhaps than all the scribes of Europe had produced since Constantine founded his city in AD 330."[28] Obviously these changes were neither sudden nor all-pervasive, but in general, from the end of the sixteenth century, "publisher-booksellers were no longer concerned with patronizing the world of letters, but merely sought to publish books whose sale was guaranteed. The richest made their fortune on books with a guaranteed market, reprints of old best-sellers, traditional religious works and, above all, the Church Fathers."[29] Others cornered the school market with glosses of scholarly lectures, grammar manuals and sheets for hornbooks.

The hornbook, in use from the sixteenth to the nineteenth century, was generally the first book put in a student's hand. Very few have survived to our time. The hornbook consisted of a thin board of wood, usually oak, about nine inches long and five or six inches wide, bearing a sheet on which were printed the alphabet, and sometimes the nine digits and the Lord's Prayer. It had a handle, and was covered in front by a transparent layer of horn to prevent it from becoming dirty; the board and the sheet of horn were then held together by a thin brass

frame. The English landscape gardener and doubtful poet William Shenstone describes the principle in *The Schoolmistress*, in these words:

> Their books of stature small they took in hand,
> Which with pellucid horn securèd are,
> To save from finger wet the letter fair.[30]

Similar books, known as "prayer boards", were used in Nigeria in the eighteenth and nineteenth centuries to teach the Koran. They were made of polished wood, with a handle at the top; the verses were written on a sheet of paper pasted directly onto the board.[31]

Books one could slip into one's pocket; books in a companionable shape; books that the reader felt could be read in any number of places; books that would not be judged awkward outside a library or a cloister: these books appeared under all kinds of guises. Throughout the seventeenth century, hawkers sold little booklets and ballads (described in *The Winter's Tale* as suitable "for man, or woman, of all sizes")[32] which became known as chap-books[33] in the following century. The preferred size of popular books had been the octavo, since a single sheet could produce a booklet of sixteen pages. In the eighteenth century, perhaps because readers now demanded fuller accounts of the events narrated in tales and ballads, the sheets were folded in twelve parts and the booklets were fattened to twenty-four paperback pages.[34] The classic series produced by Elzevir of Holland in this format achieved such popularity among less well-off readers that the snobbish Earl of Chesterfield was led to comment, "If you happen to have an Elzevir classic in your pocket, neither show it nor mention it."[35]

The pocket paperback as we now know it did not come into being until much later. The Victorian age, which saw the formation in England of the Publishers' Association, the Booksellers' Association, the first commercial agencies, the Society of Authors, the royalty system and the one-volume, six-shilling new novel, also witnessed the birth of the pocket-book series.[36] Large-format books, however, continued to encumber the shelves. In the nineteenth century, so many books were being published in huge formats that a Gustave Doré cartoon depicted a poor clerk at the Bibliothèque Nationale in Paris trying to move a single one of these huge tomes. Binding cloth replaced the costly leather (the English publisher Pickering was the first to use it, in his Diamond Classics of 1822) and, since the cloth

The booklet hawker, a sixteenth-century walking bookshop.

could be printed upon, it was soon employed to carry advertising. The object that the reader now held in his hand — a popular novel or science manual in a comfortable octavo bound in blue cloth, sometimes protected with paper wrappers on which ads might also be printed — was very different from the morocco-bound volumes of the preceding century. Now the book was a less aristocratic object, less forbidding, less grand. It shared with the reader a certain middle-class elegance that was economical and yet pleasing — a style which the designer William Morris would turn into a popular industry but which ultimately — in Morris's case — became a new luxury: a style based on the conventional beauty of everyday things. (Morris in fact modelled his ideal book on one of Aldus's volumes.) In the new books which the mid-nineteenth-century reader expected, the measure of excellence was not rarity but an alliance of pleasure and sober practicality. Private

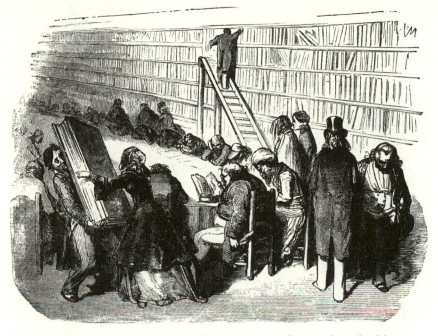

A Gustave
Doré caricature
satirizing the
new European
fad for
large-sized
books.

libraries were now appearing in bed-sitters and semi-detached homes, and their books suited the social standing of the rest of the furnishings.

In seventeenth- and eighteenth-century Europe, it had been assumed that books were meant to be read indoors, within the secluding walls of a private or public library. Now publishers were producing books meant to be taken out into the open, books made specifically to travel. In nineteenth-century England, the newly leisured bourgeoisie and the expansion of the railway combined to create a sudden urge for long journeys, and literate travellers found that they required reading material of specific content and size. (A century later, my father was still making a distinction between the green leather-bound books of his library, which no one was allowed to remove from that sanctuary, and the "ordinary paperbacks" which he left to yellow and wither on the wicker table on the patio, and which I would sometimes rescue and bring into my room as if they were stray cats.)

In 1792, Henry Walton Smith and his wife, Anna, opened a small news-vendor's shop in Little Grosvenor Street in London. Fifty-six years later W.H. Smith & Son opened the first railway bookstall, at Euston Station in London. It was soon stocking such series as Routledge's Railway Library, the Travellers' Library, the Run & Read Library and the Illustrated Novels and Celebrated Works series. The format of these

The W.H.
Smith railway
bookstall at
Blackpool
North Station,
London, 1896.

books varied slightly, but they were mainly octavos, with a few (Dickens's *A Christmas Carol*, for example) issued as smaller demi-octavo, and bound in cardboard. The bookstalls (to judge by a photograph of W.H. Smith's stall at Blackpool North, taken in 1896) sold not only these books but magazines and newspapers, so that travellers would have ample choice of reading material.

In 1841, Christian Bernhard Tauchnitz of Leipzig had launched one of the most ambitious of all paperback series; at an average of one title a week it published more than five thousand volumes in its first hundred years, bringing its circulation to somewhere between fifty and sixty million copies. While the choice of titles was excellent, the production was not equal to their content. The books were squarish, set in tiny type, with identical typographical covers that appealed neither to the hand nor to the eye.[37]

Seventeen years later, Reclam Publishers in Leipzig published a twelve-volume edition of Shakespeare in translation. It was an immediate success, which Reclam followed by subdividing the edition into twenty-five little volumes of the plays in pink paper covers at the sensational price of one decimal pfennig each. All works by German writers dead for thirty years came into the public domain in 1867, and this allowed Reclam to continue the series under the title Universal-

Bibliothek. The company began with Goethe's *Faust*, and continued with Gogol, Pushkin, Bjørnson, Ibsen, Plato and Kant. In England, imitative reprint series of "the classics" — Nelson's New Century Library, Grant Richards's World's Classics, Collins's Pocket Classics, Dent's Everyman's Library — rivalled but did not overshadow the success of the Universal-Bibliothek,[38] which remained for years the standard paperback series.

Until 1935. One year earlier, after a weekend spent with Agatha Christie and her second husband in their house in Devon, the English publisher Allen Lane, waiting for his train back to London, looked through the bookstalls at the station for something to read. He found nothing that appealed to him among the popular magazines, the expensive hardbacks and the pulp fiction, and it occurred to him that what was needed was a line of cheap but good pocket-sized books. Back at The Bodley Head, where Lane worked with his two brothers, he put forward his scheme. They would publish a series of brightly coloured paperback reprints of the best authors. They would not merely appeal to the common reader; they would tempt everyone who could read, highbrows and lowbrows alike. They would sell books not only in bookstores and bookstalls, but also at tea-shops, stationers and tobacconists.

The project met with contempt both from Lane's senior colleagues at The Bodley Head and from his fellow publishers, who had no interest in selling him reprint rights to their hardcover successes. Neither were booksellers enthusiastic, since their profits would be diminished and the books themselves "pocketed" in the reprehensible sense of the word. But Lane persevered, and in the end obtained permission to reprint several titles: two published already by The Bodley Head — André Maurois's *Ariel* and Agatha Christie's *The Mysterious Affair at Styles* — and others by such best-selling authors as Ernest Hemingway and Dorothy L. Sayers, plus a few by writers who are today less known, such as Susan Ertz and E. H. Young.

What Lane now needed was a name for his series, "not formidable like *World Classics*, not somehow patronizing like *Everyman*".[39] The first choices were zoological: a dolphin, then a porpoise (already used by Faber & Faber) and finally a penguin. Penguin it was.

On July 30, 1935, the first ten Penguins were launched at sixpence a volume. Lane had calculated that he would break even after seventeen thousand copies of each title were sold, but the first sales brought the number only to about seven thousand. He went to see the buyer for the vast Woolworth general store chain, a Mr. Clifford Prescott, who demurred; the idea of selling books like any other merchandise, together with sets of socks and tins of tea, seemed to him somehow ludicrous. By chance, at that very moment Mrs. Prescott entered her husband's office. Asked what she thought, she responded enthusiastically. Why not, she asked. Why should books not be treated as everyday objects, as necessary and as available as socks and tea? Thanks to Mrs. Prescott, the sale was made.

George Orwell summed up his reaction, both as reader and as author, to these newcomers. "In my capacity as reader," he wrote, "I applaud the Penguin Books; in my capacity as writer I pronounce them anathema. . . . The result may be a flood of cheap reprints which will cripple the lending libraries (the novelist's foster-mother) and check the output of new novels. This would be a fine thing for literature, but a very bad thing for trade."[40] He was wrong. More than its specific qualities (its vast distribution, its low cost, the

LEFT

The first ten Penguins.

RIGHT

A fifteenth-century heart-shaped book of madrigals.

excellence and wide range of its titles), Penguin's greatest achievement was symbolic. The knowledge that such a huge range of literature could be bought by almost anyone almost anywhere, from Tunis to Tucumán, from the Cook Islands to Reykjavik (such are the fruits of British expansionism that I have bought and read a Penguin in all these places), lent readers a symbol of their own ubiquity.

The invention of new shapes for books is probably endless, and yet very few odd shapes survive. The heart-shaped book fashioned towards 1475 by a noble cleric, Jean de Montchenu, containing illuminated love lyrics; the minuscule booklet held in the right hand of a young Dutch woman of the mid-seventeeth century painted by Bartholomeus van der Helst; the world's tiniest book, the *Bloemhofje* or *Enclosed*

A seventeenth-century Dutch woman portrayed by Bartholomeus van der Helst, holding an undersized volume in her right hand.

Flower-Garden, written in Holland in 1673 and measuring one-third inch by one-half inch, smaller than an ordinary postage stamp; John James Audubon's elephant-folio *Birds of America*, published between 1827 and 1838, leaving its author to die impoverished, alone and insane; the companion volumes of Brobdingnagian and Lilliputian sizes of *Gulliver's Travels* designed by Bruce Rogers for the Limited Editions Club of New York in 1950 — none of these has lasted except as a curiosity. But the essential shapes — those which allow readers to feel the physical weight of knowledge, the splendour of vast illustrations or

Books as visual
puns: a 1950
edition of
*Gulliver's
Travels*.

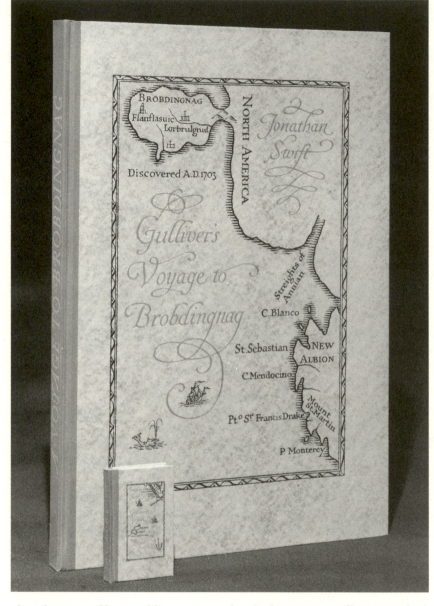

the pleasure of being able to carry a book along on a walk or into bed
— those remain.

In the mid-1980s, an international group of North American
archeologists excavating the huge Dakhleh Oasis in the Sahara found, in
the corner of a single-storey addition to a fourth-century house, two
complete books. One was an early manuscript of three political essays

LEFT

A mammoth
page from
Audubon's *Birds
of America*.

BELOW LEFT

The world's
tiniest book, the
seventeenth-
century
*Enclosed Flower-
Garden*.

BELOW RIGHT

The "Sahara
Penguin"
discovered at
the Dakhleh
Oasis.

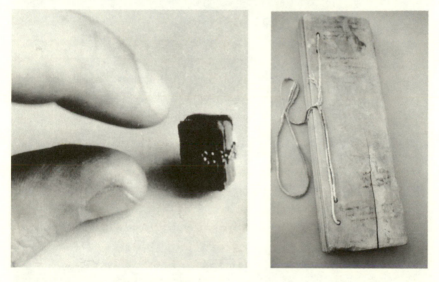

by the Athenian philosopher Isocrates; the other was a four-year record
of the financial transactions of a local estate steward. This accounts
book is the earliest complete example we have of a codex, or bound
volume, and it is much like our paperbacks except for the fact that it is
made not of paper but of wood. Each wooden leaf, five by thirteen
inches and one-sixteenth inch thick, is bored with four holes on the left
side, to be bound with a cord in eight-leaved signatures. Since the accounts book was used over a span of four years, it had to be "robust,
portable, easy to use, and durable".[41] That anonymous reader's require-
ments persist, with slight circumstantial variations, and agree with
mine, sixteen vertiginous centuries later.

PRIVATE READING

I t is summer. Sunk deep in the soft bed among feather pillows, with the inconstant rumble of carts on the cobble-stones out-side the window in the Rue de l'Hospice in the grey village of Saint-Sauveur-en-Puisaye, an eight-year-old girl is silently reading Victor Hugo's *Les Misérables*. She doesn't read many books; she rereads the same ones over and over again. She loves *Les Misérables* with what she'll later call "a reasoning passion"; she feels she can nestle in its pages "like a dog in its kennel".[1] Every night, she longs to follow Jean Valjean on his agonizing peregrinations, meet Cosette again, meet Marius, even the dreaded Javert. (In fact the only character she can't abide is the excruciatingly heroic little Gavroche.)

Outside in the back garden, among the potted trees and flowers, she has to compete for reading-matter with her father, a military man who lost his left leg during the Italian campaigns.[2] On the way to the library (his private precinct) he picks up his newspaper — *Le Temps* — and his magazine — *La Nature* — and, "his Cossack eye glittering under a grey hemp brow, swipes off the tables any printed material which will then follow him to the library and never again see the light of day".[3] Through experience, the girl has learned to keep her books out of his reach.

Her mother does not believe in fiction: "So many complications, so much passionate love in those novels," she tells her daughter. "In real life, people have other things on their minds. You be the judge: have you ever heard me whinge and whine about love as people do in those

OPPOSITE

The eighteen-year-old Colette reading in the garden at Chatillon Coligny.

149

books? And yet I'd have a right to a chapter myself, I'd say! I've had two husbands and four children!"[4] If she finds her daughter reading the Catechism for her upcoming communion, she becomes immediately incensed: "Oh, how I hate this nasty habit of asking questions! 'What is God?' 'What is this?' 'What is that?' These question marks, this obsessive probing, this inquisitiveness, I find it all so terribly indiscreet! And all this bossing about, I ask you! Who translated the Ten Commandments into this awful gibberish? Oh, I certainly don't like seeing a book like this in the hands of a child!"[5]

Reading throughout eternity: the tomb of Eleanor of Aquitaine.

Challenged by her father, lovingly watched over by her mother, the girl finds her only refuge in her room, in her bed, at night. Throughout her adult life, Colette would seek out this solitary reading-space. Either *en ménage* or alone, in small courtyard lodgings or in large country villas, in rented bed-sitters or in ample Paris apartments, she would set aside (not always successfully) an area in which the only intrusions would be those she invited herself. Now, stretched out in the muffled bed, holding the treasured book in both hands and propping it up on her stomach, she has established not only her own space but her own measure of time. (She doesn't know it, but less than three hours away, in the Abbey of Fontevrault, Queen Eleanor of Aquitaine, who died in 1204, lies sculpted in stone on the lid of her tomb, holding a book in exactly the same manner.)

I too read in bed. In the long succession of beds in which I spent the nights of my childhood, in strange hotel rooms where the lights of passing cars swept eerily across the ceiling, in houses whose smells and sounds were unfamiliar to me, in summer cottages sticky with sea spray or where the mountain air was so dry that a steaming basin of eucalyptus water was placed by my side to help me breathe, the combination of bed and book granted me a sort of home which I knew I could go back to, night after night, under whichever skies. No one would call out and ask me to do this or that; my body needed nothing, immobile under the sheets. What took place, took place in the book, and I was the story's teller. Life happened because I turned the pages. I don't think I can remember a greater *comprehensive* joy than that of coming to the few last pages and setting the book down, so that the end would not take place until at least tomorrow, and sinking back into my pillow with the sense of having actually stopped time.

I knew that not every book was suitable for reading in bed. Detective stories and tales of the supernatural were most likely to grant me a peaceful sleep. For Colette, *Les Misérables*, with its streets and forests, flights down dark sewers and across battling barricades, was the perfect book for the quiet of the bedroom. W.H. Auden agreed. He suggested that the book one reads should somehow be at odds with the place in which it's read. "I can't read Jefferies on the Wiltshire Downs," he complained, "nor browse on limericks in a smoking-room."[6] This may be true; there may be a sense of redundancy in exploring on the page a world similar to the one surrounding us at the very moment of reading. I think of André Gide reading Boileau as he was being ferried down the Congo,[7] and the counterpoint between the lush, disorderly vegetation and the chiselled, formal seventeenth-century verse seems exactly right.

But, as Colette discovered, not only do certain books demand a contrast between their contents and their surroundings; some books seem to demand particular *positions* for reading, postures of the reader's body that in turn require reading-places appropriate to those postures. (For instance, she wasn't able to read Michelet's *Histoire de France* until she found herself curled up in her father's armchair with Fanchette, "that most intelligent of cats".)[8] Often the pleasure derived from reading largely depends on the bodily comfort of the reader.

"I have sought for happiness everywhere," confessed Thomas à Kempis, early in the fifteenth century, "but I have found it nowhere except in a little corner with a little book."[9] But which little corner? And which little book? Whether we first choose the book and then an appropriate corner, or first find the corner and then decide what book will suit the corner's mood, there is no doubt that the act of reading in time requires a corresponding act of reading in place, and the relationship between the two acts is inextricable. There are books I read in armchairs, and there are books I read at desks; there are books I read in subways, on streetcars and on buses. I find that books read in trains have something of the quality of books read in armchairs, perhaps because in both I can easily abstract myself from my surroundings. "The best time for reading a good stylish story," said the English novelist Alan Sillitoe, "is in fact when one is on a train travelling alone. With strangers roundabout, and unfamiliar scenery passing by the window (at which you glance now and again) the endearing and convoluted life coming out of the pages possesses its own peculiar and imprinting effects."[10] Books read in a public library never have the same flavour as books read in the attic or the kitchen. In 1374, King Edward III paid £66 13s 4d for a book of romances "to be kept in his bedchamber",[11] where he obviously thought such a book should be read. In the twelfth-century *Life of Saint Gregory*, the toilet is described as "a retiring place where tablets can be read without interruption".[12] Henry Miller agreed: "All my good reading was done in the toilet," he once confessed. "There are passages of *Ulysses* which can be read only in the toilet — if one wants to extract the full flavor of their content."[13] In fact, the little room "destined for a more special and more vulgar use" was for Marcel Proust a place "for all my occupations which required an inviolable solitude: reading, reverie, tears and sensual pleasure".[14]

The epicurean Omar Khayyam recommended reading verse outdoors under a bough; centuries later, the punctilious Sainte-Beuve advised reading the *Memoirs* of Mme de Staël "under November's trees".[15] "My custom," wrote Shelley, "is to undress, and sit on the rocks, reading Herodotus, until the perspiration has subsided."[16] But not everyone is capable of reading under an open sky. "I seldom read on beaches or in gardens," confessed Marguerite Duras. "You can't read by two lights at once, the light of day and the light of the book. You should read by electric light, the room in shadow, and only the page lit up."[17]

One can transform a place by reading in it. During the summer holidays, Proust would sneak back into the dining-room once the rest of the family had left on its morning walk, confident that his only companions, "very respectful of reading", would be "the painted plates hung on the wall, the calendar where yesterday's page had been freshly torn away, the clock and the hearth, who speak without expecting an answer and whose babble, unlike human words, does not attempt to replace the sense of the words you are reading with another, different sense". Two full hours of bliss before the cook would appear, "far too early, to lay the table; and if at least she had laid it without speaking! But she felt obliged to say, 'You can't be comfortable like that; and if I brought you a desk?' And just by having to answer, 'No, thank you very much,' one was forced to come to a full stop and bring back from far away one's voice, which, hidden behind the lips, repeated soundlessly, and very fast, all the words read by the eyes; one had to bring one's voice to a halt, bring it into the open and, in order to say properly, 'No, thank you very much,' give it an everyday appearance, an answering intonation which it had lost."[18] Only much later — at night, well after dinner — and when there were but a few pages of the book left to read, would he relight his candle, risking punishment if discovered, and insomnia, because once the book was finished, the passion with which he had followed the plot and its heroes would make it impossible for him to sleep, and he'd pace the room or lie breathlessly, wishing for the story to continue, or wishing to know at least something more about the characters he had loved so well.

Towards the end of his life, imprisoned in a cork-lined room that gave him some respite from his asthma, propped up in a cushioned bed and working under the light of a weak lamp, Proust wrote, "True books should be born not of bright daylight and friendly conversation, but of gloom and silence."[19] In bed at night, the page lit by a dim yellow glow, I, Proust's reader, re-enact that mysterious moment of birth.

Geoffrey Chaucer — or rather, his insomniac lady in *The Book of the Duchesse* — considered reading in bed a better entertainment than a board-game:

So when I saw I might not slepe,
Til now late, this other night,
Upon my bedde I sat upright,
And bad oon reche me a book,
A romaunce, and he hit me took
To rede and dryve the night away;
For me thoghte it better play
Then playe[n] either at chesse or tables.[20]

But there is something other than entertainment which one derives from reading in bed: a particular quality of privacy. Reading in bed is a self-centred act, immobile, free from ordinary social conventions, invisible to the world, and one that, because it takes place between the sheets, in the realm of lust and sinful idleness, has something of the thrill of things forbidden. Perhaps it is the memory of those nocturnal readings that lends the detective novels of John Dickson Carr, of Michael Innes, of Anthony Gilbert — all read during summer holidays in my adolescence — a certain erotic colouring. The casual phrase "taking a book to bed" has always seemed to me laden with sensual anticipation.

The novelist Josef Skvorecky has described his reading as a boy in Communist Czechoslovakia "in a society governed by rather strict and binding rules where disobedience was punished in the good old pre-Spockian way. One such rule: light in your bedroom must be switched off at nine sharp. Boys have to get up at seven and they need ten hours of sleep every night." Reading in bed became then the forbidden thing. After the lights were switched off, Skvorecky says, "cuddled in my bed, I covered myself, head inclusive, with a blanket, from under the mattress I fished out an electric torch, and then indulged in the pleasures of reading, reading, reading. Eventually, often after midnight, I fell asleep from very pleasurable exhaustion."[21]

The writer Annie Dillard remembers how the books of her American childhood led her away from her Midwestern town "so I could fashion a life among books somewhere else. . . . And so we run to our bedrooms and read in a fever, and love the big hardwood trees outside the windows, and the terrible Midwest summers, and the terrible Midwest winters."[22] Reading in bed both closes and opens the world around us.

The notion of reading in bed is not an ancient one. The Greek bed, the *kline*, was a wooden frame set on turned, rectangular or animal-shaped legs and decorated with precious ornaments, and not really practical for reading. During social gatherings, only men and courtesans were allowed to use it. It had a low head-rest but no footboard, a mattress and pillows, and was employed both for sleeping and for reclining at leisure. In this position, it was possible to read a scroll by holding one end with the left hand, unrolling the other end with the right hand while the right elbow supported the body. But the procedure, cumbersome at the best of times, became frankly uncomfortable after a short while, and ultimately unbearable.

The Romans had a different bed (*lectus*) for each of several different purposes, including beds for reading and writing. The forms of these beds did not vary much; the legs were turned, and most were decorated with inlay and bronze mounts.[23] In the darkness of the bedroom (in the *cubiculum*, usually in the farthest corner of the house) the Roman sleeping-bed would sometimes serve as a not very congenial reading-bed; by the light of a candle made from wax-soaked cloth, the *lucubrum*, the Romans would read and "lucubrate"[24] in relative quiet. Trimalchio, the parvenu of Petronius's *Satyricon*, is brought into the banquet room "supported by piles of miniature cushions" on a bed which serves several functions. Boasting that he's not one to look down on learning — he has two libraries, "one Greek and the other Latin"

The Roman nobleman portrayed on the inside wall of his sarcophagus would have read his scrolls in this reclining position.

— he offers to compose a few impromptu lines of verse which he then reads to the assembled guests:[25] both Trimalchio's writing and the reading are performed while lying on the same ostentatious *lectus*.

In the early years of Christian Europe, and well into the twelfth century, ordinary beds were simple, disposable objects, often left behind during the forced retreats from war and famine. Since only the rich had elaborate beds, and few but the rich had books, ornate beds and books became symbols of the family's wealth. Eustathius Boilas, a Byzantine aristocrat of the eleventh century, left in his will a bible, several books of hagiography and history, a Dream Key, a copy of the popular *Romance of Alexander* and a gilded bed.[26]

Monks had plain cots in their cells, and there they could read in a little more comfort than that provided by their hard benches and desks. An illuminated manuscript of the thirteenth century shows a young, bearded monk on his cot, dressed in his habit, a white pillow behind his back and his legs wrapped up in a grey blanket. The curtain separating his bed from the rest of the room has been hitched up. On a trestle table are three open books, and three more lie on top of his legs, ready for consultation, while in his hands he holds a double wax

tablet and a stylus. Apparently he has sought refuge in bed from the
cold; his boots are sitting on a painted bench and he is working on his
reading in seemingly happy quietude.

In the fourteenth century, books passed from the exclusive hands of
the nobility and the clergy to those of the bourgeoisie. The aristocracy
became the model for the *nouveaux riches*: if the nobles read, then they

too would read (a skill the bourgeois had acquired as merchants); if the nobles slept on sculpted wood among ornate draperies, then so would they. To be seen owning books and elaborate beds became indicative of one's social standing. The bedroom became not only the room in which the bourgeois slept and made love; it became the repository of collected goods — books included — which at night could be guarded from within the stronghold of the bed.[27] Aside from the books, few other objects were on display; most of them would be shut away in chests and boxes, protected from the corruption of moths and rust.

From the fifteenth to the seventeenth century, the best bed was the grand prize of a forfeited estate.[28] Books and beds were valuable chattels (notoriously, Shakespeare bequeathed his "second-best bed" to his wife, Anne Hathaway) which, unlike most property, could be owned by individual members of the family. At a time when women were allowed to possess very few private goods, they owned books, and passed them on to their daughters more frequently than to their sons. As early as 1432, a certain Joanna Hilton of Yorkshire left a *Romance, With the 10 Commandments*, a *Romance of the Seven Sages* and a *Roman de la Rose* to her daughter in her will.[29] Excepted were the expensive prayer-books and illuminated bibles, usually part of the family patrimony and therefore of the eldest son's inheritance.[30]

The *Playfair Book of Hours*, a French illuminated volume from the late fifteenth century, shows on one of its pages the Birth of the Virgin. Saint Anne, the Virgin's mother, is being presented with the infant by the midwife. Saint Anne is depicted as a noble lady, probably not unlike Chaucer's Duchesse (in the Middle Ages, Saint Anne's family acquired a reputation for having been wealthy). Saint Anne is sitting upright in a half-tester bed that has been draped in a red cloth with a golden pattern. She is fully clothed; she's wearing a blue dress with gold embroidery, and her head and neck are decorously covered by a white mantle. (Only from the eleventh to the fifteenth century did people normally sleep naked; a thirteenth-century marriage contract included the stipulation that "a wife should not sleep in a chemise without her husband's consent".)[31] A lime-green sheet — green is the colour of birth, the triumph of spring over winter — hangs on both sides of the bed. A white sheet is folded over the red cloth that covers the bed; on this sheet, in Saint Anne's lap, lies an open book. And yet, in spite of the intimacy suggested by the little book (probably a book of prayers), in spite of the protective curtains, the room doesn't look like a very private place. The

midwife appears to have walked in quite naturally; one thinks of all
those other depictions of the birth and death of Mary, in which the bed
is assiduously surrounded by either well-wishers or mourners, men,
women and children, and sometimes even the occasional dog drinking
distractedly from a basin in a corner. This room of birth and forthcom-
ing death is not a space Saint Anne has created for herself.

In Europe in the sixteenth and seventeenth centuries, bedrooms
— like almost every other room in the house — were also passage-
ways, so that a bedroom did not necessarily guarantee peace and quiet
for such activities as reading. Even curtaining a bed and filling it with
one's personal belongings was obviously not enough; a bed required a
room of its own. (The wealthy Chinese of the fourteenth and fifteenth
centuries had two types of bed, and each one created its own private
space: the movable *k'ang*, which served the triple purpose of sleeping
platform, table and seat and was sometimes heated by pipes running
underneath it, and a free-standing construction divided into compartments, a sort of room within a room.)[32]

By the eighteenth century, even though bedrooms were still not
undisturbed spaces, staying in bed to read — in Paris, at least — had

become common enough for Saint Jean-Baptiste de La Salle, the philan-
thropic French educator canonized in 1900, to warn against the sinful
dangers of this idle pastime. "It is thoroughly indecent and unmannerly
to idly chit-chat, gossip or sport in bed," he wrote in *The Rules of Deco-
rum in Christian Civility*, published in 1703. "Imitate not certain persons
who busy themselves in reading and other matters; stay not in bed if it
be not to sleep, and your virtue shall much profit from it."[33] And
Jonathan Swift, at about the same time, ironically suggested that books
read in bed should be given an airing: "In the Time when you leave the
Windows open for Air," he advises the chamber-maid in charge of
cleaning her mistress's bedroom, "leave Books, or something else on
the Window-seat, that they may get Air too."[34] In New England in the
mid-eighteenth century, the Argand lamp, improved by Jefferson, was
supposed to have furthered the habit of reading in bed. "It was observed
at once that dinner parties, formerly lighted by candles, ceased to be as
brilliant as of old," because those who had excelled in talking now took
to their bedrooms to read.[35]

Complete privacy in the bedroom, even privacy in bed, was still
not easy to come by. Even if the family was rich enough to have individual beds and bedrooms, social conventions demanded that certain
communal ceremonies take place there. For example, it was customary
for ladies to "receive" in their bedchambers, fully dressed but lying in
bed, propped up by a multitude of pillows; visitors would sit in the *ru-
elle* or "alleyway" between the bed and the partition. Antoine de
Courtin, in his *New Treatise of Civility as Practised in France by Honest
Folk*,[36] sternly recommended "that the bed-curtains be kept drawn" to
comply with the laws of decency, and noted that "it is unbecoming, in
the presence of persons of whom one is not a superior, to fling oneself
on the bed and from there conduct a conversation." At Versailles, the
ritual of the waking of the king — the famous *lever du Roi* — became a
highly elaborate procedure in which six different hierarchies of the
nobility took turns proceeding into the royal bedchamber and carrying
out appointed honours such as slipping on — or off — the royal left or
right sleeve, or reading to the royal ear.

Even the nineteenth century was reluctant to recognize the bedroom as a private place. Demanding that attention be paid to this
"sleeping-room in which nearly half of one's life is passed," Mrs.
Haweis, in the chapter "Homes for the Happy" of her influential book
The Art of Housekeeping, complained that "bachelors — why not brides?

— sometimes disguise and adorn the bedroom, where space is precious, with sofa-beds, Chippendale or old French closed washstands, palm-plants and gipsy-tables, that it may serve as a thoroughfare without a suspicion that anybody but a canary ever sleeps in it."[37] "Commend us," wrote Leigh Hunt in 1891, "to a bedchamber of the middle order, such as it was set out about a hundred years back," in which he'd have "windows with seats, and looking upon some green place" and "two or three small shelves of books".[38]

For Edith Wharton, the aristocratic American novelist, the bedroom became the only refuge from nineteenth-century ceremony where she could read and write at ease. "Visualize her bed," suggested Cynthia Ozick in a discussion of Wharton's craft. "She used a writing board. Her breakfast was brought to her by Gross, the housekeeper, who almost alone was privy to this inmost secret of the bedchamber. (A secretary picked up the pages from the floor for typing.) Out of bed, she would have had to be, according to her code, properly dressed, and this meant stays. In bed, her body was free, and freed her pen."[39] Free also was her reading; in this private space she did not have to explain to visitors why she had chosen a book or what she thought of it. So important was this horizontal workplace that once, at the Hotel Esplanade in Berlin, Wharton had "a minor fit of hysterics because the bed in her hotel room was not properly situated; not until it had been moved to face the window did she settle down and begin to find Berlin 'incomparable'."[40]

Colette's social constraints differed from those imposed on Wharton, but on her personal life too society constantly intruded. In her time, Wharton was seen to write — at least partly — from the authority granted her by her social standing; Colette was considered far more "outrageous, audacious, perverse",[41] so that when she died, in 1954, the Catholic Church refused her religious burial. In the last years of her life Colette took to her bed, driven by illness but also by a wish to have a space entirely of her own devising. Here, in her apartment on the third floor of the Palais Royal, in her *radeau-lit* — "the bed-raft", as she christened it — she slept and ate, received her friends and acquaintances, phoned, wrote and read. The Princess of Polignac had given her a table that fitted exactly over the bed, and served her as desk. Propped up against the pillows as when she had been a child in Saint-Sauveur-en-Puisaye, with the symmetrical gardens of the Palais Royal unfurling through the window to her left, and all her collected treasures —

Colette
celebrating her
eightieth
birthday in
1953.

her glass objects, her library, her cats — spreading out to her right,[42] Colette read and reread, in what she called this *solitude en hauteur*,[43] the old books she loved best.

There is a photograph taken of her a year before her death, on her eightieth birthday. Colette is in bed, and the hands of the maid have deposited on her table — which is cluttered with magazines, cards and flowers — a birthday cake ablaze; the flames rise high, too high to seem mere candles, as if the old woman were an ancient camper in front of her familiar fire, as if the cake were a book alight, bursting into that darkness sought by Proust for literary creation. The bed has become at last so private, so intimate, that it is now a world unto itself, where everything is possible.

METAPHORS

OF READING

On March 26, 1892, Walt Whitman died in the house he had bought less than ten years before, in Camden, New Jersey — looking like an Old Testament king or, as Edmund Gosse described him, "a great old Angora Tom". A picture taken a few years before his death, by the Philadelphia artist Thomas Eakins, shows him in his shaggy white mane, sitting by his window, thoughtfully watching the world outside, which was, he had told his readers, a gloss to his writing:

> If you would understand me go to the heights or water-shore,
> The nearest gnat is an explanation, and a drop or motion of
>   waves a key,
> The maul, the oar, the hand-saw, second my words.[1]

Whitman himself is there for the reader's gaze. Two Whitmans, in fact: the Whitman in *Leaves of Grass*, "Walt Whitman, a kosmos, of Manhattan the son" but also born everywhere else ("I am of Adelaide . . . I am of Madrid . . . I belong in Moscow");[2] and the Whitman born on Long Island, who liked to read romances of adventure, and whose lovers were young men from the city, soldiers, bus drivers. Both became the Whitman who in his old age left his door open for visitors seeking "the sage of Camden", and both had been offered to the reader, some thirty years earlier, in the 1860 edition of *Leaves of Grass*:

Camerado, this is no book,
Who touches this, touches a man,
(Is it night? Are we here alone?)
It is I you hold, and who holds you,
I spring from the pages into your arms — decease calls me
    forth.[3]

Years later, in the "death-bed" edition of the often revised and augmented *Leaves of Grass*, the world does not "second" his words, but becomes the primordial voice; neither Whitman nor his verse mattered;
the world itself sufficed, since it was nothing more or less than a book
open for us all to read. In 1774, Goethe (whom Whitman read and admired) had written:

See how Nature is a living book,
Misunderstood but not beyond understanding.[4]

Now, in 1892, days before his death, Whitman agreed:

In every object, mountain, tree, and star — in every birth
    and life,
As part of each — evolv'd from each — meaning, behind
    the ostent,
A mystic cipher waits infolded.[5]

I read this for the first time in 1963, in a shaky Spanish version.
One day in high school, a friend of mine who wanted to be a poet (we
had just turned fifteen at the time) came running up to me with a book
he had discovered, a blue-covered Austral edition of Whitman's poems
printed on rough, yellowed paper and translated by someone whose
name I have forgotten. My friend was an admirer of Ezra Pound,
whom he paid the compliment of imitating, and, since readers have no
respect for the chronologies arduously established by well-paid academics, he thought Whitman was a poor imitation of Pound. Pound himself had tried to set the record straight, proposing "a pact" with
Whitman:

It was you who broke the new wood,
Now is a time for carving.

We have one sap and one root —
Let there be commerce between us.[6]

But my friend would not be convinced. I accepted his verdict for
the sake of friendship, and it wasn't until a couple of years later that I
came across a copy of *Leaves of Grass* in English and learned that Whitman had intended his book for me:

Thou reader throbbest life and pride and love the same as I,
Therefore for thee the following chants.[7]

I read Whitman's biography, first in a series intended for the young
which expurgated any reference to his sexuality and rendered him
bland to the point of non-existence, and then in Geoffrey Dutton's
Walt Whitman, instructive but somewhat too sober. Years later, Philip
Callow's biography gave me a clearer picture of the man and allowed
me to reconsider a couple of questions I had asked myself earlier: if
Whitman had seen his reader as himself, who was this reader Whitman
had in mind? And how had Whitman in turn become a reader?

Whitman learned to read in a Quaker school in Brooklyn, by what
was known as the "Lancastrian method" (after the English Quaker Joseph
Lancaster). A single teacher, helped by child monitors, was in charge of
a class of some one hundred students, ten to a desk. The youngest were
taught in the basement, the older girls on the ground floor and the
older boys on the floor above. One of his teachers commented that he
found him "a good-natured boy, clumsy and slovenly in appearance, but
not otherwise remarkable". The few textbooks were supplemented by
the books his father, a fervent democrat who named his three sons after
the founders of the United States, had at home. Many of these books
were political tracts by Tom Paine, the socialist Frances Wright and the
eighteenth-century French philosopher Constantin-François, Comte
de Volney, but there were also collections of poetry and a few novels.
His mother was illiterate but, according to Whitman, "excelled in narrative" and "had great mimetic powers".[8] Whitman first learned his letters from his father's library; their sounds he learned from the stories
he had heard his mother tell.

Whitman left school at eleven and entered the offices of the lawyer
James B. Clark. Clark's son, Edward, liked the bright boy and bought
him a subscription to a circulating library. This, said Whitman later, "was

the signal event of my life up to that time." At the library he borrowed and read the *Arabian Nights* — "every single volume" — and the novels of Sir Walter Scott and James Fenimore Cooper. A few years afterwards, at the age of sixteen, he acquired "a stout, well-cramm'd one thousand page octavo volume . . . containing Walter Scott's poetry entire" and this he avidly consumed. "Later, at intervals, summers and falls, I used to go off, sometimes for a week at a stretch, down in the country, or to Long Island's seashores — there, in the presence of outdoor influences, I went over thoroughly the Old and New Testaments, and absorb'd (probably to greater advantage for me than in any library or indoor room — it makes such difference *where* you read) Shakespeare, Ossian, the best translated versions I could get of Homer, Aeschylus, Sophocles, the old German Nibelungen, the ancient Hindu poems, and one or two other masterpieces, Dante's among them. As it happened, I read the latter mostly in an old wood." And Whitman asks, "I have wonder'd since why I was not overwhelm'd by those mighty masters. Likely because I read them, as described, in the full presence of Nature, under the sun, with the farspreading landscape and vistas, or the sea rolling in."[9] The place of reading, as Whitman suggests, is important, not only because it provides a physical setting for the text being read, but because it suggests, by juxtaposing itself with the place on the page, that both share the same hermeneutic quality, both tempting the reader with the challenge of elucidation.

Whitman didn't stay long at the lawyer's office; before the end of the year he had become an apprentice printer at the *Long Island Patriot*, learning to work a hand-press in a cramped basement under the supervision of the paper's editor and author of all its articles. There Whitman learned of "the pleasing mystery of the different letters and their divisions — the great 'e' box — the box for spaces . . . the 'a' box, 'I' box, and all the rest," the tools of his trade.

From 1836 to 1838 he worked as a country teacher in Norwich, New York. Payment was poor and erratic and, probably because school inspectors disapproved of his rowdy classrooms, he was forced to change schools eight times in those two years. His superiors cannot have been too pleased if he taught his students:

> You shall no longer take things at second or third hand,
> nor look through the eyes of the dead, nor feed on the spectres
>   in books.[10]

Or this:

> He most honors my style who learns under it to destroy the
> teacher.[11]

After learning to print and teaching to read, Whitman found that
he could combine both skills by becoming the editor of a paper: first
the *Long Islander*, in Huntington, New York, and later the Brooklyn
Daily Eagle. Here he began developing his notion of democracy as a society of "free readers", untainted by fanaticism and political schools,
whom the text-maker — poet, printer, teacher, newspaper editor —
must serve empathically. "We really feel a desire to talk on many subjects," he explained in an editorial on June 1, 1846, "to all the people
of Brooklyn; and it ain't their ninepences we want so much either.
There is a curious kind of sympathy (haven't you ever thought of it before?) that arises in the mind of a
newspaper conductor with the public
he serves. . . . Daily communion creates a sort of brotherhood and sister-
hood between the two parties."[12]

A passionate
reader,
Margaret
Fuller.

At about this time, Whitman
came across the writings of Margaret
Fuller. Fuller was an extraordinary
personality: the first full-time book
reviewer in the United States, the
first female foreign correspondent, a
lucid feminist, author of the impas-
sioned tract *Woman in the Nineteenth
Century*. Emerson thought that "all the
art, the thought and nobleness in
New England . . . seemed related to
her, and she to it".[13] Hawthorne, however, called her "a great hum-
bug",[14] and Oscar Wilde said that Venus had given her "everything except beauty" and Pallas "everything except wisdom".[15] While believing
that books could not replace actual experience, Fuller saw in them "a
medium for viewing all humanity, a core around which all knowledge,
all experience, all science, all the ideal as well as all the practical in our
nature could gather". Whitman responded enthusiastically to her
views. He wrote:

Did we count great, O soul, to penetrate the themes of
    mighty books,
Absorbing deep and full from thoughts, plays, speculations?
But now from thee to me, caged bird, to feel thy joyous
    warble,
Filling the air, the lonesome room, the long forenoon,
Is it not just as great, O soul?[16]

For Whitman, text, author, reader and world mirrored each other
in the act of reading, an act whose meaning he expanded until it served
to define every vital human activity, as well as the universe in which it
all took place. In this conjunction, the reader reflects the writer (he
and I are one), the world echoes a book (God's book, Nature's book),
the book is of flesh and blood (the writer's own flesh and own blood,
which through a literary transubstantiation become mine), the world is
a book to be deciphered (the writer's poems become my reading of the
world). All his life, Whitman seems to have sought an understanding
and a definition of the act of reading, which is both itself and the
metaphor for all its parts.

"Metaphors," wrote the German critic Hans Blumenberg, in our
time, "are no longer considered first and foremost as representing the
sphere that guides our hesitant theoretic conceptions, as an entrance
hall to the forming of concepts, as a makeshift device within specialized languages that have not yet been consolidated, but rather as the
authentic means to comprehend contexts."[17] To say that an author is a
reader or a reader an author, to see a book as a human being or a
human being as a book, to describe the world as text or a text as the
world, are ways of naming the reader's craft.

Such metaphors are very ancient ones, with roots in the earliest
Judaeo-Christian society. The German critic E.R. Curtius, in a
chapter on the symbolism of the book in his monumental *European
Literature and the Latin Middle Ages*, suggested that book metaphors
began in Classical Greece, but of these there are few examples, since
Greek society, and later Roman society as well, did not consider the
book an everyday object. Jewish, Christian and Islamic societies
developed a profound symbolic relationship with their holy books,
which were not symbols of God's Word but God's Word itself.
According to Curtius, "the idea that the world and nature are books
derives from the rhetoric of the Catholic Church, taken over by the

mystical philosophers of the early Middle Ages, and finally become a commonplace."

For the sixteenth-century Spanish mystic Fray Luis de Granada, if the world is a book, then the things of this world are the letters of the alphabet in which this book is written. In *Introducción al símbolo de la fé* (*Introduction to the Symbol of Faith*) he asked, "What are they to be, all the creatures of this world, so beautiful and so well crafted, but separated and illuminated letters that declare so rightly the delicacy and wisdom of their author? . . . And we as well . . . having been placed by you in front of this wonderful book of the entire universe, so that through its creatures, as if by means of living letters, we are to read the excellency of our Creator."[18]

"The Finger of God," wrote Sir Thomas Browne in *Religio Medici*, recasting Fray Luis's metaphor, "hath left an Inscription upon all his works, not graphical or composed of Letters, but of their several forms, constitutions, parts and operations, which, aptly joyned together, do make one word that doth express their natures."[19] To this, centuries later, the Spanish-born American philosopher George Santayana added, "There are books in which the footnotes, or the comments scrawled by some reader's hand in the margin, are more interesting than the text. The world is one of these books."[20]

Our task, as Whitman pointed out, is to read the world, since that colossal book is the only source of knowledge for mortals. (Angels, according to Saint Augustine, don't need to read the book of the world because they can see the Author Himself and receive from Him the Word in all its glory. Addressing himself to God, Saint Augustine reflects that angels "have no necessity to look upon the heavens or read them to read Your word. For they always see Your face, and there, without the syllables of time, they read Your eternal will. They read it, they choose it, they love it. They are always reading and what they read never comes to an end. . . . The book they read shall not be closed, the scroll shall not be rolled up again. For You are their book and You are eternal.")[21]

Human beings, made in the image of God, are also books to be read. Here, the act of reading serves as a metaphor to help us understand our hesitant relationship with our body, the encounter and the touch and the deciphering of signs in another person. We read expressions on a face, we follow the gestures of a loved one as in an open book. "Your face, my Thane," says Lady Macbeth to her husband, "is as a book where men may read strange matters,"[22] and the seventeenth-century poet Henry King wrote of his young dead wife:

Dear Loss! since thy untimely fate
my task has been to meditate
On Thee, on Thee: Thou art the Book,
The Library whereon I look
Though almost blind.[23]

And Benjamin Franklin, a great book-lover, composed for himself an epitaph (unfortunately not used on his tombstone) in which the image of the reader as book finds its complete depiction:

The Body of
B. Franklin, Printer,
Like the cover of an old Book,
Its Contents torn out,
And stript of its Lettering & Gilding
Lies here, Food for Worms.
But the Work shall not be lost;
For it will, as he believ'd,
Appear once more
In a new and more elegant Edition
Corrected and improved
By the Author.[24]

To say that we read — the world, a book, the body — is not enough. The metaphor of reading solicits in turn another metaphor, demands to be explained in images that lie outside the reader's library and yet within the reader's body, so that the function of reading is associated with our other essential bodily functions. Reading — as we have seen — serves as a metaphoric vehicle, but in order to be understood must itself be recognized through metaphors. Just as writers speak of cooking up a story, rehashing a text, having half-baked ideas for a plot, spicing up a scene or garnishing the bare bones of an argument, turning the ingredients of a potboiler into soggy prose, a slice of life peppered with allusions into which readers can sink their teeth, we, the readers, speak of savouring a book, of finding nourishment in it, of devouring a book at one sitting, of regurgitating or spewing up a text, of ruminating on a passage, of rolling a poet's words on the tongue, of feasting on poetry, of living on a diet of detective stories. In an essay on the art of studying, the sixteenth-century English scholar Francis Bacon catalogued the process: "Some books are to be tasted, others to be swallowed, and some few to be chewed and digested."[25]

By extraordinary chance we know on what date this curious metaphor was first recorded.[26] On July 31, 593 BC, by the river Chebar in the land of the Chaldeans, Ezekiel the priest had a vision of fire in which he saw "the likeness of the glory of the Lord" ordering him to speak to the rebellious children of Israel. "Open thy mouth, and eat what I give you," the vision instructed him.

> And when I looked, behold, an hand was sent unto me; and, lo, a roll of a book was therein;
>
> And he spread it before me; and it was written within and without: and there was written therein lamentations, and mourning, and woe.[27]

Saint John, recording his apocalyptic vision on Patmos, received the same revelation as Ezekiel. As he watched in terror, an angel came down from heaven with an open book, and a thundering voice told him not to write what he had learned, but to take the book from the angel's hand.

> And I went unto the angel, and said unto him. Give me the little book. And he said unto me, Take it, and eat it up; and it shall make thy belly bitter, but it shall be in thy mouth sweet as honey.
>
> And I took the little book out of the angel's hand, and ate it up; and it was in my mouth sweet as honey; and as soon as I had eaten it, my belly was bitter.
>
> And he said unto me, Thou must prophesy again before many peoples, and nations, and tongues, and kings.[28]

Eventually, as reading developed and expanded, the gastronomic metaphor became common rhetoric. In Shakespeare's time it was expected in literary parlance, and Queen Elizabeth I herself used it to describe her devotional reading: "I walke manie times into the pleasant fieldes of the Holye Scriptures, where I pluck up the goodlie greene

herbes of sentences, eate them by reading, chewe them up musing, and laie them up at length in the seate of memorie . . . so I may the lesse perceive the bitterness of this miserable life."[29] By 1695 the metaphor had become so ingrained in the language that William Congreve was able to parody it in the opening scene of *Love for Love*, having the pedantic Valentine say to his valet, "Read, read, sirrah! and refine your appetite; learn to live upon instruction; feast your mind, and mortify your flesh; read, and take your nourishment in at your eyes; shut up your mouth, and chew the cud of understanding." "You'll grow devilish fat upon this paper diet," is the valet's comment.[30]

Less than a century later, Dr. Johnson read a book with the same manners he displayed at the table. He read, said Boswell, "ravenously, as if he devoured it, which was to all appearance his method of studying". According to Boswell, Dr. Johnson kept a book wrapped in the tablecloth in his lap during dinner "from an avidity to have one entertainment in readiness, when he should have finished another; resembling (if I may use so coarse a simile) a dog who holds a bone in his paws in reserve, while he eats something else which has been thrown to him."[31]

However readers make a book theirs, the end is that book and reader become one. The world that is a book is devoured by a reader who is a letter in the world's text; thus a circular metaphor is created for the endlessness of reading. We are what we read. The process by which the circle is completed is not, Whitman argued, merely an intellectual one; we read intellectually on a superficial level, grasping certain meanings and conscious of certain facts, but at the same time, invisibly, unconsciously, text and reader become intertwined, creating new levels of meaning, so that every time we cause the text to yield something by ingesting it, simultaneously something else is born beneath it that we haven't yet grasped. That is why — as Whitman believed, rewriting and re-editing his poems over and over again — no reading can ever be definitive. In 1867 he wrote, by way of explanation:

> Shut not your doors to me proud libraries,
> For that which was lacking on all your well-fill'd shelves, yet
>   needed most, I bring
> Forth from the war emerging, a book I have made,
> The words of my book nothing, the drift of it every thing,
> A book separate, not link'd with the rest nor felt by the
>   intellect,
> But you ye untold latencies will thrill to every page.[32]

POWERS

of the

READER

One must be an inventor to read well.

RALPH WALDO EMERSON
The American Scholar, 1837

BEGINNINGS

I n the summer of 1989, two years before the Gulf War, I travelled to Iraq to see the ruins of Babylon and the Tower of
Babel. It was a journey I had long wanted to make. Reconstructed between 1899 and 1917 by the German archeologist
Robert Koldewey,[1] Babylon lies about forty miles south of Baghdad —
a huge maze of butter-coloured walls that was once the most powerful
city on earth, close to a clay mound which the guidebooks say is all that
is left of the tower God cursed with multiculturalism. The taxi-driver
who took me there knew the site only because it was near the town of
Hillah, where he had once or twice gone to visit an aunt. I had brought
with me a Penguin anthology of short stories, and after touring the
ruins of what was for me, as a Western reader, the starting-place of
every book, I sat down in the shade of an oleander bush and read.

Walls, oleander bushes, bituminous paving, open gateways, heaps
of clay, broken towers: part of the secret of Babylon is that what the
visitor sees is not one but many cities, successive in time but simultaneous in space. There is the Babylon of the Akkadian era, a small village
of around 2350 BC. There is the Babylon where the epic of Gilgamesh,
which includes one of the earliest accounts of Noah's Flood, was recited for the first time, one day in the second millennium BC. There is
the Babylon of King Hammurabi, of the eighteenth century BC, whose
system of laws was one of the world's first attempts at codifying the
life of an entire society. There is the Babylon destroyed by the Assyrians
in 689 BC. There is the rebuilt Babylon of Nebuchadnezzar, who around

OPPOSITE

A five-
thousand-year-
old reader, the
Sumerian scribe
Dudu.

586 BC besieged Jerusalem, sacked the Temple of Solomon and led the Jews into captivity, whereupon they sat by the rivers and wept. There is the Babylon of Nebuchadnezzar's son or grandson (genealogists are undecided), King Belshazzar, who was the first man to see the writing on the wall, in the fearful calligraphy of God's finger. There is the Babylon that Alexander the Great intended to be the capital of an empire extending from northern India to Egypt and Greece — the Babylon where the Conqueror of the World died at the age of thirty-three, in 323 BC, clutching a copy of the *Iliad*, back in the days when generals could read. There is Babylon the Great as conjured up by Saint John — the Mother of Harlots and Abominations of the Earth, the Babylon who made all nations drink of the wine of the wrath of her fornication. And then there is my taxi-driver's Babylon, a place near the town of Hillah, where his aunt lived.

Here (or at least somewhere not too far from here), archeologists have argued, the prehistory of books began. Towards the middle of the fourth millennium BC, when the climate of the Near East became cooler and the air drier, the farming communities of southern Mesopotamia abandoned their scattered villages and regrouped within and around larger urban centres which soon became city-states.[2] To maintain the scarce fertile lands they invented new irrigation techniques and extraordinary architectural devices, and to organize an increasingly complex society, with its laws and edicts and rules of commerce, towards the end of the fourth millennium the new urban dwellers developed an art that would change for ever the nature of communication between human beings: the art of writing.

In all probability, writing was invented for commercial reasons, to remember that a certain number of cattle belonged to a certain family, or were being transported to a certain place. A written sign served as a mnemonic device: a picture of an ox stood for an ox, to remind the reader that the transaction was in oxen, how many oxen, and perhaps the names of a buyer and seller. Memory, in this form, is also a document, the record of such a transaction.

The inventor of the first written tablets may have realized the advantage these pieces of clay had over the holding memory in the brain: first, the amount of information storable on tablets was endless — one could go on producing tablets *ad infinitum*, while the brain's remembering capacity is limited; second, tablets did not require the presence of the memory-holder to retrieve information. Suddenly, something intangible — a number, an item of news, a thought, an order — could be acquired without the physical presence of the message-giver; magically, it could be imagined, noted and passed on across space and beyond time. Since the earliest vestiges of prehistoric civilization, human society had tried to overcome the obstacles of geography, the finality of death, the erosion of oblivion. With a single act — the incision of a figure on a clay tablet — that first anonymous writer suddenly succeeded in all these seemingly impossible feats.

But writing is not the only invention come to life in the instant of that first incision: one other creation took place at that same time. Because the purpose of the act of writing was that the text be rescued — that is to say, read — the incision simultaneously created a reader, a role that came into being before the actual first reader acquired a physical presence. As that first writer dreamed up a new art by making marks on a piece of clay, another art became tacitly apparent, one without which the markings would have been utterly meaningless. The writer was a maker of messages, the creator of signs, but these signs and messages required a magus who would decipher them, recognize their meaning, give them voice. Writing required a reader.

The primordial relationship between writer and reader presents a wonderful paradox: in creating the role of the reader, the writer also decrees the writer's death, since in order for a text to be finished the writer must withdraw, cease to exist. While the writer remains present, the text remains incomplete. Only when the writer relinquishes the text, does the text come into existence. At that point, the existence of the text is a silent existence, silent until the moment in which a reader reads it. Only when the able eye makes contact with the markings on the tablet, does the text come to active life. All writing depends on the generosity of the reader.

This uneasy relationship between writer and reader has a beginning; it was established for all time on a mysterious Mesopotamian afternoon. It is a fruitful but anachronic relationship between a primeval creator who gives birth at the moment of death, and a post-mortem creator, or rather generations of post-mortem creators who enable the creation itself to speak, and without whom all writing is dead. From its very start, reading is writing's apotheosis.

Writing was quickly recognized as a powerful skill, and through the ranks of Mesopotamian society rose the scribe. Obviously the skill of reading was also essential to him, but neither the name given to his occupation nor the social perception of his activities acknowledged the act of reading, and instead focused almost exclusively on his ability to record. Publicly, it was safer for the scribe to be seen not as one who retrieved information (and was thereby able to imbue it with sense) but as one who merely recorded it for the public good. Though he might be the eyes and tongue of a general, or even a king, such political power was better not flaunted. For this reason, the symbol of Nisaba, Mesopotamian goddess of scribes, was the stylus, not the tablet held before the eyes.

It would be hard to exaggerate the importance of the scribe's role in Mesopotamian society. Scribes were needed to send messages, to convey news, to take down the king's orders, to register the laws, to note the astronomical data necessary for keeping the calendar, to calculate the requisite number of soldiers or workers or supplies or head of cattle, to keep track of financial and economic transactions, to record medical diagnoses and prescriptions, to accompany military expeditions and write dispatches and chronicles of war, to assess taxes, to draw contracts, to preserve the sacred religious texts and to entertain the people with readings from the epic of Gilgamesh. None of this could be achieved without the scribe. He was the hand and eye and voice through which communications were established and messages deciphered. This is why the Mesopotamian authors addressed the scribe directly, knowing that the scribe would be the one to relay the message: "To My Lord, say this: thus speaks So-and-so, your servant".[3] "Say" addresses a second person, the "you", earliest ancestor of the "Dear Reader" of later fiction. Each one of us, reading that line, becomes, across the ages, this "you".

In the first half of the second millennium BC the priests of the temple of Shamash, in Sippar, in southern Mesopotamia, erected a monument covered with inscriptions on all twelve sides, dealing with the temple's renovations and an increase in royal revenue. But instead of dating it in their own time, these primordial politicians dated it to the reign of King Manishtushu of Akkad (*circa* 2276–2261 BC), thereby establishing antiquity for the temple's financial claims. The inscriptions end with the following promise to the reader: "This is not a lie, it is indeed the truth."[4] As the scribe-reader soon discovered, his art gave him the ability to modify the historical past.

With all the power that lay in their hands, the Mesopotamian scribes were an aristocratic elite. (Many years later, in the seventh and eighth centuries of the Christian era, the scribes of Ireland still bene-fited from this exalted status: the penalty for killing an Irish scribe was equal to that for killing a bishop.)[5] In Babylon, only certain specially trained citizens could become scribes, and their function gave them pre-eminence over other members of their society. Textbooks (school tablets) have been discovered in most of the wealthier houses of Ur, from which it may be inferred that the arts of writing and reading were considered aristocratic activities. Those who were chosen to become scribes were taught, from a very early age, in a private school, an *e-dubba* or "tablet-house". A room lined with clay benches in the palace of King Zimri-Lim of Mari,[6] though it has yielded no school tablets to the scrutiny of archeologists, is considered to be a model for these schools for scribes.

The owner of the school, the headmaster or *ummia*, was assisted by an *adda e-dubba* or "father of the tablet-house" and an *ugala* or clerk. Several subjects were offered; for instance, in one of these schools a headmaster by the name of Igmil-Sin[7] taught writing, religion, history and mathematics. Discipline was in the hands of an older student who fulfilled more or less the functions of a prefect. It was important for a scribe to do well at school, and there is evidence that fathers bribed the teachers to obtain good marks for their sons.

After learning the practical skills of fashioning clay tablets and handling the stylus, the student would have to learn how to draw and recognize the basic signs. By the second millennium BC, the Mesopo-tamian script had changed from pictographic — more or less accurate depictions of the objects for which the words stood — to what we know as "cuneiform" writing (from the Latin *cuneus*, "nail"), wedge-shaped signs representing sounds, not objects. The early pictograms (of which there were more than two thousand, as there was one sign for each represented object) had evolved into abstract markings that could represent not only the objects they depicted but also associated ideas; different words and syllables pronounced the same way were repre-sented by the same sign. Auxiliary signs — phonetic or grammatical — led to an easier comprehension of the text and allowed for nuances of sense and shades of meaning. Within a short time, the system enabled the scribe to record a complex and highly sophisticated literature: epics, books of wisdom, humorous stories, love poems.[8] Cuneiform writing, in fact, survived through the successive empires of Sumer, Akkadia and Assyria, recording the literature of fifteen different languages and covering an area occupied nowadays by Iraq, western Iran and Syria. Today we cannot read the pictographic tablets as a language because we don't know the phonetic value of the early signs; we can only *recognize* a goat, a sheep. But linguists have tentatively reconstructed the pronunciation of the later Sumerian and Akkadian cuneiform texts, and we can, however rudimentarily, pronounce sounds coined thousands of years ago.

The first writing and reading skills were learned by practising the linking of signs, usually to form a name. There are numerous tablets that show these early, clumsy stages, with markings incised by an unsteady hand. The student had to learn to write following the conventions that would also allow him to read. For instance, the Akkadian word "to", *ana*, had to be written *a-na*, not *ana* or *an-a,* so that the student would stress the syllables correctly.[9]

Once the student had mastered this stage, he would be given a different kind of clay tablet, a round one on which the teacher had inscribed a short sentence, proverb or list of names. The student would study the inscription, and then turn the tablet over and reproduce the writing. To do this, he would have to bear the words in his mind from one side of the tablet to the other, becoming for the first time a transmitter of messages — from reader of the teacher's writing, to writer of that which he has read. In that small gesture a later function of the reader-scribe was born: copying a text, annotating it, glossing it, translating it, transforming it.

I speak of the Mesopotamian scribes as "he" since they were almost always male. Reading and writing were reserved for the power-holders in that patriarchal society. There are, however, exceptions. The earliest named author in history is a woman, Princess Enheduanna, born around 2300 BC, daughter of King Sargon I of Akkad, high priestess of the god of the moon, Nanna, and composer of a series of songs in honour of Inanna, goddess of love and war.[10] Enheduanna signed her name at the end of her tablets. This was customary in Mesopotamia, and much of our knowledge of scribes comes from these signatures, or colophons, which included the name of the scribe, the date and the name of the town where the writing took place. This identification enabled the reader to read a text in a given voice — in the case of the hymns to Inanna, the voice of Enheduanna — identifying the "I" in the text with a specific person and thereby creating a pseudo-fictional character, "the author", for the reader to engage with. This device, invented at the beginning of literature, is still with us more than four thousand years later.

The scribes must have been aware of the extraordinary power conferred by being the reader of a text, and guarded that prerogative jealously. Arrogantly, most Mesopotamian scribes would end their texts

Two students' tablets from Sumer. The teacher wrote on one side, the student copied the teacher's writing on the other.

with this colophon: "Let the wise instruct the wise, for the ignorant may not see."[11] In Egypt during the nineteenth dynasty, around 1300 BC, a scribe composed this encomium of his trade:

> Be a scribe! Engrave this in your heart
> So that your name might live on like theirs!
> The scroll is better than the carved stone.
> A man has died: his corpse is dust,
> And his people have passed from the land.
> It is a book which makes him be remembered
> In the mouth of the speaker who reads him.[12]

A writer can construct a text in any number of ways, choosing from the common stock of words those which seem to express the message best. But the reader receiving this text is not confined to any one interpretation. While, as we have said, the readings of a text are not infinite — they are circumscribed by conventions of grammar, and the limits imposed by common sense — they are not strictly dictated by the text itself. Any written text, says the French critic Jacques Derrida,[13] "is readable even if the moment of its production is irrevocably lost and even if I don't know what its alleged author consciously intended to say at the moment of writing it, i.e. abandoned the text to its essential drift." For that reason, the author (the writer, the scribe) who wishes to preserve and impose a meaning must also be the reader. This is the secret privilege which the Mesopotamian scribe granted himself and which I, reading in the ruins that might have been his library, have usurped.

In a famous essay, Roland Barthes proposed a distinction between *écrivain* and *écrivant*: the former fulfils a function, the latter an activity; for the *écrivain* writing is an intransitive verb; for the *écrivant* the verb always leads to an objective — indoctrinating, witnessing, explaining, teaching.[14] Possibly the same distinction can be made between two reading roles: that of the reader for whom the text justifies its existence in the act of reading itself, with no ulterior motive (not even entertainment, since the notion of pleasure is implied in the carrying out of the act), and that of the reader with an ulterior motive (learning, criticizing) for whom the text is a vehicle towards another function. The first activity takes place within a time frame dictated by the nature of the text; the second exists in a time frame imposed by the reader for the purpose of that reading. This may be what Saint Augustine believed was a distinction God Himself had established. "What My Scripture says, I say," he hears God reveal to him. "But the Scripture speaks in time, whereas time does not affect My Word, which stands for ever, equal with Me in eternity. The things which you see by My Spirit, I see, just as I speak the words which you speak by My Spirit. But while you see those things in time, it is not in time that I see them. And while you speak those words in time, it is not in time that I speak them."[15]

As the scribe knew, as society discovered, the extraordinary invention of the written word with all its messages, its laws, its lists, its literatures, depended on the scribe's ability to restore the text, to read it. With that ability lost, the text becomes once again silent markings. The ancient Mesopotamians believed birds to be sacred because their footsteps on wet clay left marks that resembled cuneiform writing, and imagined that, if they could decipher the confusion of those signs, they would know what the gods were thinking. Generations of scholars have tried to become readers of scripts whose codes we have lost: Sumerian, Akkadian, Minoan, Aztec, Mayan. . . .

Sometimes they succeeded. Sometimes they failed, as in the case of Etruscan writing, whose intricacies we have not yet decoded. The poet Richard Wilbur summed up the tragedy that befalls a civilization when it loses its readers:

TO THE ETRUSCAN POETS

Dream fluently, still brothers, who when young
Took with your mothers' milk the mother tongue,

In which pure matrix, joining world and mind,
You strove to leave some line of verse behind

Like a fresh track across a field of snow,
Not reckoning that all could melt and go.[16]

ORDAINERS OF

THE UNIVERSE

A lexandria in Egypt was founded by Alexander the Great in 331 BC. Quintus Curtius Rufus, a Roman historian who lived in the reign of Claudius and wrote more than four centuries after the event, noted in his *History of Alexander* that the founding took place immediately after Alexander's visit to the shrine of the Egyptian god Ammon, "the Hidden One", where the priest addressed Alexander as "son of Jupiter". In this recently acquired state of grace, Alexander chose for his new city the stretch of land between Lake Mareotis and the sea, and ordered his people to migrate from neighbouring cities to the new metropolis. "There is a report," wrote Rufus, "that after the king had completed the Macedonian custom of marking out the circular boundary for the future city-walls with barley-meal, flocks of birds flew down and fed on the barley. Many regarded this as an unfavourable omen, but the verdict of the seers was that the city would have a large immigrant population and would provide the means of livelihood to many countries."[1]

People of many nations did indeed flock to the new capital, but it was a different sort of immigration that ultimately made Alexandria famous. By the time of Alexander's death in 323, the city had become what we would call today a "multicultural society", divided into *politeumata* or corporations based on nationality, under the sceptre of the Ptolemaic dynasty. Of these nationalities, the most important aside from the native Egyptians was the Greeks, for whom the written word had become a symbol of wisdom and power. "Those who can

OPPOSITE

A fanciful map of Alexandria from a sixteenth-century manuscript.

read see twice as well," wrote the Attic poet Menander in the fourth century BC.[2]

Though traditionally the Egyptians had set down much of their administrative business in writing, it was probably the influence of the Greeks, who believed that society required a precise and systematically written record of its transactions, that transformed Alexandria into an intensely bureaucratic state. By the mid-third century BC, the flow of documents was becoming unwieldy. Receipts, estimates, declarations and permits were issued in writing. There are examples of documents for every kind of task, no matter how small: keeping pigs, selling beer, trading in roasted lentils, keeping a bath-house, undertaking a paint job.[3] A document dating from 258–257 BC shows that the accounting offices of the finance minister Apollonius received 434 rolls of papyrus in thirty-three days.[4] A lust for paper does not imply a love for books, but familiarity with the written word no doubt accustomed the citizens of Alexandria to the act of reading.

If the tastes of its founder were anything to go by, Alexandria was destined to become a bookish city.[5] Alexander's father, Philip of Macedon, had engaged Aristotle as a private tutor for his son, and through Aristotle's teaching Alexander became "a great lover of all kinds of learning and reading"[6] — so keen a reader, in fact, that he was seldom without a book. Once, travelling in Upper Asia and "being destitute of other books", he ordered one of his commanders to send him several; he duly received Philistus's *History*, a number of plays by Euripides, Sophocles and Aeschylus and poems by Telestes and Philoxenus.[7]

It may have been Demetrius of Phalerum — a scholar from Athens, the compiler of Aesop's fables, a critic of Homer and a student of the celebrated Theophrastus (himself a student and friend of Aristotle) — who suggested to Alexander's successor, Ptolemy I, the founding of the library that was to make Alexandria famous; so famous that 150 years after the library had perished, Athenaeus of Naucratis thought it superfluous to describe it to his readers. "And concerning the numbers of books, the establishing of libraries, and the collection in the Hall of the Muses, why need I even speak, since they are in all men's memories?"[8] This is unfortunate, because where exactly the library stood, how many books it housed, how it was run and who was responsible for its destruction are all questions for which we have no satisfactory answers.

The Greek geographer Strabo, writing towards the end of the first century BC, described Alexandria and its museum in some detail but never mentioned the library. According to the Italian historian Luciano Canfora,[9] "Strabo doesn't mention the library simply because it wasn't a separate room or building" but rather a space attached to the colonnades and common room of the museum. Canfora surmises that the *bibliothekai* or bookshelves were set in recesses along a broad covered passage or alleyway. "Every niche or recess," remarks Canfora, "must have been dedicated to a certain class of authors, each marked with an appropriate heading." This space eventually expanded until the library was said to house nearly half a million scrolls, plus forty thousand more stored in another building attached to the Temple of Serapis, in the old Egyptian quarter of Rhakotis. When we consider that, before the invention of printing, the papal library of Avignon was the only one in the Christian West to exceed two thousand volumes,[10] we begin to understand the importance of the Alexandrian collection.

The volumes had to be collected in great numbers, since the magnificent purpose of the library was to encapsulate the totality of human knowledge. For Aristotle, collecting books was part of the scholar's labours, necessary "in the way of memoranda". The library of the city founded by his disciple was simply to be a vaster version of this: the memory of the world. According to Strabo, Aristotle's collection of books was passed on to Theophrastus, from him to his relative and pupil Neleus of Scepsis, and from Neleus (though his generosity has been questioned)[11] it finally reached Ptolemy II, who acquired it for Alexandria. By the reign of Ptolemy III, no single person could have read the entire library. By royal decree, all ships stopping at Alexandria had to surrender any books they were carrying; these books were copied, and the originals (sometimes the copies) were returned to their owners while the duplicates (sometimes the originals) were kept in the library. The established texts of the great Greek dramatists, stored in Athens for actors to transcribe and study, were borrowed by the Ptolemys through the good offices of their ambassadors and copied with great care. Not all the books that entered the library were genuine; forgers, noting the passionate interest with which the Ptolemys collected the classics, sold them apocryphal Aristotelian treatises that centuries of scholarly research later proved false. Sometimes the scholars themselves produced forgeries. Under the name of a contemporary of Thucydides', the scholar Cratippus wrote a book called *Everything Thucydides Left Unsaid*, in which he made happy use of bombast and anachronism — quoting, for instance, an author who had lived four hundred years after Thucydides' death.

Accumulation of knowledge isn't knowledge. The Gallic poet Decimus Magnus Ausonius, several centuries later, mocked the confusion of the two in his *Opuscules*:

> You've bought books and filled shelves, O Lover of the Muses.
> Does that mean you're a scholar now?
> If you buy string instruments, plectrum and lyre today:
> Do you think that by tomorrow the realm of music will be
>   yours?[12]

It was obvious that a method was required to help people make use of this bookish wealth — a method that would enable any reader to trace a specific book to which his interest led him. Aristotle no doubt had a private system for retrieving the books he needed from his library (a system of which, alas, we know nothing). But the number of books shelved in the Alexandrian Library would have made it impossible for an individual reader to find a particular title, other than by an amazing stroke of good luck. The solution — and another set of problems — appeared in the guise of a new librarian, the epigrammatist and scholar Callimachus of Cyrene.

Callimachus was born in North Africa around the beginning of the third century BC and lived in Alexandria for most of his life, first teaching at a suburban school and then working at the library. He was a wonderfully prolific writer, critic, poet and encyclopedist. He began (or continued) a debate that hasn't reached its end even in our time: he believed that literature should be concise and unadorned, and denounced those who still wrote epics in the ancient manner, calling them garrulous and obsolete. His enemies accused him of being unable to write long poems and of being dry as dust in his short ones. (Centuries later, his position was taken up by the Moderns against the Ancients, the Romantics against the Classicists, the Big American Novelists against the Minimalists.) His main enemy was his superior at the library — the head librarian, Apollonius of Rhodes, whose six-thousand-line epic, *The Voyage of the Argos*, is an example of everything Callimachus detested. ("Big book, big bore," was Callimachus's laconic summation.) Neither has found great favour among modern readers: *The Voyage of the Argos* is still (if discreetly) remembered; examples of Callimachus's art survive

faintly in a translation by Catullus ("The Lock of Berenice", used by
Pope for his *Rape of the Lock*) and in William Cory's version of an elegiac
epigram on the death of Callimachus's friend Heraclitus of Halicarnas-
sus, which begins "They told me, Heraclitus, they told me you were
dead".

An imaginary
portrait of
Callimachus
from the
sixteenth
century.

Under the no doubt watchful
eye of Apollonius, Callimachus (it
remains uncertain whether he
himself ever became head librarian) began the arduous task of cataloguing the covetous library.
Cataloguing is an ancient profession; there are examples of such
"ordainers of the universe" (as
they were called by the Sumeri-
ans) among the oldest vestiges of
libraries. For instance, the catalogue of an Egyptian "House of
Books" dating from *circa* 2000 BC,
from the excavations in Edfu, be-
gins by listing several other catalogues: *The Book of What Is to Be Found in
the Temple*, *The Book of the Domains*, *The List of All Writings Engraved in
Wood*, *The Book of the Stations of the Sun and the Moon*, *The Book of Places
and What Is in Them* and so on.[13]

The system Callimachus chose for Alexandria seems to have been
based less on an orderly listing of the library's possessions than on a
preconceived formulation of the world itself. All classifications are ultimately arbitrary. That proposed by Callimachus seems a little less so
because it follows the system of thought accepted by the intellectuals
and scholars of his time, inheritors of the Greek view of the world.
Callimachus divided the library into shelves or tables (*pinakoi*)
arranged in eight classes or subjects: drama, oratory, lyric poetry, leg-
islation, medicine, history, philosophy and miscellany. He separated the
longer works by having them copied into several shorter sections
called "books", so as to have smaller rolls that would be more practical
to handle.

Callimachus was not to finish his gigantic enterprise, which was
completed by succeeding librarians. The full *pinakoi* — whose official
title was *Tables of Those Who Were Outstanding in Every Phase of Culture, and*

Their Writings — apparently extended to 120 rolls.[14] To Callimachus we also owe a cataloguing device that was to become commonplace: the custom of arranging volumes in alphabetical order. Before that time, only a few Greek inscriptions listing series of names (some dating from the second century BC) make use of alphabetical order.[15] According to the French critic Christian Jacob, Callimachus's library was the first example of "a utopian place of criticism, in which the texts can be compared, opened side by side".[16] With Callimachus, the library became an organized reading-space.

All the libraries I've known reflect that ancient library. The dark Biblioteca del Maestro (Teacher's Library) in Buenos Aires, where I could look out the windows to see jacaranda trees covering the street in blue blossoms; the exquisite Huntington Library in Pasadena, California, surrounded like an Italian villa by orderly gardens; the venerable British Library, where I sat (so I was told) in the chair Karl Marx had chosen when he wrote *Das Kapital*; the three-shelf library in the town of Djanet, in the Algerian Sahara, where among the Arabic books I saw one mysterious copy of Voltaire's *Candide* in French; the Bibliothèque Nationale in Paris, where the section reserved for erotic literature is called Hell; the beautiful Metro Toronto Reference Library, where one can watch the snow fall on the slanted glass panes as one reads — all these copy, with variations, Callimachus's systematic vision.

The Library of Alexandria and its catalogues became the models first for the libraries of imperial Rome, then for those of the Byzantine East and later for those of Christian Europe. In *De doctrina christiana*, written shortly after his conversion in 387, Saint Augustine, still under the influence of Neoplatonic thought, argued that a number of works from the Greek and Roman classics were compatible with Christian teaching, since authors such as Aristotle and Virgil had "unjustly possessed the truth" (what Plotinus called the "spirit" and Christ the "Word" or *logos*).[17] In that same eclectic spirit, the earliest known library of the Roman Church, founded in the 380s by Pope Damasus I in the Church of St. Lorenzo, contained not only the Christian books of the Bible, works of commentary and a selection of the Greek apologists, but also several Greek and Roman classics. (However, the acceptance of the ancients was still discriminatory; commenting on a friend's library in the mid-fifth century, Apollinaris Sidonius complained that pagan authors were being separated from Christian ones — the pagans near the gentlemen's seats, the Christians near the ladies'.)[18]

How then should such diverse writings be catalogued? The keepers of the first Christian libraries made shelf-lists to record their books. Bibles were listed first, then glosses, the works of the Church Fathers (Saint Augustine at the top), philosophy, law and grammar. Medical books were sometimes listed at the end. Since most books were not formally titled, a descriptive title was applied or the first words of the text were used to designate the book. The alphabet sometimes served as a key for retrieving volumes. In the tenth century, for instance, the Grand Vizier of Persia, Abdul Kassem Ismael, in order not to part with his collection of 117,000 volumes when travelling, had them carried by a caravan of four hundred camels trained to walk in alphabetical order.[19]

A rare depiction of Richard de Fournival conversing with his mistress, from a thirteenth-century illuminated manuscript.

Perhaps the earliest example of subject cataloguing in medieval Europe is that of the library of Le Puy Cathedral in the eleventh century, but for a long time this type of cataloguing was not the norm. In many cases, divisions of books were established simply for practical reasons. At Canterbury in the 1200s, the books in the Archbishop's library were listed according to the faculties that had the most use for them. In 1120, Hugh of Saint Victor proposed a cataloguing system in which the contents of each book were briefly summarized (as in a modern abstract) and placed in one of three categories corresponding to the tripartite division of the liberal arts: theoretical, practical or mechanical.

In the year 1250, Richard de Fournival, whose theories on reading and memory I described earlier, imagined a cataloguing system based on a horticultural model. Comparing his library to a garden "where-in his fellow-citizens might gather the fruits of knowledge", he divided this garden into three flowerbeds — corresponding to philosophy, the "lucrative sciences" and theology — and each flowerbed into a number of smaller plots or *areolae*, each containing a table of contents or *tabula* (like the *pinakoi* of Callimachus) of the plot's subject-matter.[20] The flowerbed of philosophy, for instance, was divided into three *areolae*:

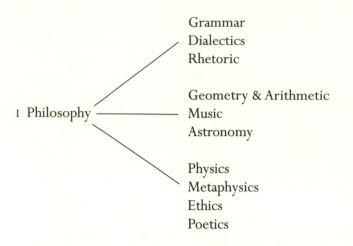

The "lucrative sciences" in the second flowerbed contained only two *areolae*, medicine and law. The third flowerbed was reserved for theology.

II   Lucrative sciences —— Medicine
                         —— Civil & Canon Law

III Theology

Within the *areolae*, each *tabula* was assigned a number of letters equal to the number of books held in it, so that one letter could be given to each of the books, and recorded on the book's cover. To avoid the confusion of having several books identified by the same letter, de Fournival used typographical and colour variations for each letter: one book of grammar would be identified by a capital rose-red A, another by an uncial A that was pansy-purple.

Even though de Fournival's library was divided into three "flowerbeds", the *tabulae* were not necessarily allocated to subcategories in order of importance, but according to the number of volumes he had collected. Dialectics, for instance, was allotted an entire table because there were more than a dozen books on the subject in his library; geometry and arithmetic, represented by only six books each, shared a single table between them.[21]

De Fournival's garden was modelled, at least in part, on the seven liberal arts into which the traditional medieval education system was

A thirteenth-century Islamic library. A group of readers is consulting one of the carefully catalogued volumes stored flat on the small shelves in the background.

divided: grammar, rhetoric, logic, arithmetic, geometry, astronomy and music. Established in the early fifth century by Martianus Capella, these seven subjects were believed to embody the entire scope of human wisdom, apart from medicine, law, and theology.[22]

About a century before de Fournival proposed his system, other bookish men such as the father of canon law, Gratian, and the theologian Peter Lombard had suggested new divisions of human knowledge based on reconsiderations of Aristotle, whose proposed universal hierarchy of existence they found deeply appealing, but their suggestions were not taken up for many years. By the mid-thirteenth century, however, the number of works of Aristotle that had begun to flood Europe (translated into Latin from the Arabic, which in turn had been translated from the Greek, by such learned men as Michael Scot and Hermannus Alemannus) obliged scholars to reconsider the division de Fournival found so natural. Beginning in 1251, the University of Paris officially incorporated the works of Aristotle into its curriculum.[23]

Like the librarians of Alexandria before them, the librarians of Europe sought out Aristotle. They found him meticulously edited and annotated by Muslim scholars such as Averroës and Avicenna, his chief Western and Eastern exponents.

Aristotle's adoption by the Arabs begins with a dream. One night early in the ninth century, the caliph al-Ma'mun, son of the almost legendary Harun al-Rashid, dreamed of a conversation. The caliph's interlocutor was a pale, blue-eyed man with a broad forehead and frowning eyebrows, sitting regally on a throne. The man (the caliph recognized him with the assurance we all have in dreams) was Aristotle, and the secret words that passed between them inspired the caliph to command the scholars at the Baghdad Academy to devote their efforts from that night onwards to the translation of the Greek philosopher.[24]

A sixteenth-century portrait of Roger Bacon.

Baghdad was not alone in collecting Aristotle and the other Greek classics. In Cairo, the Fatimid library contained, before the Sunni purges of 1175, more than 1.1 million volumes, catalogued by subject.[25] (The Crusaders, with the exaggeration induced by astonished envy, reported that there were more than 3 million books in the infidels' hold.) Following the Alexandrian model, the Fatimid library also included a museum, an archive and a laboratory. Christian scholars such as John of Gorce travelled south to make use of these invaluable resources. In Islamic Spain too there were numerous important libraries; in Andalusia alone there were more than seventy, of which the caliphal library of Córdoba listed 400,000 volumes in the reign of al-Hakam II (961–76).[26]

Roger Bacon, writing in the early thirteenth century, criticized the new cataloguing systems derived from second-hand translations of the Arabic, which in his opinion contaminated Aristotle's texts with the teachings of Islam. An experimental scientist who had studied mathematics, astronomy and alchemy in Paris, Bacon was the first European to describe in detail the manufacturing of gunpowder (which would not be used in guns until the next century) and to suggest that, thanks to the energy of the sun, it would one day be possible to have boats without rowers, coaches without horses and machines that could fly. He accused scholars such as Albert the Great and Saint Thomas Aquinas of pretending to read Aristotle in spite of their ignorance of Greek, and while he acknowledged that "something" could be learned from the Arabic commentators (he approved, for instance, of Avicenna and, as we have seen, he assiduously studied the works of al-Haytham), he considered it essential that readers base their opinions on the original text.

A scribe busy at his craft, sculpted in the thirteenth century on the Western Portal of Chartres Cathedral.

In Bacon's time, the seven liberal arts were allegorically placed under the protection of the Virgin Mary, as depicted in the tympanum over the western portal of Chartres Cathedral. In order to achieve this theological reduction, a true scholar — according to Bacon — required a thorough familiarity with science and language; for the former the study of mathematics was indispensable, for the latter the study of grammar. In Bacon's cataloguing system of knowledge (which he intended to detail in a huge, never-completed and encyclopedic *Opus principale*), the science of nature was a subcategory of the science of God. With this conviction, Bacon fought for years to have the teaching of science fully recognized as part of the university curriculum, but in 1268 the death of Pope Clement IV, who had been sympathetic to his ideas, put an end to the plan. For the rest of his life Bacon remained unpopular with his fellow intellectuals; several of his scientific theories were included in the Paris condemnation of 1277, and he was imprisoned until 1292. It is believed that he died shortly afterwards, unaware that future historians would give him the title "Doctor Mirabilis", the Wonderful Teacher, for whom every book had a place that was also its definition, and every possible aspect of human knowledge belonged to a scholarly category that aptly circumscribed it.

The categories that a reader brings to a reading, and the categories in which that reading itself is placed — the learned social and political categories, and the physical categories into which a library is divided —

constantly modify one another in ways that appear, over the years, more or less arbitrary or more or less imaginative. Every library is a library of preferences, and every chosen category implies an exclusion. After the Jesuit order was dissolved in 1773, the books stored in its Brussels house were sent to the Belgian Royal Library, which, however, had no room to accommodate them. The books were therefore kept in a vacant Jesuit church. As the church was infested with mice, the librarians had to devise a plan to protect the books. The secretary of the Belgian Literary Society was commissioned to select the best and most useful books; these were placed on shelves in the centre of the nave, while all the others were left on the floor. It was thought that the mice would gnaw their way around the edges, leaving the central core intact.[27]

There are even libraries whose categories do not accord with reality. The French writer Paul Masson, who had worked as a magistrate in the French colonies, noticed that the Bibliothèque Nationale in Paris was deficient in Latin and Italian books of the fifteenth century, and decided to remedy this by compiling a list of appropriate books under a new category that "would save the prestige of the catalogue" — a category that included only books whose titles he had made up. When Colette, a long-time friend, asked what was the use of books that did not exist, Masson's answer was an indignant "Well, I can't be expected to think of everything!"[28]

A room determined by artificial categories, such as a library, suggests a logical universe, a nursery universe in which everything has its place and is defined by it. In a celebrated story, Borges took Bacon's reasoning to its uttermost reach, imagining a library as vast as the universe itself. In this library (which in actual fact multiplies to infinity the architecture of the old Buenos Aires National Library on Calle Méjico, where Borges was the blind director) no two books are identical. Since the shelves contain all possible combinations of the alphabet, and thus rows and rows of indecipherable gibberish, every real or imaginable book is represented: "the detailed history of the future, the autobiographies of the archangels, the faithful catalogue of the Library, thousands and thousands of false catalogues, the demonstration of the falsity of these catalogues, the demonstration of the falsity of the real catalogue, the gnostic Gospel of Basilides, the commentary on that gospel, the commentary on the commentary on that gospel, the true account of your death, a version of every book in every language, the interpolation of every book in all the other books, the treatise the Venerable Bede might have written (and never wrote) on Saxon mythology, the lost books of Tacitus." In the end, Borges's narrator (who is also a librarian), wandering through the exhausting corridors, imagines that the Library itself is part of another overwhelming category of libraries, and that the almost infinite collection of books is periodically repeated throughout a bookish eternity. "My loneliness," he concludes, "is cheered by this elegant hope."[29]

Rooms, corridors, bookcases, shelves, filing cards and computerized catalogues assume that the subjects on which our thoughts dwell are actual entities, and through this assumption a certain book may be lent a particular tone and value. Filed under Fiction, Jonathan Swift's *Gulliver's Travels* is a humorous novel of adventure; under Sociology, a satirical study of England in the eighteenth century; under Children's Literature, an entertaining fable about dwarfs and giants and talking horses; under Fantasy, a precursor of science fiction; under Travel, an imaginary voyage; under Classics, a part of the Western literary canon. Categories are exclusive; reading is not — or should not be. Whatever classifications have been chosen, every library tyrannizes the act of reading, and forces the reader — the curious reader, the alert reader — to *rescue* the book from the category to which it has been condemned.

R E A D I N G

T H E   F U T U R E

I n the year 1256, the immensely well-read scholar Vincent de Beauvais gathered the opinions of such classical authors as Lactantius and Saint Augustine and, based on their writings, listed in his vast thirteenth-century encyclopedia of the world, the *Speculum majus*, the birthplaces of the ten ancient sibyls — Cumae, Cyme, Delphi, Erythrea, the Hellespont, Libya, Persia, Phrygia, Samos and Tibur.[1] The sybils, de Beauvais explained, were oracular women who spoke in riddles — divinely inspired words that human beings were supposed to decipher. In tenth-century Iceland, in a poetic monologue known as the *Voluspa*,[2] a sibyl is made to utter these blunt words as a refrain addressed to the inquisitive reader: "Well, do you understand? Or what?"

The sibyls were immortal and almost eternal: one declared that she had begun speaking the voice of her god in the sixth generation after the Flood; another maintained that she preceded the Flood itself. But they grew old. The Sibyl of Cumae, who, "dishevelled, bosom heaving, heart swollen with wild frenzy",[3] had directed Aeneas to the underworld, lived throughout the centuries in a bottle dangling in mid air, and when children asked her what she wanted she would answer, "I want to die."[4] The sibylline prophecies — many of which were accurately composed by inspired mortal poets after the events foretold — were held to be true in Greece, Rome, Palestine and Christian Europe. Collected in nine books, they were offered by the Cumaean sibyl herself to Tarquinius Superbus, the seventh and last king of Rome.[5] He

OPPOSITE

Colossal head of the first Christian Emperor, Constantine the Great.

refused to pay, and the sibyl set fire to three of the volumes. Again he refused; she burned three more. Finally the king bought the remaining three books at the price of the original nine, and they were kept in a chest in a stone vault under the Temple of Jupiter until they were consumed in a fire in 83 BC. Centuries later, in Byzantium, twelve texts attributed to the sibyls were found and collected in a single manuscript; an incomplete version was published in 1545.

The most ancient, most venerated of the sibyls was Herophile, who had prophesied the Trojan War. Apollo offered her any gift she chose; she asked him to grant her as many years as the grains of sand she held in her hand. Regrettably, like Tithonus, she forgot to ask the god for immortal youth as well. Herophile was known as the Erythrean sibyl,[6] and two towns at least claimed to be her birthplace: Marpessos, in what is today the Turkish province of Canakkale (*erythrea* means "red dirt", and the earth of Marpessos is red), and Erythrea, farther south, in Ionia,[7] in what is today roughly the province of Izmir. In the year 162, at the beginning of the Parthian Wars, Lucius Aurelius Verus, who for eight years shared the imperial Roman throne with Marcus Aurelius, seemingly settled the question. Ignoring the claims of the citizens of Marpessos, he entered the so-called Sibyl's Cave in Ionian Erythrea and set up two statues, one of the sibyl and another of her mother, declaring on her behalf, in verses engraved in stone, "No other is my country, only Erythrea."[8] The authority of the Sibyl of Erythrea was thereby established.

In the year 330, Flavius Valerius Constantinus, whom history would remember as Constantine the Great, having defeated the army of the rival emperor Licinius six years earlier, affirmed his position as head of the world's vastest empire by moving his capital from the edge of the Tiber to the edge of the Bosphorus, to Byzantium. To underline the significance of this change of waterfront he renamed the city New Rome; the emperor's vanity and his courtiers' sycophancy changed it once again, to Constantinople — the City of Constantine.

To make the city fit for an emperor, Constantine enlarged the old Byzantium both physically and spiritually. Its language was Greek; its political organization was Roman; its religion — largely through the influence of Constantine's mother, Saint Helena — was Christian. Brought up in Nicomedia, in the Eastern Roman Empire, at the court of Diocletian, Constantine had become familiar with much of the rich

Latin literature of classical Rome. In Greek he felt less comfortable; when later in life he was obliged to deliver speeches in the Greek tongue of his subjects, he would first compose them in Latin and then read out translations prepared by educated slaves. Constantine's family, originally from Asia Minor, had worshipped the sun as Apollo, the Unconquered God, whom the Emperor Aurelian had introduced as the supreme deity of Rome in 274.[9] It was from the sun that Constantine received a vision of the Cross bearing the motto *In hoc vinces* ("By this you shall be victorious") before his battle with Licinius;[10] the symbol of Constantine's new city became the sun's rayed crown made, so it was believed, from the nails of the True Cross which his mother had disinterred close to the hill of Calvary.[11] So powerful was the radiance of the sun god that barely seventeen years after Constantine's death, the date of the birth of Christ — Christmas — was transferred to the winter solstice — the birthday of the sun.[12]

In 313 Constantine and Licinius (with whom Constantine then shared the government of the empire and whom he would later betray) met in Milan to discuss "the welfare and security of the realm" and declared, in a famous edict, that "of the things that are of profit to all mankind, the worship of God ought rightly to be our first and chiefest care, and it is right that Christians and all others should have freedom to follow the kind of religion they favour."[13] With this Edict of Milan, Constantine officially ended the persecution of Christians in the Roman empire, who until then had been regarded as outlaws and traitors, and punished accordingly. But the persecuted turned persecutors: to assert the authority of the new state religion, several Christian leaders adopted the methods of their old enemies. In Alexandria, for example, where the legendary Catherine was supposed to have been martyred on a spiked and wooden wheel by the Emperor Maxentius, in 361 the bishop himself led the assault on the Temple of Mithras, the Persian god who was a favourite among soldiers and became the one really serious competitor to the religion of Christ; in 391 the patriarch Theophilus pillaged the Temple of Dionysus — the god of fertility, whose cult was celebrated in mysteries of great secrecy — and urged the Christian crowd to destroy the great statue of the Egyptian god Serapis; in 415 the patriarch Cyrillus ordered a crowd of young Christians to enter the house of Hypatia, the pagan philosopher and mathematician, drag her out into the streets, hack her to pieces and burn her remains in the public square.[14] It must be said that Cyrillus himself was not much loved.

After his death in 444, one of the bishops of Alexandria pronounced the following funeral eulogy: "At last this odious man is dead. His departure causes his survivors to rejoice, but is bound to distress the dead. They will not be long in becoming fed up with him and sending him back to us. Therefore, place a very heavy stone on his tomb so that we will not run the risk of seeing him again, even as a ghost."[15]

Christianity became, like the religion of the powerful Egyptian goddess Isis or of the Persians' Mithras, a fashionable religion, and in the Christian church of Constantinople, second only to St. Peter's in Rome, the faithful rich came and went among the faithful poor, parading such an array of silks and jewellery (on which enamelled and embroidered Christian stories had replaced the myths of the pagan gods) that Saint John Chrysostom, patriarch of the church, would stand on the steps and follow them with a reproving glare. The rich complained to no avail; from transfixing them with his eyes, Saint Chrysostom began lashing them with his tongue, denouncing from the pulpit their excesses. It was unseemly, he thundered eloquently (the name "Chrysostom" means "golden-tongued"), that a single nobleman might own ten or twenty houses and up to two thousand slaves, and possess doors carved out of ivory, floors of glittering mosaics and furniture inlaid with precious stones.[16]

But Christianity was still far from being a secure political force. There was the danger of Sassanian Persia, which from a nation of weak Parthians had become a fiercely expanding state that three centuries later was to conquer almost the entire Roman East.[17] There was the danger of heresies: the Manicheans, for instance, who believed that the universe was controlled not by one omnipotent god but by two antagonistic powers, and who, like the Christians, had missionaries and holy texts and were gaining adepts as far as Turkestan and China. There was the danger of political dissension: Constantine's father, Constantius, had controlled only the eastern part of the Roman empire, and in the farthest corners of the realm administrators were shifting their loyalties from Rome to their own domains. There was the problem of high inflation, which Constantine made more serious by flooding the market with gold expropriated from the pagan temples. There were the Jews, with their books and religious arguments. And there were still the pagans. What Constantine needed was not the tolerance preached in his own Milan edict, but a strict, no-nonsense, far-reaching, authoritarian Christianity, with deep roots in the past and a stern promise for the future, established through earthly powers and laws and customs for the greater glory of both emperor and God.

In May 325, in Nicaea, Constantine presented himself to his bishops as "the bishop of external things" and declared his recent military campaigns against Licinius to have been "a war against corrupt paganism".[18] For his efforts, Constantine would be seen from then on as a leader sanctioned by divine power, an emissary of the godhead itself. (When he died in 337, he was buried in Constantinople next to the cenotaphs of the twelve Apostles, the implication being that he had become a posthumous thirteenth. After his death, he was usually depicted in ecclesiastical iconography as receiving the imperial crown from the hand of God Himself.)

Constantine saw that it was necessary to establish the exclusivity of the religion he had chosen for his state. To do this, he decided to wield against the pagans the pagan heroes themselves. On Good Friday of that same year, 325, in Antioch, the emperor addressed a congregation of Christian followers, including bishops and theologians, and spoke to them about what he called "the eternal truth of Christianity". "My desire," he said to the assembly — which he called "the Assembly of Saints" — "is to derive even from foreign sources a testimony to the Divine nature of Christ. For on such testimony it is evident that even those who blaspheme His name must acknowledge that He is God, and the Son of God, if indeed they will accredit the words of those whose sentiments coincided with their own."[19] To prove this, Constantine invoked the Erythrean sibyl.

Constantine told his audience how the sibyl, in times long past, had been given over "by the folly of her parents" to the service of Apollo, and how "in the sanctuary of her vain superstition" she had answered the questions of Apollo's followers. "On one occasion, however," he explained, the sibyl "became really filled with inspiration from above, and declared in prophetic verses the future purposes of God, plainly indicating the advent of Jesus by the initial letters of a series of verses that formed an acrostic with these words: JESUS CHRIST, SON OF GOD, SAVIOUR, CROSS." Then Constantine proceeded to declaim the sibyl's poem.

Magically, the poem (which in English translation begins "Judgement! Earth's oozing pores shall mark the day") indeed contains the divine acrostic. To refute any possible skeptics, Constantine immediately acknowledged the obvious explanation: "that some one professing our faith, and not unacquainted with the poetic art, was the composer of these verses." But this possibility he dismissed: "Truth, however, in this case is evident, since the diligence of our countrymen has made a careful computation of the times, so that there is no room to suspect that this poem was composed after the advent and condemnation of

A woodcut of the Erythrean Sibyl in a 1473 edition of Boccaccio's *De claris mulieribus*.

Christ." Furthermore, "Cicero was acquainted with this poem, which he translated into the Latin tongue, and incorporated with his own works." Unfortunately, the passage in which Cicero mentions the sibyl — the Cumaean, not the Erythrean — contains no reference to either these verses or the acrostic, and is in fact a refutation of prophetic predictions.[20] Nevertheless, so convenient was this marvellous revelation that for many centuries afterwards the Christian world accepted the sibyl among its forebears. Saint Augustine gave her a home among the blessed in his City of God.[21] At the end of the twelfth century, the architects of the Cathedral of Laon sculpted on its façade the Erythrean sibyl (decapitated during the French Revolution) carrying her oracular tablets, shaped like those of Moses, and inscribed at her feet the second line of the apocryphal poem[22] And four hundred years later Michelangelo placed her on the ceiling of the Sistine Chapel, as one of the four sibyls complementing the four Old Testament prophets.

The Sibyl was the pagan oracle, and Constantine had made her speak in the name of Jesus Christ. Constantine now turned his attention to pagan poetry and announced that the "prince of Latin poets" had also been inspired by a Saviour he could not have known. Virgil had written an eclogue to honour his patron, Gaius Asinius Pollio, founder of Rome's first public library; the eclogue announced the arrival of a new golden age, born in the guise of a baby boy:

Begin, sweet boy! with smiles thy mother know,
Who ten long months did with thy burden go.

No mortal parents smiled upon thy birth:
No nuptial joy thou know'st, no feast on earth.[23]

Traditionally, prophecies were held to be infallible, so it was easier to change the historical circumstances than to alter the words of a prophecy. A century earlier, Ardashir, the first Sassanian king, had rearranged historical chronology to make a Zoroastrian prophecy benefit his empire. Zoroaster had prophesied that the Persian empire and religion would be destroyed after a thousand years. He had lived about 250 years before Alexander the Great, who had died 549 years before Ardashir's reign. In order to add two centuries to his dynasty, Ardashir proclaimed that his reign had begun only 260 years after Alexander. Constantine chose to alter neither history nor the prophetic words; instead he had Virgil translated into Greek with an elastic poetic licence that achieved his political purpose.

Constantine read out passages from the translated poem to his audience, and now everything the Good Book chronicled was here, in Virgil's ancient words: the Virgin, the long-desired Messiah King, the righteous elect, the Holy Spirit. Constantine discreetly chose to forget those passages in which Virgil mentioned the pagan gods, Apollo, Pan and Saturn. Ancient characters who couldn't be omitted became metaphors of Christ's coming. "Another Helen shall other wars create, / And great Achilles urge the Trojan fate," Virgil had written. This, said Constantine, was Christ "proceeding to the war against Troy, understanding by Troy the world itself." In other cases, Constantine told his audience, the pagan references were devices by which Virgil fooled the Roman authorities. "I suppose," he said (and we can imagine him lowering his voice after the loud declamation of Virgil's verses), "he was restrained by a sense of danger which threatened one who should assail the credit of ancient religious practice. Cautiously, therefore, and securely, as far as possible, he presents the truth to those who have faculties to understand it."

"Those who have faculties to understand it": the text became a ciphered message that could be read by only a select few who possessed the necessary "faculties". It was not open to any number of interpretations; for Constantine, only one reading was the true one, and to that reading he and his fellow believers alone held the key. The Edict of Milan had offered freedom of faith to all Roman citizens; the Council of Nicaea limited this freedom to those who held Constantine's creed.

In barely twelve years, people who had in Milan been granted the public right to read as they pleased and what they pleased were now, under
pain of lawful punishment, told in Antioch and again in Nicaea that
only one reading was true. To stipulate a single reading for a religious
text was necessary in Constantine's conception of a unanimous empire; more original and less comprehensible is the notion of a single
orthodox reading for a secular text such as Virgil's poems.

Every reader imparts to certain books a certain reading, albeit not as
far-fetched nor as far-reaching as Constantine's. To see a parable of exile
in *The Wizard of Oz*, as Salman Rushdie does,[24] is very different from
reading into Virgil a foretelling of the coming of Christ. And yet something of the same sleight of hand or expression of faith takes place in
both these readings, something that allows the readers, if not to be con-
vincing, at least to show themselves convinced. At the age of thirteen or
fourteen I developed a literary longing for London, and I read the Sherlock Holmes stories with absolute certainty that the smoky Baker
Street room, with its Turkish slipper for tobacco and its table stained
with foul chemicals, faithfully resembled the lodgings I would someday
have when I too was in Arcadia. The obnoxious creatures Alice found on
the other side of the looking-glass, petulant, peremptory and constantly nagging, foreshadowed so many of the adults of my adolescent
life. And when Robinson Crusoe began building his hut, "a Tent under
the Side of a Rock, surrounded with a strong Pale of Posts and Cables",
I knew he was describing the one I would build myself one summer, on
the beach in Punta del Este. The novelist Anita Desai, who as a child in
India was known in her family as a *Lese Ratte* or "reading rat", a bookworm, remembers how, when she discovered *Wuthering Heights* at the
age of nine, her own world "of an Old Delhi bungalow, its verandas and
plastered walls and ceiling fans, its garden of papaya and guava trees full
of shrieking parakeets, the gritty dust that settled on the pages of a
book before one could turn them, all receded. What became real, daz-
zlingly real, through the power and magic of Emily Brontë's pen, were
the Yorkshire moors, the storm-driven heath, the torments of its
anguished inhabitants who roamed thereon in rain and sleet, crying out
from the depths of their broken hearts and hearing only ghosts reply."[25]
The words Emily Brontë wrote to describe a young girl in England in
1847 served to illuminate a young girl in India in 1946.

Using random passages of books to foretell one's future has a long tradition in the West, and, well before Constantine, Virgil was the preferred source for pagan divination in the empire; copies of his poems were kept for consultation in several of the temples dedicated to the Goddess Fortune.[26] The first reference[27] to this custom, known as *sortes Vergilianae*, appears in Aelius Spartianus's life of Hadrian, which says that the young Hadrian, wishing to know what the Emperor Trajan thought of him, consulted Virgil's *Aeneid* at random and found the lines in which Aeneas sees "the Roman king whose laws shall establish Rome anew". Hadrian was satisfied; indeed, it came to pass that Trajan adopted him as his son and Hadrian became the new emperor of Rome.[28]

In encouraging a new version of the *sortes Vergilianae*, Constantine was following the trend of his time. By the end of the fourth century, the prestige attached to spoken oracles and soothsayers had shifted to the written word, to Virgil but also to the Bible, and a form of divination known as "gospel cleromancy" had developed.[29] Four hundred years later, the art of divination, which had been proscribed as "an abomination unto the Lord"[30] in the time of the prophets, had become so popular that in 829 the Council of Paris had to condemn it officially. To no avail — writing a personal memoir in Latin, published in 1434 in a French translation, the scholar Gaspar Peucer confessed that as a child he had "made a book out of paper and written therein the principal divinatory verses of Virgil, from which I'd draw conjectures — in play and merely as entertainment — about everything I found pleasing, such as the life and death of princes, about my adventures and about other things, in order to better and more vividly impress those verses in my mind."[31] Peucer insisted that the game had a mnemonic and not a divinatory intention, but the context makes it hard to believe his protestations.

In the sixteenth century the divinatory game was still so firmly established that Rabelais could parody the custom in Pantagruel's advice to Panurge on whether or not to marry. Panurge, Pantagruel says, must resort to the *sortes Vergilianae*. The correct method, he explains, is this: a page is chosen by opening the book at random; then three dice are thrown, and the sum of them indicates a line on a page.[32] When the method is put into practice, Pantagruel and Panurge come up with opposing and equally possible interpretations of the verses.

Bomarzo, the vast novel on the Italian Renaissance by the Argentinian Manuel Mujica Láinez, alludes to how familiar seventeenth-century society was with divination through Virgil: "I would trust my fate to the decision of other gods, more sovereign than the Orsini, by means of the *sortes Vergilianae*. At Bomarzo we used to practise this popular form of divination, which trusted the resolution of difficult or trivial problems to the fortuitous oracle of a book. Did not the blood of magicians run through Virgil's veins? Do we not, thanks to Dante's charm, consider him a wizard, a soothsayer? I'd submit to what the *Aeneid* decreed."[33]

Perhaps the most famous example of the *sortes* is that of King Charles I visiting a library in Oxford during the Civil Wars, at the end of 1642 or the beginning of 1643. To entertain him, Lord Falkland suggested that the king "make a trial of his fortunes by the *sortes Vergilianae*, which everybody knows was an usual kind of augury some ages past." The king opened the book to a passage in Book IV of the *Aeneid* and read, "May he be harried in war by audacious tribes, and exiled from his own land".[34] On Tuesday, January 30, 1649, condemned as a traitor by his own people, Charles I was beheaded at Whitehall.

Some seventy years later, Robinson Crusoe was still availing himself of a similar method on his inhospitable island: "One Morning," he wrote, "being very sad, I open'd the Bible upon these Words, *I will never, never leave thee, nor forsake thee*; immediately it occur'd, That these Words were to me, Why else should they be directed in such a Manner, just at the Moment when I was mourning over my Condition, as one forsaken of God and Man?"[35] And just over 150 years after that, Bathsheba still turned to the Bible to find out whether she should marry Mr. Boldwood in *Far from the Madding Crowd*.[36]

Robert Louis Stevenson astutely noted that the oracular gift of a writer such as Virgil has less to do with supernatural gifts than with poetry's mimetic qualities, which allow a line of verse to signal, intimately and powerfully, to readers across the ages. In *The Ebb Tide* one of Stevenson's characters, lost on a faraway island, seeks to know his fortune in a tattered copy of Virgil, and the poet, replying from the page "with no very certain or encouraging voice", stirs in the outcast visions of his native land. "For it is the destiny of those grave, restrained and classic writers," wrote Stevenson, "with whom we make enforced and often painful acquaintanceship at school, to pass into the blood and become native in the memory; so that a phrase of Virgil speaks not so much of Mantua or Augustus, but of English places and the student's own irrevocable youth."[37]

Constantine was the first to read prophetic Christian meanings into Virgil, and through his reading Virgil became the most prestigious of all oracular writers. From imperial poet to Christian visionary, Virgil assumed an important role in Christian mythology, enabling him, ten centuries after Constantine's encomium, to guide Dante through hell and purgatory. His prestige even flowed backwards; a story preserved in verse in the medieval Latin Mass tells that Saint Paul himself travelled to Naples to weep over the ancient poet's tomb.

What Constantine discovered on that distant Good Friday, and for all time, is that the meaning of a text is enlarged by the reader's capabilities and desires. Faced with a text, the reader can transform the words into a message that deciphers for him or her a question historically unrelated to the text itself or to its author. This transmigration of meaning can enlarge or impoverish the text itself; invariably it imbues the text with the circumstances of the reader. Through ignorance, through faith, through intelligence, through trickery and cunning, through illumination, the reader rewrites the text with the same words of the original but under another heading, re-creating it, as it were, in the very act of bringing it into being.

THE SYMBOLIC
READER

OPPOSITE

"Hospice de Beaune" by André Kertész.

I n 1929, in the Hospice de Beaune, in France, the Hungarian photographer André Kertész, who had trained himself in the craft during his service with the Austro-Hungarian army, took a picture of an old woman sitting up in her bed, reading.[1] It is a perfectly framed composition. In the centre is the diminutive woman, wrapped in a black shawl and wearing a black night-cap that unexpectedly reveals the gathered hair at the back of her head; white pillows prop her up and a white coverlet drapes her feet. Around and behind her, white bunched-up curtains hang among the bed's black wooden columns of Gothic design. Further inspection reveals, on the top frame of the bed, a small plaque with the number 19, a knotted cord dangling from the bed's ceiling (to call for assistance? to draw the front curtain?) and a night-table bearing a box, a jug and a cup. On the floor, under the table, is a tin basin. Have we seen everything? No. The woman is reading, holding the book open at a fair distance from her obviously still keen eyes. But *what* is she reading? Because she's an old woman, because she's in bed, because the bed is in an old people's home in Beaune, in the heart of Catholic Burgundy, we believe that we can guess the nature of her book: a devotional volume, a compendium of sermons? If it were so — close inspection with a magnifying glass tells us nothing — the image would somehow be coherent, complete, the book defining its reader and identifying her bed as a spiritually quiet place.

But what if we were to discover that the book was in fact something else? What if, for instance, she was reading Racine, Corneille —

a sophisticated, cultured reader — or, more surprisingly, Voltaire? Or what if the book turned out to be Cocteau's *Les Enfants terribles*, that scandalous novel of bourgeois life published the same year Kertész took her picture? Suddenly the commonplace old woman is no longer commonplace; she becomes, through the tiny act of holding one book in her hands instead of another, a questioner, a spirit still burning with curiosity, a rebel.

Sitting across from me in the subway in Toronto, a woman is reading the Penguin edition of Borges's *Labyrinths*. I want to call out to her, to wave a hand and signal that I too am of that faith. She, whose face I have forgotten, whose clothes I barely noticed, young or old I can't say, is closer to me, by the mere act of holding that particular book in her hands, than many others I see daily. A cousin of mine from Buenos Aires was deeply aware that books could function as a badge, a sign of alliance, and always chose a book to take on her travels with the same care with which she chose her handbag. She would not travel with Romain Rolland because she thought it made her look too pretentious, or with Agatha Christie because it made her look too vulgar. Camus was appropriate for a short trip, Cronin for a long one; a detective story by Vera Caspary or Ellery Queen was acceptable for a weekend in the country; a Graham Greene novel was suitable for travelling by ship or plane.

The association of books with their readers is unlike any other between objects and their users. Tools, furniture, clothes — all have a symbolic function, but books inflict upon their readers a symbolism far more complex than that of a simple utensil. The mere possession of books implies social standing and a certain intellectual richness; in eighteenth-century Russia, during the reign of Catherine the Great, a certain Mr. Klostermann made a fortune by selling long rows of binding stuffed with waste paper, which allowed courtiers to create the illusion of a library and thereby garner the favour of their bookish empress.[2] In our day, interior decorators line walls with yards of books to give a room a "sophisticated" atmosphere, or offer wallpaper that creates the illusion of a library,[3] and TV talk-show producers believe that a background of bookshelves adds a touch of intelligence to a set. In these cases, the general notion of books is enough to denote lofty pursuits, just as red velvet furniture has come to suggest sensual pleasures. So important is the symbol of the book that its presence or absence can, in the eyes of the viewer, lend or deprive a character of intellectual power.

In the year 1333 the painter Simone Martini completed an Annunciation for the central panel of an altarpiece for the Duomo of Siena — the first surviving Western altar dedicated to this subject.[4] The scene is inscribed within three Gothic arches: a high arch in the centre containing a formation of angels in dark gold, encircling the Holy Spirit in the shape of a dove, and a smaller arch to each side. Beneath the arch on the viewer's left a kneeling angel in embroidered vestments holds an

olive branch in his left hand; he raises the index finger of his right hand
to indicate silence with the rhetorical gesture common in ancient
Greek and Roman statuary. Beneath the right arch, on a gilded throne
inlaid with ivory, sits the Virgin in a purple cloak fringed with gold.
Next to her, in the middle of the panel, is a vase of lilies. The immacu-
lately white flower, with its asexual blooms and lack of stamens, served
as a perfect emblem of Mary, whose purity Saint Bernard compared to
the "inviolate chastity of the lily".[5] The lily, the fleur-de-lis, was also the
symbol of the city of Florence, and towards the end of the Middle Ages
it replaced the herald's staff borne by the angel in Florentine Annunci-
ations.[6] Sienese painters, arch-enemies of the Florentines, could not
entirely delete the traditional fleur-de-lis from depictions of the Virgin, but they would not honour Florence by allowing the angel to carry
the city's flower. Therefore Martini's angel bears an olive branch, the
plant symbolic of Siena.[7]

For someone seeing the painting in Martini's time, every object
and every colour had a specific significance. Though blue later became
the Virgin's colour (the colour of heavenly love, the colour of truth
seen after the clouds are dispelled),[8] purple, the colour of authority
and also of pain and penitence, stood in Martini's day as a reminder of
the Virgin's coming sorrows. In a popular account of her early life, in
the apocryphal second-century *Protoevangelion* of James[9] (a remarkable
bestseller throughout the Middle Ages, with which Martini's public
would have been familiar), it is told that the council of priests required
a new veil for a temple. Seven undefiled virgins from the tribe of David
were chosen, and lots were cast to see who would spin the wool for
each of the seven requisite colours; the colour purple fell to Mary.
Before starting to spin, she went to the well to draw water and there
heard a voice that said to her, "Hail thou art full of grace, the Lord is
with thee; thou art blessed among women." Mary looked right and left
(the protoevangelist notes with a novelist's touch), saw no one and,
trembling, entered her house and sat down to work at her purple
wool. "And behold the angel of the Lord stood by her, and said, Fear
not, Mary, for thou hast found favour in the sight of God."[10] Thus, before Martini, the herald angel, the purple cloth and the lily — representing in turn acceptance of the word of God, acceptance of suffering
and immaculate virginity — marked the qualities for which the Christian Church wanted Mary to be honoured.[11] Then, in 1333, Martini
placed in her hands a book.

Traditionally, in Christian iconography, the book or scroll belonged to the male deity, to either God the Father or the triumphant
Christ, the new Adam, in whom the word of God had been made
flesh.[12] The book was the repository of God's law; when the governor
of Roman Africa asked a group of Christian prisoners what they had
brought with them to defend themselves in court, they replied, "Texts
by Paul, a just man".[13] The book also conferred intellectual authority,
and from the earliest representations Christ was often depicted exercising the rabbinical functions of teacher, interpreter, scholar, reader.
To the woman belonged the Child, affirming her role as mother.

Not everyone agreed. Two centuries before Martini, Peter
Abelard, the canon of Notre Dame in Paris who had been castrated as
a punishment for seducing his pupil Heloise, initiated a correspon-
dence with his old beloved, now abbess of the Paraclete, that was to
become famous. In these letters Abelard, who had been condemned
by the councils of Sens and Soissons and prohibited either to teach or
to write by Pope Innocent II, suggested that women were in fact closer
to Christ than any man. Against man's obsession with war, violence,
honour and power, Abelard counterpoised woman's refinement of
soul and intelligence, "capable of conversing with God the Spirit in the
inner kingdom of the soul on terms of intimate friendship".[14] A
contemporary of Abelard, the abbess Hildegard of Bingen, one of the
greatest intellectual figures of her century, maintained that the weakness of the Church was a male weakness, and that women were to
make use of the strength of their sex in this *tempus muliebre*, this Age of
Woman.[15]

But the entrenched hostility against women was not to be overcome easily. God's admonition to Eve in Genesis 3: 16 was used again
and again to preach the virtues of womanly meekness and mildness:
"thy desire shall be to thy husband, and he shall rule over thee."
"Woman was created to be man's helpmate," paraphrased Saint Thomas
Aquinas.[16] In Martini's time, Saint Bernardine of Siena, perhaps the
most popular preacher of his age, saw Martini's Mary not as conversant
with God the Spirit but as an example of the submissive, dutiful
woman. "It seems to me," he wrote, reviewing the painting, "surely the
most beautiful, the most reverent, the most modest pose you ever saw
in an Annunciation. You see she does not gaze at the angel, but sits with
that almost frightened pose. She knew well it was an angel, so why
should she be disturbed? What would she have done if it had been a

man? Take her as an example, girls, of what you should do. Never talk to a man unless your father or mother is present."[17]

In such a context, to associate Mary with intellectual power was a bold act. In the introduction to a textbook written for his students in Paris, Abelard made clear the value of intellectual curiosity: "By doubting we come to questioning, and by questioning we learn truth".[18] Intellectual power came from curiosity, but for Abelard's detractors — whose misogynistic voices Saint Bernardine echoed — curiosity, especially in women, was a sin, the sin that had led Eve to taste the forbidden fruit of knowledge. The virginal innocence of women was to be preserved at all costs.[19]

In Saint Bernardine's view, education was the dangerous result of, and the cause of more, curiosity. As we have seen, most women throughout the fourteenth century — indeed throughout most of the Middle Ages — were educated only as far as was useful to a man's household. Depending on their social standing, the young girls familiar to Martini would receive little or no intellectual teaching. If they were brought up in an aristocratic family, they would be trained as ladies-in-waiting or taught to run an estate, for which they required only rudimentary instruction in reading and writing, though many became quite literate. If they belonged to the merchant class, they would develop some business ability, for which a little reading, writing and mathematics was essential. Merchants and artisans sometimes taught their trades to their daughters, who were then expected to become unpaid assistants. Peasant children, both male and female, usually received no education at all.[20] In the religious orders women sometimes followed intellectual pursuits, but they did so under the constant censorship of their male religious superiors. As schools and universities were mostly closed to women, the artistic and scholarly blooming of the late twelfth to fourteenth century centred around the men.[21] The women whose remarkable work emerged during that time — such as Hildegard of Bingen, Julian of Norwich, Christine de Pisan and Marie de France — succeeded against seemingly impossible odds.

In this context, Martini's Mary requires a second, less cursory look. She sits awkwardly, her right hand tightly gripping her cloak beneath her chin, turning her body away from the strange presence, her eyes fixed not on the angelic eyes but (contrary to Saint Bernardine's biased description) on the angelic lips. The words the angel pronounces stream from his mouth to Mary's gaze, written in large letters of gold; Mary can not only hear but see the Annunciation. Her left hand holds the book she was reading, keeping it open with her thumb. It is a fair-sized volume, probably an octavo, bound in red.

But what book is it?

Twenty years before Martini's painting was completed, Giotto had given the Mary of his Annunciation a small blue Book of Hours, in one of the frescoes of the Arena Chapel in Padua. From the thirteenth century onwards, the Book of Hours (apparently developed in the eighth century by Benedict of Anane as a supplement to the canonical office) had been the common private prayer-book for the rich, and its popularity continued well into the fifteenth and sixteenth centuries — as seen in numerous depictions of the Annunciation, in which the Virgin is represented reading her Book of Hours much as any royal or noble lady would have done. In many of the wealthier households, the Book of Hours was the only book, and mothers and nurses would use it to teach their children to read.[22]

A detail of Giotto's *Annunciation* in the Arena of Padua.

It is possible that Martini's Mary is simply reading a Book of Hours. But it might also be another book. According to the tradition that saw in the New Testament the fulfilment of the prophecies made in the Old — a popular belief in Martini's day — Mary would have been aware, after the Annunciation, that the events of her life and her Son's had been foretold in Isaiah and in the so-called Wisdom Books of the Bible: Proverbs, Job and Ecclesiastes, and two books of the Apocrypha, *The Wisdom of Jesus, the Son of Sirach* and *The Wisdom of Solomon.*[23] In the sort of literary parallelism that delighted medieval audiences, Martini's Mary might have been reading, just before the arrival of the angel, the very chapter of Isaiah that announces her own fate: "Behold, a virgin shall conceive, and bear a son, and shall call his name Immanuel."[24]

But it is even more illuminating to surmise that Martini's Mary is reading the Books of Wisdom.[25]

In the ninth chapter of the Book of Proverbs, Wisdom is represented as a woman who "hath builded her house, she hath hewn out her seven pillars: . . . She hath sent forth her maidens: she crieth upon the highest places of the city, Whoso is simple, let him turn in hither: as for him that wanteth understanding, she saith to him, Come, eat of my bread, and drink of the wine which I have mingled".[26] And in two other sections of Proverbs, Lady Wisdom is described as originating from God. Through her He "hath founded the earth" (3: 19) at the beginning of all things; "I was set up from everlasting, from the beginning, or ever the earth was" (8: 23). Centuries later, the Rabbi of Lublin explained that Wisdom was called "Mother" because "when a man confesses and repents, when his heart accepts Understanding and is converted by it, he becomes like a new-born child, and his own turning to God is like turning to his mother."[27]

Lady Wisdom is the protagonist of one of the most popular books of the fifteenth century, *L'Orloge de Sapience* (*The Hourglass of Wisdom*), written in (or translated into) French in 1389 by a Franciscan friar from Lorraine, Henri Suso.[28] Sometime between 1455 and 1460, an artist known to us as the Master of Jean Rolin created for it a series of exquisite illuminations. One of these miniatures depicts Wisdom sitting on her throne, surrounded by a garland of crimson angels, holding in her left arm the globe of the world and in her right hand an open book.

The Virgin represented with the attributes of Wisdom in an illuminated manuscript of Henri Suso's *L'Orloge de Sapience*.

Above her, on both sides, larger angels kneel in a starry sky; below her, to her right, five monks discuss two scholarly tomes open in front of them; to her left a crowned donor, with a book set open on a draped lectern, is praying to her. Her position is identical to that of God the Father, who sits on just such a golden throne in countless other illuminations, usually as a companion piece to the Crucifixion, holding an orb in His left hand and a book in His right, and circled by similar fiery angels.

Carl Jung, associating Mary with the Eastern Christian concept of Sophia or Wisdom, suggested that Sophia-Mary "reveals herself to men as a friendly helper and advocate against Yahweh, and shows them the bright side, the kind, just, and amiable aspect of their God".[29] Sophia, the Lady Wisdom of the Proverbs and of Suso's *Orloge*, stems from the ancient tradition of the Mother Goddess whose carved images, the so-called Venus figurines, are found all over Europe and Northern Africa, dating back to between 25,000 and 15,000 BC, and throughout the world at later dates.[30] When the Spaniards and Portuguese arrived in the New World carrying their swords and their crosses, the Aztecs and Incas (among other native peoples) transferred their beliefs in various earth-mother deities such as Tonantzin and Pacha Mama to an androgynous Christ still evident in Latin American religious art today.[31]

Around the year 500 the Frankish emperor Clovis, after converting to Christianity and reinforcing the role of the Church, banned the worship of the Goddess of Wisdom under her several guises — Diana, Isis, Athena — and closed down the last of her temples.[32] Clovis's decision followed to the letter Saint Paul's declaration (I Corinthians 1: 24) that only Christ is "the wisdom of God". The attribute of wisdom, now usurped from the female deity, became exemplified in the vast and ancient iconography depicting Christ as a book-bearer. About twenty-five years after Clovis's death, the Emperor Justinian attended the consecration of Constantinople's newly finished cathedral, Hagia Sophia (Holy Wisdom) — one of the largest man-made structures of antiquity. There, tradition has it, he exclaimed, "Solomon, I have outdone thee!"[33] Not one of the famous mosaics of Hagia Sophia — not even the majestic Virgin Enthroned of 867 — allows Mary a book. Even in her own temple, Wisdom remained subservient.

Against this historical background, Martini's portrayal of Mary as the inheritor — perhaps the incarnation — of Holy Wisdom may be regarded as an effort to restore the intellectual power denied to the female godhead. The book Mary is holding in Martini's painting, whose text is hidden from us and whose title we can only guess, might suggest itself as the last utterance of the dethroned goddess, a goddess older than history, silenced by a society that has chosen to make its god in the image of a man. Suddenly, in this light, Martini's *Annunciation* becomes subversive.[34]

Little is known of Simone Martini's life. It is likely that he was a disciple of Duccio di Buoninsegna, the father of Sienese painting; Martini's first dated work, his *Maestà* of 1315, is based on Duccio's model. He worked in Pisa, Assisi and of course Siena, and in 1340 moved to Avignon, to the papal court, where two ruined frescoes on the portal of the cathedral are all that remain of his work.[35] We know nothing of his education, of his intellectual influences, of the discussions he may have had about women and power and the Mother of God and Our Lady of

Wisdom, but in the red-bound book that he painted sometime during the year 1333 for the Siena cathedral he left perhaps a clue to those questions, and possibly a statement.

Martini's *Annunciation* was copied at least seven times.[36] Technically it provided painters with an alternative to the sober realism put forward by Giotto in his Padua *Annunciation*; philosophically it may have enlarged the scope of Mary's reading from Giotto's minute Book of Hours to an entire theological compendium with roots in the earliest beliefs in the wisdom of the goddess. In later depictions of Mary,[37] the Christ Child rumples or tears a page of the book she is reading, indicating His intellectual superiority. The Child's gesture represents the New Testament brought by Christ superseding the old one, but for late-medieval viewers, to whom Mary's relation to the Books of Wisdom may still have been apparent, the image served also as a reminder of Saint Paul's misogynist dictum.

The Child Jesus tearing the pages of the Old Testament, showing that the New One is coming into being, in Rogier van der Weyden's *Virgin and Child*, c. 1450.

I know that, for me, seeing someone reading creates in my mind a curious metonymy in which the reader's identity is coloured by the book and the setting in which it is being read. It seems appropriate that Alexander the Great, who shares in the popular imagination the mythical landscape of Homer's heroes, always carried with him a copy of the *Iliad* and the *Odyssey*.[38] I'd love to know what book Hamlet held in his hands when he dismissed Polonius's question — "What do you read, my lord?" — with "Words, words, words"; that elusive title might tell me a little more about the prince's cloudy character.[39] The priest who saved Joan Martorell's *Tirant lo Blanc* from the pyre to which he and the barber had destined Don Quixote's maddening library,[40] rescued for future generations an extraordinary novel of chivalry; by knowing exactly *what* book Don Quixote was reading we can understand a little of the world which fascinated the doleful knight — a reading through which we too can become, for a moment, Don Quixote.

Sometimes the process is reversed, and knowing the reader affects our judgement of a book: "I used to read him by candle-light, or by moonlight with the help of a huge magnifying glass," said Adolf Hitler

Islamic fundamentalists burning a copy of Salman Rushdie's *The Satanic Verses.*

of the adventure-story writer Karl May,[41] thereby condemning the author of such Wild West novels as *The Treasure of the Silver Lake* to the fate of Richard Wagner, whose music wasn't publicly performed in Israel for years because Hitler had praised it.

During the early months of the *fatwa* against Salman Rushdie, when it became public knowledge that an author had been threatened with death for writing a novel, the American TV reporter John Innes kept a copy of *The Satanic Verses* on his desk whenever he delivered one of his commentaries on any number of subjects. He made no reference to the book or to Rushdie, or to the Ayatollah, but the novel's presence by his elbow indicated one reader's solidarity with the fate of the book and its author.

READING

WITHIN WALLS

T he stationery shop around the corner from my house in Buenos Aires had a fair selection of books for children. I had (and have still) a lustful craving for notebooks (which in Argentina used to carry the profile of one of our national heroes on the cover, and sometimes a detachable page of gummed stickers depicting natural history or battle scenes) and I often hung about the shop. The stationery was in the front; in the back were the rows of books. There were the large, illustrated books of the Editorial Abril, with big letters and bright drawings, written for little children by Constancio C. Vigil (who, at his death, was discovered to have amassed one of the largest collections of pornographic literature in Latin America). There were (as I've mentioned) the yellow-covered books of the Robin Hood series. And there were twin rows of books with cardboard covers in a pocket format, some bound in green and some bound in pink. In the green series were the adventures of King Arthur, dreadful Spanish translations of the Just William books, *The Three Musketeers*, the animal stories of Horacio Quiroga. In the pink series were the novels of Louisa May Alcott, *Uncle Tom's Cabin*, the stories of the Comtesse de Ségur, the entire Heidi saga. One of my girl cousins loved to read (later, one summer, I borrowed from her John Dickson Carr's *The Black Spectacles* and was hooked on detective fiction for the rest of my life) and we both read Salgari's pirate adventures, bound in yellow. Sometimes she borrowed a Just William book from me, in the series bound in green. But the pink-bound series, which she read with impunity, was (at the age of

OPPOSITE

Court women of medieval times depicted in a woodcut by Hishikawa Moronobu in the 1681 edition of the *Ukiyo Hyakunin Onna*.

ten I distinctly knew) forbidden to me. Its covers were a warning, brighter than any spotlight, that these were books no proper boy would read. These books were for girls.

The notion that certain books are intended for the eyes of certain groups only is almost as ancient as literature itself. Some scholars have suggested that, as the Greek epics and theatre were directed primarily at a male audience, the early Greek novels were most likely intended for a predominantly female one.[1]

Though Plato wrote that in his ideal republic schooling would be compulsory for both boys and girls,[2] one of his disciples, Theophrastus, argued that women should be taught only as much as was necessary to manage a household, because advanced education "turns a woman into a quarrelling, lazy gossip". Since literacy among Greek women was low (though it has been suggested that the courtesans were "thoroughly literate"),[3] educated slaves would read novels out loud to them. Because of the sophistication of the authors' language and the relatively small number of fragments that survive, the historian William V. Harris has argued that these novels were not massively popular, but rather the light reading of a limited female public with a certain degree of education.[4]

The subject was love and adventure; the hero and heroine were always young, beautiful and well born; misfortune befell them but the end was always happy; trust in the gods was expected, as well as virginity or chastity (at least in the heroine).[5] From the earliest novels, the contents were made clear to the reader. The author of the earliest Greek novel that survives in full, who lived around the beginning of the Christian era,[6] introduced himself and his subject in the first two lines: "My name is Chariton, of Aphrodisias [a town in Asia Minor], and I am clerk to the lawyer Athenagoras. I'm going to tell you a love story that took place in Syracuse." "Love story" — *pathos erotikon*: from the very first lines, the books allotted to women were associated with what would later be called romantic love. Reading this permitted fiction, from the patriarchal society of first-century Greece all the way to twelfth-century Byzantium (when the last of these romances were written), women must have found in the pap some form of intellectual stimulation: in the labours and perils and agonies of loving couples, the women sometimes discovered unsuspected food for thought. Centuries later, as a child reading novels of chivalry (sometimes inspired by the Greek romances), Saint Teresa found much of the imagery that she

Forbidden Fruit,
an 1865
engraving
after a painting
by Auguste
Toulmouche.

would develop in her devotional writing. "I became accustomed to reading them, and that small fault made me cool my desire and will to do my other tasks. And I thought nothing of spending many hours a day and night in this vain exercise, hidden from my father. My rapture in this was so great that, unless I had a new book to read, it seemed to me that I could not be happy."[7] Vain the exercise may have seemed, yet the stories of Marguerite de Navarre, *La Princesse de Clèves* by Mme de La

Fayette and the novels of the Brontë sisters and Jane Austen owe much to the reading of romances. As the English critic Kate Flint points out, reading these novels not only provided a means for the woman reader occasionally "to withdraw into the passivity induced by the opiate of fiction. Far more excitingly, it allowed her to assert her sense of selfhood, and to know that she was not alone in doing so."[8] From early days, women readers found ways of subverting the material that society placed on their shelves.

Setting aside a group of books or a genre for a specific group of readers (whether Greek novels or the pink-covered series of my childhood) not only creates an enclosed literary space which those readers are encouraged to explore; it also, quite often, makes that space off limits for others. I was told that those pink-bound books were for girls, and being seen with one of them in my hands would have labelled me effeminate; I remember the look of surprised reproval on the face of the Buenos Aires shopkeeper when I once bought one of the pink-covered books, and how I had to explain quickly that I meant it as a gift for a girl. (Later I was to come across a similar prejudice when, after co-editing an anthology of male gay fiction, I was told by "straight" friends that they would be embarrassed to be seen with the book in public, for fear of being thought gay.) To venture into the literature society sets aside, condescendingly, for a "less privileged" or "less accepted" group is to risk being tainted by association, since the same caution did not apply to my cousin who could trespass into the green series without provoking any more comment than a quip from her mother about her "eclectic tastes".

But sometimes the reading material of a segregated group is created, deliberately, by readers within the group itself. Such a creation took place among the women of the Japanese court sometime in the eleventh century.

In 894 — a hundred years after the founding of the new capital, Heian-Kyo, in what is now Kyoto — the Japanese government decided to stop sending official envoys to China. For the three previous centuries the ambassadors had been bringing back the art and teachings of Japan's vast millennial neighbour, and Japanese fashion had been ruled by the customs of China; now, with that break from Chinese influence, Japan began to develop a life-style of its own devising, which

Women are being spied on in their quarters, in an illustration by Tosa Mitsuyoshi for *The Tale of Genji*.

reached its peak in the late tenth century under the regent Fujiwara no Michinaga.[9]

As in any aristocratic society, those who enjoyed the benefits of this renaissance were very few. Women in the Japanese court, even though they were very much privileged in comparison to women of the lower classes,[10] were subject to a large number of rules and limitations. Closed off from most of the outside world, forced to follow monotonous routines, limited by language itself (since, with very few exceptions, they were not instructed in the vocabularies of history, law, philosophy "and every other form of scholarship"[11] and their exchanges were normally conducted by letters rather than through conversations), the women had to develop on their own — in spite of reams of restrictions — sly methods to explore and read about the world they lived in, as well as the world beyond their paper walls. Speaking of a young princess, Prince Genji, the hero of Lady Murasaki's *Tale of Genji*, observes that "I do not think we need worry too much about her education. Women should have a general knowledge of several subjects, but it gives a bad impression if they show themselves to be attached to a particular branch of learning. I would not have her completely ignorant in any field. The important thing is that she should appear to have a gentle, easy-going approach even to those subjects that she takes most seriously."[12]

Appearance was all-important, and as long as an apparent indifference to knowledge and an untampered ignorance were feigned, the women at court could manage certain ways of escape from their condition. Under such circumstances, it is astounding that they managed to create the foremost literature of this period, inventing some genres themselves in the process. To be at the same time the creator and the enjoyer of literature — to form, as it were, a closed circle that produces and consumes what it produces, all within the strictures of a society that wants that circle to remain subservient — must be seen as an extraordinary act of courage.

At court, the women's days were spent mostly "gazing into space" in an agony of leisure ("suffering from leisure" is a recurrent phrase) something akin to the European melancholy. The largely empty rooms, with their silk hangings and screens, were almost constantly in darkness. But this didn't afford privacy. The thin walls and latticed parapets allowed sounds to travel easily, and hundreds of paintings depict voyeurs spying upon the activities of the women.

The long leisure hours they were forced to spend, barely broken by yearly festivals and occasional visits to fashionable temples, moved them to practise music and calligraphy, but above all to read out loud or to be read to. Not all books were permitted. In Heian Japan, as in ancient Greece, in Islam, in post-Vedic India and so many other societies, women were excluded from reading what was regarded as "serious" literature: they were expected to confine themselves to the realm of banal and frivolous entertainment, which Confucian scholars frowned upon, and a clear-cut distinction was made between literature and language that were "male" (the themes being heroic and philosophical, and the voice public) and those that were "female" (trivial, domestic and intimate). This distinction was carried into many different areas: for instance, since Chinese ways continued to be admired, Chinese painting was called "male" while the lighter Japanese painting was called "female".

Even if all the libraries of Chinese and Japanese literature had been opened to them, the Heian women would not have found the sound of their own voices in most of the books of the period. Therefore, partly to augment their stock of reading material and partly to gain access to reading material that would respond to their unique preoccupations, they created their own literature. To record it, they developed a phonetic transcription of the tongue they were allowed to speak, the *kanabungaku*, a Japanese purged of almost all Chinese word constructions. This written language came to be known as "women's writing" and, being restricted to the female hand, it acquired, in the eyes of the men who ruled them, an erotic quality. To be attractive, a Heian woman needed not only to possess physical charms but also to write elegant calligraphy, as well as to be versed in music and able to read, interpret and compose poetry. These accomplishments, however, were never considered comparable to those of male artists and scholars.

"Of all the ways of acquiring books," commented Walter Benjamin, "writing them oneself is regarded as the most praiseworthy method."[13] In some cases, as the Heian women had discovered, it is the only method. In their new language, the Heian women wrote some of the most important works in Japanese literature, and perhaps of all time. The most famous of these are Lady Murasaki's monumental *The Tale of Genji*, which the English scholar and translator Arthur Waley considered to be the world's first real novel, probably begun in 1001 and finished not before 1010; and *The Pillow Book of Sei Shonagon*, so called because it was composed, at about the same time as *Genji*, in the author's bed-chamber, and probably kept in the drawers of her wooden pillow.[14]

In books such as *Genji* and *The Pillow Book*, the cultural and social life of both men and women is explored in great detail, but little attention is paid to the political manoeuvring that took up so much of the male court officials' time. Waley found that the "extraordinary vagueness of women concerning purely male activities"[15] in these books was disconcerting; being kept away from both the language and the performance of politics, women such as Sei Shonagon and Lady Murasaki undoubtedly could not have given more than hearsay descriptions of these activities. In any case, these women were essentially writing for themselves — holding up mirrors to their own lives. They required from literature not the images their male counterparts indulged in and were interested in, but a reflection of that other world where time was slow and conversation was meagre, and the landscape hardly changed except as the seasons themselves brought change. *The Tale of Genji*, while displaying a huge canvas of contemporary life, was intended to be read mainly by women like the author herself; women who shared her intelligence and acute perspicacity in matters psychological.

Sei Shonagon's *Pillow Book* is a seemingly casual record of impressions, descriptions, gossip, lists of pleasing or displeasing things — full of whimsical opinions, prejudiced and conceited, utterly dominated by the notion of hierarchy. Her comments have an outspoken ring that she says (are we to believe her?) comes from the fact that "I never thought that these notes would be read by anyone else, and so I included everything that came into my head, however strange or unpleasant." Her simplicity accounts for much of her charm. Here are two examples of "things that are delightful":

> Finding a large number of tales that one has not read before. Or acquiring the second volume of a tale whose first volume one has enjoyed. But often it is a disappointment.

> Letters are commonplace enough, yet what splendid things they are! When someone is in a distant province and one is worried about him, and then a letter suddenly arrives, one feels as though one were seeing him face to face. And it is a great comfort to have expressed one's feelings in a letter — even though one knows it cannot yet have arrived.[16]

Like *The Tale of Genji*, *The Pillow Book*, with its paradoxical adoration of the imperial power yet scorn for the ways of men, lends value to the enforced leisure and places women's domestic lives on the same literary level as the "epic" lives of men. Lady Murasaki, however, for whom the women's narrative needed to be brought to light within the men's epics and not, frivolously, within the confines of their paper walls, found Sei Shonagon's writing "full of imperfections": "She is a gifted woman, to be sure. Yet, if one gives free rein to one's emotions even under the most inappropriate circumstances, if one has to sample each interesting thing that comes along, people are bound to regard one as frivolous. And how can things turn out well for such a woman?"[17]

At least two different sorts of reading seem to take place within a segregated group. In the first, the readers, like imaginative archeologists, burrow their way through the official literature in order to rescue from between the lines the presence of their fellow outcasts, to find mirrors for themselves in the stories of Clytemnestra, of Gertrude, of Balzac's courtesans. In the second, the readers become writers, inventing for themselves new ways of telling stories in order to redeem on the page the everyday chronicles of their excluded lives in the laboratory of the kitchen, in the studio of the sewing-room, in the jungles of the nursery.

There is perhaps a third category somewhere between these two. Many centuries after Sei Shonagon and Lady Murasaki, across the sea, the English writer George Eliot, writing about the literature of her day, described what she called "silly novels by Lady Novelists . . . a genus with many species, determined by the particular quality of silliness that predominates in them — the frothy, the prosy, the pious, or the pedantic. But it is a mixture of all these — a composite order of feminine fatuity, that produces the largest class of such novels, which we shall distinguish as the *mind-and-millinery* species. . . . The standing apology for women who become writers without any special qualification is, that society shuts them out from other spheres of occupation. Society is a very culpable entity, and has to answer for the manufacture of many unwholesome commodities, from bad pickles to bad poetry. But society, like 'matter', and Her Majesty's Government, and other lofty abstractions, has its share of excessive blame as well as excessive praise." She concluded, " 'In all labour there is profit'; but ladies' silly novels, we imagine, are less the result of labour than of busy idleness."[18] What George Eliot was describing was fiction which, though written within the group, does little more than echo the official stereotypes and prejudices that led to the creation of the group in the first place.

Silliness was also the fault which Lady Murasaki, as a reader, saw in the writing of Sei Shonagon. The obvious difference, however, was that Sei Shonagon was not offering her readers a stultified version of their own image as consecrated by the men. What Lady Murasaki found frivolous was Sei Shonagon's subject-matter: the everyday world within which she herself moved, whose triviality Sei Shonagon had documented with as much attention as if it had been the shining world of Genji himself. Lady Murasaki's criticism notwithstanding, Sei Shonagon's intimate, seemingly banal style of literature flourished among the women readers of her time. The earliest known example of this period is the diary of a Heian court lady known only as the "Mother of Michitsuna", the *Journal of Summer's End* or *Fleeting Journal*. In it, the author tried to chronicle, as faithfully as possible, the reality of her existence. Speaking of herself in the third person, she wrote, "As the days drifted away monotonously, she read through the old novels and found most of them a collection of gross inventions. Perhaps, she said to herself, the story of her wearisome existence, written in the form of a journal, might provoke some degree of interest. Perhaps she might even be able to answer the question: is this an appropriate life for a well-born lady?"[19]

In spite of Lady Murasaki's criticism, it is easy to understand why the confessional form, the page on which a woman could appear to be giving "free rein to one's emotions", became the favourite reading matter among Heian women. *Genji* presented something of the lives of women in the characters who surrounded the prince, but *The Pillow Book* allowed women readers to become their own historians.

"There are four ways to write a woman's life," argues the American critic Carolyn G. Heilbrun. "The woman herself may tell it, in what she chooses to call an autobiography; she may tell it in what she chooses to call fiction; a biographer, woman or man, may write the woman's life in what is called a biography; or the woman may write her own life in advance of living it, unconsciously, and without recognizing or naming the process."[20]

Carolyn Heilbrun's cautious labelling of forms also vaguely corresponds to the shifting literatures the Heian women writers produced — *monogatari* (novels), pillow-books, and others. In these texts, their readers found their own lives lived or unlived, idealized or fantasized, or chronicled with documentary prolixity and faithfulness. This is usually the case for segregated readers: the literature they require is confessional, autobiographical, even didactic, because readers whose identities are denied have no other place to find their stories except in the literature they themselves produce. In an argument applied to gay reading — which can fairly be applied to women's reading, to the reading of any group excluded from the realm of power — the American writer Edmund White notes that as soon as someone notices that he (we can add "or she") is different, that person must account for it, and that such accounts are a kind of primitive fiction, "the oral narrations told and retold as pillow talk or in pubs or on the psychoanalytic couch". Telling "each other — or the hostile world around them — the stories of their lives, they're not just reporting the past but also shaping the future, forging an identity as much as revealing it."[21] In Sei Shonagon, as well as in Lady Murasaki, lie the shadows of the women's literature we read today.

A generation after George Eliot, in Victorian England, Oscar Wilde's Gwendolen in *The Importance of Being Earnest* declared that she never travelled without her diary because "one should always have something sensational to read in the train"; she was not exaggerating. Her counterpart, Cecily, defined a diary as "simply a very young girl's record of her own thoughts and impressions, and consequently meant for publication".[22] Publication — that is to say, the reproduction of a text in order to multiply its readers through manuscript copies, through reading out loud or through the press — allowed women to find voices similar to their own, to discover that their plight was not unique, to find in the confirmation of experience a solid basis upon which to build an authentic image of themselves. This was as true for the Heian women as it was for George Eliot.

Unlike the stationery shop of my childhood, a bookstore today carries not only the books marketed for women by outside commercial interests, to determine and limit that which a woman should read, but also the books created from within the group, in which women write for themselves that which is absent in the official texts. This sets out the reader's task, which the Heian writers may have foreseen: to climb over the walls: to take whatever book seems appealing, strip it of its colour-coded covers and place it among those volumes which chance and experience have put upon her bedside shelf.

G Lebre

STEALING BOOKS

I am once again about to move house. Around me, in the secret dust from unsuspected corners now revealed by the shifting of furniture, stand unsteady columns of books, like the wind-carved rocks of a desert landscape. As I build pile after pile of familiar volumes (I recognize some by their colour, others by their shape, many by a detail on the jackets whose titles I try to read upside down or at an odd angle) I wonder, as I have wondered every other time, why I keep so many books that I know I will not read again. I tell myself that, every time I get rid of a book, I find a few days later that this is precisely the book I'm looking for. I tell myself that there are no books (or very, very few) in which I have found nothing at all to interest me. I tell myself that I've brought them into my house for a reason in the first place, and that this reason may hold good again in the future. I invoke excuses of thoroughness, of scarcity, of faint scholarship. But I know that the main reason I hold onto this ever-increasing hoard is a sort of voluptuous greed. I enjoy the sight of my crowded bookshelves, full of more or less familiar names. I delight in knowing that I'm surrounded by a sort of inventory of my life, with intimations of my future. I like discovering, in almost forgotten volumes, traces of the reader I once was — scribbles, bus tickets, scraps of paper with mysterious names and numbers, the occasional date and place on the book's flyleaf which take me back to a certain café, a distant hotel room, a far-away summer so long ago. I could, if I had to, abandon these books of mine and begin again, somewhere else; I have done so before, several

OPPOSITE

The possessive reader, Count Guglielmo Libri.

237

times, out of necessity. But then I have also had to acknowledge a grave, irreparable loss. I know that something dies when I give up my books, and that my memory keeps going back to them with mournful nostalgia. And now, with the years, my memory can recall less and less, and seems to me like a looted library: many of the rooms have been closed, and in the ones still open for consultation there are huge gaps on the shelves. I pull out one of the remaining books and see that several of its pages have been torn out by vandals. The more decrepit my memory becomes, the more I wish to protect this repository of what I've read, this collection of textures and voices and scents. Possessing these books has become all-important to me, because I've become jealous of the past.

The French Revolution attempted to abolish the notion that the past was the property of a single class. It succeeded in at least one aspect: from an aristocratic entertainment, the collecting of ancient things became a bourgeois hobby, first under Napoleon, with his love for the trappings of Ancient Rome, and later in the republic. By the turn of the nineteenth century, the displaying of fusty bric-à-brac, of old masters' paintings, of early books, had become a fashionable European pastime. Curiosity shops flourished. Antique dealers amassed caches of pre-revolutionary treasures which were bought and then displayed in the home museums of the *nouveaux riches*. "The collector," wrote Walter Benjamin, "dreams that he is not only in a distant or past world but also, at the same time, in a better one in which, although men are as unprovided with what they need as in the everyday world, things are free of the drudgery of being useful."[1]

In 1792 the Louvre Palace was turned into a museum for the people. Voicing a haughty complaint against the notion of a common past, the novelist Viscount François-René de Chateaubriand protested that works of art thus assembled "had no longer anything to say either to the imagination or to the heart". When, a few years later, the artist and antiquarian Alexandre Lenoir founded the Museum of French Monuments to preserve the statuary and masonry of the mansions and monasteries, palaces and churches that the revolution had plundered, Chateaubriand dismissively described it as "a collection of ruins and tombs from every century, assembled without rhyme or reason in the cloisters of the Petits-Augustins."[2] In both the official world and the private world of collectors of the past's ruins, Chateaubriand's criticism went staunchly unheard.

Books were among the most copious remains left behind by the revolution. The private libraries of eighteenth-century France were family treasures, preserved and expanded from generation to generation among the nobility, and the books they contained were as much symbols of social standing as finery and deportment. One imagines the Count d'Hoym,[3] one of the most celebrated bibliophiles of his time (he died at the age of forty in 1736), drawing from one of his overpopulated shelves a volume of Cicero's *Orations*, which he would regard not as one among many hundreds or thousands of identical printed copies dispersed through numerous libraries but as a unique object, bound according to his specifications, annotated by his hand and bearing his family arms embossed in gold.

From roughly the end of the twelfth century, books became recognized as items of trade, and in Europe the commercial value of books was sufficiently established for money-lenders to accept them as collateral; notes recording such pledges are found in numerous medieval books, especially those belonging to students.[4] By the fifteenth century the trade had become sufficiently important for books to be placed on the schedule of goods sold at the trade fairs of Frankfurt and Nördlingen.[5]

Some books, of course, were unique because of their rarity, and were valued at exorbitant prices (the rare *Epistolae* of Petrus Delphinus, of 1524, was sold for 1,000 *livres* in 1719 — about US $30,000 in today's currency),[6] but most had the value of intimate objects — family heirlooms, objects that only their hands and the hands of their children would ever touch. For that reason, libraries became one of the obvious targets of the revolution.

The raided libraries of the clergy and aristocracy, symbols of the "enemies of the republic", ended up in huge depots in several French cities — Paris, Lyons, Dijon and others — where they waited, preyed upon by humidity, dust and vermin, for the revolutionary authorities to decide on their fate. The problem of storing such quantities of books became so serious that the authorities began organizing sales to rid themselves of part of the booty. However, at least up to the creation of the Bank of France as a private institution in 1800, most French bibliophiles (those who were not dead or in exile) were too impoverished to become customers, and only foreigners, mainly English and Germans, were able to profit from the situation. To satisfy this foreign clientele, local booksellers began acting as scouts and agents. In one of the last expurgatory sales, in Paris in 1816, the bookseller and publisher Jacques-Simon Merlin bought enough books to fill from cellar to attic two five-storey houses that he had acquired specially for the purpose.[7] These volumes, in many cases precious and rare, sold for the weight of the paper, and this at a time when new books were still very expensive. For instance, during the first decade of the nineteenth century a recently published novel would have cost one-third of a French farmhand's monthly wages, while a first edition of Paul Scarron's *Le Roman comique* (1651) might have been picked up for a tenth of that sum.[8]

The books which the revolution had requisitioned and which had been neither destroyed nor sold abroad were eventually distributed among public reference libraries, but few readers made use of them. Throughout the first half of the nineteenth century, the hours of access to these *bibliothèques publiques* were restricted, a dress code was enforced, and the precious books once again gathered dust on the shelves,[9] forgotten and unread.

But not for long.

Guglielmo Bruto Icilio Timoleone, Conte Libri-Carucci della Sommaia, was born in Florence in 1803 of an old and noble Tuscan family. He studied both law and mathematics, and became so successful at the latter that at the age of twenty he was offered the chair of mathematics at the University of Pisa. In 1830, supposedly under threats from a nationalistic organization, the Carbonari, he emigrated to Paris and shortly thereafter became a French citizen. His resounding name reduced now to Count Libri, he was welcomed by French academics, elected a member of the Institut de France, made a professor of science at the University of Paris and awarded the Legion of Honour for his scholarly credentials. But Libri was interested in more than science; he had also developed a passion for books, and by 1840 he had amassed a notable collection and was trading in manuscripts and rare printed volumes. Twice he tried to obtain a post at the Royal Library, and failed. Then, in 1841, he was appointed secretary of a commission charged with overseeing the official "general and detailed catalogue of all the manuscripts, in tongues both ancient and modern, existing today in all departmental public libraries".[10]

This is how Sir Frederic Madden, keeper of the Department of Manuscripts of the British Museum, described his first encounter with Libri, on May 6, 1846, in Paris: "In his external appearance [he] seemed as if he had never used soap and water or a brush. The room, in which we were introduced, was not more than about 16 feet wide, but filled with manuscripts on shelves up to the ceiling. The windows had double sashes and a fire of coal and coke burnt in the grate, the heat of which, added to the smell of the pile of vellum around, was so unsufferable, that I gasped for breath. M. Libri perceived the inconvenience we suffered and opened one of the windows, but it was easy to see that a breath of air was disagreeable to him, and his ears were stuffed with cotton, as if to prevent his feeling sensible of it! M. Libri is a rather corpulent person, of good humoured but broad features."[11] What Sir Frederic did not know — then — was that Count Libri was one of the most accomplished book thieves of all time.

According to the seventeenth-century gossipmonger Tallemant des Réaux, stealing books is not a crime unless the books are sold.[12] The pleasure of holding a rare volume in one's hands, of turning pages which no one else will turn without one's permission, no doubt prompted Libri to some degree. But whether the sight of so many beautiful volumes unexpectedly tempted the learned bibliophile, or whether the lust for books had prompted him to seek out the position in the first place, we will never know. Armed with official credentials, dressed in a huge cloak under which he concealed his treasures, Libri gained access to libraries across France, where his specialized knowledge enabled him to pick out the hidden plums. In Carpentras, Dijon, Grenoble, Lyons, Montpellier, Orléans, Poitiers and Tours, he not only stole entire volumes but also cut out single pages, which he then exhibited and sometimes sold.[13] Only in Auxerre did he not carry out his spoiling. The obsequious librarian, anxious to please the official whose papers announced him as *Monsieur le Secrétaire* and *Monsieur l'Inspecteur Général*, willingly authorized Libri to work in the library at night, but insisted that a guard be at his elbow to attend to monsieur's every need.[14]

The first accusations against Libri date from 1846, but — perhaps because they sounded so improbable — they were ignored, and Libri continued to raid the libraries. He also began to organize important sales of some of the stolen books, sales for which he prepared excellent and detailed catalogues.[15] Why did this passionate bibliophile sell the books he had stolen at such great risk? Perhaps he believed, like Proust, that "desire makes all things flourish, possession withers them all".[16] Perhaps he required only a precious few which he selected as the rare pearls of his booty. Perhaps he sold them out of mere greed — but that is a far less interesting supposition. Whatever his reasons, the sale of stolen books could no longer be ignored. The accusations grew, and a year later the public prosecutor initiated discreet enquiries — which were hushed up by the president of the Ministerial Council, M. Guizot, a friend of Libri's and a witness at his marriage. It is probable that the affair would not have gone any further had not the Revolution of 1848, which ended the July Monarchy and proclaimed the Second Republic, uncovered Libri's file hidden away in Guizot's desk. Libri was warned and he and his wife escaped to England, but not without taking along eighteen cases of books valued at 25,000 francs.[17] At the time, a skilled labourer was earning about 4 francs a day.[18]

A host of politicians, artists and writers rallied (in vain) to Libri's defence. Some had profited from his schemes and didn't want to be implicated in the scandal; others had accepted him as an honourable scholar and didn't wish to appear as dupes. The writer Prosper Mérimée in particular was ardent in Libri's defence.[19] Libri had shown Mérimée, at the apartment of a friend, the celebrated Tours Pentateuch, a seventh-century illuminated volume; Mérimée, who had travelled widely through France and visited numerous libraries, remarked that he had seen this Pentateuch in Tours; Libri, quick on his feet, explained to Mérimée that what he had seen was a French copy of the original acquired by Libri himself in Italy. Mérimée believed him. Writing to Édouard Delessert on June 5, 1848, Mérimée insisted, "For me, who has always said that the love of collecting leads people to crime, Libri is the most honest of collectors, and I know of no man except Libri who would return to the libraries the books that others have stolen."[20] Finally, two years after Libri had been found guilty, Mérimée published in *La Revue des Deux Mondes*[21] such a loud defence of his friend that the courts ordered him to appear before them, accused of contempt.

Under the burden of evidence, Libri was condemned *in absentia* to ten years in prison and loss of his public postings. Lord Ashburnham, who had bought from Libri through the intermediary of the bookseller Joseph Barrois another rare illuminated Pentateuch (this one he had stolen from the public library of Lyons), accepted the proofs of Libri's guilt and returned the book to the French ambassador in London. The

Pentateuch was the only book Lord Ashburnham returned. "The congratulations addressed from all sides to the author of such a liberal act, did not prompt him however to repeat the experience with other manuscripts in his library," commented Léopold Delisle,[22] who in 1888 assembled a catalogue of Libri's spoils.

But by then Libri had long turned the final page of his last stolen book. From England he left for Italy and settled in Fiesole, where he died on September 28, 1869, unvindicated and destitute. And yet, in the end, he had his revenge on his accusers. The year of Libri's death, the mathematician Michel Chasles, who had been elected to fill Libri's chair at the Institut, purchased an incredible collection of autographs which he was certain would bring him envy and fame. It included letters from Julius Caesar, Pythagoras, Nero, Cleopatra, the elusive Mary Magdalen — and they were all eventually proved to be fakes, the handicraft of the famous forger Vrain-Lucas, whom Libri had asked to pay his successor a visit.[23]

The theft of books was not a new crime in Libri's time. "The history of bibliokleptomania," writes Lawrence S. Thompson, "goes back to the beginning of libraries in Western Europe, and undoubtedly can be traced back even further through the history of Greek and Oriental libraries."[24] The earliest Roman libraries were composed largely of Greek volumes because the Romans had so thoroughly ransacked Greece. The Royal Macedonian Library, the library of Mithridates of Pontus, the library of Apellicon of Teos (later used by Cicero), were all raided by the Romans and transferred to Roman soil. The early Christian centuries were not spared: the Coptic monk Pachomius, who had set up a library in his monastery at Tabennisi in Egypt in the first few decades of the third century, carried out an inventory check every evening to assure that the books had been returned.[25] In their raids on Anglo-Saxon England, the Vikings stole the illuminated manuscripts of the monks, probably for the sake of the gold in the bindings. One of these rich volumes, the *Codex Aureus*, was stolen sometime in the eleventh century but had to be ransomed back to its original owners, because the thieves were unable to find a market for it elsewhere. Book thieves plagued the Middle Ages and the Renaissance; in 1752 Pope Benedict XIV proclaimed a bull in which book thieves were punished with excommunication.

Other threats were more worldly, as this admonition inscribed in a valuable Renaissance tome proves:

My Master's name above you see,
Take heede therefore you steale not mee;
For if you doe, without delay
Your necke . . . for me shall pay.
Looke doune below and you shall see
The picture of the gallowstree;
Take heede therefore of thys in time,
Lest on this tree you highly clime![26]

Or this one, inscribed in the library of the monastery of San Pedro, in Barcelona:

For him that steals, or borrows and returns not, a book from its owner, let it change into a serpent in his hand and rend him. Let him be struck with palsy, and all his members blasted. Let him languish in pain crying aloud for mercy, and let there be no surcease to his agony till he sing in dissolution. Let bookworms gnaw at his entrails in token of the Worm that dieth not. And when at last he goes to his final punishment, let the flames of Hell consume him for ever.[27]

And yet no curses seem to deter those readers who, like crazed lovers, are determined to make a certain book theirs. The urge to possess a book, to be its sole owner, is a species of covetousness unlike any other. "A book reads the better," confessed Charles Lamb, Libri's contemporary, "which is our own, and has been so long known to us, that we know the topography of its blots, and dog's ears, and can trace the dirt in it to having read it at tea with buttered muffins."[28]

The act of reading establishes an intimate, physical relationship in which all the senses have a part: the eyes drawing the words from the page, the ears echoing the sounds being read, the nose inhaling the familiar scent of paper, glue, ink, cardboard or leather, the touch caressing the rough or soft page, the smooth or hard binding; even the taste, at times, when the reader's fingers are lifted to the tongue (which is how the murderer poisons his victims in Umberto Eco's *The Name of the Rose*). All this, many readers are unwilling to share — and if the book they wish to read is in someone else's possession, the laws of property are as hard to uphold as those of faithfulness in love. Also, physical ownership becomes at times synonymous with a sense of intellectual apprehension. We come to feel that the books we own are the books we know, as if possession were, in libraries as in courts, nine-tenths of the law; that to glance at the spines of the books we call ours, obediently standing guard along the walls of our room, willing to speak to us and us alone at the mere flick of a page, allows us to say, "All this is mine," as if their presence alone fills us with their wisdom, without our actually having to labour through their contents.

In this I have been as guilty as Count Libri. Even today, submerged as we are by dozens of editions and thousands of identical copies of the same title, I know that the volume I hold in my hands, that volume and no other, becomes the Book. Annotations, stains, marks of one kind or another, a certain moment and place, characterize that volume as surely as if it were a priceless manuscript. We may be loath to justify Libri's thefts, but the underlying longing, the urge to be, even for a moment, the only one able to call a book "mine", is common to more honest men and women than we may be willing to acknowledge.

THE AUTHOR

AS READER

One evening at the end of the first century AD, Gaius Plinius Caecilius Secundus (known to future readers as Pliny the Younger to distinguish him from his erudite uncle, Pliny the Elder, who died in the eruption of Mount Vesuvius in AD 79) left the house of a friend in Rome in a state of righteous anger. As soon as he reached his study, Pliny sat down and, in order to collect his thoughts (and perhaps with an eye to the volume of letters he would one day assemble and publish), wrote about that night's events to the lawyer Claudius Restitutus. "I have just left in indignation a reading at a friend of mine's, and I feel I have to write to you at once, as I can't tell you about it personally. The text that was read was highly polished in every possible way, but two or three witty people — or so they seemed to themselves and a few others — listened to it like deaf-mutes. They never opened their lips or moved a hand, or even stretched their legs to change from their seated postures. What's the point of all this sober demeanour and scholarship, or rather of this laziness and conceit, this lack of tact and good sense, which makes one spend an entire day doing nothing but causing grief and turning into an enemy the man one came to hear as one's dearest friend?"[1]

It is somewhat difficult for us, at a distance of twenty centuries, to understand Pliny's dismay. In his time, authors' readings had become a fashionable social ceremony[2] and, as with any other ceremony, there was an established etiquette for both the listeners and the authors. The listeners were expected to provide critical response, based on which the

OPPOSITE

Pliny the Younger, sculpted on the façade of Como Cathedral.

author would improve the text — which is why the motionless audience had so outraged Pliny; he himself sometimes tried out a first draft
of a speech on a group of friends and then altered it according to their
reaction.[3] Furthermore, the listeners were expected to attend the entire function, whatever its length, so as not to miss any part of the work
being read, and Pliny felt that those who used readings as mere social di-
versions were little better than hoodlums. "Most of them sit around in
the waiting-rooms," he fumed to another friend, "wasting their time instead of paying attention, and ordering their servants to tell them every
so often if the reader has arrived and has read the introduction, or if he
has reached the end. Only then, and most reluctantly, do they straggle
in. And they don't stay long but leave before the end, some trying to escape unnoticed, others walking out with no shame. . . . More praise and
honour are due to those whose love of writing and reading out loud is
not affected by the bad manners and arrogance of their audience."[4]

The author too was obliged to follow certain rules if his reading
was to be successful, for there were all sorts of obstacles to overcome.
First of all, an appropriate reading-space had to found. Rich men fan-
cied themselves poets, and recited their work to large crowds of acquaintances at their opulent villas, in the *auditorium* — a room built
specially for that purpose. Some of these wealthy poets, such as Titinius
Capito,[5] were generous and lent their *auditoria* for the performances of
others, but mostly these recital-spaces were for the exclusive use of
their owners. Once his friends had gathered at the appointed place, the
author had to face them from a chair on a dais, wearing a new toga and
displaying all his rings.[6] According to Pliny, this custom doubly hindered him: "he is at a great disadvantage by the mere fact of sitting
down, even though he may be as gifted as speakers who stand"[7] and he
had the "two main aids to his delivery, i.e., eyes and hands" occupied
with holding his text. Oratorical skills were therefore essential. Praising
one reader for his performance, Pliny noted that "he showed an appropriate versatility in raising or lowering his tone, and the same dexterity
in going from loftier subjects to baser ones, from simple to complex, or
passing from lighter subjects to more serious ones. His remarkably
pleasant voice was another advantage, and was improved by his mod-
esty, his blushes and nervousness, which always add charm to a reading.
I don't know why, but shyness suits an author better than confidence."[8]

Those who had doubts about their reading skills could resort to
certain stratagems. Pliny himself, confident when reading speeches but

uncertain about his ability to read verse, came up with the following idea for an evening of his poetry. "I'm planning to give an informal reading to a few friends," he wrote to Suetonius, the author of *Lives of the Twelve Caesars*, "and I'm thinking of using one of my slaves. I'll be showing my friends no great civility, since the man I've chosen is not really a good reader, but I think he'll be better than I'd be, as long as he's not too nervous. . . . The question is: what should I do while he is reading? Should I sit still and silent like a spectator, or do as some people do and follow his words by mouthing them with my lips, eyes and gestures?" We do not know if Pliny gave that night one of the first lip-synch performances in history.

Many of these readings must have seemed interminable; Pliny attended one that lasted three days. (This particular reading doesn't seem to have bothered him, perhaps because the reader had announced to his audience, "But what do I care for the poets of the past, since I know Pliny?")[9] Ranging from several hours to half a week, public readings became practically unavoidable for anyone who wished to be known as an author. Horace complained that educated readers no longer seemed interested in the actual writings of a poet, but had "transferred all their pleasure from the ear to the shifting and empty delights of the eye".[10] Martial became so fed up with being pestered by poetasters anxious to read their work out loud that he complained:

> I ask you, who can endure these efforts?
> You read to me when I'm standing,
> You read to me when I'm sitting,
> You read to me when I'm running,
> You read to me when I'm shitting.[11]

Pliny, however, approved of authors' readings, and saw in them the signs of a new golden literary age. "There was hardly a day all through-out April when there wasn't someone giving a public reading," he remarked, very pleased. "I'm delighted to see literature flourishing and talent blooming."[12] Future generations disagreed with Pliny's verdict, and chose to forget the names of most of these performing poets.

And yet, if fame was to be one's lot, thanks to these public readings, an author no longer had to wait till after death for consecration. "Opinions differ," wrote Pliny to his friend Valerius Paulinus, "but my idea of the truly happy man is one who enjoys the anticipation of a good and lasting reputation, and, confident in the verdict of posterity, lives in the knowledge of the fame to come."[13] Present fame was important to him. He was delighted when someone at the races thought the writer Tacitus (whom he much admired) might be Pliny. "If Demosthenes had the right to be pleased when the old woman of Attica recognized him with the words 'That's Demosthenes!', I may surely be glad when my name is well known. In fact, I *am* glad and I admit it."[14] His work was published and read, even in the wilds of Lugdunum (Lyons). He wrote to another friend, "I didn't think there were any booksellers in Lugdunum, so I was all the more pleased to learn from your letter that my efforts are being sold. I'm glad they retain abroad the popularity they won in Rome, and I'm beginning to think my work must really be quite good when public opinion in such widely different places is agreed about it."[15] However, he much preferred the accolade of a listening audience to the silent approval of anonymous readers.

Pliny suggested a number of reasons why reading in public was a beneficial exercise. Celebrity was no doubt a very important factor, but there was also the delight of hearing one's own voice. He justified this self-indulgence by noting that listening to a text led the audience to buy the published piece, thereby causing a demand that would satisfy both the authors and the bookseller-publishers.[16] Reading publicly was, in his view, the best way for an author to acquire an audience. In fact, reading publicly was in itself a rudimentary form of publishing.

As Pliny accurately remarked, reading in public was a performance, an act undertaken with the whole body for others to perceive. The author who reads in public — then as now — overrides the words with certain sounds and enacts them with certain gestures; this performance gives the text a tone which is (supposedly) the one the author had in mind at the moment of its conception, and therefore grants the listener the feeling of being close to the author's intentions; it also gives the text a seal of authenticity. But at the same time the author's reading also distorts the text, by improving (or impoverishing) it with interpretation. The Canadian novelist Robertson Davies brought layers and layers of characterization to his readings, acting out rather than reciting his fiction. The French novelist Nathalie Sarraute instead reads in a monotone that does no justice to her lyrical texts. Dylan Thomas chanted his poetry, striking the stresses like gongs and leaving enormous pauses.[17] T.S. Eliot muttered his as if he were a sulky vicar cursing his flock.

Read out to an audience, a text is not exclusively determined by the relationship between its intrinsic characteristics and those of its arbitrary, ever-changing public, since the members of that public are no longer at liberty (as ordinary readers would be) to go back, reread, delay, and to give the text their own connotative intonation. It becomes instead dependent on the author-performer who assumes the role of reader of readers, the presumptive incarnation of each and every member of the captive audience for whom the reading is being held, teaching them how to read. Authors' readings can become thoroughly dogmatic.

Public readings were not unique to Rome. The Greeks read publicly. Five centuries before Pliny, for instance, Herodotus read his own work at the Olympic festivals, where a large and enthusiastic audience was assembled from all over Greece, to avoid having to travel from city to city. But in the sixth century public readings effectively ceased because there no longer seemed to be an "educated public". The last description known to us of a Roman audience at a public reading is in the letters of the Christian poet Apollinaris Sidonius, written in the second half of the fifth century. By then, as Sidonius himself lamented in his letters, Latin had become a specialized, foreign tongue, "the language of the liturgy, of the chancelleries and of a few scholars".[18] Ironically, the Christian Church, which had adopted Latin to spread the gospel to "all men in all places", found that the language had become incomprehensible to the vast majority of the flock. Latin became part of the Church's "mystery", and in the eleventh century the first Latin dictionaries appeared, to help students and novices for whom Latin was no longer the mother tongue.

But authors continued to require the stimulation of an immediate public. By the late thirteenth century, Dante was suggesting that the "vulgar tongue" — that is to say, the vernacular — was even more noble than Latin, for three reasons: because it was the first tongue spoken by Adam in Eden; because it was "natural", while Latin was "artificial" since it was only learned in schools; and because it was universal, since all men spoke a vulgar tongue and only a few knew Latin.[19] Though this defence of the vulgar tongue was written, paradoxically, in Latin, it is probable that towards the end of his life, at the court of Guido Novello da Polenta in Ravenna, Dante himself read out passages from his *Commedia* in the "vulgar tongue" he had so eloquently defended. What is certain is that in the fourteenth and fifteenth centuries

authors' readings were once again common; there are many instances
in both secular and religious literature. In 1309, Jean de Joinville addressed his *Life of St. Louis* to "you and your brothers, and others who
will hear it read".[20] In the late fourteenth century Froissart, the French
historian, braved the storm in the middle of the night for six long winter weeks to read his romance *Méliador* to the insomniac Count du
Blois.[21] The prince and poet Charles d'Orléans, taken prisoner by the
English at Agincourt in 1415, wrote numerous poems during his long
captivity, and after his release in 1440 read them to the court at Blois
during literary evenings to which other poets, such as François Villon,
were invited. *La Celestina*, by Fernando de Rojas, made clear in its introduction of 1499 that the lengthy play (or novel in the form of a
play) was intended to be read out loud "when some ten people get together to listen to this comedy";[22] it is likely that the author (of whom
we know very little, except that he was a converted Jew and not anxious to bring his work to the attention of the Inquisition) had tried the
"comedy" out on his friends.[23] In January 1507, Ariosto read his unfinished *Orlando Furioso* to the convalescent Isabella Gonzaga, "causing
two days to pass not only without boredom but with the greatest of
pleasure".[24] And Geoffrey Chaucer, whose books are full of references
to literature being read out loud, most certainly read his work to a listening audience.[25]

The son of a prosperous wine merchant, Chaucer was probably educated in London, where he discovered the works of Ovid, Virgil and
the French poets. As was common with children of wealthy families,
he entered the service of a noble household — that of Elizabeth,
Countess of Ulster, married to the second son of King Edward III. Tradition has it that one of his first poems was a hymn to the Virgin, written at the request of a noble lady, Blanche of Lancaster (for whom he
later wrote *The Book of the Duchesse*) and read out loud to her and her
attendants. One can imagine the young man, nervous at first, then
warming up to his task, stammering a little, reading out his poem
much as a student today would read an essay in front of the class.
Chaucer must have persevered; the readings of his poetry continued. A
manuscript of *Troilus and Criseyde* now in Corpus Christi College, Cambridge, depicts a man standing at an outside pulpit and addressing an
audience of lords and ladies, an open book laid out in front of him. The

man is Chaucer; the royal couple next to him, King Richard II and Queen Anne.

Chaucer's style combines devices borrowed from the classical rhetoricians with the colloquialisms and catch-phrases of the minstrel tradition, so that a reader following his words from across the centuries hears as well as sees the text. Because Chaucer's audience were going to "read" his poems through their ears, devices such as rhyme, cadence, repetition, and the voices of different characters were essential elements of his poetic composition; reading out loud, he would be able to alter these devices according to the audience's reaction. When the text was set down in written form, whether for someone else to read out loud or for someone to read silently, it was obviously important to retain the effect of these aural tricks. For that reason, just as certain punctuation marks had been developed through silent reading, equally practical signs were now developed for reading out loud. For instance, the *diple* — a scribe's mark in the shape of a horizontal arrowhead, placed in the margin to draw attention to some element in the text — now became the sign we recognize today as inverted commas, to indicate first quotations, and then passages of direct speech. As well, the scribe who copied out *The Canterbury Tales* in the late-fourteenth-century Ellesmere manuscript resorted to slashes (the *solidus*) to mark the rhythm of the verse spoken out loud:

In Southwerk / at the Tabard / as I lay
Redy / to wenden on my pilgrimage[26]

By 1387, however, Chaucer's contemporary John of Trevisa, who was translating an immensely popular epic, the *Polychronicon*, from the Latin, chose to render it into English prose rather than verse — a medium less adapted to a public reading — because he knew that his audience no longer expected to listen to a recitation, and would instead, in all probability, read the book by themselves. The death of the author, it was thought, enabled the reader to have freer commerce with the text.

And yet the author, the magical creator of the text, retained an incantatory prestige. What intrigued new readers was meeting that maker, the body that lodged the mind that had dreamt up Dr. Faust, Tom Jones, Candide. And for the authors there was a parallel act of magic: meeting that literary invention, the public, the "dear reader",

Chaucer reading to King Richard II, in an early fifteenth-century manuscript of *Troilus and Criseyde*.

those who for Pliny were well- or ill-behaved people of visible eyes and
ears and who now, centuries later, had become a mere hope beyond the
page. "Seven copies," reflects the protagonist of Thomas Love Peacock's
early nineteenth-century novel *Nightmare Abbey*, "have been sold. Seven
is a mystical number, and the omen is good. Let me find the seven purchasers of my seven copies, and they shall be the seven golden candle-
sticks with which I will illuminate the world."[27] To meet their allotted
seven (and seven times seven, if the stars were lucky), authors started
once again to read their work in public.

As Pliny had explained, public readings by the author were meant
to bring the text not only to the public but back to the author as well.
Chaucer no doubt emended the text of *The Canterbury Tales* after his
public readings (perhaps putting some of the complaints he heard into
the mouths of his pilgrims — such as the Man of Law, who finds
Chaucer's rhymes pretentious). Molière, three centuries later, habitu-
ally read his plays out loud to his housemaid. "If Molière ever did read
to her," the English novelist Samuel Butler commented in his *Notebooks*,
"it was because the mere act of reading aloud put his work before him
in a new light and, by constraining his attention to every line, made
him judge it more rigorously. I always intend to read, and generally do
read, what I write aloud to someone; any one almost will do, but he
should not be so clever that I am afraid of him. I feel weak places at
once when I read aloud where I thought, as long as I read to myself
only, that the passage was all right."[28]

Sometimes it was not self-improvement but censorship that led
the author back to reading in public. Jean-Jacques Rousseau, forbidden
by the French authorities to publish his *Confessions*, instead read
throughout the long cold winter of 1768, in various aristocratic Paris
households. One of these readings lasted from nine in the morning
until three in the afternoon. According to one of his listeners, when
Rousseau came to the passage describing how he had abandoned his
children, the audience, at first embarrassed, was reduced to tears of
grief.[29]

Throughout Europe, the nineteenth century was the golden age of
authors' readings. In England the star was Charles Dickens. Always interested in amateur theatrics, Dickens (who did in fact act on stage a
number of times, notably in his own collaboration with Wilkie Collins,
The Frozen Deep, in 1857) used his histrionic talent in readings of his
own work. These, like Pliny's, were of two kinds: reading to his friends

Dickens reading
"The Chimes"
to a group
of friends.

to polish his final drafts and gauge the effect of his fiction on his public; and public readings, performances for which he became famous in later life. Writing to his wife, Catherine, about reading his second Christmas story, *The Chimes*, he exulted, "If you had seen Macready [one of Dickens's friends] last night — undisguisedly sobbing, and crying on the sofa, as I read — you would have felt (as I did) what a thing it is to have Power". "Power over others," one of his biographers adds. "Power to move and to sway. The Power of his writing. The Power of his voice."To Lady Blessington, regarding the reading of *The Chimes*, Dickens wrote, "I am in great hopes that I shall make you cry, bitterly."[30]

At about the same time, Alfred, Lord Tennyson began haunting London drawing-rooms with readings of his most famous (and very long) poem, *Maud*. Tennyson sought not power in the reading, as Dickens did, but rather continued applause, confirmation that his work did indeed have an audience. "Allingham, would it disgust you if I read *Maud*? Would you expire?" he asked a friend in 1865.[31] Jane Carlyle recalled him going about at a party asking people if they had liked *Maud*, and reading *Maud* aloud, "talking Maud, Maud, Maud" and "as sensitive to criticisms as if they were imputations on his honour".[32] She was a patient listener; at the Carlyle home in Chelsea, Tennyson had forced her to approve the poem by reading it to her three times in succession.[33] According to another witness, Dante Gabriel Rossetti, Tennyson read his own work with the emotion he sought in his audience, shedding tears and "with such intensity of feeling that he seized and kept quite unconsciously twisting in his powerful hands a large brocaded cushion".[34] Emerson missed that intensity when reading Tennyson's poems aloud himself. "It is a pretty good test of a ballad, as of all poetry," he confided in his notebooks, "the facility of reading it aloud. Even in Tennyson, the voice grows solemn and drowsy."[35]

Dickens was a much more professional performer. His version of the text — the tone, the emphasis, even the deletions and amendments to make the story better suited to an oral delivery — made it clear to everyone that there was to be one and only one interpretation. This became evident on his celebrated reading tours. The first extensive tour, beginning in Clifton and ending in Brighton, comprised some eighty readings in more than forty towns. He "read in warehouses, assembly rooms, booksellers, offices, halls, hotels and pump rooms." At a high desk, and later at a lower one, to allow his audience to see his gestures better, he entreated them to try to create the impression of "a small group of friends assembled to hear a tale told". The public reacted as Dickens wished. One man cried openly and then "covered his face with both hands, and lay down on the back of the seat before him, and really shook with emotion." Another, whenever he felt a certain character was about to reappear, would "laugh and wipe his eyes afresh, and when he came he gave a kind of cry, as if it were too much for him." Pliny would have approved.

The effect was laboriously obtained; Dickens had spent at least two months working on his delivery and gestures. He had scripted his reactions. In the margins of his "reading books" — copies of his work which he had edited for these tours — he had noted reminders to himself of the tone to use, such as "Cheerful. . . . Stern. . . . Pathos. . . . Mystery. . . . Quick on", as well as gestures: "Beckon down. . . . Point. . . . Shudder. . . . Look Round in Terror. . . ."[36] Passages were revised according to the effect produced on the audience. But, as one of his biographers notes, "he did not act out the scenes, but suggest them, evoke them, intimate them. He remained a reader, in other words, and not an actor. No mannerisms. No artifice. No affectations. Somehow he created his startling effects by an economy of means which was unique to himself, so it is truly as if the novels themselves spoke through him."[37] After the reading, he never acknowledged the applause. He would bow, leave the stage and change his clothes, which would be drenched with sweat.

This was, in part, what Dickens's audience came for, and what brings the audiences of today to public readings: to watch the writer perform, not as an actor, but as a writer; to hear the voice the writer had in mind when a character was created; to match the writer's voice to the writing. Some readers come out of superstition. They want to know what a writer looks like, because they believe that writing is an act of magic; they want to see the face of someone who can create a novel or a poem in the same way that they would want to see the face of a small god, creator of a little universe. They hunt for autographs, thrusting books under the author's nose in the hope that they will come away with the blessed inscription "To Polonius, best wishes, the Author."Their enthusiasm led William Golding to say (during the 1989 literary festival in Toronto) that "one day, someone will find an unsigned William Golding novel and it will be worth a fortune."They are driven by the same curiosity that makes children look behind a puppet theatre or take apart a clock. They want to kiss the hand that wrote *Ulysses* even though, as Joyce remarked, "it did lots of other things, too."[38] The Spanish writer Dámaso Alonso was not impressed. He considered public readings "an expression of snobbish hypocrisy and of the incurable superficiality of our time." Distinguishing between the gradual discovery of a book read silently, in solitude, and a quick acquaintance with an author in a crowded amphitheatre, he described the latter as "the true fruit of our unconscious haste. That is to say, of our barbarism. Because culture is slowness."[39]

At authors' readings, at writers' festivals in Toronto, Edinburgh, Melbourne or Salamanca, readers expect that they will become part of the artistic process. The unexpected, the unrehearsed, the event that will prove somehow unforgettable, may, they hope, happen in front of their eyes, making them witnesses to a moment of creation — a joy denied even to Adam — so that when someone asks them in their gossipy old age, as Robert Browning once asked ironically, "And did you once see Shelley plain?" the answer will be yes.

In an essay on the plight of the panda, the biologist Stephen Jay Gould wrote that "zoos are changing from institutions of capture and display to havens of preservation and propagation."[40] At the best of literary festivals, at the most successful public readings, writers are both preserved and propagated. Preserved because they are made to feel (as Pliny confessed) that they have an audience that attaches importance to their work; preserved, in the crudest sense, because they get paid (as Pliny wasn't) for their labours; and propagated because writers breed readers, who in turn breed writers. The listeners who buy books after a reading multiply that reading; the author who realizes that he or she may be writing on a blank page but is at least not speaking to a blank wall may be encouraged by the experience, and write more.

THE TRANSLATOR

AS READER

I n a café not far from the Rodin Museum in Paris, I laboriously pick my way through a small paperback edition of Rainer Maria Rilke's translations into German of the sonnets of Louise Labé, a sixteenth-century poet from Lyons. Rilke worked as Rodin's secretary for several years, and later became the sculptor's friend, writing an admirable essay on the old man's craft. He lived for a time in the building that was to become the Rodin Museum, in a sunlit room with ornate plaster mouldings, overlooking the over-grown French garden, mourning something he imagined was always to be beyond his grasp — a certain poetic truth that generations of read-ers since have believed could be found in Rilke's own writing. The room was one of his many transitory dwellings, from hotel to hotel and from castle to sumptuous castle. "Never forget that solitude is my lot," he wrote from Rodin's house to one of his women lovers, as transitory as his rooms. "I implore those who love me to love my solitude."[1] From my table at the café I can see the solitary window that was Rilke's; if he were there today, he could see me far below, reading the book he was one day to write. Under his ghost's vigilant eye, I repeat the end of Sonnet XIII.

Er küßte mich, es mundete mein Geist
auf seine Lippen; und der Tod war sicher
noch süßer als das dasein, seliglicher.

[He kissed me, my soul transformed itself
Upon his lips; and death was certainly
Sweeter than living, even more blessed.]

I stop for a long moment at that last word, *seliglicher*. *Seele* is "soul"; *selig* means "blessed" but also "overjoyed", "blissful". The augmentative, *-icher*, allows the soulful word to trip gently off the tongue four times before ending. It seems to extend that blessed joy given by the lover's kiss; it remains, like the kiss, in the mouth until the *-er* exhales it back onto the lips. All the other words in those three lines ring out mono-chordally, one by one; only *seliglicher* holds onto the voice for a much longer moment, reluctant to let go.

I look up the sonnet's original in another paperback, this time the *Oeuvres poétiques* of Louise Labé,[2] who has, through the miracle of publishing, become Rilke's contemporary on my café table. She had written:

Lors que souef plus il me baiserait,
Et mon esprit sur ses lèvres fuirait,
Bien je mourrais, plus que vivante, heureuse.

[When he softly kisses me further,
And my soul escapes onto his lips,
I will surely die, happier than when I lived.]

Leaving aside the modern connotation of *baiserait* (which in Labé's time meant nothing more than kissing, but has since acquired the meaning of full sexual intercourse), the French original seems to me conventional, though pleasantly direct. To be happier in the death throes of love than in the miseries of living is one of the oldest poetic claims; the soul exhaled in a kiss is equally ancient and equally trite. What did Rilke uncover in Labé's poem that allowed him to convert the ordinary *heureuse* into the memorable *seliglicher*? What enabled him to provide me, who might otherwise have leafed distractedly through Labé's poems, with this complex and disturbing reading? How far does the reading of a gifted translator such as Rilke affect our knowledge of the original? And what happens in this case to the reader's reliance on an author's authority? I believe that some shape of an answer formed itself, in Rilke's mind, one winter in Paris.

Carl Jacob Burckhardt — not the celebrated author of *The Civilisation of the Renaissance in Italy* but a younger, far less notorious fellow Swiss and fellow historian — had left his native Basel to study in France, and in the early 1920s found himself working at the Bibliothèque Nationale in Paris. One morning, he entered a barbershop near the Madeleine and asked to have his hair washed.[3] As he was sitting with his eyes closed in front of the mirror, he heard behind him a rising quarrel. In a deep voice, someone was shouting:

"Sir, that could be everyone's excuse!"
A woman's voice piped up:
"Unbelievable! And he even asked for the Houbigant lotion!"
"Sir, we don't know you. You're a complete stranger to us. We
    don't take kindly to this sort of thing here!"
A third voice, weak and whining, which seemed to come
    from another dimension — rustic, with a Slavic accent
    — was attempting to explain: "But you must forgive
    me, I forgot my wallet, I'll simply go and fetch it at the
    hotel. . . ."
At the risk of filling his eyes with soap, Burckhardt looked
    round. Three barbers were gesticulating wildly. Behind
    the desk, the cashier was watching, purple lips pursed
    tight with righteous indignation. And in front of them a
    small, unobtrusive man with a high forehead and a long
    moustache was pleading, "I promise you, you can phone
    the hotel to make sure. I am . . . I am . . . the poet Rainer
    Maria Rilke."
"Of course. That's what *everyone* says," growled the barber.
    "You're certainly not anyone *we* know."
Burckhardt, hair dripping, jumped off his chair, and putting
    his hand into his pocket, loudly announced: "*I'll* pay!"

Burckhardt had met Rilke some time earlier, but hadn't been aware that the poet was now back in Paris. For a long moment Rilke didn't recognize his saviour; when he did, he burst out laughing and offered to wait until Burckhardt was ready and then take him for a walk across the river. Burckhardt agreed. After a while, Rilke said he was tired and, since it was too early for lunch, suggested that they visit a second-hand bookstore not far from the Place de l'Odéon. As the two men entered, the old bookseller greeted them by rising from his seat and waving at them the small leather-bound volume he had been reading. "This, gentlemen," he called out to them, "is the 1867 Ronsard, Blanchemin's edition." Rilke answered with delight that he loved Ronsard's poems. The

A contemporary portrait of Louise Labé.

mention of one author led to another, and finally the bookseller quoted some verses by Racine which he believed were a literal translation of Psalm 36.[4] "Yes," Rilke agreed. "They are the same human words, the same concepts, the same experience and intuitions." And then, as if making a sudden discovery: "Translation is the purest procedure by which the poetic skill can be recognized."

This was to be Rilke's last Paris sojourn. He was to die two years later, at the age of fifty-one, on December 29, 1926, of a rare form of leukemia which he never dared mention, even to those who were closest to him. (With poetic licence, in his last days he encouraged his friends to think he was dying from the prick of a rose thorn.) The first time he had come to settle in Paris, in 1902, he had been poor, young and almost unknown; now he was Europe's best-known poet, praised and famous (though obviously not among barbers). In the meantime he had returned to Paris several times, on each occasion attempting to "start again" on his quest for "the ineffable truth". "The beginning here is always a judgement,"[5] he wrote about Paris to a friend shortly after finishing his novel *The Notebooks of Malte Laurids Brigge*, a task which he felt had emptied him of creative sap. In an attempt to resume his own writing, he decided to undertake several translations: a romantic novella by Maurice de Guérin, an anonymous sermon on the love of Mary Magdalen, and the sonnets of Louise Labé, whose book he had discovered in his wanderings through the city.

The sonnets had been written in Lyons, a city which in the sixteenth century rivalled Paris as the centre of French culture. Louise Labé — Rilke preferred the old-fashioned spelling, "Louize" — "was known in all Lyons and beyond not only for her beauty but for her accomplishments. She was as skilled in military exercises and games as her brothers were, and rode with such daring that friends, in fun and admiration, called her Capitaine Loys. She was renowned for her playing of that difficult instrument, the lute, and for her singing. She was a woman of letters, leaving a volume published by Jean de Tournes in 1555 which contained a Dedicatory Epistle, a play, three elegies, twenty-four sonnets, and poems written in her honour by some of the most distinguished men of her time. In her library were to be found books in Spanish, Italian, and Latin as well as French."[6]

At the age of sixteen she fell in love with a soldier and rode out to fight by his side in the Dauphin's army, during the siege of Perpignan. Legend has it that from that love (though attributing sources of inspiration to a poet is a notoriously hazardous occupation) sprang the two dozen sonnets for which she is remembered. The collection, presented to another Lyonnaise woman of letters, Mademoiselle Clémence de Bourges, carries an illuminating dedication: "The past," Labé writes there, "gives us pleasure and is of more service than the present; but the delight of what we once felt is dimly lost, never to return, and its memory is as distressing as the events themselves were then delectable. The other voluptuous senses are so strong that whatever memory returns to us it cannot restore our previous disposition, and however strong the images we impress in our minds, we still know that they are but shadows of the past misusing us and deceiving us. But when we happen to put our thoughts in writing, how easily, later on, does our mind race through an infinity of events, incessantly alive, so that when a long time afterwards we take up those written pages we can return to the same place and to the same disposition in which we once found ourselves."[7] For Louise Labé, the reader's ability is to re-create the past.

But whose past? Rilke was one of those poets who, in his reading, was constantly reminding himself of his own biography: his miserable childhood, his domineering father who forced him into military school, his snobbish mother who regretted not having a daughter and dressed him in girl's clothes, his inability to maintain amorous relationships, torn as he was between the seductions of chic society and the life of a hermit. He began reading Labé three years before the outbreak of the First World War, at a loss in his own work in which he seemed to recognize the desolation and horror to come.

> For when I gaze until I disappear
> In my own gaze, I seem to carry death.[8]

In a letter he wrote, "I don't think of work, only of gradually regaining my health through reading, rereading, reflecting."[9] It was a multitudinous activity.

Recasting Labé's sonnets into German, Rilke was engaged in many readings at once. He was recapturing — as Labé had suggested — the past, though not Labé's, of which he knew nothing, but his own. In "the same human words, the same concepts, the same experience and intuitions", he was able to read what Labé had never evoked.

He was reading for the sense, deciphering a text in a language which was not his but in which he had become sufficiently fluent to write his own poetry. Sense is often dictated by the language being used. Something is said, not necessarily because the author chooses to say it in a particular way, but because in that specific language a certain sequence of words is required to constellate a sense, a certain music is deemed agreeable, certain constructions are eschewed as cacophonous or carry a double sense or appear to have fallen out of use. All the fashionable trappings of language conspire to favour one set of words over another.

He was reading for the meaning. Translating is the ultimate act of comprehending. For Rilke, the reader who reads in order to translate engages on a "purest procedure" of questions and answers by which that most elusive of notions, the literary meaning, is gleaned. Gleaned but never made explicit, because in the particular alchemy of this kind of reading the meaning is immediately transformed into another, equivalent text. And the poet's meaning progresses from words to words, metamorphosed from one language into another.

He was reading the long ancestry of the book he was reading, since the books we read are also the books others have read. I don't mean that vicarious pleasure of holding in our hands a volume that once belonged to another reader, conjured up like a ghost through the whisper of a few scribbled words on the margin, a signature on the flyleaf, a dried leaf left as a marker, a tell-tale wine-stain. I mean that every book has been engendered by long successions of other books whose covers you may never see and whose authors you may never know but which echo in the one you now hold in your hand. What were the books that stood so preciously in Labé's proud library? We don't know exactly but we can guess. Spanish editions of Garcilaso de la Vega, for instance, the poet who introduced the Italian sonnet to the rest of Europe, were no doubt known to her, since his work was being translated in Lyons. And her publisher, Jean de Tournes, had brought out French editions of Hesiod and Aesop, and had published editions of Dante and Petrarch in Italian, as well as the works of several other Lyonnais poets,[10] and it is likely that she had received from him copies of several of these. In Labé's sonnets, Rilke was also reading her readings of Petrarch, of Garcilaso, of Labé's contemporary the great Ronsard, whom Rilke was to discuss with the Odéon bookseller on a winter afternoon in Paris.

Like every reader, Rilke was also reading through his own experience. Beyond the literal sense and the literary meaning, the text we read acquires the projection of our own experience, the shadow, as it were, of who we are. Louise Labé's soldier, who may have inspired her ardent verses is, like Labé herself, a fictional character for Rilke, reading her in his room four centuries later. Of her passion he could know nothing: her restless nights, the fruitless waiting by the door pretending to be happy, the overheard mention of the soldier's name that made her catch her breath, the shock of seeing him ride past her window and almost immediately realizing that it was not he but someone who resembled his matchless figure — all these were absent from the book Rilke kept by his bedside table. All he could bring to the printed words that Labé had penned years afterwards — when she was happily married to the middle-aged ropemaker Ennemond Perrin, and her soldier had become little more than a somewhat embarrassing memory — was his own desolation. It sufficed, of course, because we readers, like Narcissus, like to believe that the text into which we gaze holds our reflection. Even before contemplating possession of the text through translation, Rilke must have read Labé's poems as if her first-person singular were also his.

Reviewing Rilke's translations of Labé, George Steiner reproved him *because* of their excellence, allying himself with Dr. Johnson. "A translator is to be like his author," wrote Johnson; "it is not his business to excel him." And Steiner added, "Where he does so, the original is subtly injured. And the reader is robbed of a just view."[11] The clue to Steiner's criticism lies in the epithet "just". Reading Louise Labé today — reading her in the original French outside Labé's own time and place — necessarily lends the text the reader's optic. Etymology, sociology, studies of fashion and the history of art — all these enrich a reader's understanding of a text, but ultimately much of this is mere archeology. Louise Labé's twelfth sonnet, which begins *Luth, compagnon de ma calamité*, ("Lute, companion of my misfortune"), addresses the lute, in the second quatrain, in these terms:

Et tant le pleur piteux t'a molesté
Que, commençant quelque son délectable,
Tu le rendais tout soudain lamentable,
Feignant le ton que plein avais chanté.

A literal word-by-word translation might read:

And the pitiable weeping so upset you
That, as I began (to play) some pleasant sound,
All of a sudden you turned it pitiful,
Pretending (to play as minor) the key which I had sung as
    major.

Here Labé makes use of an arcane musical language which she, as a lute player, must have known well, but which is incomprehensible to us without a historical dictionary of musical terms. *Plein ton* meant, in the sixteenth century, the major key, as opposed to the *ton feint* — the minor key. *Feint* literally means "false, pretended". The line suggests that the lute plays in a minor key that which the poet has sung in a "full" (i.e., major) key. To understand this, the contemporary reader must acquire a knowledge that was common to Labé, must become (in equivalent terms) far more instructed than Labé merely to keep up with her in her time. The exercise is, of course, futile if the purpose is to assume the position of Labé's audience: we cannot become the reader for whom her poem was intended. Rilke, however, reads:

[. . .] Ich riß
dich so hinein in diesen Gang der Klagen,
drin ich befangen bin, daß, wo ich je
seligen Ton versuchend angeschlagen,
da unterschlugst du ihn und tontest weg.

[. . .] I led
You so deep along the path of sorrow
In which I'm trapped, that anywhere

I try to strike a blissful tone,
There you conceal and mute it until it dies away.

No knowledge of specialized German is required here, and yet
every musical metaphor in Louise Labé's sonnet is faithfully preserved.
But German allows further explorations, and Rilke charges the quatrain with a more complex reading than Labé, writing in French, *could*
have perceived. The homophonies between *anschlagen* ("to strike") and
unterschlagen ("to embezzle, to pocket, to stash away") serve him to
compare the two amorous attitudes: that of Labé, the distressed lover,
attempting to "strike a blissful tone", and that of her lute, her faithful
companion, the witness of her true feelings, who will not allow her to
sound a "dishonest", "false" tone and who, paradoxically, will "embezzle
it", "conceal it", in order to allow her to become, at last, silent. Rilke
(and here is where the reader's experience bears down on the text)
reads into Labé's sonnets images of travel, cloistered sorrow, silence
preferable to the false expression of feelings, the unyielding supremacy
of the poetic instrument over any social niceties such as pretence of
happiness, which are the features of his own life. Labé's setting is
chambered, like that of her distant sisters in Heian Japan; she is a
woman alone, mourning her love; in Rilke's time, the image, commonplace in the Renaissance, is no longer resonant and requires an explanation of how she came to be "trapped" in this place of sorrow.
Something of Louise Labé's simplicity (dare one say banality?) is lost,
but much is gained in depth, in tragic feeling. It is not that Rilke's reading distorts Labé's poem more than any other reading beyond her century; it is a better reading than most of us are capable of, one that
makes our reading possible, since any other reading of Labé must remain, for us on this side of time, at the level of our impoverished individual intellectual skills.

Asking why, of the work of all the twentieth-century poets,
Rilke's difficult poetry acquired such popularity in the West, the
critic Paul de Man suggested that it might be because "many have read
him as if he addressed the most secluded parts of their selves,
revealing depths they hardly suspected or allowing them to share in
ordeals he helped them to understand and to overcome."[12] Rilke's
reading of Labé "solves" nothing, in the sense of rendering Labé's
simplicity even more explicit; instead, his task seems to have been the
deepening of her poetic thought, carrying it further than the original

was prepared to go, seeing, as it were, more in Labé's words than Labé herself saw.

As early as Labé's time, the respect accorded to the authority of a text had long been in abeyance. In the twelfth century, Abelard had denounced the habit of attributing one's opinions to others, to Aristotle or to the Arabs, in order to avoid being directly criticized;[13] this — "the argument of authority", which Abelard compared to the chain by which beasts are attached and led on blindly — was possible because in the mind of the reader the classical text and its acknowledged author were deemed infallible. And if the accepted reading was infallible, what room was there for interpretations?

Even the text judged most infallible of all — God's Word itself, the Bible — underwent a long series of transformations in the hands of its successive readers. From the Old Testament canon established in the second century AD by Rabbi Akiba ben Joseph to John Wycliffe's English translation in the fourteenth century, the book called the Bible was at times the Greek Septuagint of the third century BC (and the basis for subsequent Latin translations), the so-called Vulgate (Saint Jerome's Latin version of the late fourth century) and all the later Bibles of the Middle Ages: Gothic, Slavic, Armenian, Old English, West Saxon, Anglo-Norman, French, Frisian, German, Irish, Netherlandish, Central Italian, Provençal, Spanish, Catalan, Polish, Welsh, Czech, Hungarian. Each one of these was, for its readers, *the* Bible, yet each allowed for a different reading. In this multiplicity of Bibles, some saw the humanists' dream being accomplished. Erasmus had written, "I wish that even the weakest woman should read the Gospel — should read the Epistles of Paul. And I wish that these were translated into all the languages so that they might be read and understood, not only by Scots and Irishmen, but also by Turks and Saracens. . . . I long that the husbandman should sing portions of them to himself as he follows the plough, that the weaver should hum them to the tune of his shuttle."[14] Now was their chance.

In the face of this explosion of multiple possible readings, the authorities sought a way to retain control over the text — a single authoritative book in which the word of God could be read as He intended. On January 15, 1604, at Hampton Court, in the presence of King James I, the Puritan Dr. John Rainolds "moved His Majesty that there be a new translation of the Bible because those which were allowed in the reign of Henry VIII and Edward VI were corrupt and not answerable to the truth of the original" — to which the Bishop of London answered that "if every man's humour should be followed, there would be no end to the translating."[15]

In spite of the bishop's sage warning, the king agreed and ordered that the Dean of Westminster and the regius professors of Hebrew at Cambridge and Oxford put forward a list of scholars able to undertake such a stupendous task. James was unhappy with the first list presented, since several of the men on it had "either no ecclesiastical preferment at all, or else very small", and asked the Archbishop of Canterbury to seek further suggestions from his fellow bishops. One name appeared on no one's list: that of Hugh Broughton, a great Hebrew scholar who had already completed a new translation of the Bible but whose irascible temper had made him few friends. Broughton, however, required no invitation, and sent the king himself a list of recommendations for the enterprise.

For Broughton, textual fidelity could be sought through a vocabulary that specified and updated the terms used by those who set down God's Word in a past of desert shepherds. Broughton suggested that to render exactly the technical fabric of the text, artisans should be brought in to help with specific terms, "as embroiderers for Aaron's ephod, geometricians, carpenters, masons about the Temple of Solomon and Ezekiel; and gardeners for all the boughs and branches of Ezekiel's tree."[16] (A century and a half later, Diderot and d'Alembert would proceed in exactly this manner to get the technical details right for their extraordinary *Encyclopédie*.)

Broughton (who had, as mentioned, already translated the Bible on his own) argued that a multiplicity of minds were needed to solve the endless problems of sense and meaning, preserving, at the same time, an overall coherence. To achieve this, he proposed that the king "have many to translate a part, and when they have brought a good English style and true sense, others should make an uniformity that diverse words might not be used when the original word was the same."[17] Here perhaps begins the Anglo-Saxon tradition of editing, the habit of a super-reader revising the text before publication.

One of the bishops on the scholarly committee, Bishop Bancroft, drew up a list of fifteen rules for the translators. They would follow, as closely as possible, the earlier Bishops' Bible of 1568 (a revised edition of the so-called Great Bible, which was in turn a revision of the Matthew's Bible, itself a composite of the incomplete Bible of William Tyndale and the first printed edition of a complete English Bible, produced by Miles Coverdale).

The translators, working with the Bishops' Bible in front of them, referring intermittently to the other English translations and to a wealth of Bibles in other languages, incorporated all those previous readings into their own.

Tyndale's Bible, cannibalized in successive editions, gave them much material which they now took for granted. William Tyndale, scholar and printer, had been condemned by Henry VIII as a heretic (he had earlier offended the king by criticizing his divorce from Catherine of Aragon) and in 1536 had been first strangled and then burnt at the stake for his translation of the Bible from Hebrew and Greek. Before undertaking his translation, Tyndale had written, "Because I had perceived by experience how that it was impossible to establish the lay-people in any truth, except the scriptures were plainly laid before their eyes in their mother tongue, that they might see the process, order, and meaning of the text." In order to achieve this, he had rendered the ancient words into a language both simple and artfully crafted. He introduced into the English language the words "passover", "peace-maker", "long-suffering" and (this I find inexplicably moving) the adjective "beautiful". He was the first to use the name *Jehovah* in an English Bible.

Miles Coverdale had complemented and completed Tyndale's work, publishing the first complete English Bible in 1535. A Cambridge scholar and Augustinian friar who, some say, assisted Tyndale in parts of his translation, Coverdale undertook an English version sponsored by Thomas Cromwell, Lord Chancellor of England, and drawn not from the original Hebrew and Greek but from other translations. His Bible is sometimes known as the "Treacle Bible" because it gives Jeremiah 8: 22 as "Is there treacle in Gilead" instead of "balm", or the "Bugs Bible" because the fifth verse of Psalm 91 became "Thou shalt not need be afraid of any bugs by night" for "the terror by night". It is to Coverdale that the new translators owed the phrase "the valley of the shadow of death" (Twenty-third Psalm).

But the King James translators did much more than copy out old readings. Bishop Bancroft had indicated that the vulgar forms of names and ecclesiastical words were to be kept; even if the original suggested a more accurate translation, traditional usage would prevail over exactness. In other words, Bancroft acknowledged that an established reading overrode that of the author. He wisely understood that to restore an original name would be to introduce a startling novelty that was absent in the original. For the same reason, he precluded marginal notes, recommending instead that they be "briefly and fitly" included in the text itself.

The King James translators worked in six groups: two in Westminster, two in Cambridge and two in Oxford. These forty-nine men achieved, in their private interpretations and communal blendings, an extraordinary balance of accuracy, a respect for traditional phrasing and an overall style that read not like a new work but like something long-existing. So accomplished was their result that several centuries later, when the King James Bible was established as one of the masterpieces of English prose, Rudyard Kipling imagined a story in which Shakespeare and Ben Jonson collaborated on the translation of a few verses of Isaiah for the great project.[18] Certainly the King James Bible has a poetic depth that enlarges the text beyond any mere rendering of sense. The difference between a correct but dry reading, and a precise and resonant one, can be judged by comparing, for instance, the famous Twenty-third Psalm in the Bishops' Bible to its version in the King James. The Bishops' Bible reads:

> God is my shepherd, therefore I can lose nothing;
> he will cause me to repose myself in pastures full of grass,
> and he will lead me unto calm waters.

The King James translators transformed this into:

> The Lord is my shepherd; I shall not want.
> He maketh me to lie down in green pastures:
> he leadeth me beside the still waters.

Officially the King James translation was supposed to clarify and restore meaning. Yet any successful translation is necessarily *different* from the original, since it assumes the original text as something already digested, divested of its fragile ambiguity, interpreted. It is in the translation that the innocence lost after the first reading is restored under another guise, since the reader is once again faced with a new

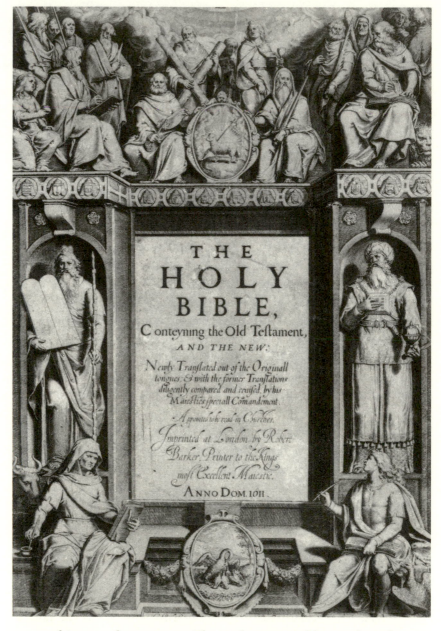

text and its attendant mystery. That is the inescapable paradox of translation, and also its wealth.

For King James and his translators the purpose of the colossal enterprise was avowedly political: to produce a Bible that people could
read singly and yet, because it was a common text, communally. Print-

ing gave them the illusion of being able to produce the same book *ad infinitum*; the act of translation heightened that illusion, but seemed to replace different versions of the text with a single one, officially approved, nationally endorsed, religiously acceptable. The King James Bible, published after four years of hard labour in 1611, became the "authorized" version, the "Everyman's Bible" in the English language, the same one that we, travelling in an English-speaking country today, find by our bedsides in our hotel rooms, in an ancient effort to create a commonwealth of readers through a unified text.

In their "Preface to the Reader", the King James translators wrote, "Translation it is that openeth the window, to let in the light; that breaketh the shell, that we may eat the kernell; that putteth aside the curtain, that we may look into the most holy place; that removeth the cover of the well, that we may come by the water." This meant not being afraid "of the light of Scripture" and entrusting the reader with the possibility of illumination; not proceeding archeologically to restore the text to an illusory pristine state, but to free it from the constraints of time and place; not simplifying for the sake of a shallow explanation, but allowing the depths of meaning to become apparent; not glossing the text in the scholastic manner, but constructing a new and equivalent text. "For is the kingdome of God become words or syllables?" asked the translators. "Why should we be in bondage to them if we may be free. . . ?" The question was still being asked several centuries later.

As Rilke, in Burckhardt's silent presence, became more and more engaged in literary chit-chat with the Odéon bookseller, an old man, obviously a habitual customer, entered the shop and, as readers are known to do when the subject is books, uninvitedly joined the conversation. Their talk soon turned to the poetic merits of Jean de La Fontaine, whose *Fables* Rilke admired, and to the Alsatian writer Johann Peter Hebel, whom the bookseller considered La Fontaine's "sort of younger brother". "Can Hebel be read in French translation?" asked Rilke, disingenuously. The old man pulled the book out of the poet's hands. "A translation of Hebel!" he cried. "A French translation! Have you ever read a French translation of a German text that is even bearable? The two languages are diametrically opposed. The only Frenchman who could have translated Hebel, supposing he had known German, and then he would not have been the same man, was La Fontaine."

"In paradise," interrupted the bookseller, who had thus far remained silent, "they no doubt speak to one another in a language we have forgotten."

To which the old man growled angrily, "Oh, to hell with paradise!"

But Rilke agreed with the bookseller. In the eleventh chapter of Genesis, the King James translators wrote that, before God confused the tongues of men to prevent the building of the Tower of Babel, "the whole earth was of one language, and of one speech." This primordial language, which the cabbalists believed was also the language of paradise, has been ardently sought many times throughout our history — always unsuccessfully.

In 1836 the German scholar Alexander von Humboldt[19] suggested that each language possesses an "inner linguistic shape" which expresses the particular universe of the people who speak it. This would imply that no word in any given language is exactly identical to any word in any other language, rendering translation an impossible task, like coining the face of the wind or braiding a cord of sand. Translation can only exist as the unruly and informal activity of understanding through the translator's language that which lies irretrievably concealed within the original.

As we read a text in our own language, the text itself becomes a barrier. We can go into it as far as its words allow, embracing all their possible definitions; we can bring other texts to bear upon it and to reflect it, as in a hall of mirrors; we can construct another, critical text that will extend and illuminate the one we are reading; but we cannot escape the fact that its language is the limit of our universe. Translation proposes a sort of parallel universe, another space and time in which the text reveals other, extraordinary possible meanings. For these meanings, however, there are no words, since they exist in the intuitive no man's land between the language of the original and the language of the translator.

According to Paul de Man, Rilke's poetry promises a truth that, in the end, the poet must confess is but a lie. "Rilke," said de Man, "can only be understood if one realizes the urgency of this promise together with the equally urgent, and equally poetic, need of retracting it at the very instant he seems to be on the point of offering it to us."[20] In this ambiguous place to which Rilke brings Labé's verses, the words (Labé's or Rilke's — the possessive author no longer matters) become so brilliantly rich that no further translation is possible. The reader

(I am that reader, sitting at my café table with the French and German poems open in front of me) must apprehend those words intimately, no longer through any explicatory language but as an overwhelming, immediate, *wordless* experience that both re-creates and redefines the world, through the page and far beyond it — what Nietzsche called "the movement of style" in a text. Translation may be an impossibility, a betrayal, a fraud, an invention, a hopeful lie — but in the process, it makes the reader a wiser, better listener: less certain, far more sensitive, *seliglicher*.

FORBIDDEN

READING

In 1660, Charles II of England, son of the king who had so unfortunately consulted Virgil's oracle, known to his subjects as the Merrie Monarch for his love of pleasure and loathing of business, decreed that the Council for Foreign Plantations should instruct natives, servants and slaves of the British colonies in the precepts of Christianity. Dr. Johnson, who from the vantage point of the following century admired the king, said that "he had the merit of endeavouring to do what he thought was for the salvation of the souls of his subjects, till he lost a great empire."[1] The historian Macaulay,[2] who from a distance of two centuries did not, argued that for Charles "the love of God, the love of country, the love of family, the love of friends, were phrases of the same sort, delicate and convenient synonyms for the love of self."[3]

It isn't clear why Charles issued this decree in the first year of his reign, except that he imagined it to be a way of laying out new grounds for religious tolerance, which Parliament opposed. Charles, who in spite of his pro-Catholic tendencies proclaimed himself loyal to the Protestant faith, believed (as far as he believed anything) that, as Luther had taught, the salvation of the soul depended on each individual's ability to read God's word for himself or herself.[4] But British slave-owners were not convinced. They feared the very idea of a "literate black population" who might find dangerous revolutionary ideas in books. They did not believe those who argued that a literacy restricted to the Bible would strengthen the bonds of society; they realized that if slaves could

OPPOSITE

A rare photograph of a slave reading, taken c. 1856 in Aiken, South Carolina.

read the Bible, they could also read abolitionist tracts, and that even in the Scriptures the slaves might find inflammatory notions of revolt and freedom.[5] The opposition to Charles's decree was strongest in the American colonies, and strongest of all in South Carolina, where, a century later, strict laws were proclaimed forbidding all blacks, whether slaves or free men, to be taught to read. These laws were in effect until well into the mid-nineteenth century.

For centuries, Afro-American slaves learned to read against extraordinary odds, risking their lives in a process that, because of the difficulties set in their way, sometimes took several years. The accounts of their learning are many and heroic. Ninety-year-old Belle Myers Carothers — interviewed by the Federal Writers' Project, a commission set up in the 1930s to record, among other things, the personal narratives of former slaves — recalled that she had learned her letters while looking after the plantation owner's baby, who was playing with alphabet blocks. The owner, seeing what she was doing, kicked her with his boots. Myers persisted, secretly studying the child's letters as well as a few words in a speller she had found. One day, she said, "I found a hymn book . . . and spelled out 'When I Can Read My Title Clear'. I was so happy when I saw that I could really read, that I ran around telling all the other slaves."[6] Leonard Black's master once found him with a book and whipped him so severely "that he overcame my thirst for knowledge, and I relinquished its pursuit until after I absconded".[7] Doc Daniel Dowdy recalled that "the first time you was caught trying to read or write you was whipped with a cow-hide, the next time with a cat-o-nine-tails and the third time they cut the first joint off your forefinger."[8] Throughout the South, it was common for plantation owners to hang any slave who tried to teach the others how to spell.[9]

Under these circumstances, slaves who wanted to be literate were forced to find devious methods of learning, either from other slaves or from sympathetic white teachers, or by inventing devices that allowed them to study unobserved. The American writer Frederick Douglass, who was born into slavery and became one of the most eloquent abolitionists of his day, as well as founder of several political journals, recalled in his autobiography: "The frequent hearing of my mistress reading the Bible aloud . . . awakened my curiosity in respect to this *mystery* of reading, and roused in me the desire to learn. Up to this time I had known nothing whatever of this wonderful art, and my ignorance and inexperience of what it could do for me, as well as my confidence in my mistress, emboldened me to ask her to teach me to read. . . . In an incredibly short time, by her kind assistance, I had mastered the alphabet and could spell words of three or four letters.... [My master] forbade her to give me any further instruction . . . [but] the determination which he expressed to keep me in ignorance only rendered me the more resolute to seek intelligence. In learning to read, therefore, I am not sure that I do not owe quite as much to the opposition of my master as to the kindly assistance of my amiable mistress."[10] Thomas Johnson, a slave who later became a well-known missionary preacher in England, explained that he had learned to read by studying the letters in a Bible he had stolen. Since his master read aloud a chapter from the New Testament every night, Johnson would coax him to read the same chapter over and over, until he knew it by heart and was able to find the same words on the printed page. Also, when the master's son was studying, Johnson would suggest that the boy read part of his lesson out loud. "Lor's over me," Johnson would say to encourage him, "read that again," which the boy often did, believing that Johnson was admiring his perfomance. Through repetition, he learned enough to be able to read the newspapers by the time the Civil War broke out, and later set up a school of his own to teach others to read.[11]

Learning to read was, for slaves, not an immediate passport to freedom but rather a way of gaining access to one of the powerful instruments of their oppressors: the book. The slave-owners (like dictators, tyrants, absolute monarchs and other illicit holders of power) were strong believers in the power of the written word. They knew, far better than some readers, that reading is a strength that requires barely a few first words to become overwhelming. Someone able to read one sentence is able to read all; more important, that reader has now the possibility of reflecting upon the sentence, of acting upon it, of giving it a meaning. "You can play dumb with a sentence," said the Austrian playwright Peter Handke. "Assert yourself with the sentence against other sentences. Name everything that gets in your way and move it out of the way. Familiarize yourself with all objects. Make all objects into a sentence with the sentence. You can make all objects into your sentence. With this sentence, all objects belong to you. With this sentence, all objects are yours."[12] For all these reasons, reading had to be forbidden.

As centuries of dictators have known, an illiterate crowd is easiest to rule; since the craft of reading cannot be untaught once it has been acquired, the second-best recourse is to limit its scope. Therefore, like

A sixteenth-
century Chinese
woodblock
depicting the
burning of
books by the
First Emperor
Shih Huang-ti.

no other human creation, books have been the bane of dictatorships. Absolute power requires that all reading be official reading; instead of whole libraries of opinions, the ruler's word should suffice. Books, wrote Voltaire in a satirical pamphlet called "Concerning the Horrible Danger of Reading", "dissipate ignorance, the custodian and safeguard of well-policed states".[13] Censorship, therefore, in some form or another, is the corollary of all power, and the history of reading is lit by a seemingly endless line of censors' bonfires, from the earliest papyrus scrolls to the books of our time. The works of Protagoras were burned in 411 BC in Athens. In the year 213 BC the Chinese emperor Shih Huang-ti tried to put an end to reading by burning all the books in his realm. In 168 BC, the Jewish Library in Jerusalem was deliberately destroyed during the Maccabean uprising. In the first century AD, Augustus exiled the poets Cornelius Gallus and Ovid and banned their works. The emperor Caligula ordered that all books by Homer, Virgil and Livy be burned (but his edict was not carried out). In 303, Diocletian condemned all Christian books to the fire. And these were only the beginning. The young Goethe, witnessing the burning of a book in Frankfurt, felt that he was attending an execution. "To see an inanimate object being punished," he wrote, "is in and of itself something truly terrible."[14] The illusion cherished by those who burn books is that, in doing so, they are able to cancel history and abolish the past. On May 10, 1933, in Berlin,

The Nazi burning of books in Berlin, 10 May 1933.

as the cameras rolled, propaganda minister Paul Joseph Goebbels spoke during the burning of more than twenty thousand books, in front of a cheering crowd of more than one hundred thousand people: "Tonight you do well to throw in the fire these obscenities from the past. This is a powerful, huge and symbolic action that will tell the entire world that the old spirit is dead. From these ashes will rise the phoenix of the new spirit." A twelve-year-old boy, Hans Pauker, later head of the Leo Baeck Institute for Jewish Studies in London, was present at the burning, and recalled that, as the books were thrown into the flames, speeches were made to add solemnity to the occasion.[15] "Against the exaggeration of unconscious urges based on destructive analysis of the psyche, for the nobility of the human soul, I commit to the flames the works of Sigmund Freud," one of the censors would declaim before burning Freud's books. Steinbeck, Marx, Zola, Hemingway, Einstein, Proust, H.G. Wells, Heinrich and Thomas Mann, Jack London, Bertolt Brecht and hundreds of others received the homage of similar epitaphs.

In 1872, a little over two centuries after Charles II's optimistic decree, Anthony Comstock — a descendant of the old colonialists who had objected to their sovereign's educating urges — founded in New York the Society for the Suppression of Vice, the first effective censorship board in the United States. All things considered, Comstock would have preferred that reading had never been invented ("Our father Adam could not read in Paradise," he once affirmed), but since it had, he was determined to regulate its use. Comstock saw himself as a reader's reader, who knew what was good literature and what was bad, and did everything in his power to impose his views on others. "As for me," he wrote in his journal a year before the society's founding, "I am resolved that I will not in God's strength yield to other people's opinion but will if I feel and believe I am right stand firm. Jesus was never moved from the path of duty, however hard, by public opinion. Why should I be?"[16]

Anthony Comstock was born in New Canaan, Connecticut, on March 7, 1844. He was a hefty man, and in the course of his censoring career he many times used his size to defeat his opponents physically. One of his contemporaries described him in these terms: "Standing about five feet in his shoes, he carries his two hundred and ten pounds of muscle and bone so well that you would judge him to weigh not over a hundred and eighty. His Atlas shoulders of enormous girth, surmounted by a bull-like neck, are in keeping with a biceps and a calf of exceptional size and iron solidarity. His legs are short, and remind one somewhat of tree trunks."[17]

Comstock was in his twenties when he arrived in New York with $3.45 in his pocket. He found a job as a dry-goods salesman and was soon able to save the $500 necessary to buy a little house in Brooklyn. A few years later, he met the daughter of a Presbyterian minister, ten years his elder, and married her. In New York, Comstock discovered much that he found objectionable. In 1868, after a friend told him how he had been "led astray and corrupted and diseased" by a certain book (the title of this powerful work has not come down to us), Comstock bought a copy at the store and then, accompanied by a policeman, had the shopkeeper arrested and the stock seized. The success of his first raid was such that he decided to continue, regularly causing the arrest of small publishers and printers of titillating material.

A contemporary American caricature of the self-appointed censor Anthony Comstock.

With the assistance of friends in the YMCA, who supplied him with $8,500, Comstock was able to set up the society for which he became famous. Two years before his death, he told an interviewer in New York, "In the forty-one years I have been here, I have convicted persons enough to fill a passenger train of sixty-one coaches, sixty coaches containing sixty passengers each and the sixty-first almost full. I have destroyed 160 tons of obscene literature."[18]

Comstock's fervour was also responsible for at least fifteen suicides. After he had a former Irish surgeon, William Haynes, thrown in prison "for publishing 165 different kinds of lewd literature", Haynes killed himself. Shortly afterwards, Comstock was about to catch the Brooklyn ferry (he later recalled) when "a Voice" told him to proceed to Haynes's house. He arrived as the widow was unloading the printing-plates of the forbidden books from a delivery wagon. With great agility Comstock leapt onto the wagoner's seat and rushed the wagon to the YMCA, where the plates were destroyed.[19]

What books did Comstock read? He was an unwitting follower of Oscar Wilde's facetious advice: "I never read a book I must review; it prejudices you so." Sometimes, however, he dipped into the books before destroying them, and was aghast at what he read. He found the literature of France and Italy "little better than histories of brothels and prostitutes in these lust-crazed nations. How often are found in these villainous stories, heroines, lovely, excellent, cultivated, wealthy, and charming in every way, who have for their lovers married men; or, after marriage, lovers flock about the charming young wife, enjoying privileges belonging only to the husband!" Even the classics were not above reproach. "Take, for instance, a well-known book written by Boccaccio," he wrote in his book, *Traps for the Young*. The book was so filthy that he would do anything "to prevent this, like a wild beast, from breaking loose and destroying the youth of the country."[20] Balzac, Rabelais, Walt Whitman, Bernard Shaw and Tolstoy were among his victims. Comstock's everyday reading was, he said, the Bible.

Comstock's methods were savage but superficial. He lacked the perception and patience of more sophisticated censors, who will mine a text with excruciating care in search of buried messages. In 1981, for instance, the military junta led by General Pinochet banned *Don Quixote* in Chile, because the general believed (quite rightly) that it contained a plea for individual freedom and an attack on conventional authority.

Comstock's censoring limited itself to placing suspect works, in a rage of abuse, on a catalogue of the damned. His access to books was also limited; he could only chase them as they appeared in public, by which time many had escaped into the hands of eager readers. The Catholic Church was far ahead of him. In 1559, the Sacred Congregation of the Roman Inquisition had published the first *Index of Forbidden Books* — a list of books that the Church considered dangerous to the faith and morals of Roman Catholics. The *Index*, which included books censored in advance of publication as well as immoral books already published, was never intended as a complete catalogue of all the books banned by the Church. When it was abandoned in June 1966, however, it contained — among hundreds of theological works — hundreds of others by secular writers from Voltaire and Diderot to Colette and Graham Greene. No doubt Comstock would have found such a list useful.

"Art is not above morals. Morals stand first," Comstock wrote. "Law ranks next as the defender of public morals. Art only comes in conflict with the law when its tendency is obscene, lewd or indecent." This led the *New York World* to ask, in an editorial, "Has it really been determined that there is nothing wholesome in art unless it has clothes on?"[21] Comstock's definition of immoral art, like that of all censors, begs the question. Comstock died in 1915. Two years later, the American essayist H.L. Mencken defined Comstock's crusade as "the new Puritanism", . . . "not ascetic but militant. Its aim is not to lift up saints but to knock down sinners."[22]

Comstock's conviction was that what he called "immoral literature" perverted the minds of the young, who

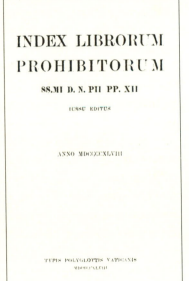

INDEX LIBRORUM PROHIBITORUM

SS.MI D. N. PII PP. XII

IUSSU EDITUS

ANNO MDCCCCXLVIII

TYPIS POLYGLOTTIS VATICANIS
MDCCCCXLVIII

Title-page of the Catholic *Index*, revised for the last time in 1948 and not reprinted after 1966.

should busy themselves with higher spiritual matters. This concern is ancient, and not exclusive to the West. In fifteenth-century China, a collection of tales from the Ming Dynasty known as *Stories Old and New* was so successful that it had to be placed in the Chinese index so as not to distract young scholars from the study of Confucius.[23] In the Western world, a milder form of this obsession has expressed itself in a general fear of fiction — at least since the days of Plato, who banned poets from his ideal republic. Madame Bovary's mother-in-law argued that novels were poisoning Emma's soul, and convinced her son to stop Emma's subscription to a book-lender, plunging her further into the swamp of boredom.[24] The mother of the English writer Edmund Gosse would allow no novels of any kind, religious or secular, to enter the house. As a very small child, in the early 1800s, she had amused herself and her brothers by reading and making up stories, until her Calvinist governess found out and lectured her severely, telling her that her pleasures were wicked. "From that time forth," wrote Mrs. Gosse in her diary, "I considered that to invent a story of any kind was a sin." But "the longing to invent stories grew with violence; everything I heard or read became food for my distemper. The simplicity of truth was not sufficient for me; I must needs embroider imagination upon it, and the folly, vanity and wickedness which disgraced my heart are more than I am able to express. Even now, tho' watched, prayed and striven against, this is still the sin that most easily besets me. It has hindered my prayers and prevented my improvement, and therefore has humbled me very much."[25] This she wrote at the age of twenty-nine.

In this belief she brought up her son. "Never in all my early childhood, did anyone address to me the affecting preamble, 'Once upon a time!' I was told about missionaries, but never about pirates; I was familiar with humming-birds, but I had never heard of fairies," Gosse remembered. "They desired to make me truthful; the tendency was to make me positive and sceptical. Had they wrapped me in the soft folds of supernatural fancy, my mind might have been longer content to follow their traditions in an unquestioning spirit."[26] The parents who took the Hawkins County Public Schools to court in Tennessee in 1980 had obviously not read Gosse's claim. They argued that an entire elementary school series, which included *Cinderella*, *Goldilocks* and *The Wizard of Oz*, violated their fundamentalist religious beliefs.[27]

Authoritarian readers who prevent others from learning to read, fanatical readers who decide what can and what cannot be read, stoical readers who refuse to read for pleasure and demand only the retelling of facts that they themselves hold to be true: all these attempt to limit the reader's vast and diverse powers. But censors can also work in different ways, without need of fire or courts of law. They can reinterpret books to render them serviceable only to themselves, for the sake of justifying their autocratic rights.

In 1967, when I was in my fifth year of high school, a military coup took place in Argentina, led by General Jorge Rafael Videla. What followed was a wave of human-rights abuses such as the country had never seen before. The army's excuse was that it was fighting a war against terrorists; as General Videla defined it, "a terrorist is not just someone with a gun or bomb, but also someone who spreads ideas that are contrary to Western and Christian civilization."[28] Among the thousands kidnapped and tortured was a priest, Father Orlando Virgilio Yorio. One day, Father Yorio's interrogator told him that his reading of the Gospel was false. "You interpreted Christ's doctrine in too literal a way," said the man. "Christ spoke of the poor, but when he spoke of the poor he spoke of the poor in spirit and you interpreted this in a literal way and went to live, literally, with poor people. In Argentina those who are poor in spirit are the rich and in the future you must spend your time helping the rich, who are those who really need spiritual help."[29]

Thus, not all the reader's powers are enlightening. The same act that can bring a text into being, draw out its revelations, multiply its meanings, mirror in it the past, the present and the possibilities of the future, can also destroy or attempt to destroy the living page. Every reader makes up readings, which is not the same as lying; but every reader can also lie, wilfully declaring the text subservient to a doctrine, to an arbitrary law, to a private advantage, to the rights of slave-owners or the authority of tyrants.

They are all common gestures: pulling the glasses out of a case, cleaning them with a tissue or the hem of the blouse or the tip of the tie, perching them on the nose and steadying them behind the ears before peering at the now lucid page held in front of us. Then pushing them up or sliding them down the glistening bridge of the nose in order to bring the letters into focus and, after a while, lifting them off and rubbing the skin between the eyebrows, screwing the eyelids shut to keep out the siren text. And the final act: taking them off, folding them and inserting them between the pages of the book to mark the place where we left off reading for the night. In Christian iconography, Saint Lucy is represented carrying a pair of eyes on a tray; glasses are, in effect, eyes that poor-sighted readers can pull off and put on at will. They are a detachable function of a body, a mask through which the world can be observed, an insect-like creature carried along like a pet praying mantis. Unobtrusive, sitting cross-legged on a pile of books or standing expectantly in a cluttered corner of a desk, they have become the reader's emblem, a mark of the reader's presence, a symbol of the reader's craft.

It is bewildering to imagine the many centuries before the invention of glasses, during which readers squinted their way through the nebulous outlines of a text, and moving to imagine their extraordinary relief, once glasses were available, at suddenly seeing, almost without effort, a page of writing. A sixth of all humankind is myopic;[1] among readers the proportion is much higher, closer to 24 per cent. Aristotle,

OPPOSITE

Sebastian Brant, author of *The Ship of Fools*.

Luther, Samuel Pepys, Schopenhauer, Goethe, Schiller, Keats, Tennyson, Dr. Johnson, Alexander Pope, Quevedo, Wordsworth, Dante
Gabriel Rossetti, Elizabeth Barrett Browning, Kipling, Edward Lear,
Dorothy L. Sayers, Yeats, Unamuno, Rabindranath Tagore, James Joyce
— all had impaired sight. In many people the condition deteriorates,
and a remarkable number of famous readers have gone blind in their
old age, from Homer to Milton, and on to James Thurber and Jorge
Luis Borges. Borges, who began losing his sight in the early thirties and
was appointed head of the Buenos Aires National Library in 1955,
when he could no longer see, commented on the peculiar fate of the
failing reader who is one day granted the realm of books:

> Let no one demean to tears or reproach
> This declaration of the skill of God
> Who with such magnificent irony
> Gave me at the same time darkness and the books.[2]

Borges compared the fate of this reader in the blurred world of
"pale vague ashes resembling oblivion and sleep" to the fate of King
Midas, condemned to die of hunger and thirst surrounded by food and
drink. An episode of the television series *The Twilight Zone* concerns
one such Midas, a voracious reader who alone of all mankind survives a
nuclear disaster. All the books in the world are now at his disposal;
then, accidentally, he breaks his glasses.

Before the invention of glasses, at least a quarter of all readers
would have required extra-large letters to decipher a text. The strain
on the eyes of medieval readers was great: the rooms in which they
tried to read were darkened in summer to protect them from the heat;
in winter the rooms were naturally dark because the windows, necessarily small to keep out the icy drafts, let in only a dusty light. Medieval scribes constantly complained about the conditions in which
they had to work, and often scribbled notes about their troubles in the
margins of their books, like the one penned in the mid-thirteenth century by a certain Florencio of whom we know virtually nothing except
his first name and this mournful description of his craft: "It is a painful
task. It extinguishes the light from the eyes, it bends the back, it
crushes the viscera and the ribs, it brings forth pain to the kidneys,
and weariness to the whole body."[3] For poor-sighted readers the work
must have been even harder; Patrick Trevor-Roper suggested that they

likely felt somewhat more comfortable at night "because darkness is a great equalizer".[4]

In Babylon and Rome and Greece, readers whose sight was poor had no other resource than to have their books read to them, usually by slaves. A few found that looking through a disk of clear stone helped. Writing about the properties of emeralds,[5] Pliny the Elder noted in passing that the short-sighted Emperor Nero used to watch gladiator combats through an emerald. Whether this magnified the gory details or simply gave them a greenish hue we can't tell, but the story persisted throughout the Middle Ages and scholars such as Roger Bacon and his teacher, Robert Grosseteste, commented on the jewel's remarkable property.

But few readers had access to precious stones. Most were condemned to live out their reading hours depending on vicarious reading, or on a slow and painstaking progress as the muscles of their eyes strained to remedy the defect. Then, sometime in the late thirteenth century, the fate of the poor-sighted reader changed.

We don't know exactly when the change happened, but on February 23, 1306, from the pulpit of the church of Santa Maria Novella in Florence, Giordano da Rivalto of Pisa delivered a sermon in which he reminded his flock that the invention of eyeglasses, "one of the most useful devices in the world", was already twenty years old. He added, "I've seen the man who, before anyone else, discovered and made a pair of glasses, and I spoke to him."[6]

Nothing is known of this remarkable inventor. Perhaps he was a contemporary of Giordano, a monk named Spina of whom it was said that "he made glasses and freely taught the art to others".[7] Perhaps he was a member of the Guild of Venetian Crystal Workers, where the craft of eyeglass-making was known as early as 1301, since one of the guild's rules that year explained the procedure to be followed by anyone "wishing to make eyeglasses for reading".[8] Or perhaps the inventor was a certain Salvino degli Armati, whom a funeral plaque still visible in the church of Santa Maria Maggiore in Florence calls "inventor of eyeglasses" and adds, "May God forgive his sins. A.D. 1317". Another candidate is Roger Bacon, whom we have already encountered as master cataloguer and whom Kipling, in a late story, made witness to the use of an early Arab microscope smuggled into England by an illuminator.[9] In the year 1268, Bacon had written, "If anyone examines letters or small objects through the medium of a crystal or glass if it be shaped like the lesser segment of a sphere, with all the convex side towards the eye, he will see the letters far better and larger. Such an instrument is useful to all persons."[10] Four centuries later, Descartes was still praising the invention of glasses: "All the management of our lives depends on the senses, and since that of sight is the most comprehensive and the noblest of these, there is no doubt that inventions that serve to augment its power are among the most useful there can be."[11]

The first painted depiction of eyeglasses, on the nose of Cardinal Hugo de Saint Cher, painted by Tommaso da Modena in 1352.

The earliest known depiction of eyeglasses is in a 1352 portrait of Cardinal Hugo de St. Cher, in Provence, by Tommaso da Modena.[12] It shows the cardinal in full costume, seated at his table, copying from an open book on a shelf slightly above him, to his right. The glasses, known as "rivet spectacles", consist of two round lenses held in thick frames and hinged above the bridge of the nose, so that the grip can be regulated.

Until well into the fifteenth century, reading-glasses were a luxury; they were expensive, and comparatively few people needed them, since books themselves were in the possession of a select few. After the invention of the printing press and the relative popularization of books, the demand for eyeglasses increased; in England, for instance, pedlars travelling from town to town sold "cheap continental spectacles". Makers of spectacles and clips became known in Strasbourg in 1466, barely eleven years after the publication of Gutenberg's first Bible; in Nuremberg in 1478; and in Frankfurt in 1540.[13] It is possible that more and better glasses allowed more readers to become better readers, and to buy more books, and that for this reason glasses became associated with the intellectual, the librarian, the scholar.

From the fourteenth century on, glasses were added to numerous paintings, to mark the studious and wise nature of a character. In many depictions of the Dormition or Death of the Virgin, several of the doctors and wise men surrounding her death-bed found themselves wearing eyeglasses of various kinds; in the anonymous eleventh-century Dormition now at the Neuberg Monastery in Vienna, a pair of glasses was added several centuries later to a white-bearded sage being shown

An eleventh-century *Dormition of the Virgin* in Neuberg Monastery, Vienna. Second from the right, one of the doctors attending her is wearing a pair of scholarly glasses added more than three centuries later to lend him authority.

a hefty volume by a disconsolate younger man. The implication seems to be that even the wisest among scholars do not possess sufficient wisdom to heal the Virgin and change her destiny.

In Greece, Rome and Byzantium, the scholar-poet — the *doctus poeta*, represented as holding a tablet or a scroll — had been considered a paragon, but this role was confined to mortals. The gods never busied themselves with literature; Greek and Latin divinities were never shown holding a book.[14] Christianity was the first religion to place a book in the hands of its god, and from the mid-fourteenth century onwards the emblematic Christian book was accompanied by another image, that of the eyeglasses. The perfection of Christ and of God the Father would not justify their representation as short-sighted, but the Fathers of the Church — Saint Thomas Aquinas, Saint Augustine — and the ancient authors admitted into the Catholic canon — Cicero, Aristotle — were at times depicted carrying a learned tome and wearing the sage spectacles of knowledge.

By the end of the fifteenth century, eyeglasses were sufficiently familiar to symbolize not only the prestige of reading but also its abuses. Most readers, then and now, have at some time experienced the humiliation of being told that their occupation is reprehensible. I remember being laughed at, during one recess in grade six or seven, for staying indoors and reading, and how the taunting ended with me sprawled face down on the floor, my glasses kicked into one corner, my book into another. "You wouldn't enjoy it" was the verdict of my cousins who, having seen my book-lined bedroom, assumed that I would not want to accompany them to see yet another Western. My grandmother, seeing me read on Sunday afternoons, would sigh, "You're day-dreaming," because my inactivity seemed to her a wasteful idleness and a sin against the joy of living. Slothful, feeble, pretentious, pedantic, elitist — these are some of the epithets that eventually became associated with the absent-minded scholar, the poor-sighted reader, the bookworm, the nerd. Buried in books, isolated from the world of facts and flesh, feeling superior to those unfamiliar with the words preserved between dusty covers, the bespectacled reader who pretended to know what God in His wisdom had hidden was seen as a fool, and glasses became emblematic of intellectual arrogance.

In February 1494, during the famous Carnival of Basel, the young doctor of law Sebastian Brant published a small volume of allegorical verse in German entitled *Das Narrenschiff*, or *The Ship of Fools*. Its success was immediate: in the first year the book was reprinted three times and in Strasbourg, Brant's birthplace, an enterprising publisher, anxious to share in the profits, commissioned an unknown poet to increase the book by four thousand lines. Brant complained about this form of plagiarism, but in vain. Two years later, Brant asked his friend Jacques Locher, professor of poetry at the University of Freiburg, to translate the book into Latin.[15] Locher did so, but rearranged the order of the chapters and included variations of his own. Whatever the changes to Brant's original text, the book's readership kept increasing until well into the seventeenth century. Its success was partly due to the accompanying woodcuts, many by the hand of the twenty-two-year-old Albrecht Dürer. But largely the merit was Brant's own. Brant had meticulously surveyed the follies or sins of his society, from adultery and gambling to lack of faith and ingratitude, in precise, up-to-date terms: for instance, the discovery of the New World, which had taken place less than two years earlier, is mentioned halfway through the book to exemplify the follies of covetous curiosity. Dürer and other artists offered Brant's readers common images of these new sinners, recognizable at once among their peers in everyday life, but it was Brant himself who roughed out the illustrations intended as accompaniments to his text.

One of these images, the first after the frontispiece, illustrates the folly of the scholar. The reader opening Brant's book would be confronted by his own image: a man in his study, surrounded by books. There are books everywhere: on the shelves behind him, on both sides of his lectern-desk, inside the compartments of the desk itself. The man is wearing a nightcap (to hide his ass's ears) while a fool's hood with bells hangs behind him, and he holds in his right hand a duster with which he swats at the flies come to settle on his books. He is the *Büchernarr*, the "book fool", the man whose folly consists in burying himself in books. On his nose sits a pair of glasses.

These glasses accuse him: here is a man who will not see the world directly, but relies instead on peering at the dead words on a printed page. "It is for a very good reason," says Brant's foolish reader, "that I'm the first to climb into the ship. For me the book is everything, more precious even than gold. / I have great treasures here, of which I understand not a word." He confesses that, in the company of learned men who quote from wise books, he loves to be able to say, "I have all those volumes at home"; he compares himself to Ptolemy II of Alexandria, who accumulated books but not knowledge.[16] Through Brant's book, the image of the bespectacled and foolish scholar quickly became a common icon; as early as 1505, in the *De fide concubinarum* of Olearius, an ass is sitting at an identical desk, glasses on his nose and fly-swatter in his hoof, reading from a big open book to a class of student-beasts.

So popular was Brant's book that in 1509 the humanist scholar Geiler von Kaysersberg began preaching a series of sermons based on

Albrecht
Dürer's
frontispiece
for Sebastian
Brant's first
edition of *The
Ship of Fools*.

Brant's cast of fools, one for every Sunday.[17] The first sermon, corresponding to the first chapter of Brant's book, was of course on the Book Fool. Brant had lent the fool words to describe himself; Geiler used the description to divide this bookish folly into seven types, each recognizable by the tinkling of one of the Fool's bells. According to Geiler, the first bell announces the Fool who collects books for the sake of glory, as if they were costly furniture. In the first century AD, the Latin philosopher Seneca (whom Geiler liked to quote) had already denounced the ostentatious accumulation of books: "Many people without a school education use books not as tools for study but as decorations for the dining-room."[18] Geiler insists, "He

Armed with a lectern, a book, a bundle of birches and a pair of glasses, an ass teaches a class of beasts in Olearius's satirical *De fide concubinarum* of 1505.

who wants books to bring him fame must learn something from them; he must store them not in his library but in his head. But this first Fool has put his books in chains and made them his prisoners; could they free themselves and speak, they would haul him in front of the magistrate, demanding that he, not they, be locked up." The second bell rings in the Fool who wants to grow wise through the consumption of too many books. Geiler compares him to a stomach upset by too much food, and to a military general hampered in his siege by having too many soldiers. "What should I do? you ask. Should I throw all my books away then?" — and we can imagine Geiler pointing his finger at one particular parishioner in his Sunday audience. "No, that you should not. But you should select those that are useful to you, and make use of them at the right moment." The third bell rings in the Fool who collects books without truly reading them, merely flicking through them to satisfy his idle curiosity. Geiler compares him to a madman running through the town, trying to observe in detail, as he tears along, the signs and emblems on the house-fronts. This, he says, is impossible, and a sorry waste of time.

The fourth bell calls the Fool who loves sumptuously illuminated books. "Is it not a sinful folly," asks Geiler, "to feast one's eyes on gold and silver when so many of God's children go hungry? Don't your eyes have the sun, the moon, the stars, the many flowers and other things to please you?" What need do we have for human figures or flowers in a book? Are not the ones God provided enough? And Geiler concludes that this love of painted images "is an insult to wisdom." The fifth bell announces the Fool who binds his books in rich cloth. (Here again Geiler borrows silently from Seneca, who protested against the collector "who gets his pleasure from bindings and labels" and in whose illiterate household "you can see the complete works of orators and historians on shelves up to the ceiling, because, like bathrooms, a library has become an essential ornament of a rich house.")[19] The sixth bell calls in the Fool who writes and produces badly written books without having read the classics, and without any knowledge of spelling, grammar or rhetoric. He is the reader turned writer, tempted to add his scribbled thoughts to stand beside the works of the great. Finally — in a paradoxical switch future anti-intellectuals would ignore — the seventh and last Book Fool is he who despises books entirely and scorns the wisdom that can be obtained from them.

Through Brant's intellectual imagery, Geiler, the intellectual, provided arguments for the anti-intellectuals of his time who lived uncertainly in an age that saw the civil and religious structures of European society split through dynastic wars that altered their concept of history, geographical explorations that shifted their concepts of space and of commerce, religious schisms that changed for ever their concept of who and why and what they were on earth. Geiler armed them with a whole catalogue of accusations which allowed them, as a society, to see fault not in their own actions but in the *thoughts* about their actions, in their imaginations, their ideas, their readings.

Many of those who sat in Strasbourg Cathedral Sunday after Sunday, listening to Geiler's railings against the follies of the misguided reader, probably believed that he was echoing the popular grudge against the man of books. I can imagine the uncomfortable feeling of those who, like myself, wore glasses, perhaps taking them off surreptitiously as these meek helpers suddenly became a badge of dishonour. But it was not the reader and his glasses that Geiler was attacking. Far from it; his arguments were those of a humanist cleric, critical of untrained or vacuous intellectual competition, but equally strong in defending the need for literate knowledge and the value of books. He did not share the resentment growing among the general population, who saw scholars as undeservedly privileged, suffering from what John Donne described as "defects of loneliness",[20] hiding away from the real labours of the world in what several centuries later Sainte-Beuve was to call "the ivory tower", the haven "to which the intellectual reader could climb to isolate himself from the crowd",[21] far from the gregarious occupations of the common folk. Three centuries after Geiler, Thomas Carlyle, speaking in defence of the scholar-reader, lent him heroic features: "He, with his copy-rights and his copy-wrongs, in his squalid garret, in his rusty coat; ruling (for this is what he does), from his grave, after death, whole nations and generations who would, or would not, give him bread while living."[22] But the prejudiced view persisted of the reader as an absent-minded egghead, an absconder from the world, a day-dreamer with glasses mousing through a book in a secluded corner.

The Spanish writer Jorge Manrique, a contemporary of Geiler's, divided humankind between "those who live by their hands, and the rich".[23] Soon that division was perceived as between "those who live by their hands" and "the Book Fool", the bespectacled reader. It is curious that glasses have never lost this unworldly association. Even those who wish to appear wise (or at least bookish) in our time take advantage of the symbol; a pair of glasses, whether prescription or not, undermines the sensuality of a face and suggests instead intellectual preoccupations. Tony Curtis wears a pair of stolen glasses while attempting to convince Marilyn Monroe that he is nothing but a naive millionaire in *Some Like It Hot*. And in Dorothy Parker's famous words, "Men seldom make passes / At girls who wear glasses." Opposing the strength of the body to the power of the mind, separating the *homme moyen sensuel* from the scholar, calls for elaborate argumentations. On one side are the workers, the slaves with no access to books, the creatures of bone and sinew, the majority of humankind; on the other, the minority, the thinkers, the elite of scribes, the intellectuals supposedly allied with authority. Discussing the meaning of happiness, Seneca granted the minority the stronghold of wisdom and scorned the opinion of the majority. "The best," he said, "should be preferred by the majority, and instead the populace chooses the worst. . . . Nothing is as noxious as listening to what people say, considering right that which is approved by most, and taking as one's model the behaviour of the masses, who live not according to reason but in order to conform."[24] The English scholar John Carey, analysing the relationship between intellectuals and the masses at the turn of our century, found Seneca's views echoed in many of the most famous British writers of the late Victorian and Edwardian ages. "Given the multitudes by which the individual is surrounded," Carey concluded, "it is virtually impossible to regard everyone else as having an individuality equivalent to one's own. The mass, as a reductive and dismissive concept, is invented to ease this difficulty."[25]

The argument that opposes those with the right to read, because they can read "well" (as the fearful glasses seem to indicate), and those to whom reading must be denied, because they "wouldn't understand", is as ancient as it is specious. "Once a thing is put into writing," Socrates argued, "the text, whatever it might be, is taken from place to place and falls into the hands *not only of those who understand it, but also of those who have no business with it* [the italics are mine]. The text doesn't know how to address the right people, and how not to address the wrong ones. And when it is ill-treated and unfairly abused, it always needs its parent to come to its help, being unable to defend or help itself." Right and wrong readers: for Socrates there appears to be a "correct" interpretation of a text, available only to a few informed specialists. In Victorian England, Matthew Arnold would echo this splendidly arrogant opinion: "We . . . are for giving the heritage neither to the Barbarians nor to the Philistines, nor yet to the Populace."[26] Trying to understand exactly what that heritage was, Aldous Huxley defined it as the special accumulated knowledge of any united family, the common property of all its members. "When we of the great Culture Family meet," wrote Huxley, "we exchange reminiscences about Grandfather Homer, and that awful old Dr Johnson, and Aunt Sappho, and poor Johnny Keats. 'And do you remember that absolutely priceless thing Uncle Virgil said? You know. *Timeo Danaos.* . . . Priceless; I shall never forget it.' No, we shall never forget it; and what's more, we shall take good care that those horrid people who have had the impertinence to call on us, those wretched outsiders who never knew dear mellow old Uncle V., shall never forget it either. We'll keep them constantly reminded of their outsideness."[27]

Which came first? The invention of the masses, which Thomas Hardy described as "a throng of people . . . containing a certain minority who have sensitive souls; these, and the aspects of these, being what is worth observing",[28] or the invention of the bespectacled Book Fool, who thinks himself superior to the rest of the world and whom the world passes by, laughing?

Their chronology hardly matters. Both stereotypes are fictions and both are dangerous, because under the pretence of moral or social criticism they are employed in an attempt to curtail a craft that, in its essence, is neither limited nor limiting. The reality of reading lies elsewhere. Trying to discover in ordinary mortals an activity akin to creative writing, Sigmund Freud suggested that a comparison could be drawn between the inventions of fiction and those of day-dreaming, since in reading fiction "our actual enjoyment of an imaginative work proceeds from a liberation of tensions in our mind . . . enabling us thenceforward to enjoy our own day-dreaming without self-reproach or shame".[29] But surely that is not the experience of most readers. Depending on the time and the place, our mood and our memory, our experience and our desire, the enjoyment of reading, at its best, tightens rather than liberates the tensions of our mind, drawing them taut to make them sing, making us *more*, not less, aware of their presence. It is true that on occasion the world of the page passes into our conscious *imaginaire* — our everyday vocabulary of images — and then we wander aimlessly in those fictional landscapes, lost in wonder, like Don Quixote.[30] But most of the time we tread firmly. We know that we are reading even while suspending disbelief; we know why we read even when we don't know how, holding in our mind at the same time, as it were, the illusionary text and the act of reading. We read to find the end, for the story's sake. We read not to reach it, for the sake of the reading itself. We read searchingly, like trackers, oblivious of our surroundings. We read distractedly, skipping pages. We read contemptuously, admiringly, negligently, angrily, passionately, enviously, longingly. We read in gusts of sudden pleasure, without knowing what brought the pleasure along. "What in the world is this emotion?" asks Rebecca West after reading *King Lear*. "What is the bearing of supremely great works of art on my life which makes me feel so glad?"[31] We don't know: we read ignorantly. We read in slow, long motions, as if drifting in space, weightless. We read full of prejudice, malignantly. We read generously, making excuses for the text, filling gaps, mending faults. And sometimes, when the stars are kind, we read with an intake of breath, with a shudder, as if someone or something had "walked over our grave", as if a memory had suddenly been rescued from a place deep within us — the recognition of something we never knew was there, or of something we vaguely felt as a flicker or a shadow, whose ghostly form rises and passes back into us before we can see what it is, leaving us older and wiser.

This reading has an image. A photograph taken in 1940, during the bombing of London in the Second World War, shows the remains of a

FOLLOWING PAGE

Readers browsing through the severely damaged library of Holland House in West London, wrecked by a fire bomb on 22 October 1940.

caved-in library. Through the torn roof can be seen ghostly buildings outside, and in the centre of the store is a heap of beams and crippled furniture. But the shelves on the walls have held fast, and the books lined up along them seem unharmed. Three men are standing amidst the rubble: one, as if hesitant about which book to choose, is apparently reading the titles on the spines; another, wearing glasses, is reaching for a volume; the third is reading, holding an open book in his hands. They are not turning their backs on the war, or ignoring the destruction. They are not choosing the books over life outside. They are trying to persist against the obvious odds; they are asserting a common right to ask; they are attempting to find once again — among the ruins, in the astonished recognition that reading sometimes grants — an understanding.

E N D P A P E R

P A G E S

*Patient as one of the alchemists, I've always imagined
and attempted something else, and would be willing
to sacrifice all satisfaction and vanity for its sake, just
as in the old days they used to burn their furniture
and the beams of their roofs to feed their furnace for
the magnum opus. What is it? Difficult to say: simply
a book, in several volumes, a book that is truly a book,
architecturally sound and premeditated, and not a
collection of casual inspirations however wonderful
that might be. . . . So there, dear friend, is the bare
confession of this vice which I've rejected a
thousand times. . . . But it holds me in its sway and
I may yet be able to succeed, not in the completion of
this work as a whole (one would have to be
God-knows-who for that!) but in showing a
successful fragment. . . . proving through finished
portions that this book does exist, and that
I was aware of what I wasn't able to accomplish.*

STÉPHANE MALLARMÉ
Letter to Paul Verlaine, November 16, 1869

I n Hemingway's celebrated story "The Snows of Kilimanjaro", the protagonist, who is dying, recalls all the stories he will now never write. "He knew at least twenty good stories from out there and he had never written one. Why?"[1] He mentions a few but the list, of course, must be endless. The shelves of books we haven't written, like those of books we haven't read, stretches out into the darkness of the universal library's farthest space. We are always at the beginning of the beginning of the letter *A*.

Among the books I haven't written — among the books I haven't read but would like to read — is *The History of Reading*. I can see it, just there, at the exact point where the light of this section of the library ends and the darkness of the next section begins. I know exactly what it looks like. I can picture its cover and imagine the feel of its rich cream pages. I can guess, with prurient accuracy, the sensual dark cloth binding beneath the jacket, and the embossed golden letters. I know its sober title page, and its witty epigraph and moving dedication. I know it possesses a copious and curious index which will give me intense delight, with headings such as (I fall by chance on the letter T) *Tantalus for readers, Tarzan's library, Tearing pages, Toes (reading with), Tolstoy's canon, Tombstones, Torment by recitation, Tortoise (see Shells and animal skins), Touching books, Touchstone and censorship, Transmigration of readers' souls (see Lending books)*. I know the book has, like veins in marble, signatures of illustrations that I have never seen before: a seventh-century mural depicting the Library of Alexandria as seen by a contemporary artist; a photograph of the poet Sylvia Plath reading out loud in a garden, in the rain; a sketch of Pascal's room at Port-Royal, showing the books he kept on his desk; a photograph of the sea-sodden books saved by one of the passengers on the *Titanic*, without which she would not abandon ship; Greta Garbo's Christmas list for 1933, drawn up in her own hand, showing that among the books she was going to buy was Nathanael West's *Miss Lonelyhearts*; Emily Dickinson in bed, a frilly bonnet tied snugly under her chin and six or seven books lying around her, whose titles I can just barely make out.

I have the book open in front of me, on my table. It is amicably written (I have an exact sense of its tone), accessible and yet erudite, informative and yet reflective. The author, whose face I've seen in the handsome frontispiece, is smiling agreeably (I can't tell if it's a man or a woman; the clean-shaven face could be either, and so could the initials of the name) and I feel I'm in good hands. I know that as I proceed through the chapters I will be introduced to that ancient family of readers, some famous, many obscure, to which I belong. I will learn of their manners, and the changes in those manners, and the transformation they underwent as they carried with them, like the magi of old, the power of transforming dead signs into living memory. I will read of their triumphs and persecutions and almost secret discoveries. And in the end I will better understand who I, the reader, am.

That a book does not exist (or does not yet exist) is not a reason to ignore it any more than we would ignore a book on an imaginary subject. There are volumes written on the unicorn, on Atlantis, on gender equality, on the Dark Lady of the Sonnets and the equally dark Youth. But the history this book records has been particularly difficult to grasp; it is made, so to speak, of its digressions. One subject calls to another, an anecdote brings a seemingly unrelated story to mind, and the author proceeds as if unaware of logical causality or historical continuity, as if defining the reader's freedom in the very writing about the craft.

And yet, in this apparent randomness, there is a method: this book I see before me is the history not only of reading but also of common readers, the individuals who, through the ages, chose certain books over others, accepted in a few cases the verdict of their elders, but at other times rescued forgotten titles from the past, or put upon their library shelves the elect among their contemporaries. This is the story of their small triumphs and their secret sufferings, and of the manner in which these things came to pass. How it all happened is minutely chronicled in this book, in the daily life of a few ordinary people discovered here and there in family memoirs, village histories, accounts of life in distant places long ago. But it is always individuals who are spoken of, never vast nationalities or generations whose choices belong not to the history of reading but to that of statistics. Rilke once asked, "Is it possible that the whole history of the world has been misunderstood? Is it possible that the past is false, because we've always spoken about its masses, as if we were telling about a gathering of people, instead of talking about the one person they were standing around, because he was a stranger and was dying? Yes, it's possible."[2] This misunderstanding the author of *The History of Reading* has surely recognized.

Here then, in Chapter Fourteen, is Richard de Bury, Bishop of Durham and treasurer and chancellor to King Edward II, who was born on January 24, 1287, in a little village near Bury St. Edmund's, in Suffolk, and who, on his fifty-eighth birthday, completed a book, explaining that "because it principally treats of the love of books, we have chosen after the fashion of the ancient Romans fondly to name it by a Greek word, *Philobiblon*". Four months later, he died. De Bury had collected books with a passion; he had, it was said, more books than all the other bishops of England put together, and so many lay piled around his bed that it was hardly possible to move in his room without treading on them. De Bury, thank the stars, was not a scholar, and just read what he liked. He thought the *Hermes Trismegistus* (a Neoplatonic volume of Egyptian alchemy from around the third century AD) an excellent scientific book "from before the Flood", attributed the wrong works to Aristotle and quoted some terrible verses as if they were by Ovid. It didn't matter. "In books," he wrote, "I find the dead as if they were alive; in books I foresee things to come; in books warlike affairs are set forth; from books come forth the laws of peace. All things are corrupted and decay in time; Saturn ceases not to devour the children that he generates: all the glory of the world would be buried in oblivion, unless God had provided mortals with the remedy of books."[3] (Our author doesn't mention it, but Virginia Woolf, in a paper read at school, echoed de Bury's contention: "I have sometimes dreamt," she wrote, "that when the Day of Judgement dawns and the great conquerors and lawyers and statesmen come to receive their rewards — their crowns, their laurels, their names carved indelibly upon imperishable marble — the Almighty will turn to Peter and will say, not without a certain envy when He sees us coming with our books under our arms, 'Look, these need no re-ward. We have nothing to give them. They have loved reading.'")[4]

Chapter Eight is devoted to an almost forgotten reader whom Saint Augustine, in one of his letters, praises as a formidable scribe and to whom he dedicated one of his books. Her name was Melania the Younger (to distinguish her from her grandmother, Melania the Elder) and she lived in Rome, in Egypt and in North Africa. She was born around 385 and died in Bethlehem in 439. She was passionately fond of books, and copied out for herself as many as she could find, thereby collecting an important library. The scholar Gerontius, writing in the fifth century, described her as "naturally gifted" and so fond of reading that "she would go through the *Lives* of the Fathers as if she were eating dessert". "She read books that were bought, as well as books she chanced upon with such diligence that no word or thought remained unknown to her. So overwhelming was her love of learning, that when she read in Latin, it seemed to everyone that she did not know Greek and, on the other hand, when she read in Greek, it was thought that she did not know Latin."[5] Brilliant and transient, Melania the Younger drifts through *The History of Reading* as one of the many who sought comfort in books.

From a century closer to us (but the author of *The History of Reading* doesn't care for these arbitrary conventions, and invites him into Chapter Six) another eclectic reader, the genial Oscar Wilde, makes his appearance. We follow his reading progress, from the Celtic fairy-tales given to him by his mother to the scholarly volumes he read at Magdalen College in Oxford. It was here at Oxford that, for one of his examinations, he was asked to translate from the Greek version of the story of the Passion in the New Testament, and since he did so easily and accurately the examiners told him it was enough. Wilde continued, and once again the examiners told him to stop. "Oh, do let me go on," Wilde said, "I want to see how it ends."

For Wilde, it was as important to know what he liked as it was to know what he should avoid. For the benefit of the subscribers to the *Pall Mall Gazette* he issued, on February 8, 1886, these words of advice on what "To Read, or Not to Read":

Books not to read at all, such as Thomson's *Seasons*, Rogers' *Italy*, Paley's *Evidences*, all the Fathers, except St Augustine, all John Stuart Mill, except the essay on Liberty, all Voltaire's plays without any exception, Butler's *Analogy*, Grant's *Aristotle*, Hume's *England*, Lewes' *History of Philosophy*, all argumentative books, and all books that try to prove anything. . . . To tell people what to read is as a rule either useless or harmful, for the true appreciation of literature is a question of temperament not of teaching, to Parnassus there is no primer, and nothing that one can learn is ever worth learning. But to tell people what not to read is a very different matter, and I venture to recommend it as a mission to the University Extension Scheme.

Private and public reading tastes are discussed quite early in the book, in Chapter Four. The role of reader as anthologist is considered, as collector of material either for oneself (the commonplace book of Jean-Jacques Rousseau is the example given) or for others (Palgrave's *Golden Treasury*), and our author very amusingly shows how concepts of audience modify the choice of an anthologist's texts. To support this "micro-history of anthologies" our author quotes Professor Jonathan Rose on the "five common fallacies to reader response":

- first, all literature is political, in the sense that it always influences the political consciousness of the reader;
- second, the influence of a given text is directly proportional to its circulation;
- third, "popular" culture has a much larger following than "high" culture, and therefore it more accurately reflects the attitudes of the masses;
- fourth, "high" culture tends to reinforce acceptance of the existing social and political order (a presumption widely shared by both the left and the right); and
- fifth, the canon of "great books" is defined solely by social elites. Common readers either do not recognize that canon, or else they accept it only out of deference to elite opinion.[6]

As our author makes quite clear, we the readers are commonly guilty of subscribing to at least some, if not all, of these fallacies. The chapter also mentions "ready-made" anthologies collected and come upon by chance, such as the ten thousand texts assembled in a curious Jewish archive in Old Cairo, called the Geniza and discovered in 1890 in the sealed lumber-room of a medieval synagogue. Because of the Jewish reverence for the name of God, no paper was thrown away for fear it might bear His name, and therefore everything from marriage contracts to grocery lists, from love poems to booksellers' catalogues (one of which included the first known reference to *The Arabian Nights*), was assembled here for a future reader.[7]

Not one but three chapters (Thirty-one, Thirty-two and Thirty-three) are devoted to what our author calls "The Invention of the Reader". Every text assumes a reader. When Cervantes begins his introduction to the first part of *Don Quixote* with the invocation "Leisured reader,"[8] it is I who from the first words become a character in the fiction, a person with time enough to indulge in the story that is about to begin. To me Cervantes addresses the book, to me he explains the facts of its composition, to me he confesses the book's shortcomings. Following the advice of a friend, he has written himself a few laudatory poems recommending the book (today's less inspired version is to ask well-known personalities for praise and stick their panegyrics on the book's jacket). Cervantes undermines his own authority by taking me into his confidence. I, the reader, am put on my guard and, by that very action, disarmed. How can I protest what has been explained to me so clearly? I agree to play the game. I accept the fiction. I don't close the book.

My open deception continues. Eight chapters into the first part of *Don Quixote*, I am told that these are the extent of Cervantes's telling and that the rest of the book is a translation from the Arabic by the historian Cide Hamete Benengeli. Why the artifice? Because I, the reader, am not easily convinced, and while I don't fall for most tricks by which the author swears truthfulness, I enjoy being pulled into a game in which the levels of reading are constantly shifting. I read a novel, I read a true adventure, I read the translation of a true adventure, I read a corrected version of the facts.

The History of Reading is eclectic. The invention of the reader is followed by a chapter on the invention of the writer, another fictional character. "I've had the misfortune of beginning a book with the word 'I'," wrote Proust, "and immediately it was thought that instead of attempting to discover general laws, I was analysing myself in the individual and detestable sense of the word."[9] This leads our author to discuss the use of the first person singular, and how that fictitious "I" forces the reader into a semblance of dialogue from which, however, the reader is excluded by the physical reality of the page. "Only when the reader reads *beyond* the writer's authority does the dialogue take place", says our author, and draws his examples from the *nouveau roman*, notably from Michel Butor's *La Modification*,[10] written entirely in the second person. "Here," says our author, "the cards are on the table, and the writer neither expects us to believe in the 'I' nor presumes us to assume the role of the condescended to 'dear reader'."

In a fascinating aside (Chapter Forty of *The History of Reading*) our author advances the original suggestion that the form in which the reader is addressed leads to the creation of the principal literary genres — or at least to their categorization. In 1948, in *Das Sprachliche Kunstwerk,* the German critic Wolfgang Kayser suggested that the concept of genre derived from the three persons that exist in every known language: "I", "you" and "he, she or it". In lyrical literature, the "I" expresses itself emotionally; in drama, the "I" becomes a second person, "you", and engages with another "you" in a passionate dialogue. Finally, in the epic, the protagonist is the third person, "he, she or it", who narrates objectively. Furthermore, each genre requires from the reader three distinct attitudes: a lyrical attitude (that of song), a dramatic attitude (which Kayser calls "apostrophe") and an epic attitude, or enunciation.[11] Our author enthusiastically embraces this argument, and proceeds to illustrate it through three readers: a nineteenth-century French schoolgirl, Éloise Bertrand, whose diary survived the Franco-Prussian War of 1870 and who faithfully recorded her reading of Nerval; Douglas Hyde, who was prompter at the performance of *The Vicar of Wakefield* at the Court Theatre in London, with Ellen Terry as Olivia; and Proust's housekeeper, Céleste, who read (partially) her employer's extensive novel.

In Chapter Sixty-eight (this *History of Reading* is a comfortingly fat tome) our author raises the question of how (and why) certain readers will preserve a reading long after most other readers have relinquished it to the past. The example given is from a London journal published sometime in 1855, when most English papers were full of news of the war in Crimea:

John Challis, an old man about 60 years of age, dressed in the pastoral garb of a shepherdess of the golden age, and George Campbell, aged 35, who described himself as a lawyer, and appeared completely equipped in female attire of the present day, were placed at the bar before Sir R. W. Carden, charged with being found disguised as women in the Druids'-hall, in Turnagain Lane, an unlicensed dancing room, for the purpose of exciting others to commit an unnatural offence.[12]

"A shepherdess of the golden age": by 1855 the literary pastoral ideal was very much a thing of the past. Codified in Theocritus's *Idylls* in the third century BC, appealing to writers in one form or another until well into the seventeenth century, tempting such disparate writers as Milton, Garcilaso de la Vega, Giambattista Marino, Cervantes, Sidney and Fletcher, the pastoral found a very different reflection in novelists such as George Eliot and Elizabeth Gaskell, Émile Zola and Ramón del Valle Inclán, who were giving readers other, less sunlit visions of country life in their books: *Adam Bede* (1859), *Cranford* (1853), *La Terre* (1887), *Tirano Banderas* (1926). These reconsiderations were not new. As early as the fourteenth century, the Spanish writer Juan Ruiz, archpriest of Hita, in his *Libro de buen amor* (*The Book of Loving Well*), had subverted the convention in which a poet or lonely knight meets a beautiful shepherdess whom he gently seduces, by having the narrator encounter in the hills of Guadarrama four wild, burly and headstrong shepherdesses. The first two rape him, he escapes from the third by falsely promising to marry her, while the fourth offers him lodging in exchange for clothes, jewels, a wedding or hard cash. Two hundred years later, there were few such as the elderly Mr. Challis, who still believed in the symbolic appeal of the loving shepherd and his shepherdess, or in the amorous gentleman and the innocent country maiden. According to the author of *The History of Reading*, this is one of the ways (extreme, no doubt) in which readers preserve and retell the past.

Several chapters, in different parts of the book, address the duties of fiction as opposed to what the reader accepts as fact. The chapters on reading fact are a touch dry, ranging from the theories of Plato to the criticisms of Hegel and Bergson; even though these chapters feature the possibly apocryphal fourteenth-century English travel writer Sir John Mandeville, they are somewhat too dense to lend themselves to summary. The chapters on reading fiction, however, are more concise. Two opinions, equally prescriptive and utterly opposed, are set forth. According to one, the reader is meant to believe in and act like the characters in a novel. According to the other, the reader must dismiss these characters as mere fabrications with no bearing whatsoever on "the real world". Henry Tilney, in Jane Austen's *Northanger Abbey*, voices the first opinion when he interrogates Catherine after the breaking off of her friendship with Isabella; he expects her feelings to follow the conventions of fiction:

> "You feel, I suppose, that, in losing Isabella, you lose half your-self: you feel a void in your heart which nothing else can oc-cupy. Society is becoming irksome; and as for the amusements in which you were wont to share at Bath, the very idea of them without her is abhorrent. You would not, for instance, now go to a ball for the world. You feel that you have no longer any friend to whom you can speak with unreserve; on whose re-gard you can place dependence; or whose counsel, in any diffi-culty, you could rely on. You feel all this?"
>
> "No," said Catherine, after a few moments' reflection, "I do not — ought I?"[13]

The reader's tone and how it affects the text are discussed in Chap-ter Fifty-one, through the character of Robert Louis Stevenson reading stories to his neighbours in Samoa. Stevenson attributed his sense of the dramatic and the music of his prose to the bedtime stories of his childhood nurse, Alison Cunningham, "Cummie". She read him ghost stories, religious hymns, Calvinist tracts and Scottish romances, all of which eventually found their way into his fiction. "It's you that gave me the passion for the drama, Cummie," he confessed to her as a grown man. "Me, Master Lou? I never put foot inside a playhouse in my life." "Ay woman," he answered. "But it was the grand dramatic way ye had of reciting the hymns."[14] Stevenson himself did not learn to read until the age of seven, not out of laziness but because he wanted to prolong the delights of hearing the stories come to life. This our author calls "the Scheherazade syndrome".[15]

Reading fiction is not our author's only preoccupation. The read-ing of scientific tracts, dictionaries, parts of a book such as indexes, footnotes and dedications, maps, newspapers — each merits (and re-ceives) its own chapter. There is a short but telling portrait of the nov-elist Gabriel García Márquez, who every morning reads a couple of pages of a dictionary (any dictionary except the pompous *Diccionario de la Real Academia Española*) — a habit our author compares to that of Stendhal, who perused the Napoleonic Code so as to learn to write in a terse and exact style.

The topic of reading borrowed books occupies Chapter Fifteen. Jane Carlyle (Thomas Carlyle's wife, and a celebrated letter writer) leads us through the intricacies of reading books that don't belong to us, "like having an illicit affair", and of taking out from libraries books that might affect our reputation. One afternoon in January 1843, having chosen from the respectable London Library several *risqué* novels by the French writer Paul de Kock, she brazenly entered her name in the ledger as that of Erasmus Darwin, the dry-as-dust invalid grandfather of the more famous Charles, to the astonishment of the librarians.[16]

Here also are the reading ceremonies of our own era and previous times (Chapters Forty-three and Forty-five). Here are the marathon readings of *Ulysses* on Bloomsday, the nostalgic radio readings of a book before bedtime, the library readings in big crowded halls and in far, empty, snowbound places, the readings by the bedsides of the sick, the ghost-story readings by the winter fire. Here is the curious science of bibliotherapy (Chapter Twenty-one), defined in Webster's as "the use of selected reading materials as therapeutic adjuvants in medicine and psychiatry", by which certain doctors claim they can heal the sick in body and spirit with *The Wind in the Willows* or *Bouvard and Pécuchet*.[17]

Here are the book-bags, the *sine qua non* of every Victorian voyage. No traveller left home without a suitcase full of appropriate reading, whether travelling to the Côte d'Azur or to Antarctica. (Poor Amundsen: our author tells us that, on his way to the South Pole, the explorer's book-bag sank under the ice, and he was obliged to spend many months in the company of the only volume he was able to rescue: Dr. John Gauden's *The Portraiture of His Sacred Majesty in His Solitudes and Sufferings*.)

One of the final chapters (not the last) concerns the writer's explicit acknowledgement of the reader's power. Here are the books left open for the reader's construction, like a box of Lego: Laurence Sterne's *Tristram Shandy*, of course, which allows us to read it any which way, and Julio Cortázar's *Hopscotch*, a novel built out of interchangeable chapters whose sequence the reader determines at will. Sterne and Cortázar inevitably lead to the New Age novels, the hypertexts. The term (our author tells us) was coined in the 1970s by a computer specialist, Ted Nelson, to describe the nonsequential narrative space made possible by computers. "There are no hierarchies in these topless (and bottomless) networks," our author quotes the novelist Robert Coover as saying, describing hypertext in an article in *The New*

York Times, "as paragraphs, chapters and other conventional text divisions are replaced by evenly empowered and equally ephemeral window-sized blocks of text and graphics".[18] The reader of a hypertext can enter the text at almost any point; change the narrative course, demand insertions, correct, expand or delete. Neither do these texts have an end, since the reader (or the writer) can always continue or retell a text: "If everything is middle, how do you know when you are done, either as reader or writer?" asks Coover. "If the author is free to take a story anywhere at any time and in so many directions as she or he wishes, does that not become the *obligation* to do so?" In brackets, our author questions the freedom implicit in such an obligation.

The History of Reading, fortunately, has no end. After the final chapter and before the already-mentioned copious index, our author has left a number of blank pages for the reader to add further thoughts on reading, subjects obviously missed, apposite quotations, events and characters still in the future. There is some consolation in that. I imagine leaving the book by the side of my bed, I imagine opening it up tonight, or tomorrow night, or the night after that, and saying to myself, "It's not finished."

N O T E S

I have not provided a separate bibliography since
most of the books that I drew upon are mentioned
in the following notes. In any case, the vastness of
the subject and the limitations of the author, would
make such a list, gathered under the prestigious
title of "Bibliography", seem both mysteriously
erratic and hopelessly incomplete.

THE LAST PAGE
pages 2–25

1. Claude Lévi-Strauss, *Tristes Tropiques* (Paris, 1955). Lévi-Strauss calls societies without writing "cold societies" because their cosmology attempts to annul the sequence of events that constitutes our notion of history.

2. Philippe Descola, *Les Lances du crépuscule* (Paris, 1994).

3. Miguel de Cervantes Saavedra, *El Ingenioso Hidalgo Don Quixote de la Mancha*, 2 vols., ed. Celina S. de Cortázar & Isaías Lerner (Buenos Aires, 1969), I: 9.

4. Gershom Scholem, *Kabbalah* (Jerusalem, 1974).

5. Miguel de Unamuno, untitled sonnet in *Poesía completa* (Madrid, 1979).

6. Virginia Woolf, "Charlotte Brontë", in *The Essays of Virginia Woolf, Vol. 2: 1912–1918*, ed. Andrew McNeillie (London, 1987).

7. Jean-Paul Sartre, *Les Mots* (Paris, 1964).

8. James Hillman, "A Note on Story", in *Children's Literature: The Great Excluded, Vol. 3*, ed. Francelia Butler & Bennett Brockman (Philadelphia, 1974).

9. Robert Louis Stevenson, "My Kingdom", *A Child's Garden of Verses* (London, 1885).

10. Michel de Montaigne, "On the Education of Children", in *Les Essais*, ed. J. Plattard (Paris, 1947).

11. Walter Benjamin, "A Berlin Chronicle", in *Reflections*, ed. Peter Demetz; trans. Edmund Jephcott (New York, 1978).

12. Samuel Butler, *The Notebooks of Samuel Butler* (London, 1912).

13. Jorge Luis Borges, "Pierre Menard, autor del *Quijote*", in *Ficciones* (Buenos Aires, 1944).

14. Spinoza, *Tractatus Theologico-Politicus*, trans. R.H.M. Elwes (London, 1889).

15. Quoted in John Willis Clark, *Libraries in the Medieval and Renaissance Periods* (Cambridge, 1894).

16. Traditio Generalis Capituli *of the English Benedictines* (Philadelphia, 1866).

17. Jamaica Kincaid, *A Small Place* (New York, 1988).

18. At the time, neither Borges nor I knew that Kipling's bundled message was not an invention. According to Ignace J. Gelb (*The History of Writing* [Chicago, 1952]), in Eastern Turkestan, a young woman sent her lover a message consisting of a lump of tea, a leaf of grass, a red fruit, a dried apricot, a piece of coal, a flower, a piece of sugar, a pebble, a falcon's feather and a nut. The message read, "I can no longer drink tea, I'm pale as grass without you, I blush to think of you, my heart burns as coal, you are beautiful as a flower, and sweet as sugar, but is your heart of stone? I'd fly to you if I had wings, I am yours like a nut in your hand."

19. Borges analysed Wilkins's language in an essay, "El idioma analítico de John Wilkins", in *Otras Inquisiciones* (Buenos Aires, 1952).

20. Evelyn Waugh, "The Man Who Liked Dickens", a chapter in *A Handful of Dust* (London, 1934).

21. Ezequiel Martínez Estrada, *Leer y escribir* (Mexico, D.F., 1969).

22. Jorge Semprún, *L'Écriture ou la vie* (Paris, 1994).

23. Jorge Luis Borges, review of *Men of Mathematics*, by E.T. Bell, in *El Hogar*, Buenos Aires, July 8, 1938.

24. P.K.E. Schmöger, *Das Leben der Gottseligen Anna Katharina Emmerich* (Freiburg, 1867).

25. Plato, *Phaedrus*, in *The Collected Dialogues*, ed. Edith Hamilton & Huntington Cairns (Princeton, 1961).

26. Hans Magnus Enzensberger, "In Praise of Illiteracy", in *Die Zeit*, Hamburg, Nov. 29, 1985.

27. Allan Bloom, *The Closing of the American Mind* (New York, 1987).

28. Charles Lamb, "Detached Thoughts on Books and Reading", in *Essays of Elia* (London, 1833).

29. Orhan Pamuk, *The White Castle*, trans. Victoria Holbrook (Manchester, 1990).

READING SHADOWS

pages 26–39

1. This is not to say that all writing has its roots in these Sumerian tablets. It is generally accepted that Chinese and Central American scripts, for example, developed independently. See Albertine Gaur, *A History of Writing* (London, 1984).

2. "Early Writing Systems", in *World Archeology* 17/3, Henley-on-Thames, Feb. 1986. The Mesopotamian invention of writing probably influenced other writing systems: the Egyptian, shortly after 3000 BC, and the Indian, around 2500 BC.

3. William Wordsworth, writing in 1819, described a similar feeling: "O ye who patiently explore / The wreck of Herculanean lore, / What rapture! Could ye seize / Some Theban fragment, or unrol / One precious, tender-hearted scroll / Of pure Simonides."

4. Cicero, *De oratore*, Vol. I, ed. E.W. Sutton & H. Rackham (Cambridge, Mass., & London, 1967), II, 87: 357.

5. Saint Augustine, *Confessions* (Paris, 1959), X, 34.

6. M.D. Chenu, *Grammaire et théologie au XIIᵉ et XIIIᵉ siècles* (Paris, 1935–36).

7. Empedocles, Fragment 84DK, quoted in Ruth Padel, *In and Out of the Mind: Greek Images of the Tragic Self* (Princeton, 1992).

8. Epicurus, "Letter to Herodotus", in Diogenes Laërtius, *Lives of Eminent Philosophers*, 10, quoted in David C. Lindberg, *Studies in the History of Medieval Optics* (London, 1983).

9. Ibid.

10. For a lucid explanation of this complex term, see Padel, *In and Out of the Mind*.

11. Aristotle, *De anima*, ed. W.S. Hett (Cambridge, Mass., & London, 1943).

12. Quoted in Nancy G. Siraisi, *Medieval & Early Renaissance Medicine* (Chicago & London, 1990).

13. Saint Augustine, *Confessions*, X, 8–11.

14. Siraisi, *Medieval & Early Renaissance Medicine*.

15. Kenneth D. Keele & Carlo Pedretti, eds., *Leonardo da Vinci: Corpus of the Anatomical Studies in the Collection of Her Majesty the Queen at Windsor Castle*, 3 vols. (London, 1978–80).

16. Albert Hourani, *A History of the Arab Peoples* (Cambridge, Mass., 1991).

17. Johannes Pedersen, *The Arabic Book*, trans. Geoffrey French (Princeton, 1984).

18. Sadik A. Assaad, *The Reign of al-Hakim bi Amr Allah* (London, 1974).

19. These rather elaborate explanations are developed in Saleh Beshara Omar's *Ibn al-Haytham's Optics: A Study of the Origins of Experimental Science* (Minneapolis & Chicago, 1977).

20. David C. Lindberg, *Theories of Vision from al-Kindi to Kepler* (Oxford, 1976).

21. Émile Charles, *Roger Bacon, sa vie, ses ouvrages, ses doctrines d'après des textes inédits* (Paris, 1861).

22. M. Dax, "Lésions de la moitié gauche de l'encéphale coincidant avec l'oubli des signes de la pensée", *Gazette hebdomadaire de médecine et de chirurgie*, 2 (1865), and P. Broca, "Sur le siège de la faculté du langage articulé", *Bulletin de la Societé d'anthropologie*, 6 337–393 (1865), in André Roch Lecours et al., "Illiteracy and Brain Damage (3): A Contribution to the Study of Speech and Language Disorders in Illiterates with Unilateral Brain Damage (Initial Testing)", *Neuropsychologia 26/4*, London, 1988.

23. André Roch Lecours, "The Origins and Evolution of Writing", in *Origins of the Human Brain* (Cambridge, 1993).

24. Daniel N. Stern, *The Interpersonal World of the Infant: A View from Psychoanalysis and Developmental Psychology* (New York, 1985).

25. Roch Lecours et al., "Illiteracy and Brain Damage (3)".

26. Jonathan Swift, *Gulliver's Travels*, ed. by Herbert Davis (Oxford, 1965).

27. Personal interview with André Roch Lecours, Montreal, Nov. 1992.

28. Émile Javal, eight articles in *Annales d'oculistique*, 1878–79, discussed in Paul A. Kolers, "Reading", lecture delivered at the Canadian Psychological Association meeting, Toronto, 1971.

29. Oliver Sacks, "The President's Speech", in *The Man Who Mistook His Wife for a Hat* (New York, 1987).

30. Merlin C. Wittrock, "Reading Comprehension", in *Neuropsychological and Cognitive Processes in Reading* (Oxford, 1981).

31. Cf. D. LaBerge & S.J. Samuels, "Toward a Theory of Automatic Information Processing in Reading", in *Cognitive Psychology* 6, London, 1974.

32. Wittrock, "Reading Comprehension".

33. E.B. Huey, *The Psychology and Pedagogy of Reading* (New York, 1908), quoted in Kolers, "Reading".

34. Quoted in Lindberg, *Theories of Vision from al-Kindi to Kepler*.

THE SILENT READERS
pages 40–53

1. Saint Augustine, *Confessions* (Paris, 1959), V, 12.

2. Donald Attwater, "Ambrose", in *A Dictionary of Saints* (London, 1965).

3. W. Ellwood Post, *Saints, Signs and Symbols* (Harrisburg, Penn., 1962).

4. Saint Augustine, *Confessions*, VI, 3.

5. In 1927, in an article titled "Voces Paginarum" (*Philologus* 82) the Hungarian scholar Josef Balogh tried to prove that silent reading was almost completely unknown in the ancient world. Forty-one years later, in 1968, Bernard M.W. Knox ("Silent Reading in Antiquity", in *Greek, Roman and Byzantine Studies* 9/4 [Winter 1968]) argued against Balogh that "ancient books were normally read aloud, but there is nothing to show that silent reading of books was anything extraordinary." And yet the examples Knox gives (several of which I quote) seem to me too weak to support his thesis, and appear to be *exceptions* to reading out loud, rather than the rule.

6. Knox, "Silent Reading in Antiquity".

7. Plutarch, "On the Fortune of Alexander", Fragment 340a, in *Moralia*, Vol. IV, ed. Frank Cole Babbitt (Cambridge, Mass., & London, 1972): "In fact it is recorded that once, when he had broken the seal of a confidential letter from his mother and was reading it silently to himself, Hephaestion quietly put his head beside Alexander's and read the letter with him; Alexander could not bear to stop him, but took off his ring and placed the seal on Hephaestion's lips."

8. Claudius Ptolemy, *On the Criterion*, discussed in *The Criterion of Truth*, ed. Pamela Huby & Gordon Neal (Oxford, 1952).

9. Plutarch, "Brutus", V, in *The Parallel Lives*, ed. B. Perrin (Cambridge, Mass., & London, 1970). It doesn't seem odd that Caesar should have read this note silently. In the first place, he may not have wanted a love-letter overheard; secondly, it may have been part of his plan to irritate his enemy, Cato, and lead

him to suspect a conspiracy — which is exactly what happened, according to Plutarch. Caesar was forced to show the note and Cato was ridiculed.

10. Saint Cyril of Jerusalem, *The Works of Saint Cyril of Jerusalem*, Vol. I, trans. L.P. McCauley & A.A. Stephenson (Washington, 1968).

11. Seneca, *Epistulae Morales*, ed. R.M. Gummere (Cambridge, Mass., & London, 1968), Letter 56.

12. The refrain *tolle, lege* doesn't appear in any ancient children's game known to us today. Pierre Courcelle suggests that the formula is one used in divination and quotes Marc le Diacre's *Life of Porphyrus*, in which the formula is uttered by a figure in a dream, to induce consultation of the Bible for divinatory purposes. See Pierre Courcelle, "L'Enfant et les 'sortes bibliques'", in *Vigiliae Christianae*, Vol. 7 (Nîmes, 1953).

13. Saint Augustine, *Confessions*, IV, 3.

14. Saint Augustine, "Concerning the Trinity", XV, 10: 19, in *Basic Writings of Saint Augustine*, ed. Whitney J. Oates (London, 1948).

15. Martial, *Epigrams*, trans. J.A. Pott & F.A. Wright (London, 1924), I. 38.

16. Cf. Henri Jean Martin, "Pour une histoire de la lecture", *Revue française d'histoire du livre* 46, Paris, 1977. According to Martin, Sumerian (not Aramaic) and Hebrew lack a specific verb meaning "to read".

17. Ilse Lichtenstadter, *Introduction to Classical Arabic Literature* (New York, 1974).

18. Quoted in Gerald L. Bruns, *Hermeneutics Ancient and Modern* (New Haven & London, 1992).

19. Julian Jaynes, *The Origin of Consciousness in the Breakdown of the Bicameral Mind* (Princeton, 1976).

20. Cicero, *Tusculan Disputations*, ed. J.E. King (Cambridge, Mass., & London, 1952), Disputation V.

21. Albertine Gaur, *A History of Writing* (London, 1984).

22. William Shepard Walsh, *A Handy-Book of Literary Curiosities* (Philadelphia, 1892).

23. Quoted in M.B. Parkes, *Pause and Effect: An Introduction to the History of Punctuation in the West* (Berkeley & Los Angeles, 1993).

24. Suetonius, *Lives of the Caesars*, ed. J.C. Rolfe (Cambridge, Mass., & London, 1970).

25. T. Birt, *Aus dem Leben der Antike* (Leipzig, 1922).

26. Gaur, *A History of Writing*.

27. Pierre Riché, *Les Écoles et l'enseignement dans l'Occident chrétien de la fin du Vᵉ siècle au milieu du XIᵉ siècle* (Paris, 1979).

28. Parkes, *Pause and Effect*.

29. Saint Isaac of Syria, "Directions of Spiritual Training", in *Early Fathers from the Philokalia*, ed. & trans. E. Kadloubovsky & G.E.H. Palmer (London & Boston, 1954).

30. Isidoro de Sevilla, *Libri sententiae*, III, 13: 9, quoted in *Etimologías*, ed. Manuel C. Díaz y Díaz (Madrid, 1982–83).

31. Isidoro de Sevilla, *Etimologías*, I, 3: 1.

32. David Diringer, *The Hand-Produced Book* (London, 1953).

33. Parkes, *Pause and Effect*.

34. Carlo M. Cipolla, *Literacy and Development in the West* (London, 1969).

35. Quoted in Wilhelm Wattenbach, *Das Schriftwesen im Mittelalter* (Leipzig, 1896).

36. Alan G. Thomas, *Great Books and Book Collectors* (London, 1975).

37. Saint Augustine, *Confessions*, VI, 3.

38. Psalms 91: 6.

39. Saint Augustine, *Confessions*, VI, 3.

40. David Christie-Murray, *A History of Heresy* (Oxford & New York, 1976).

41. Robert I. Moore, *The Birth of Popular Heresy* (London, 1975).

42. Heiko A. Oberman, *Luther: Mensch zwischen Gott und Teufel* (Berlin, 1982).

43. E.G. Léonard, *Histoire générale du protestantisme*, Vol. I (Paris, 1961–64).

44. Van Wyck Brooks, *The Flowering of New England, 1815–1865* (New York, 1936).

45. Ralph Waldo Emerson, *Society and Solitude* (Cambridge, Mass., 1870).

THE BOOK OF MEMORY
pages 54–65

1. Saint Augustine, "Of the Origin and Nature of the Soul", IV, 7: 9, in *Basic Writings of Saint Augustine*, ed. Whitney J. Oates (London, 1948).

2. Cicero, *De oratore*, Vol. I, ed. E.W. Sutton & H. Rackham (Cambridge, Mass., & London, 1957), II, 86: 354.

3. Louis Racine, *Mémoires contenant quelques particularités sur la vie et les ouvrages de Jean Racine*, in Jean Racine, *Oeuvres complètes*, Vol. I, ed. Raymond Picard (Paris, 1950).

4. Plato, *Phaedrus*, in *The Collected Dialogues*, ed. Edith Hamilton & Huntington Cairns (Princeton, 1961).

5. Mary J. Carruthers, *The Book of Memory* (Cambridge, 1990).

6. Ibid.

7. Eric G. Turner, "I Libri nell'Atene del V e IV secolo A.C.", in Guglielmo Cavallo, *Libri, editori e pubblico nel mondo antico* (Rome & Bari, 1992).

8. John, 8:8.

9. Carruthers, *The Book of Memory*.

10. Ibid.

11. Aline Rousselle, *Porneia* (Paris, 1983).

12. Frances A. Yates, *The Art of Memory* (London, 1966).

13. Petrarch, *Secretum meum*, II, in *Prose*, ed. Guido Martellotti et al. (Milan, 1951).

14. Victoria Kahn, "The Figure of the Reader in Petrarch's *Secretum*", in *Petrarch: Modern Critical Views*, ed. Harold Bloom (New York & Philadelphia, 1989).

15. Petrarch, *Familiares*, 2.8.822, quoted in ibid.

LEARNING TO READ
pages 66–83

1. Claude Lévi-Strauss, *Tristes Tropiques* (Paris, 1955).

2. A. Dorlan, "Casier descriptif et historique des rues & maisons de Sélestat" (1926), in *Annuaire de la Société des Amis de la Bibliothèque de Sélestat* (Sélestat, 1951).

3. Quoted in Paul Adam, *Histoire de l'enseignement secondaire à Sélestat* (Sélestat, 1969).

4. Herbert Grundmann, *Vom Ursprung der Universität im Mittelalter* (Frankfurt-am-Main, 1957).

5. Ibid.

6. Edouard Fick, Introduction to *La Vie de Thomas Platter écrite par lui-même* (Geneva, 1862).

7. Paul Adam, *L'Humanisme à Sélestat: L'École, les humanistes, la bibliothèque* (Sélestat, 1962).

8. Thomas Platter, *La Vie de Thomas Platter écrite par lui-même*, trans. Edouard Fick (Geneva, 1862).

9. Israel Abrahams, *Jewish Life in the Middle Ages* (London, 1896).

10. I am grateful to Professor Roy Porter for this caveat.

11. Mateo Palmieri, *Della vita civile* (Bologna, 1944).

12. Leon Battista Alberti, *I Libri della famiglia*, ed. R. Romano & A. Tenenti (Turin, 1969).

13. Quintilian, *The Institutio Oratoria of Quintilian*, trans. H.E. Butler (Oxford, 1920–22), I i 12.

14. Quoted in Pierre Riche & Daniele Alexandre-Bidon, *L'Enfance au Moyen Age*. Catalogue of exhibition at the Bibliothèque Nationale, Paris, Oct. 26, 1994–Jan. 15, 1995 (Paris, 1995).

15. Ibid.

16. M.D. Chenu, *La Théologie comme science au XIIIe siècle*, 3rd ed. (Paris, 1969).

17. Dominique Sourdel & Janine Sourdel-Thomine, eds., *Medieval Education in Islam and the West* (Cambridge, Mass., 1977).

18. Alfonso el Sabio, *Las Siete Partidas*, ed. Ramón Menéndez Pidal (Madrid, 1955), 2 31 IV.

19. We have a letter, from about the same time, from a student requesting that his mother obtain some books for him, without concern about the cost: "I also want Paul to buy the *Orationes Demosthenis Olynthiacae*, have it bound and send it to me." Steven Ozment, *Three Behaim Boys: Growing Up in Early Modern Germany* (New Haven & London, 1990).

20. Adam, *Histoire de l'enseignement secondaire à Sélestat*.

21. Jakob Wimpfeling, *Isidoneus*, XXI, in J. Freudgen, *Jakob Wimphelings pädagogische Schriften* (Paderborn, 1892).

22. Isabel Suzeau, "Un Écolier de la fin du XVe siècle: À propos d'un cahier inédit de l'école latine de Sélestat sous Crato Hofman", in *Annuaire de la Société des Amis de la Bibliothèque de Sélestat* (Sélestat, 1991).

23. Jacques Le Goff, *Les Intellectuels au Moyen Age*, rev. ed. (Paris, 1985).

24. Letter from L. Guidetti to B. Massari dated Oct. 25, 1465, in *La critica del Landino*, ed. R. Cardini (Florence, 1973). Quoted in Anthony Grafton, *Defenders of the Text: The Traditions of Scholarship in an Age of Science, 1450–1800* (Cambridge, Mass., 1991).

25. Wimpfeling, *Isidoneus*, XXI.

26. Adam, *L'Humanisme à Sélestat*.

27. Ibid.

28. In the end, Dringenberg's preference became prevalent: in the early years of the sixteenth century, as a reaction to the Reformation, the teachers at the Latin school eliminated all pagan writers deemed "suspect", i.e., not "canonized" by authorities such as Saint Augustine, and insisted on a strict Catholic education.

29. Jakob Spiegel, "Scholia in Reuchlin Scaenica progymnasmata", in G. Knod, *Jakob Spiegel aus Schlettstadt: Ein Beitrag zur Geschichte des deutschen Humanismus* (Strasbourg, 1884).

30. Jakob Wimpfeling, "*Diatriba*" IV, in G. Knod, *Aus der Bibliothek des Beatus Rhenanus: Ein Beitrag zur Geschichte des Humanismus* (Sélestat, 1889).

31. Jerôme Gebwiler, quoted in *Schlettstadter Chronik des Schulmeisters Hieronymus Gebwiler*, ed. J. Geny (Sélestat, 1890).

32. Nicolas Adam, "Vraie manière d'apprendre une langue quelconque", in *Dictionnaire pédagogique* (Paris, 1787).

33. Keller, Helen, *The Story of My Life*, 3rd ed. (London, 1903).

34. Quoted in E.P. Goldschmidt, *Medieval Texts and Their First Appearance in Print*, suppl. to *Biographical Society Transactions 16* (Oxford, 1943).

35. The Catholic Church did not revoke the ban on Copernicus's writings until 1758.

THE MISSING FIRST PAGE
pages 84–93

1. Franz Kafka, *Erzählungen* (Frankfurt-am-Main, 1967).

2. Cf. Goethe (quoted in Umberto Eco, *The Limits of Interpretation* [Bloomington & Indianapolis, 1990]): "Symbolism transforms the experience into an idea and an idea into an image, so that the idea expressed through the image remains always active and unattainable and, even though expressed in all languages, remains inexpressible. Allegory transforms experience into a concept and a concept into an image, but so that the concept remains always defined and expressible by the image."

3. Paul de Man, *Allegories of Reading: Figural Language in Rousseau, Nietzsche, Rilke,*

and Proust (New Haven, 1979).

4. Dante, *Le Opere di Dante. Testo critico della Società Dantesca Italiana*, ed. M. Barbi et al. (Milan, 1921–22).

5. Ernst Pawel, *The Nightmare of Reason: A Life of Franz Kafka* (New York, 1984).

6. Franz Kafka, *Brief an den Vater* (New York, 1953).

7. Quoted in Pawel, *The Nightmare of Reason*.

8. Gustav Janouch, *Conversations with Kafka*, trans. Goronwy Rees, 2nd ed., revised and enlarged (New York, 1971).

9. Martin Buber, *Tales of the Hasidim*, 2 vols., trans. Olga Marx (New York, 1947).

10. Marc-Alain Ouaknin, *Le Livre brûlé: Philosophie du Talmud* (Paris, 1986).

11. Pawel, *The Nightmare of Reason*.

12. Janouch, *Conversations with Kafka*.

13. Walter Benjamin, *Illuminations*, trans. Harry Zohn (New York, 1968).

14. Ibid.

15. Fyodor Dostoevsky, *The Brothers Karamazov*, trans. David Magarshack, Vol. I (London, 1958).

16. Janouch, *Conversations with Kafka*.

17. Eco, *The Limits of Interpretation*.

18. Pawel, *The Nightmare of Reason*.

19. Janouch, *Conversations with Kafka*.

20. Quoted in Gershom Sholem, *Walter Benjamin: The Story of a Friendship*, trans. Harry Zohn (New York, 1981).

21. Marthe Robert, *La Tyrannie de l'imprimé* (Paris, 1984).

22. Jorge Luis Borges, "Kafka y sus precursores", in *Otras Inquisiciones* (Buenos Aires, 1952).

23. Robert, *La Tyrannie de l'imprimé*.

24. Vladimir Nabokov, "Metamorphosis", in *Lectures on Literature* (New York, 1980).

25. Pawel, *The Nightmare of Reason*.

PICTURE READING

pages 94–107

1. Luigi Serafini, *Codex Seraphinianus*, intr. by Italo Calvino (Milan, 1981).

2. John Atwatter, *The Penguin Book of Saints* (London, 1965).

3. K. Heussi, "Untersuchungen zu Nilus dem Asketem", in *Texte und Untersuchungen*, Vol. XLII, Fasc. 2 (Leipzig, 1917).

4. Louis-Sébastien Le Nain de Tillemont, *Mémoires pour servir à l'histoire ecclésiastique des six premiers siècles*, Vol. XIV (Paris, 1693–1712).

5. *Dictionnaire de théologie catholique* (Paris, 1903–50).

6. Saint Nilus, *Epistula LXI:* "Ad Olympidoro Eparcho", in *Patrologia Graeca*, LXXIX, 1857–66.

7. Quoted in F. Piper, *Über den christlichen Biderkreis* (Berlin, 1852).

8. Quoted in Claude Dagens, *Saint Grégoire le Grand: Culture et experience chrétienne* (Paris, 1977).

9. Synod of Arras, Chapter 14, in *Sacrorum Nova et Amplissima Collectio*, ed. J.D. Mansi (Paris & Leipzig, 1901–27), quoted in Umberto Eco, *Il problema estetico di Tommaso d'Aquino* (Milan, 1970).

10. Exodus 20: 4; Deuteronomy 5: 8.

11. I Kings 6–7.

12. André Grabar, *Christian Iconography: A Study of Its Origins* (Princeton, 1968).

13. Matthew 1: 22; also Matthew 2: 5; 2: 15; 4: 14; 8: 17; 13: 35; 21: 4; 27: 35.

14. Luke 24: 44.

15. *A Cyclopedic Bible Concordance* (Oxford, 1952).

16. Saint Augustine, "In Exodum" 73, in *Quaestiones in Heptateuchum*, II, *Patrologia Latina*, XXXIV, Chapter 625, 1844–55.

17. Eusebius of Caesare, *Demostratio evangelium*, IV, 15, *Patrologia Graeca*, XXII, Chapter 296, 1857–66.

18. Cf. "For they drank of that spiritual Rock that followed them: and that Rock was Christ", I Corinthians 10: 4.

19. Grabar, *Christian Iconography*.

20. Quoted in Piper, *Über den christlichen Bilderkreis*.

21. Allan Stevenson, *The Problem of the Missale Speciale* (London, 1967).

22. Cf. Maurus Berve, *Die Armenbibel* (Beuron, 1989). The *Biblia Pauperum* is catalogued as Ms. 148 at the Heidelberg University Library.

23. Gerhard Schmidt, *Die Armenbibeln des XIV Jahrhunderts* (Frankfurt-am-Main, 1959).

24. Karl Gotthelf Lessing, *G.E. Lessings Leben* (Frankfurt-am-Main, 1793–95).

25. G.E. Lessing, "Ehemalige Fenstergemälde im Kloster Hirschau", in *Zur Geschichte und Literatur aus der Herzoglichen Bibliothek zu Wolfenbüttel* (Braunschweig, 1773).

26. G. Heider, "Beitrage zur christlichen Typologie", in *Jahrbuch der K.K. Central-Comission zur Erforschung der Baudenkmale*, Vol. V (Vienna, 1861).

27. Marshall McLuhan, *Understanding Media: The Extensions of Man* (New York, 1964).

28. François Villon, *Oeuvres complètes*, ed. P.L. Jacob (Paris, 1854).

29. Ibid., "Ballade que Villon fit à la requeste de sa mère pour prier Nostre-Dame", in *Le Grand Testament*:

> *Femme je suis povrette et ancienne,*
> *Ne rien ne scay; oncques lettre ne leuz;*
> *Au monstier voy, dont suis parroissienne,*
> *Paradis painct, ou sont harpes et luz,*
> *Et ung enfer ou damnez sont boulluz:*

L'ung me faict paour; l'autre, joye et liesse."

30. Berve, *Die Armenbibel*.

31. Schmidt, *Die Armenbibeln des XIV Jahrhunderts*; also Elizabeth L. Einsenstein, *The Printing Revolution in Early Modern Europe* (Cambridge, 1983).

BEING READ TO
pages 108–123

1. Philip S. Foner, *A History of Cuba and Its Relations with the United States*, Vol. II (New York, 1963).

2. José Antonio Portuondo, *'La Aurora' y los comienzos de la prensa y de la organización en Cuba* (Havana, 1961).

3. Ibid.

4. Foner, *A History of Cuba*.

5. Ibid.

6. Hugh Thomas, *Cuba; the Pursuit of Freedom* (London, 1971).

7. L. Glenn Westfall, *Key West: Cigar City U.S.A.* (Key West, 1984).

8. Manuel Deulofeu y Lleonart, *Martí, Cayo Hueso y Tampa: La emigración* (Cienfuegos, 1905).

9. Kathryn Hall Proby, *Mario Sánchez: Painter of Key West Memories* (Key West, 1981). Also personal interview, Nov. 20, 1991.

10. T.F. Lindsay, *St Benedict, His Life and Work* (London, 1949).

11. Borges's story "The Aleph", in *El Aleph* (Buenos Aires, 1949), from which this description is taken, centres around one such universal vision.

12. García Colombas & Inaki Aranguren, *La regla de San Benito* (Madrid, 1979).

13. "Thus there are two Books from whence I collect my Divinity; besides that written one of God, another of his servant Nature, that universal and publick Manuscript, that lies expans'd unto the Eyes of all." Sir Thomas Browne, *Religio Medici* (London, 1642), I: 16.

14. "The Rule of S. Benedict", in *Documents of the Christian Church*, ed. Henry Bettenson (Oxford, 1963).

15. John de Ford, in his *Life of Wulfric of Haselbury*, compares this "love of silence" to the Bride's entreaties for the quiet in the Song of Songs 2: 7. In Pauline Matarasso, ed., *The Cistercian World: Monastic Writings of the Twelfth Century* (London, 1993).

16. "I tell you brothers, no misfortune can touch us, no situation so galling or distressing can arise that does not, as soon as Holy Writ seizes hold of us, either fade into nothingness or become bearable." Aelred of Rievaulx, "The Mirror of Charity", in Matarasso, ibid.

17. Cedric E. Pickford, "Fiction and the Reading Public in the Fifteenth Century", in the *Bulletin of the John Rylands University Library of Manchester*, Vol. 45 II, Manchester, Mar. 1963.

18. Gaston Paris, *La Littérature française au Moyen Age* (Paris, 1890).

19. Quoted in Urban Tigner Holmes, Jr., *Daily Living in the Twelfth Century* (Madison, Wisc., 1952).

20. Pliny the Younger, *Lettres I–IX*, ed. A.M. Guillemin, 3 vols. (Paris, 1927–28), IX: 36.

21. J.M. Richard, *Mahaut, comtesse d'Artois et de Bourgogne* (Paris, 1887).

22. Iris Cutting Origo, *The Merchant of Prato: Francesco di Marco Datini* (New York, 1957).

23. Emmanuel Le Roy Ladurie, *Montaillou: Village occitan de 1294 à 1324* (Paris, 1978).

24. Madeleine Jeay, ed., *Les Évangiles des quenouilles* (Montreal, 1985). The distaff, the cleft stick that holds wool or flax for spinning, symbolizes the female sex. In English, "the distaff side of the family" means "the female branch".

25. Miguel de Cervantes Saavedra, *El Ingenioso Hidalgo Don Quijote de la Mancha* (Madrid, 1605), I: 34.

26. Fourteen chapters earlier, Don Quixote himself has reproved Sancho for telling a story "full of interruptions and digressions", instead of the linear narration that the bookish knight expects. Sancho's defence is that "this is how they tell tales in my part of the country; I don't know any other way and it isn't fair of Your Grace to ask me to undertake new manners." *Ibid.*, I: 20.

27. William Chambers, *Memoir of Robert Chambers with Autobiographic Reminiscences*, 10th ed. (Edinburgh, 1880). This wonderful anecdote was given to me by Larry Pfaff, reference librarian at the Art Gallery of Ontario.

28. *Ibid.*

29. Jean Pierre Pinies, "Du choc culturel á l'ethnocide: La Pénétration du livre dans les campagnes languedociennes du XVIIe au XIXe siècles", in *Folklore* 44/3 (1981), quoted in Martyn Lyons, *Le Triomphe du livre* (Paris, 1987).

30. Quoted in Amy Cruse, *The Englishman and His Books in the Early Nineteenth Century* (London, 1930).

31. Denis Diderot, "Lettre à sa fille Angélique", July 28, 1781, in *Correspondance littéraire, philosophique et critique*, ed. Maurice Tourneux; trans. P.N. Furbank (Paris, 1877–82), XV: 253–54.

32. Benito Pérez Galdós, "O'Donnell", in *Episodios Nacionales, Obras Completas* (Madrid, 1952).

33. Jane Austen, *Letters*, ed. R.W. Chapman (London, 1952).

34. Denis Diderot, *Essais sur la peinture*, ed. Gita May (Paris, 1984).

THE SHAPE OF THE BOOK
pages 124–147

1. David Diringer, *The Hand-Produced Book* (London, 1953).

2. Pliny the Elder, *Naturalis Historia*, ed. W.H.S. Jones (Cambridge, Mass., &

London, 1968), XIII, 11.

3. The earliest extant Greek codex on vellum is an *Iliad* from the third century AD (Biblioteca Ambrosiana, Milan).

4. Martial, *Epigrammata*, XIV: 184, in *Works*, 2 vols., ed. W.C.A. Ker (Cambridge, Mass., & London, 1919–20).

5. François I, *Lettres de François Ier au Pape* (Paris, 1527).

6. John Power, *A Handy-Book about Books* (London, 1870).

7. Quoted in Geo. Haven Putnam, *Books and Their Makers during the Middle Ages*, Vol. I (New York, 1896–97).

8. Janet Backhouse, *Books of Hours* (London, 1985).

9. John Harthan, *Books of Hours and Their Owners* (London, 1977).

10. Now in the Municipal Library of Sémur-en-Auxois, France.

11. Johannes Duft, *Stiftsbibliothek Sankt Gallen: Geschichte, Barocksaal, Manuskripte* (St. Gall, 1990). The antiphonary is catalogued as Codex 541, *Antiphonarium officii* (parchment, 618 pp.), Abbey Library, St. Gall, Switzerland.

12. D.J. Gillies, "Engineering Manuals of Coffee-Table Books: The Machine Books of the Renaissance", in *Descant* 13, Toronto, Winter 1975.

13. Benjamin Franklin, *The Autobiography of B.F.* (New York, 1818).

14. Elizabeth L. Eisenstein, *The Printing Revolution in Early Modern Europe* (Cambridge, 1983).

15. Victor Scholderer, *Johann Gutenberg* (Frankfurt-am-Main, 1963).

16. Quoted in Guy Bechtel, *Gutenberg et l'invention de l'imprimerie* (Paris, 1992).

17. Paul Needham, director of the Books and Manuscripts Dept. at Sotheby's, New York, has suggested two other possible reactions from Gutenberg's public: surprise that the new method used metallurgical technology to produce letters, instead of quill or reed, and also that this "holy art" came from the backwaters of barbaric Germany instead of from learned Italy. Paul Needham, "Haec sancta ars: Gutenberg's Invention As a Divine Gift", in *Gazette of the Grolier Club*, Number 42, 1990, New York, 1991.

18. Svend Dahl, *Historia del libro*, trans. Albert Adell; rev. Fernando Huarte Morton (Madrid, 1972).

19. Konrad Haebler, *The Study of Incunabula* (London, 1953).

20. Warren Chappell, *A Short History of the Printed Word* (New York, 1970).

21. Sven Birkerts, *The Gutenberg Elegies: The Fate of Reading in an Electronic Age* (Boston & London, 1994).

22. Catalogue: *Il Libro della Bibbia, Esposizione di manoscritti e di edizioni a stampa della Biblioteca Apostolica Vaticana dal Secolo III al Secolo XVI* (Vatican City, 1972).

23. Alan G. Thomas, *Great Books and Book Collectors* (London, 1975).

24. Lucien Febvre & Henri-Jean Martin, *L'Apparition du livre* (Paris, 1958).

25. Marino Zorzi, introduction to *Aldo Manuzio e l'ambiente veneziano 1494–1515*, ed. Susy Marcon & Marino Zorzi (Venice, 1994). Also: Martin Lowry, *The World of Aldus Manutius*, Oxford, 1979.

26. Anthony Grafton, "The Strange Deaths of Hermes and the Sibyls", in *Defenders*

of the Text: The Traditions of Scholarship in an Age of Science, 1450–1800 (Cambridge, Mass., & London, 1991).

27. Quoted in Alan G. Thomas, *Fine Books* (London, 1967).

28. Quoted in Eisenstein, *The Printing Revolution in Early Modern Europe*. (No source given.)

29. Febvre & Martin, *L'Apparition du livre*.

30. William Shenstone, *The Schoolmistress* (London, 1742).

31. In the exhibition "Into the Heart of Africa", Royal Ontario Museum, Toronto, 1992.

32. Shakespeare, *The Winter's Tale*, Act IV, Scene 4.

33. The word apparently derives from the journeymen or "chapmen" who sold these books, "chapel" being the collective term for the journeymen attached to a particular printing house. See John Feather, ed., *A Dictionary of Book History* (New York, 1986).

34. John Ashton, *Chap-books of the Eighteenth Century* (London, 1882).

35. Philip Dormer Stanhope, 4th earl of Chesterfield, "Letter of Feb. 22 1748", *Letters to His Son, Philip Stanhope, Together with Several Other Pieces on Various Subjects* (London, 1774).

36. John Sutherland, "Modes of Production", in *The Times Literary Supplement*, London, Nov. 19, 1993.

37. Hans Schmoller, "The Paperback Revolution", in *Essays in the History of Publishing in Celebration of the 250th Anniversary of the House of Longman 1724–1974*, ed. Asa Briggs (London, 1974).

38. Ibid.

39. J.E. Morpurgo, *Allen Lane, King Penguin* (London, 1979).

40. Quoted in Schmoller, "The Paperback Revolution".

41. Anthony J. Mills, "A Penguin in the Sahara", in *Archeological Newsletter of the Royal Ontario Museum*, II: 37, Toronto, March 1990.

PRIVATE READING

pages 148–161

1. Colette, *La Maison de Claudine* (Paris, 1922).

2. Claude & Vincenette Pichois (with Alain Brunet), *Album Colette* (Paris, 1984).

3. Colette, *La Maison de Claudine*.

4. Ibid.

5. Ibid.

6. W.H. Auden, "Letter to Lord Byron", in *Collected Longer Poems* (London, 1968).

7. André Gide, *Voyage au Congo* (Paris, 1927).

8. Colette, *Claudine à l'École* (Paris, 1900).

9. Quoted in Gerald Donaldson, *Books: Their History, Art, Power, Glory, Infamy and*

Suffering According to Their Creators, Friends and Enemies (New York, 1981).

10. *Bookmarks*, edited and introduced by Frederic Raphael (London, 1975).

11. Maurice Keen, *English Society in the Later Middle Ages, 1348–1500* (London, 1990).

12. Quoted in Urban Tigner Holmes, Jr., *Daily Living in the Twelfth Century* (Madison, Wisc., 1952).

13. Henry Miller, *The Books in My Life* (New York, 1952).

14. Marcel Proust, *Du Côté de chez Swann* (Paris, 1913).

15. Charles-Augustin Sainte-Beuve, *Critiques et portraits littéraires* (Paris, 1836–39).

16. Quoted in N.I. White, *Life of Percy Bysshe Shelley*, 2 vols. (London, 1947).

17. Marguerite Duras, interview in *Le Magazine littéraire* 158, Paris, March 1980.

18. Marcel Proust, *Journées de lecture*, ed. Alain Coelho (Paris, 1993).

19. Marcel Proust, *Le Temps retrouvé* (Paris, 1927).

20. Geoffrey Chaucer, "The Proem", *The Book of the Duchesse*, 44–51, in *Chaucer: Complete Works*, ed. Walter W. Skeat (Oxford, 1973).

21. Josef Skvorecky, "The Pleasures of the Freedom to Read", in *Anteus*, No. 59, Tangier, London & New York, Autumn 1987.

22. Annie Dillard, *An American Childhood* (New York, 1987).

23. Hollis S. Barker, *Furniture in the Ancient World* (London, 1966).

24. Jerôme Barker, *La Vie quotidienne à Rome à l'apogée de l'empire* (Paris, 1939).

25. Petronius, *The Satyricon*, trans. William Arrowsmith (Ann Arbor, 1959).

26. *Byzantine Books and Bookmen* (Washington, 1975).

27. Pascal Dibie, *Ethnologie de la chambre à coucher* (Paris, 1987).

28. C. Gray & M. Gray, *The Bed* (Philadelphia, 1946).

29. Keen, *English Society in the Later Middle Ages*.

30. Margaret Wade Labarge, *A Small Sound of the Trumpet: Women in Medieval Life* (London, 1986).

31. Eileen Harris, *Going to Bed* (London, 1981).

32. G. Ecke, *Chinese Domestic Furniture* (London, 1963).

33. Jean-Baptiste De la Salle, *Les Régles de la bienséance de la civilité chrétienne* (Paris, 1703).

34. Jonathan Swift, *Directions to Servants* (Dublin, 1746).

35. Van Wyck Brooks, *The Flowering of New England, 1815–1865* (New York, 1936).

36. Antoine de Courtin, *Nouveau Traité de la civilité qui se pratique en France parmi les honnestes gens* (Paris, 1672).

37. Mrs. Haweis, *The Art of Housekeeping* (London, 1889), quoted in Asa Briggs, *Victorian Things* (Chicago, 1988).

38. Leigh Hunt, *Men, Women and Books: A Selection of Sketches, Essays, and Critical Memoirs* (London, 1891).

39. Cynthia Ozick, "Justice (Again) to Edith Wharton", in *Art & Ardor* (New York, 1983).

40. R.W.B. Lewis, *Edith Wharton: A Biography* (New York, 1975), quoted ibid.

41. Colette, *Lettres à Marguerite Moreno* (Paris, 1959).

42. Pichois & Vincenette, *Album Colette*.

43. Germaine Beaumont & André Parinaud, *Colette par elle-même* (Paris, 1960).

METAPHORS OF READING
pages 162–173

1. Walt Whitman, "Song of Myself", in *Leaves of Grass*, 1856, in *The Complete Poems*, ed. Francis Murphy (London, 1975).

2. Ibid.

3. Walt Whitman, "Song of Myself", in *Leaves of Grass*, 1860, ibid.

4. Goethe, "Sendscreiben", quoted in E.R. Curtius, *Europäische Literatur und lateinisches Mittelalter* (Berne, 1948).

5. Walt Whitman, "Shakespeare-Bacon's Cipher", in *Leaves of Grass*, 1892, in *The Complete Poems*.

6. Ezra Pound, *Personae* (New York, 1926).

7. Walt Whitman, "Inscriptions", in *Leaves of Grass*, 1881, in *The Complete Poems*.

8. Quoted in Philip Callow, *Walt Whitman: From Noon to Starry Night* (London, 1992).

9. Walt Whitman, "A Backward Glance O'er Travel'd Roads", introduction to *November Boughs*, 1888, in *The Complete Poems*.

10. Walt Whitman, "Song of Myself", in *Leaves of Grass*, 1856, in ibid.

11. Ibid.

12. Quoted in Thomas L. Brasher, *Whitman As Editor of the Brooklyn "Daily Eagle"* (Detroit, 1970).

13. Quoted in William Harlan Hale, *Horace Greeley, Voice of the People* (Boston, 1942).

14. Quoted in Randall Stewart, *Nathaniel Hawthorne* (New York, 1948).

15. Quoted in Arthur W. Brown, *Margaret Fuller* (New York, 1951).

16. Walt Whitman, "My Canary Bird", in *November Boughs*, 1888, in *The Complete Poems*.

17. Hans Blumenberg, *Schiffbruch mit Zuschauer* (Frankfurt-am-Main, 1979).

18. Fray Luis de Granada, *Introducción al símbolo de la fe* (Salamanca, 1583).

19. Sir Thomas Browne, *Religio Medici*, ed. Sir Geoffrey Keynes (London, 1928–31), I: 16.

20. George Santayana, *Realms of Being*, Vol. II (New York, 1940).

21. Quoted in Henri de Lubac, *Augustinisme et théologie moderne* (Paris, 1965). Pierre Bersuire, in the *Repertorium morale*, extended the image to the Son: "For Christ is a sort of book written upon the skin of the virgin. . . . That book was spoken in the disposition of the Father, written in the conception of the

mother, exposited in the clarification of the nativity, corrected in the passion, erased in the flagellation, punctuated in the imprint of the wounds, adorned in the crucifixion above the pulpit, illuminated in the outpouring of blood, bound in the resurrection, and examined in the ascension." Quoted in Jesse M. Gellrich, *The Idea of the Book in the Middle Ages: Language Theory, Mythology, and Fiction* (Ithaca & London, 1985).

22. Shakespeare, *Macbeth*, Act I, Scene 5.

23. Henry King, "An Exequy to His Matchlesse Never to Be Forgotten Friend", in *Baroque Poetry*, ed. J.P. Hill & E. Caracciolo-Trejo (London, 1975).

24. Benjamin Franklin, *The Papers of Benjamin Franklin*, ed. Leonard W. Labaree (New Haven, 1959).

25. Francis Bacon, "Of Studies", in *The Essayes or Counsels* (London, 1625).

26. Joel Rosenberg, "Jeremiah and Ezekiel", in *The Literary Guide to the Bible*, ed. Robert Alter & Frank Kermode (Cambridge, Mass., 1987).

27. Ezekiel 2: 9–10.

28. Revelation, 10: 9–11.

29. Elizabeth I, *A Book of Devotions: Composed by Her Majesty Elizabeth R.*, ed. Adam Fox (London, 1970).

30. William Congreve, *Love for Love*, Act I, Scene 1, in *The Complete Works*, 4 vols., ed. Montague Summers (Oxford, 1923).

31. James Boswell, *The Life of Samuel Johnson*, ed. John Wain (London, 1973).

32. Walt Whitman, "Shut Not Your Doors", in *Leaves of Grass*, 1867, in *The Complete Poems*.

BEGINNINGS
pages 176–185

1. Joan Oates, *Babylon* (London, 1986).

2. Georges Roux, *Ancient Iraq* (London, 1964).

3. Ibid.

4. Mark Jones, ed., *Fake? The Art of Deception* (Berkeley & Los Angeles, 1990).

5. Alan G. Thomas, *Great Books and Book Collectors* (London, 1975).

6. A. Parrot, *Mission archéologique à Mari* (Paris, 1958–59).

7. C.J. Gadd, *Teachers and Students in the Oldest Schools* (London, 1956).

8. C.B.F. Walker, *Cuneiform* (London, 1987).

9. Ibid.

10. William W. Hallo & J.J.A. van Dijk, *The Exaltation of Inanna* (New Haven, 1968).

11. Catalogue of the exhibition *Naissance de l'écriture*, Bibliothèque Nationale, Paris, 1982.

12. M. Lichtheim, *Ancient Egyptian Literature*, Vol. 1 (Berkeley, 1973–76).

13. Jacques Derrida, *De la grammatologie* (Paris, 1976).

14. Roland Barthes, "Écrivains et écrivants", in *Essais critiques* (Paris, 1971).

15. Saint Augustine, *Confessions* (Paris, 1959), XIII, 29.

16. Richard Wilbur, "To the Etruscan Poets", in *The Mind Reader* (New York, 1988), and *New and Collected Poems* (London, 1975).

ORDAINERS OF THE UNIVERSE
pages 186–199

1. Quintus Curtius Rufus, *The History of Alexander*, ed. & trans. John Yardley (London, 1984), 4.8.1–6.

2. Menander, *Sententiae* 657, in *Works*, ed. W.G. Arnott (Cambridge, Mass., & London, 1969).

3. M.I. Rostovtzeff, *A Large Estate in Egypt in the Third Century B.C.* (Madison, 1922), quoted in William V. Harris, *Ancient Literacy* (Cambridge, Mass., 1989).

4. *P.Col.Zen.* 3.4, plus *P.Cair.Zen.* 4.59687, in Harris, ibid.

5. I take a certain pride in the fact that, in our time, the only city in the world to have been founded with a library was Buenos Aires. In 1580, after a first unsuccessful attempt to found on the banks of the Rio de la Plata, a second city was erected. The books of the Adelantado Pedro de Mendoza became the new city's first library, and those in the crew who were literate (including St Teresa's younger brother, Rodrigo de Ahumada) were able to read Erasmus and Virgil under the southern cross. See Enrique de Gandia's Introduction to Ruy Díaz de Guzmán's *La Argentina* (Buenos Aires, 1990).

6. Plutarch, "Life of Alexander", in *The Parallel Lives*, ed. B. Perrin (Cambridge, Mass., & London, 1970).

7. Ibid.

8. Athenaeus, *Deipnosophistai*, Vol. I, quoted in Luciano Canfora, *La biblioteca scomparsa* (Palermo, 1987).

9. Canfora, ibid.

10. Anthony Hobson, *Great Libraries* (London, 1970). Hobson notes that in 1968 the annual intake of the British Museum Library was 128,706 volumes.

11. Howard A. Parsons, *The Alexandrian Library: Glory of the Hellenic World* (New York, 1967).

12. Ausonius, *Opuscules*, 113, quoted in Guglielmo Cavallo, "Libro e pubblico alla fine del mondo antico", in *Libri, editori e pubblico nel mondo antico* (Rome & Bari, 1992).

13. James W. Thompson, *Ancient Libraries* (Hamden, Conn., 1940).

14. P.M. Fraser, *Ptolemaic Alexandria* (Oxford, 1972).

15. David Diringer, *The Alphabet: A Key to the History of Mankind,* 2 vols. (London, 1968).

16. Christian Jacob, "La Leçon d'Alexandrie", in *Autrement*, No. 121, Paris, Apr. 1993.

17. Prosper Alfaric, *L'Évolution intellectuelle de Saint Augustin* (Tours, 1918).

18. Sidonius, *Epistolae*, II: 9.4, quoted in Cavallo, "Libro e pubblico alla fine del mondo antico".

19. Edward G. Browne, *A Literary History of Persia*, 4 vols. (London, 1902–24).

20. Alain Besson, *Medieval Classification and Cataloguing: Classification Practices and Cataloguing Methods in France from the 12th to 15th Centuries* (Biggleswade, Beds., 1980).

21. Ibid.

22. Almost fifteen centuries later, the American librarian Melvil Dewey augmented the number of categories by three, dividing all knowledge into ten groups and assigning to each group a hundred numbers whereby any given book might be classified.

23. Titus Burckhardt, *Die maurische Kultur in Spanien* (Munich, 1970).

24. Johannes Pedersen, *The Arabic Book*, trans. Geoffrey French (Princeton, 1984). Pedersen notes that al-Ma'mun was not the first to establish a library of translations; the son of an Umayyad caliph, Khalid ibn Yazid ibn Mu'awiya, is said to have preceded him.

25. Jonathan Berkey, *The Transmission of Knowledge in Medieval Cairo: A Social History of Islamic Education* (Princeton, 1992).

26. Burckhardt, *Die maurische Kultur in Spanien*.

27. Hobson, *Great Libraries*.

28. Colette, *Mes apprentissages* (Paris, 1936).

29. Jorge Luis Borges, "La Biblioteca de Babel", in *Ficciones* (Buenos Aires, 1944).

READING THE FUTURE

pages 200–211

1. Michel Lemoine, "L'Oeuvre encyclopédique de Vincent de Beauvais", in Maurice de Gandillac et al., *La Pensée encyclopédique au Moyen Age* (Paris, 1966).

2. *Voluspa*, ed. Sigurdur Nordal, trans. Ommo Wilts (Oxford, 1980).

3. Virgil, *Aeneid*, ed. H.R. Fairclough (Cambridge, Mass., & London), VI: 48–49.

4. Petronius, *Satyricon*, ed. M. Heseltine (Cambridge, Mass., & London, 1967), XV. 48.

5. Aulus Gellius, *Noctes Atticae*, ed. J.C. Rolfe (Cambridge, Mass., & London, 1952).

6. Pausanias, *Description of Greece*, ed. W.H.S. Jones (Cambridge, Mass., & London, 1948), X. 12–1; Euripides, prologue to *Lamia*, ed. A.S. Way (Cambridge, Mass., & London, 1965).

7. In *The Greek Myths* (London, 1955), II. 132.5, Robert Graves notes that "the whereabouts of Erytheia, also called Erythrea or Erythria, is disputed." According to Graves, it might be an island beyond the ocean, or off the coast of Lusitania, or it might be a name given to the island of Leon on which the earliest city of Gades was built.

8. Pausanias, *Description of Greece*, X. 12.4–8.

9. Aurelian, *Scriptores Historiae Augustae*, 25, 4–6, quoted in John Ferguson, *Utopias of the Classical World* (London, 1975).

10. Eusebius Pamphilis, *Ecclesiastical History: The Life of the Blessed Emperor Constantine, in Four Books* (London, 1845), Ch. XVIII.

11. Ferguson, *Utopias of the Classical World*.

12. Bernard Botte, *Les Origines de la Noël et de l'Épiphanie* (Paris, 1932). Despite a reference in the *Liber pontificalis* indicating that Pope Telesphorus initiated the celebration of Christmas in Rome between 127 and 136, the first certain mention of December 25 as the date of Christ's birthday is in the *Deposito martyrum* of the Philocalian Calendar of 354.

13. The Edict of Milan, in Henry Bettenson, ed., *Documents of the Christian Church* (Oxford, 1943).

14. The English novelist Charles Kingsley made the Neoplatonic philosopher the heroine of his now neglected novel *Hypatia, or New Foes with an Old Face* (London, 1853).

15. Jacques Lacarrière, *Les Hommes ivres de Dieu* (Paris, 1975).

16. C. Baur, *Der heilige Johannes Chrysostomus und seine Zeit*, 2 vols. (Frankfurt, 1929–30).

17. Garth Fowden, *Empire to Commonwealth: Consequences of Monotheism in Late Antiquity* (Princeton, 1993). Also, see the remarkable Jacques Giès & Monique Cohen, *Sérinde, Terre de Bouddha. Dix siècles d'art sur la Route de la Soie*. Catalogue of the exhibition at the Grand Palais, Paris, 1996.

18. J. Daniélou & H.I. Marrou, *The Christian Centuries*, Vol. I (London, 1964).

19. Eusebius, *Ecclesiastical History*.

20. Cicero, *De Divinatione*, ed. W.A. Falconer (Cambridge, Mass., & London, 1972), II. 54.

21. Saint Augustine, *The City of God*, Vol. VI, ed. W.C. Greene (London & Cambridge, Mass., 1963).

22. Lucien Broche, *La Cathédrale de Laon* (Paris, 1926).

23. Virgil, "Eclogue IV", as quoted in Eusebius, *Ecclesiastical History*.

24. Salman Rushdie, *The Wizard of Oz*, British Film Institute Film Classics (London, 1992).

25. Anita Desai, "A Reading Rat on the Moors", in *Soho Square III*, ed. Alberto Manguel (London, 1990).

26. Aelius Lampridius, *Vita Severi Alexandri*, 4.6, 14.5, quoted in L.P. Wilkinson, *The Roman Experience* (London, 1975).

27. Cf. Helen A. Loane, "The Sortes Vergilianae", in *The Classical Weekly* 21/24, New York, Apr. 30, 1928. Loane quotes De Quincey, according to whom tradition held that the name of Virgil's maternal grandfather was Magus. The people of Naples, says De Quincey, mistook the name for a profession and held that Virgil "had stepped by mere succession and right of inheritance into his wicked old grandpapa's infernal powers and knowledge, both of which he exercised for centuries without blame, and for the benefit of the faithful." Thomas

De Quincey, *Collected Writings* (London, 1896), III. 251–269.

28. Aelius Spartianus, *Vita Hadriani*, 2.8, in *Scriptores Historiae Augustae*, quoted in Loane, "The Sortes Vergilianae". Not only Virgil was consulted in this manner. Cicero, writing in the first century BC (*De Natura Deorum*, II. 2) tells of the augur Tiberius Sempronius Gracchus, who in 162 BC "caused the resignation of the consuls at whose election he had presided in the previous year, basing his decision on a fault in the auspices, of which he became aware 'when reading the books'."

29. William V. Harris, *Ancient Literacy* (Cambridge, 1989).

30. "There shall not be found among you any one that maketh his son or his daughter to pass through the fire, or that useth divination, or an observer of times, or an enchanter, or a witch, Or a charmer, or a consulter with familiar spirits, or a wizard, or a necromancer. For all that do these things are an abomination unto the Lord. . . ." Deuteronomy 18: 10–12.

31. Gaspar Peucer, *Les Devins ou Commentaire des principales sortes de devinations*, trans. Simon Goulard (?) (Sens [?], 1434).

32. Rabelais, *Le Tiers Livre de Pantagruel*, 10–12.

33. Manuel Mujica Láinez, *Bomarzo* (Buenos Aires, 1979), Ch. II.

34. William Dunn Macray, *Annals of the Bodleian Library, A.D. 1598 to A.D. 1867* (London, 1868).

35. Daniel Defoe, *The Life and Strange Surprizing Adventures of Robinson Crusoe, of York, Mariner*, ed. J.D. Crowley (London & Oxford, 1976).

36. Thomas Hardy, *Far from the Madding Crowd* (London, 1874).

37. Robert Louis Stevenson (with Lloyd Osbourne), *The Ebb Tide* (London, 1894).

THE SYMBOLIC READER

pages 212–233

1. André Kertész, *On Reading* (New York, 1971).

2. Michael Olmert, *The Smithsonian Book of Books* (Washington, 1992).

3. Beverley Smith, "Homes of the 1990s to stress substance", *The Globe and Mail*, Toronto, Jan. 13, 1990.

4. Andrew Martindale, *Gothic Art from the Twelfth to Fifteenth Centuries* (London, 1967).

5. Quoted in Réau, Louis, *Iconographie de l'art chrétien*, Vol. II (Paris, 1957).

6. *Marienbild in Rheinland und Westfalen*, catalogue of an exhibition at Villa Hugel, Essen, 1968.

7. George Ferguson, *Signs and Symbols in Christian Art* (Oxford, 1954).

8. *De Madonna in de Kunst*, catalogue of an exhibition, Antwerp, 1954.

9. *The Lost Books of the Bible and the Forgotten Books of Eden*, intr. by Frank Crane (New York, 1974).

10. *Protoevangelion*, ibid., IX, 1–9.

11. Mary at the well and Mary at the spinning-wheel are the most common images of the Annunciation in early Christian art, especially in Byzantine depictions from the fifth century onwards. Before that time, portrayals of the Annunciation are scarce and schematic. The earliest extant depiction of Mary and the angel precedes Martini's *Annunciation* by ten centuries. Painted in grubby colours on one wall of the Catacomb of St. Priscilla, in the outskirts of Rome, it shows a featureless seated Virgin listening to a standing man — an angel wingless and uncrowned.

12. John 1: 14.

13. Robin Lane Fox, *Pagans and Christians* (New York, 1986).

14. *The Letters of Peter Abelard*, ed. Betty Radice (London, 1974).

15. Hildegard of Bingen, *Opera omnia*, in *Patrologia Latina*, Vol. LXXII (Paris, 1844–55).

16. Quoted in Carol Ochs, *Behind the Sex of God: Toward a New Consciousness — Transcending Matriarchy and Patriarchy* (Boston, 1977).

17. San Bernardino, *Prediche volgari*, in Creighton E. Gilbert, *Italian Art, 1400–1500: Sources and Documents* (Evanston, 1980).

18. Victor Cousin, ed., *Petri Abaelardi Opera*, 2 vols. (London, 1849–59).

19. Five centuries later not much seemed to have changed, as witness the sermon delivered by the learned J.W. Burgon in 1884, on the occasion of a proposal made at Oxford to admit women to the university: "Will none of you have the generosity or the candour to tell [Woman] what a very disagreeable creature, in Man's account, she will inevitably become? If she is to compete successfully with men for 'honours', you must needs put the classic writers of antiquity unreservedly into her hands — in other words, must introduce her to the obscenities of Greek and Roman literature. Can you seriously intend it? . . . I take leave of the subject with a short Allocution addressed to the other sex. . . . Inferior to us God made you: and our inferiors to the end of time you will remain." Quoted in Jan Morris, ed., *The Oxford Book of Oxford* (Oxford, 1978).

20. S. Harksen, *Women in the Middle Ages* (New York, 1976).

21. Margaret Wade Labarge, *A Small Sound of the Trumpet: Women in Medieval Life* (London, 1986).

22. Janet Backhouse, *Books of Hours* (London, 1985).

23. Paul J. Achtemeier, ed., *Harper's Bible Dictionary* (San Francisco, 1985).

24. Isaiah 7: 14.

25. Anna Jameson, *Legends of the Madonna* (Boston & New York, 1898).

26. Proverbs 9: 1, 9: 3–5.

27. Martin Buber, *Erzählungen der Chassidim* (Berlin, 1947).

28. E.P. Spencer, "L'Horloge de Sapience" (Brussels, Bibliothèque Royale, Ms. IV 111), in *Scriptorium*, 1963, XVII.

29. C.G. Jung, "Answer to Job", in *Psychology and Religion, West and East* (New York, 1960).

30. Merlin Stone, *The Paradise Papers: The Suppression of Women's Rites* (New York, 1976).

31. Carolyne Walker Bynum, *Jesus As Mother: Studies in the Spirituality of the High Middle Ages* (Berkeley & London, 1982).

32. St. Gregoire de Tours, *L'Histoire des Rois Francs*, ed. J.J.E. Roy, pref. by Erich Aurebach (Paris, 1990).

33. Heinz Kahlen & Cyril Mango, *Hagia Sophia* (Berlin, 1967).

34. In "The Fourteenth-Century Common Reader", an unpublished paper delivered at the Kalamazoo Conference of 1992, referring to the image of the reading Mary in the fourteenth-century Book of Hours, Daniel Williman suggests that "without apology, the Book of Hours embodies women's appropriation of an *opus Dei* and of literacy".

35. Ferdinando Bologna, *Gli affreschi di Simone Martini ad Assisi* (Milan, 1965).

36. Giovanni Paccagnini, *Simone Martini* (Milan, 1957).

37. Colyn de Coter, *Virgin and Child Crowned by Angels*, 1490–1510, in the Chicago Art Institute; the anonymous *Madonna auf der Rasenbank*, Upper Rhine, *circa* 1470–80, in the Augustinermuseum, Freiburg; and many others.

38. Plutarch, "On the Fortune of Alexander", 327: 4, in *Moralia*, Vol. IV, ed. Frank Cole Babbitt (Cambridge, Mass., & London, 1972). Also Plutarch, "Life of Alexander", VIII and XXVI, in *The Parallel Lives*, ed. B. Perrin (Cambridge, Mass., & London, 1970).

39. Act II, scene ii. George Steiner has suggested that the book is Florio's translation of Montaigne's *Essais* ("Le trope du livre-monde dans Shakespeare", conference at the Bibliothèque Nationale, Paris, Mar. 23, 1995).

40. Miguel de Cervantes, *Don Quixote*, ed. Celina S. de Cortázar & Isaías Lerner (Buenos Aires, 1969), I: 6.

41. Martin Bormann, *Hitler's Table Talk*, intr. by Hugh Trevor-Roper (London, 1953).

READING WITHIN WALLS
pages 224–235

1. Thoas Hägg, *The Novel in Antiquity*, English ed. (Berkeley & Los Angeles, 1983).

2. Plato, *Laws*, ed. Rev. R.G. Bury (Cambridge, Mass., & London, 1949), VII, 804 c–e.

3. William V. Harris, *Ancient Literacy* (Cambridge, Mass., 1989).

4. Ibid.

5. Reardon, *Collected Ancient Greek Novels*.

6. C. Ruiz Montero, "Una observación para la cronología de Caritón de Afrodisias", in *Estudios Clásicos* 24 (Madrid, 1980).

7. Santa Teresa de Jesús, *Libro de la Vida*, II:1, in *Obras Completas*, Biblioteca de Autores Cristianos (Madrid, 1967).

8. Kate Flint, *The Woman Reader, 1837–1914* (Oxford, 1993).

9. Ivan Morris, *The World of the Shining Prince: Court Life in Ancient Japan* (Oxford, 1964).

10. "The vast majority of women in Murasaki's day toiled arduously in the fields, were subject to harsh treatment by their men, bred young and frequently, and died at an early age, without having given any more thought to material independence or cultural enjoyments than to the possibility of visiting the moon." Ibid.

11. Ibid.

12. Quoted ibid.

13. Walter Benjamin, "Unpacking My Library", in *Illuminations*, trans. Harry Zohn (New York, 1968).

14. Ivan Morris, introduction to Sei Shonagon, *The Pillow Book of Sei Shonagon* (Oxford and London, 1967).

15. Quoted in Morris, *The World of the Shining Prince*.

16. Sei Shonagon, *The Pillow Book of Sei Shonagon*, trans. Ivan Morris (Oxford and London, 1967).

17. Quoted in Morris, *The World of the Shining Prince*.

18. George Eliot, "Silly Novels by Lady Novelists", in *Selected Critical Writings*, ed. Rosemary Ashton (Oxford, 1992).

19. Rose Hempel, *Japan zur Heian-Zeit: Kunst und Kultur* (Freiburg, 1983).

20. Carolyn G. Heilbrun, *Writing a Woman's Life* (New York, 1989).

21. Edmund White, Foreword to *The Faber Book of Gay Short Stories* (London, 1991).

22. Oscar Wilde, "The Importance of Being Earnest", Act II, in *The Works of Oscar Wilde*, ed. G.F. Mayne (London & Glasgow, 1948).

STEALING BOOKS
pages 236–245

1. Walter Benjamin, "Paris, Capital of the Nineteenth Century", in *Reflections*, ed. Peter Demetz; trans. Edmund Jephcott (New York, 1978).

2. François-René Chateaubriand, *Mémoires d'outre-tombe* (Paris, 1849–50).

3. Jean Viardot, "Livres rares et pratiques bibliophiliques", in *Histoire de l'édition française*, Vol. II (Paris, 1984).

4. Michael Olmert, *The Smithsonian Book of Books* (Washington, 1992).

5. Geo. Haven Putnam, *Books and Their Makers during the Middle Ages*, Vol. I (New York, 1896–97).

6. Ibid.

7. P. Riberette, *Les Bibliothèques françaises pendant la Révolution* (Paris, 1970).

8. Bibliothèque Nationale, *Le Livre dans la vie quotidienne* (Paris, 1975).

9. Simone Balayé, *La Bibliothèque Nationale des origines à 1800* (Geneva, 1988).

10. Madeleine B. Stern & Leona Rostenberg, "A Study in 'Bibliokleptomania'", in *Bookman's Weekly*, No. 67, New York, June 22, 1981.

11. Quoted in A.N.L. Munby, "The Earl and the Thief: Lord Ashburnham and Count Libri", in *Harvard Literary Bulletin*, Vol. XVII, Cambridge, Mass., 1969.

12. Gédéon Tallemant des Réaux, *Historiettes* (Paris, 1834).

13. Albert Cim, *Amateurs et Voleurs de Livres* (Paris, 1903).

14. Ibid.

15. Léopold Delisle, *Les Manuscrits des Fonds Libri et Barrois* (Paris, 1888).

16. Marcel Proust, *Les Plaisirs et les jours* (Paris, 1896).

17. Munby, "The Earl and the Thief".

18. Philippe Vigier, "Paris pendant la monarchie de juillet 1830–1848", in *Nouvelle Histoire de Paris* (Paris, 1991).

19. Jean Freustié, *Prosper Mérimée, 1803–1870* (Paris, 1982).

20. Prosper Mérimée, *Correspondance*, établie et annotée par Maurice Parturier *Vol. v: 1847–1849* (Paris, 1946).

21. Prosper Mérimée, "Le Procès de M. Libri", in *Revue des Deux Mondes*, Paris, Apr. 15, 1852.

22. Delisle, *Les Manuscrits des Fonds Libri et Barrois*.

23. Cim, *Amateurs et voleurs de livres*.

24. Lawrence S. Thompson, "Notes on Bibliokleptomania", in *The Bulletin of the New York Public Library*, New York, Sept. 1944.

25. Rudolf Buchner, *Bücher und Menschen* (Berlin, 1976).

26. Thompson, "Notes on Bibliokleptomania".

27. Cim, *Amateurs et voleurs de livres*.

28. Charles Lamb, *Essays of Elia*, second series (London, 1833).

THE AUTHOR AS READER
pages 246–259

1. Pliny the Younger, *Lettres I–IX*, ed. A.M. Guillemin, 3 vols. (Paris, 1927–28), VI: 17.

2. Even the Emperor Augustus attended these readings "with both goodwill and patience": Suetonius, "Augustus", 89: 3, in *Lives of the Twelve Caesars*, ed. J.C. Rolfe (Cambridge, Mass., & London, 1948).

3. Pliny the Younger, *Lettres I–IX*, V: 12, VII: 17.

4. Ibid., I: 13.

5. Ibid., VIII: 12.

6. Juvenal, VII: 39–47, in *Juvenal and Persius: Works*, ed. G.G. Ramsay (Cambridge, Mass., & London, 1952).

7. Pliny the Younger, *Lettres I–IX*, II: 19.

8. Ibid., V: 17.

9. Ibid., IV: 27.

10. Horace, "A Letter to Augustus", in *Classical Literary Criticism*, ed. D.A. Russell & M. Winterbottom (Oxford, 1989).

11. Martial, *Epigrammata*, III: 44, in *Works*, ed. W.C.A. Ker (Cambridge, Mass., & London, 1919-20).

12. Pliny the Younger, *Lettres I–IX*, I: 13.

13. Ibid., IX: 3.

14. Ibid., IX: 23.

15. Ibid., IX: 11.

16. Ibid., VI: 21.

17. According to the poet Louis MacNeice, after one of Thomas's readings "an actor who had been standing dazzled in the wings said to him with amazement, 'Mr Thomas, one of your pauses was fifty seconds!' Dylan drew himself up, injured (a thing he was good at): 'Read as fast as I could', he said haughtily." John Berryman, "After Many A Summer: Memories of Dylan Thomas", in *The Times Literary Supplement*, London, Sept. 3, 1993.

18. Erich Auerbach, *Literatursprache und Publikum in der lateinischen Spätantike und im Mittelalter* (Berne, 1958).

19. Dante, *De vulgare eloquentia*, trans. & ed. Vittorio Coletti (Milan, 1991).

20. Jean de Joinville, *Histoire de saint Louis*, ed. Noël Corbett (Paris, 1977).

21. William Nelson, "From 'Listen Lordings' to 'Dear Reader'", in *University of Toronto Quarterly* 47/2 (Winter 1976–77).

22. Fernando de Rojas, *La Celestina: Tragicomedia de Calisto y Melibea*, ed. Dorothy S. Severin (Madrid, 1969).

23. María Rosa Lida de Malkiel, *La originalidad artística de La Celestina* (Buenos Aires, 1967).

24. Ludovico Ariosto, *Tutte le opere*, ed. Cesare Segre (Milan, 1964), I: XXXVIII, quoted in Nelson, "From 'Listen Lordings' to 'Dear Reader'".

25. Ruth Crosby, "Chaucer and the Custom of Oral Delivery", in *Speculum: A Journal of Medieval Studies* 13, Cambridge, Mass., 1938.

26. Quoted in M.B. Parkes, *Pause and Effect: An Introduction to the History of Punctuation in the West* (Berkeley & Los Angeles, 1993).

27. Thomas Love Peacock, *Nightmare Abbey* (London, 1818).

28. Samuel Butler, *The Notebooks of Samuel Butler*, ed. Henry Festing Jones (London, 1921).

29. P.N. Furbank, *Diderot* (London, 1992).

30. Peter Ackroyd, *Dickens* (London, 1991).

31. Paul Turner, *Tennyson* (London, 1976).

32. Charles R. Saunders, "Carlyle and Tennyson", PMLA 76 (March 1961), London.

33. Ralph Wilson Rader, *Tennyson's Maud: The Biographical Genesis* (Berkeley & Los Angeles, 1963).

34. Charles Tennyson, *Alfred Tennyson* (London, 1950).

35. Ralph Waldo Emerson, *The Topical Notebooks*, ed. Ronald A. Bosco (New York & London, 1993).

36. Kevin Jackson, review of Peter Ackroyd's lecture "London Luminaries and Cockney Visionaries" at the Victoria and Albert Museum, in *The Independent*, London, Dec. 9, 1993.

37. Ackroyd, *Dickens*.

38. Richard Ellman, *James Joyce*, rev. ed. (London, 1982).

39. Dámaso Alonso, "Las conferencias", in *Insula* 75, Mar. 15, 1952, Madrid.

40. Stephen Jay Gould, *The Panda's Thumb* (New York, 1989).

THE TRANSLATOR AS READER

pages 260–277

1. Rainer Maria Rilke, letter to Mimi Romanelli, May 11, 1911, in *Briefe 1907–1914* (Frankfurt-am-Main, 1933).

2. Louise Labé, *Oeuvres poétiques*, ed. Françoise Charpentier (Paris, 1983).

3. Carl Jacob Burckhardt, *Ein Vormittag beim Buchhandler* (Basel, 1944).

4. Racine's poem, a translation of only the second half of Psalm 36, begins, "Grand Dieu, qui vis les cieux se former sans matière".

5. Quoted in Donald Prater, *A Ringing Glass: The Life of Rainer Maria Rilke* (Oxford, 1986).

6. Alta Lind Cook, *Sonnets of Louise Labé* (Toronto, 1950).

7. Labé, *Oeuvres poétiques*.

8. Rainer Maria Rilke, "Narcissus", in *Sämtliche Werke*, ed. Rilke-Archiv (Frankfurt-am-Main, 1955–57).

9. Quoted in Prater, *A Ringing Glass*.

10. Natalie Zemon Davis, "Le Monde de l'imprimerie humaniste: Lyon", in *Histoire de l'édition française*, 1 (Paris, 1982).

11. George Steiner, *After Babel* (Oxford, 1973).

12. Paul de Man, *Allegories of Reading: Figural Language in Rousseau, Nietzsche, Rilke, and Proust* (New Haven & London, 1979).

13. D.E. Luscombe, *The School of Peter Abelard: The Influence of Abelard's Thought in the Early Scholastic Period* (Cambridge, 1969).

14. Quoted in Olga S. Opfell, *The King James Bible Translators* (Jefferson, N.C., 1982).

15. Ibid.

16. Quoted ibid.

17. Ibid.

18. Rudyard Kipling, "Proofs of Holy Writ", in *The Complete Works of Rudyard Kipling*, "Uncollected Items", Vol. XXX, Sussex Edition (London, 1939).

19. Alexander von Humboldt, *Über die Verschiedenheit des menschlischen Sprachbaues und ihren Einfluß auf die geistige Entwicklung des Menschengeschlechts*, quoted in Umberto Eco, *La Ricerca della Lingua Perfetta* (Rome & Bari, 1993).

20. De Man, *Allegories of Reading*.

FORBIDDEN READING
pages 278–289

1. James Boswell, *The Life of Samuel Johnson*, ed. John Wain (London, 1973).

2. T.B. Macaulay, *The History of England*, 5 vols. (London, 1849–61).

3. Charles was nevertheless viewed as a worthy king by most of his subjects, who believed that his small vices corrected his greater ones. John Aubrey tells of a certain Arise Evans who "had a fungous Nose, and said it was revealed to him, that the King's Hand would Cure him: And at the first coming of King Charles II into St. James's Park, he kiss'd the King's Hand, and rubbed his Nose with it; which disturbed the King, but Cured him": John Aubrey, *Miscellanies*, in *Three Prose Works*, ed. John Buchanan-Brown (Oxford, 1972).

4. Antonia Fraser, *Royal Charles: Charles II and the Restoration* (London, 1979).

5. Janet Duitsman Cornelius, *When I Can Read My Title Clear: Literacy, Slavery, and Religion in the Antebellum South* (Columbia, S.C., 1991).

6. Quoted ibid.

7. Ibid.

8. Ibid.

9. Ibid.

10. Frederick Douglass, *The Life and Times of Frederick Douglass* (Hartford, Conn., 1881).

11. Quoted in Duitsman Cornelius, *When I Can Read My Title Clear*.

12. Peter Handke, *Kaspar* (Frankfurt-am-Main, 1967).

13. Voltaire, "De l'Horrible Danger de la Lecture", in *Mémoires, Suivis de Mélanges divers et precédés de "Voltaire Démiurge" par Paul Souday* (Paris, 1927).

14. Johann Wolfgang von Goethe, *Dichtung und Wahrheit* (Stuttgart, 1986), IV: I.

15. Margaret Horsfield, "The Burning Books" on "Ideas", CBC Radio Toronto, broadcast Apr. 23, 1990.

16. Quoted in Heywood Broun & Margaret Leech, *Anthony Comstock: Roundsman of the Lord* (New York, 1927).

17. Charles Gallaudet Trumbull, *Anthony Comstock, Fighter* (New York, 1913).

18. Quoted in Broun & Leech, *Anthony Comstock*.

19. Ibid.

20. Ibid.

21. Ibid.

22. H.L. Mencken, "Puritanism as a Literary Force", in *A Book of Prefaces* (New York, 1917).

23. Jacques Dars, Introduction to *En Mouchant la chandelle* (Paris, 1986).

24. Gustave Flaubert, Madame Bovary, II, 7 (Paris, 1857).

25. Edmund Gosse, *Father and Son* (London, 1907).

26. Ibid.

27. Joan DelFattore, *What Johnny Shouldn't Read: Textbook Censorship in America* (New Haven & London, 1992).

28. Quoted from *The Times* of London, Jan. 4, 1978, reprinted in Nick Caistor's Foreword to *Nunca Más: A Report by Argentina's National Commission on Disappeared People* (London, 1986).

29. In *Nunca Más*.

THE BOOK FOOL

pages 290–306

1. Patrick Trevor-Roper, *The World through Blunted Sight* (London, 1988).

2. Jorge Luis Borges, "Poema de los dones", in *El Hacedor* (Buenos Aires, 1960).

3. Royal Ontario Museum, *Books of the Middle Ages* (Toronto, 1950).

4. Trevor-Roper, *The World through Blunted Sight*.

5. Pliny the Elder, *Natural History*, ed. D.E. Eichholz (Cambridge, Mass., & London, 1972), Book XXXVII: 16.

6. A. Bourgeois, *Les Bésicles de nos ancêtres* (Paris, 1923) (Bourgeois gives no day or month, and the wrong year). See also Edward Rosen, "The Invention of Eyeglasses", in *The Journal of the History of Medicine and Allied Sciences* 11 (1956).

7. Redi, *Lettera sopra l'invenzione degli occhiali di nazo* (Florence, 1648).

8. Rosen, "The Invention of Eyeglasses".

9. Rudyard Kipling, "The Eye of Allah", in *Debits and Credits* (London, 1926).

10. Roger Bacon, *Opus maius*, ed. S. Jebb (London, 1750).

11. René Descartes, *Traité des passions* (Paris, 1649).

12. W. Poulet, *Atlas on the History of Spectacles*, Vol. II (Godesberg, 1980).

13. Hugh Orr, *An Illustrated History of Early Antique Spectacles* (Kent, 1985).

14. E.R. Curtius, quoting F. Messerschmidt, *Archiv fur Religionswissenschaft* (Berlin, 1931), notes that the Etruscans did, however, represent several of their gods as scribes or readers.

15. Charles Schmidt, *Histoire littéraire de l' Alsace* (Strasbourg, 1879).

16. Sebastian Brant, *Das Narrenschiff*, ed. Friedrich Zarncke (Leipzig, 1854).

17. Geiler von Kaysersberg, *Nauicula siue speculum fatuorum* (Strasbourg, 1510).

18. Seneca, "De tranquillitate", in *Moral Essays*, ed. R.M. Gummere (Cambridge, Mass., & London, 1955).

19. Ibid.

20. John Donne, "The Extasie", in *The Complete English Poems*, ed. C.A. Patrides (New York, 1985).

21. Gérard de Nerval, "Angélique", in *Les Filles du feu*, ed. Béatrice Didier (Paris, 1972).

22. Thomas Carlyle, "The Hero As Man of Letters", in *Selected Writings*, ed. Alan Shelston (London, 1971).

23. Jorge Manrique, "Coplas a la muerte de su padre", in *Poesías*, ed. F. Benelcarría (Madrid, 1952).

24. Seneca, "De vita beata", in *Moral Essays*.

25. John Carey, *The Intellectuals and the Masses: Pride and Prejudice among the Literary Intelligentsia, 1880–1939* (London, 1992).

26. Matthew Arnold, *Culture and Anarchy* (London, 1932). To be fair to Arnold, his argument continues: "but we are for the transformation of each and all of these according to the law of perfection."

27. Aldous Huxley, "On the Charms of History", in *Music at Night* (London, 1931).

28. Thomas Hardy, writing in 1887, quoted in Carey, *The Intellectuals and the Masses*.

29. Sigmund Freud, "Writers and Day-Dreaming", in *Art and Literature*, Vol. 14 of the Pelican Freud Library, trans. James Strachey (London, 1985).

30. And even Don Quixote is not entirely lost in fiction. When he and Sancho mount the wooden horse, convinced that it is the flying steed Clavileño, and the incredulous Sancho wants to take off the kerchief that covers his eyes in order to see if they are really up in the air and near the sun, Don Quixote orders him not to do so. Fiction would be destroyed by prosaic proof. (*Don Quixote*, II, 41.) The suspension of disbelief, as Coleridge rightly pointed out, must be willing; beyond that willingness lies madness.

31. Rebecca West, "The Strange Necessity", in *Rebecca West — A Celebration* (New York, 1978).

ENDPAPER PAGES
pages 308–319

1. Ernest Hemingway, "The Snows of Kilimanjaro", in *The Snows of Kilimanjaro and Other Stories* (New York, 1927).

2. Rainer Maria Rilke, *Die Aufzeichnungen des Malte Laurids Brigge*, ed. Erich Heller (Frankfurt-am-Main, 1986).

3. Richard de Bury, *The Philobiblon*, ed. & trans. Ernest C. Thomas (London, 1888).

4. Virginia Woolf, "How Should One Read a Book?", in *The Common Reader*, second series (London, 1932).

5. Gerontius, *Vita Melaniae Janioris*, trans. & ed. Elizabeth A. Clark (New York & Toronto, 1984).

6. Jonathan Rose, "Rereading the English Common Reader: A preface to a History of Audiences", in the *Journal of the History of Ideas*, 1992.

7. Robert Irwin, *The Arabian Nights: A Companion* (London, 1994).

8. Miguel de Cervantes Saavedra, *El Ingenioso Hidalgo Don Quijote de la Mancha*, 2 vols., ed. Celina S. de Cortázar & Isaías Lerner (Buenos Aires, 1969).

9. Marcel Proust, *Journées de lecture*, ed. Alain Coelho (Paris, 1993).

10. Michel Butor, *La Modification* (Paris, 1957).

11. Wolfgang Kayser, *Das Sprachliche Kunstwerk* (Leipzig, 1948).

12. Quoted in Thomas Boyle, *Black Swine in the Sewers of Hampstead: Beneath the Surface of Victorian Sensationalism* (New York, 1989).

13. Jane Austen, *Northanger Abbey* (London, 1818), xxv.

14. Graham Balfour, *The Life of Robert Louis Stevenson*, 2 vols. (London, 1901).

15. "Perhaps improperly so," comments Professor Simone Vauthier, of the University of Strasbourg, in a review of the book. "One would rather have expected the 'King Shahryar Syndrome' or if, following American novelist John Barth, we pay attention to Sheherazade's other listener, her younger sister, 'The Dunyazade Syndrome'."

16. John Wells, *Rude Words: A Discursive History of the London Library* (London, 1991).

17. Marc-Alain Ouaknin, *Bibliothérapie: Lire, c'est guérir* (Paris, 1994).

18. Robert Coover, "The End of Books", in *The New York Times*, June 21, 1992.

PLATE

CREDITS

Musée de Cluny, Paris. © photo R.M.N; *bottom*: Musée de Cluny, Paris, © photo R.M.N. P.76 Oeffentliche Kunstsammlung Basel, Kunstmuseum. Photo: Oeffentliche Kunstsammlung Basel, Martin Bühler, (detail). P.77 © cliché Bibliothèque Nationale de France, Paris. P.80 Library of Congress LC-USZ 62-78985. P.81 Humanist Library, Sélestat. P.84 Bildarchiv Preussischer Kulturbesitz, Berlin. P.87 Photo Scala, Florence. P.92 National Gallery of Prague. P.94 Franco Maria Ricci. P.98 Israel Museum, Jerusalem. P.99 St. Bavon, Ghent, photo Copyright IRPA-KIK, Brussels, (detail). P.100 S. Sabina, Rome. Photograph Alinari-Giraudon. P.102 Universitätsbibliothek Heidelberg. P.104 Das Gleimhaus, Halberstadt, Germany. P.105 TBWA/V & S Vin & Sprit AB. P.106 Swiss National Museum, Zürich. Inv.Nr.LM7211, Neg Nr.11308. P.107 Schnütgen-Museum, Cologne/Rheinisches Bildarchiv, Cologne. P.108 © Bibliothèque Nationale, Paris/Archives Seuil. P.112 Library of Congress LC-USZ 65011. P.113 Key West Art & Historical Society. P.114 Archives of the Abbey of Monte-Cassino, Italy/G. Dagli Orti, Paris. P.118 Musée Condé, Chantilly/Lauros-Giraudon. P.124 Biblioteca Nazionale Marciana, Venice. Photo Toso. P.128 Author's collection. P.129 By permission of The British Library Add Ms. 63493, f.112v. P.130, *left*: Stiftsbibliothek St Gallen, Switzerland; *right*: by courtesy of the Board of Trustees of the Victoria & Albert Museum. P.131 By courtesy of the Board of Trustees of the Victoria & Albert Museum. P.132 Mary Evans Picture Library/Institution of Civil Engineers. P.134 Author's collection. P.136 By permission of The British Library G.9260. P.137 By permission of the British Library IB24504. P.139, *left*: by permission of The Folger Shakespeare Library; *right*: courtesy of the Royal Ontario Museum. P.140 © cliché Bibliothèque Nationale de France, Paris. P.141 Mary Evans Picture Library. P.142 WH Smith Ltd. P.144, *left*: Penguin Books; *right*: © cliché Bibliothèque Nationale de France, Paris. P.145 Courtesy of the Fogg Art Museum. Harvard University Art Museums, Bequest of James P. Warburg. P.146 Beinecke Rare Book and Manuscript Library, Yale University. P.147, *top*: by permission of The British Library, NL.Tab.2; *bottom left*: Associated Press; *bottom right*: © The Dakhleh Oasis Project. Photo Alan Hollet. P.148 Photo Jean-Loup Charmet. P.150 Fonterrault, France. Photo AKG, London/Erich Lessing. P.155 National Museum of Antiquities, Leiden. P.156 Bibliothèque Mazarine, Paris. Photo Jean-Loup Charmet. P.158 By courtesy of the Board of Trustees of the Victoria & Albert Museum. P.161 Paris-Match/Walter Carone. P.162 Yale Collection of American Literature, Beinecke Rare Book and Manuscript Library, Yale University. P.167 Library of Congress LC-USZ62-70956. P.172 By permission of The British Library LR413G1 798(31). P.173 Mary Evans Picture Library. P.176 © Iraq Museum, Baghdad; courtesy J. Oates. P.183 (*both*): copyright British Museum. P.186 Bibliothèque Nationale/ photo © Collection Viollet. P.191 Mary Evans Picture Library. P.193 Author's collection. P.195 © cliché Bibliothèque Nationale de France, Paris. P.196 Mary Evans Picture Library. P.197 Chartres. Photo Giraudon. P.200 AKG, London. P.206 By permission of The British Library IB9110. P.212 © Estate of André Kertész. P.215 Galleria degli Uffizi, Florence. Photo Scala, Florence. P.219 Arena de Padua. Photo Scala, Florence. P.220 ©

INDEX